For all those who
appreciate and responsibly enjoy
Utah's spectacular public lands
MW00770094

Acknowledgments

Sincere thanks are due to the people who helped make this book more inclusive and accurate. They include Josh Winkler of the BLM office in Price; Myron Jeffs of the Henry Mountains Field Station; Joanne Stenton and Cody Clark of the Fishlake National Forest; Bob Emrich, Sandy Borthwick, and Deb Clark. Al Hendricks, retired superintendent of Capitol Reef National Park, generously reviewed a significant part of the draft. Very special thanks to Gary Lenhart for his invaluable help and counsel. The support, advice, and warmth of the Captiol Reef community have ultimately made this book and the companion Capitol Reef book possible. Lastly, Shirley Torgerson and the entire Capitol Reef Natural History Association staff and board have been wonderfully supportive of our work at Capitol Reef and this project.

Contents

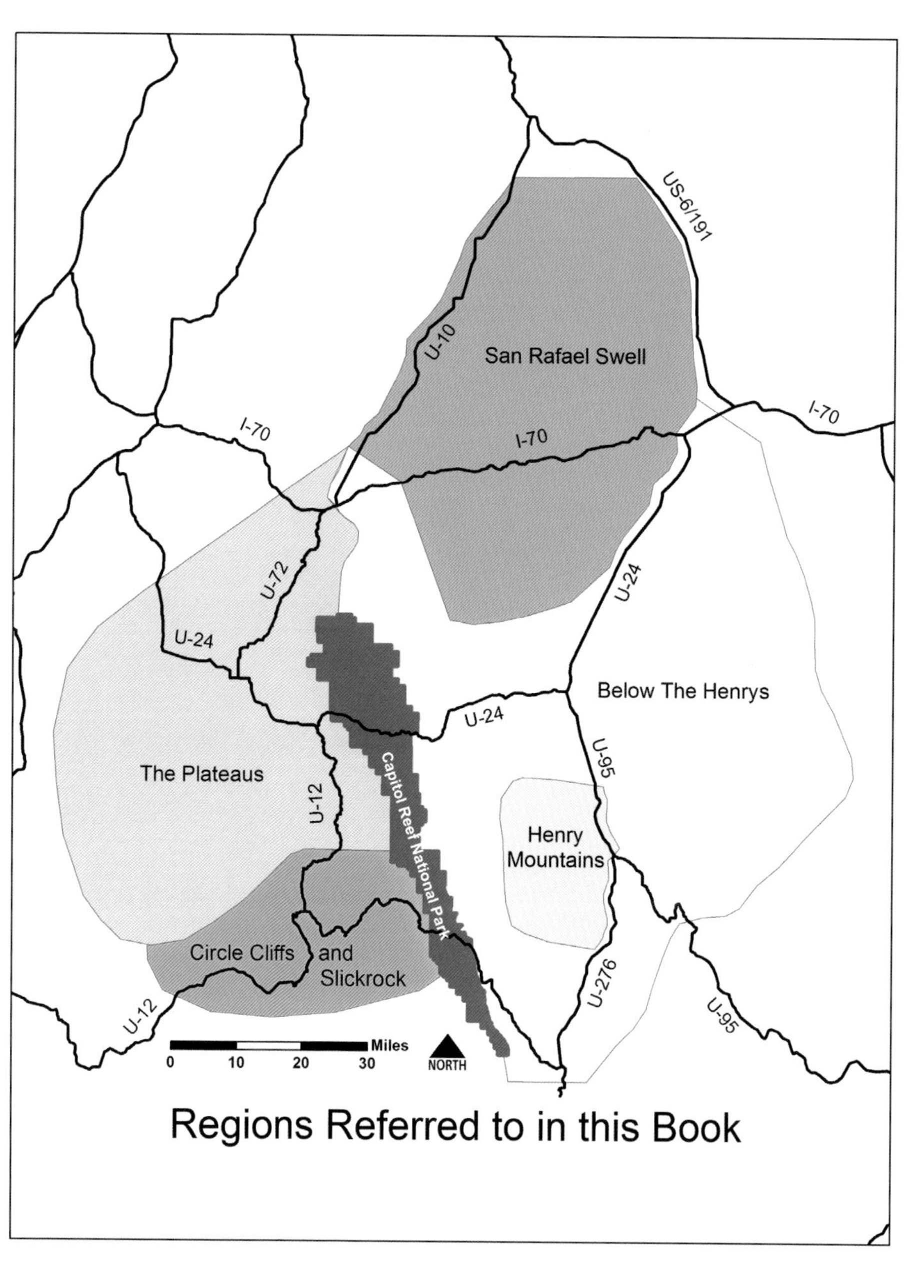

Regions Referred to in this Book

Head of Sinbad

Introduction

Utah is graced with five spectacular national parks that each year attract millions of visitors from around the world. Capitol Reef is the least known, but annually about three-quarters of a million people somehow find their way to this secluded wonderland of red rock, antiquity, history, and, in season, fresh fruit. Many come by tour bus, others by rental RV or car, most in their own vehicle, and a surprising number on bicycles. They stop in the park, take the Scenic Drive, visit the Gifford House, pick some apricots, peaches, or apples, and usually enjoy at least a short hike. Some come back year after year, exploring the backcountry for challenge, beauty, and solitude. One can easily spend three months a year in the park for a decade and not run out of new places to explore in Capitol Reef. We know, because we have.

Still … parks are defined by lines on a map. Those lucky enough to spend considerable time in south-central Utah will find that this vast land, often empty of human presence, presents a banquet of recreational opportunities, limited more by time and imagination than anything else. The universal quest to see something new, or beautiful, or intriguing, or to have an experience that expands a life, can be pursued here.

One of the singular virtues of the region is dominance of the natural world. Of course, it is not perfect; the spider web of old roads and tracks that enable people to get around is decidedly not natural. A stray cow or a thousand head of sheep that wander through your campsite may also be less than enchanting, even if interesting. On the other hand, you could be the only one at McMillan Springs Campground high in the Henry Mountains, lying flat on your back on a soft bed of ponderosa pine needles, and gazing up at stars brighter than you have ever seen before. If the air is calm, there may be no sound save the blood pulsing through your head. As you look out to the west over Capitol Reef, not a single light may be seen, and the view encompasses hundreds and hundreds of square miles. Probably the only other evidence of human activity would be the twinkling lights of infrequent jets high above, just beginning their glide path into Las Vegas. Soon, those passengers will disembark at McCarran Airport and find their way onto the Strip with its ersatz pirate ships, dancing fountains, ringing casinos, and glitzy hotel lobbies. South-central Utah is the anti-Vegas, even if you are in downtown Hanksville, but in the Henrys, or the San Rafael Swell, on Thousand Lake Mountain, or in Death Hollow, it may well seem that the entire world is yours alone.

This book assumes that its readers are inquisitive people, the kind who see a plant that is new to their experience and wonder, what is that, why is it here, how does it fit in, what is that beetle doing on it? These folks want to know about the rocks and why the scenery is so spectacular in one place, and pedestrian a few miles away, and why Utah is so over-blessed with slot canyons. What brought the early people here, and how did they live? Why are there so many dirt roads and tracks anyway? We believe that questions of this kind are best answered in context with an example right in front of you. Thus, while there are short overviews of several major areas of general interest, much of the information in this book is presented within the descriptions of the various hikes, road trips, and other activities.

This book covers a variety of outdoor activities, spread across several thousand square miles of south-central Utah. They range from long hikes and fairly difficult slot canyons to drive-up rock art panels. From the Pedestal Alley hike to the top of Mount Ellen is more than 7,500 vertical feet, sandy desert to near timberline, warm sun to deep snow at times. If you are traveling through the national parks and monuments there may be times when you need to go higher or lower for comfortable weather, or you might want a change of pace, or, perhaps, a bit of an escape from your fellow travelers. This part of Utah easily obliges on all counts, as few places do.

Upper Calf Creek Falls

How to Use this Guide

The guide is organized by region, and carefully cross-indexed by activity. For each region a general summary is followed by descriptions of two- and four-wheel drive options for exploring the area. The travel-logs reference hikes, slot canyons, rock art sites, and rock collecting opportunities, each of which is then described in later sections. Two of the regions are well defined in the minds of most people familiar with south-central Utah: the San Rafael Swell, neatly bisected by Interstate 70, and the stand-alone Henry Mountains that dominate the skyline east of Capitol Reef's Waterpocket Fold. The other three areas are a little more squishy. One, the Plateaus, combines the three flat-topped mountains west of Capitol Reef, namely, Boulder, Thousand Lake, and Fish Lake Mountains. Another region is the area south of Boulder Mountain, east of the Escalante River, and west of Capitol Reef, which we labeled Circle Cliffs and Slickrock. The final area, which we are calling Below the Henry Mountains, is bounded by the Green and Colorado Rivers on the east and southeast, the San Rafael Swell to the north, and Capitol Reef to the west. The Henry Mountains are the hole in this doughnut. In sum, these regions entirely surround Capitol Reef National Park, providing a buffet of things to do in combination with a visit to the park.

These regions are presented in a more or less circular geographic pattern, beginning with the San Rafael Swell to the north, and continuing with Below the Henry Mountains, the Henrys themselves, Circle Cliffs and Slickrock, and concluding with the Plateaus. A good first step in getting oriented would be to look at the south-central Utah map and pick out the highways that are the primary access points for each area. The San Rafael Swell sites covered here are entered from Highways 10 and 24, and Interstate 70. The Henry Mountains and the region around them are served by Highways 24, 95, and 276, while the Circle Cliffs and plateau mountains are reached from the Burr Trail and Highways 12, 24, and 72.

Many of the sites and hikes covered in this guide have paved road access, but a larger number do not. It is surprising how many people we talk with at the Capitol Reef visitor center are very reluctant to even consider driving on a gravel road. In good weather, there are several important roads in south-central Utah that are well maintained and usually just fine for passenger cars. These include the main routes in the Swell north of the San Rafael River, the portion of the Burr Trail linking Highways 276 and 12, and the Posey Lake Road between Escalante and Highway 24. The primary north-south route through the Swell, the Temple Mountain Road from the Goblin Valley access road to the San Rafael River, is a little rougher, but can usually be negotiated in a well-driven, moderate-clearance passenger car; other routes in this category include the Hells Backbone Road, almost all of the road to Horseshoe Canyon, the road to the edge of Boulder Mountain from the northwest, the Hancock Flat Road, and the road up to the ridge of Thousand Lake Mountain from Highway 72.

When the road quality dips below the levels above, we have tried to be careful in describing the conditions you might expect. The big problem, however, is that adverse weather can change things in a hurry, and with lasting effect, even on the best of the gravel roads. The storms of September 2013, for example, rendered many back roads impassable for weeks. There were huge washouts and stream cuts, along with deposits of sand and mud, and persistent bogs without an alternate way around. For safety, it is therefore folly to enter the backcountry without knowledge of the weather forecast, and to avoid disappointment from weather events in the past, make sure to stop in at the relevant public lands or tourism office to get an update on conditions. Rest assured, though, that normally a standard SUV will access the vast majority of activities described in this book.

Then there is the matter of four-wheel drive (4WD) tracks. If you are an experienced driver of a short wheelbase high-clearance vehicle, there is nothing covered here that should be too challenging. On the other hand, if you are renting a standard 4WD SUV and have no experience with obstacles, steep pitches, sand, and mud, then we cannot stress enough the importance of using caution and good judgment before attempting, say, any of the 4WD tracks on top of Boulder Mountain. This is particularly critical because of the isolation and great distance from help up there. Keep in mind that we drive a Toyota pickup truck, an able and high clearance 4WD vehicle; if you have something longer and/or lower, the more difficult tracks will probably not be possible.

Buckhorn Wash

As noted above, and often in the text that follows, this guide is best enjoyed with a fine, up-to-date weather report. This doesn't mean that a 20 percent chance of showers in the middle of a period of nice sunny weather should necessarily keep you on paved roads, though it ought to cause you to choose some other activity than clambering through a slot canyon. On a broader scale, climate and elevation should factor into your trip planning. It is cold enough in the winter (mid-November through mid-March) that travel in this part of the world is very limited, even at low elevations. Spring is popular at low elevation as it offers long days, the onset of floral abundance, and generally pleasant temperatures. This is the windiest time, however, in the American Southwest, and access to the mountains may still be limited by snow. Summer is very hot down low, while the mountains provide welcome relief from the heat. July through September is the time of a monsoonal shift in the weather pattern, resulting in thunderstorms with occasional heavy rains that can make backcountry travel and hiking hazardous. Fall is a prime travel time, offering moderate temperatures and good color as the aspen and cottonwoods turn, but by autumn, cold fronts with associated severe weather can make it into the region. Insect pests, namely gnats and biting flies, can be annoying at lower elevations especially during May and June, and mosquitoes can be an issue near breeding areas during the summer.

It is important to know what this guide does *not* cover. Technical canyoneering and climbing routes, of which there are many, are left to other books. In the same vein, highly technical four-wheel drive roads and ATV tracks are beyond the scope of most visitors and are not included here. Please note, however, that some slot canyon routes and some 4WD tracks that are described may be beyond your personal comfort level. We have tried to offer the appropriate cautions, but you alone know your limits and must make good decisions. We do not describe little-known rock art sites, even though seeking them out is one of our most enjoyable activities. The reason is well known to rock art aficionados: the best protection for these fragile panels is the very fact that they are unknown to most, sadly not all, of those who would vandalize them. The sites we do cover are located and named on widely available maps.

Some of the hikes that are described in this book lack well-defined trails, or any trail at all. In these cases, GPS coordinates are usually included for important points. The next section covers GPS use in some detail; for experienced users of the technology, the coordinates are based on NAD 27.

Even though we are tempted, we do not discuss lodging, dining, and guide services available in south-central Utah. Our experience is that many of these come and go, some quickly, and that ownership and quality can change over time, for better or worse. In the Resources section at the end of the book, we have included websites for local travel councils, which contain addresses for many businesses that serve travelers.

Please Come Back and Visit Again

It will take many, many trips to even begin to feel that you have done justice to south-central Utah. So, let's be blunt: if you mess up and die in a flash flood, you will miss a lot. Even if you just have bad tires and two of them give up the ghost 17 miles from the nearest help and you forgot to bring more than a couple of cans of root beer and it is 95 degrees in the shade, the experience may not be one that leaves you thinking about the next trip even before you get back to your driveway on this one.

Many who spend considerable time rambling around in the backcountry can become complacent about the dangers there. It seems that every time this happens to us, Mother Nature (we call her "Mom") sends us a reminder. We have gotten lost. We have climbed up slopes that unexpectedly became cliffs, with no good way to reverse field. We have heard nearby thunder from inside slot canyons. We have watched good solid clay roads turn to goo in a matter of minutes. We have been caught in storms at high elevations on days predicted to be sunny and warm. We have fallen and seen others fall. One of us has had giardia not once, but three times. And we have flailed futilely against hordes of gnats. All this, yet we think of ourselves as cautious, thoughtfully regarding what we do, and well prepared. Even if you consider yourself to be all these things as well, Mom would like you to review the information in the rest of this section.

Flash Floods

Flash flood debris in Swett Canyon

Probably the gravest danger is an ironic one in this desert: flash floods. Capitol Reef gets about 8 inches of precipitation in a year, but is one of the most flash-flood prone places on earth. A look around is all it takes to figure out why. There is a lot of bare rock and gradients are steep. A moderate thunderstorm can generate big waterfalls off normally dry cliffs in minutes. If the water gets funneled into a slot canyon there may be no escape. Eleven people perished in such an event in Antelope Canyon near Page, Arizona, in 1997. Most of the best and deepest slots have

Flash flood in North Wash

logs and rocks wedged between the walls high above the canyon floor. While some slots have relatively small watersheds above them, others may get floods from many miles away, too far sometimes to even hear thunder from the storm.

Any time of the year it should be obvious that careful attention paid to the weather forecast is important, but it becomes absolutely critical during the monsoon season that often begins in July and continues well into September. Reading the local forecast discussion on www.weather.gov can be helpful, even with the jargon they use. Also important is to fully understand the characteristics of the drainage system above a slot. Of course, nothing can substitute for good judgment: plain and simple, if there is even a chance of rain, don't enter a slot, and if you are in one and hear thunder, get out. No exceptions.

GPS Technology

Not too long ago, just after global positioning system (GPS) technology became available to citizens, some eschewed its use as somehow tainting the wilderness experience. Now, altogether too many people rely on a cell phone to get them out of trouble in the backcountry, but the number of folks who have and know how to use a handheld GPS unit remains surprisingly small, even when they rely on the system in their car. In the region covered in this book, that situation can lead to real problems, since cell coverage is spotty at best, and often impossible. At least if you have a GPS and think to take a waypoint on your vehicle, you have a better chance of heading in the right direction even if the land is a spiderweb of canyons and mesas.

Then there is the quaint old-time skill of map reading. In many cases, having a topographic map and knowing how to visualize a three-dimensional landscape from that two-dimensional sheet of paper is enough. This is especially true if there is a prominent landmark close enough to your target to be helpful. Sadly, in country that is dissected by numerous drainages, a topo map may not be enough. The most powerful solution is to combine GPS coordinates with a map. For this reason the GPS readings in this guide use NAD 27 since the topographic maps are based on it as well. The metric (UTM) system is used because it permits easier interpolations on maps in the field. All coordinates are in Zone 12, so this notation is omitted in the text.

Complete dependence on a GPS unit is not a good approach, however, since batteries fail, signals can be lost in canyons, and accuracy can be affected by several factors. In the end, if you know what you are doing in terms of both map reading and GPS use, problems in finding your way should be rare. If you do not know how to use either aid, hike with someone who does, or stay on well-defined trails.

Being Prepared

There are several drives described in this book where it is likely that you will not see another vehicle all day, depending on the day of the week and time of the year. Additionally, when some critical vehicle part reaches its breaking point, or all the oil finally leaks out because the guy at the lube shop forgot to tighten the plug, or you lose your keys on the hike from the end of the road, you may be a long way from any kind of help, and well out of cell phone range. If no one in the party is capable of walking, say, 15 miles in the heat, such a situation could be very serious. Anyone who has heard of Aron Ralston's ordeal (as depicted in the movie *127 Hours*) knows to let a responsible person know where s/he is hiking and when the return will be, but the same principle applies to people driving off well-traveled roadways. It also doesn't take a lot of effort to take along items that could mean the difference between the experience being relatively comfortable and thus making for a great story back in Memphis or Munich, or becoming life threatening.

The list of those items is largely based on common sense: water, preferably a five gallon jug; plenty of food; extra clothing, including raingear; and the means to be comfortable if you have to spend the night. In some vehicles the seats fold down and a couple of air mattresses and sufficient blankets for the season are enough. Otherwise, why not throw in a tent? A second key (not left in the locked vehicle!) could be a wonderful thing. Extra medications are an obvious need. If you have the know-how, extra vehicle belts and related tools are handy to have.

Self-Rescue

Being prepared for self-rescue if you get stuck is very important, since this is probably more likely than a mechanical problem. Getting stuck usually requires rain or sand. The roads at moderate elevations in this part of the world are often mere gradings of the existing terrain, or just untended two tracks. We have found it surprising that roads on silt or sandy geologic formations can still become impassible with modest rainfall. Roads on clay, well, you can guess the result when a thunderstorm passes overhead. Self-rescue when these roads go bad consists of waiting for them to dry out. This can be a short process if it is warm and the sun comes out, or a much longer one in cooler months. Either way, preparation is the key to enjoying the break from driving.

Sand is a different story. Obviously, it makes the most sense to not bog down in the first place. Momentum is the key in many circumstances. Driven fast enough, two-wheel drive vehicles can get through short patches that might stop four-wheel drive (4WD) vehicles driven too tentatively. Of course, all other things equal, 4WD is critical for many sandy roads, and it can reduce the need to go too fast and thus lose control. If you do get to feel the dread of your vehicle slowly coming to a stop in the middle of a stretch of sand, the first thing to do is to let off on the accelerator; if you don't it will take only seconds for the tires to dig vast holes that will soon lower the frame onto the sand. This is not good, as you may imagine. Assuming that you had the discipline to not make matters worse, if you are prepared it may be possible to extricate your vehicle even if it is not equipped with a winch (if it does have a winch, we are going to assume that you know how to operate it effectively and safely).

The essentials are a good shovel and several lengths of solid dimension lumber. We always have a small spade in the truck, and a full size one if there is a chance of sand. A good strong grain scoop–type of shovel can move a lot of sand quickly as well. It is often the case that the layer of dry sand may be thin enough that simply digging down to firmer or wetter material may be sufficient to get the vehicle out. This is especially likely if there are drifts of sand across a road that are separated by bare spots. When digging is not enough, four lengths of lumber may be. These should be at least 2 by 8 inches (2x10s are much better) and several feet long. Getting the wheels up onto the boards will require plenty of digging in most cases. If you think about it, it is even good to have four more boards to link up with the ones the truck is already on.

An important trick in driving through sand, or getting out of it, is to lower the pressure in your tires, perhaps as low as 10 pounds per square inch. Traction increases significantly if you do this. Once again, preparation is important: if you have canned air you can continue with your drive rather than limp back very slowly to the nearest gas station after you get out of the sand. Ultimately, experience is the key. If you have any doubt at all about getting through sand (or mud for that matter), simply turn around and enjoy the rest of the day.

Falling Rock

Many rescues in Utah's backcountry are the result of falls, or being hit by falling rock. The Navajo Sandstone is a true Jekyll and Hyde story in this regard. Much of the time the Navajo is firm and steady, solid as a rock. All too often, however, the cementing agent, usually calcite, is weak, and the sandstone can literally crumble in your hand.

Weathering also accelerates in and along cracks, and large pieces of rock can detach from cliffbands, even slopes. Rocks that are already free of bedrock may be turning to sand underneath, and can topple without notice. Every rock unit on the Colorado Plateau has some idiosyncrasy that can wreak havoc on the unwary or careless hiker, characteristics that are even more dangerous for those who do their sightseeing while walking, rather than pausing and truly taking in the scenery. The fresh scars of rockfalls, perhaps best illustrated in the Wingate Sandstone, are testimony to that risk as well.

Heat-Related Dangers

Awareness of heat-related dangers has increased, but it is still altogether common to see people several miles from a trailhead on a hot day with a single 20-ounce bottle of water, or, frequently, an empty 20-ounce container. You no doubt know the drill already, but heat problems can sneak up on almost anyone. There are various prescriptions for the amount of water to take on a hike or pack, but people are very different, and one size does not fit all. We have gone through a gallon of water each when we expected to need only a couple of quarts. In the desert, temperatures and the low humidity may make mornings cool, and it is easy to decide against carrying that extra couple or four pounds of water. Go ahead and put those bottles into the pack anyway. Drink early and often. Wear light-colored clothing and a big floppy hat that would make Grandma nostalgic. Importantly, stay within your physical limits. Consider what might happen if you get lost.

Hyponatremia

If the danger of dehydration is becoming more well known, less progress is occurring in terms of its sister threat, hyponatremia. It occurs when electrolytes become unbalanced and the proportion of sodium in the fluid outside of body cells falls below normal levels. This can happen due to numerous causes. Even healthy people can become victims if they consume only water during long periods of strenuous activity. As brain cells respond by swelling, disorientation can occur, followed by very serious, even life-threatening symptoms. This kind of hyponatremia can usually be prevented by adding electrolyte drinks and making sure to eat along with drinking. Mom also says that long hikes are not an appropriate time to limit your calories, so take along food you really like, and enjoy it.

Perils

Excessive reliance on guidebooks, especially for those new to backcountry exploration, can lead to trouble as well. No matter how carefully researched, no guidebook can cover everything, and it is not possible to discern readers' particular skills and deficiencies and account for them all. That said, perhaps the most significant problem is that things change on the ground, often in profound ways. Slot canyons are the obvious example: all it takes is one storm to alter a perfectly pleasant walk-through slot into a nightmare of tangled tree debris, deep pools, or impassable obstacles. Roads, too, can be washed out, covered by slides, or simply disappear from lack of use, not to mention the temporary nature of signs. When you encounter something that doesn't square with the description here, be prepared to adjust and use good judgment.

The list of perils, of course, goes on and on: snakes, scorpions, spiders, rabid bats, mountain lions, sharp pointy things like cactus and Russian olive, quicksand, sunstroke, sunburn, lightning, hypothermia, altitude sickness, spousal or significant other arguments, excessive alcohol consumption, giardia, forest fire, high winds, missing tent poles, and, most serious, a wreck on the Interstate getting to Utah. If even the remotest possibility of any of these things scares you to death, it may be that you should stay within sight of a Walmart at all times. Otherwise, simply keep your common sense on active duty, be flexible, and let this exquisitely beautiful part of the world lift your spirit.

August hail on Boulder Mountain

The Colorado Plateau

The area covered in this guide is situated on the west side of the Colorado Plateau. The continental United States is divided by the U.S. Geological Survey (USGS) into ten geological provinces, large areas that share similar features and origins. Five of the provinces are east of the Front Range of the Rocky Mountains, and five to the west. The Colorado Plateau is one of them, an area of approximately 140,000 square miles. It is bounded by the Rocky Mountains Province on the east and north, and the Basin and Range Province to the south and west. In terms of prominent markers, the Colorado Plateau extends to the base of the Uinta Mountains to the north; the Uncompahgre Plateau, San Juan Mountains, and Sangre de Christo Range on the east; the Mogollon Rim to the south; and to the Wasatch Plateau on the west. Boundaries of the province are, of course, subject to discussion and new evidence, and many geologists include the Wasatch Plateau as part of the Colorado Plateau (CP).

The CP is characterized by a thick sequence of sedimentary rocks that lie notably flat compared to the strata all around the province. There are exceptions to this rule, such as the sharply tilted (dipping) limbs of monoclines and asymmetrical anticlines like the Waterpocket Fold of Capitol Reef and the San Rafael Reef. Farther east, beds dip due to the influence of the movement of salt evaporites in an ancient basin around Moab. Despite these localized anomalies, most CP rock layers are horizontal, or close to it.

Mancos Shale near Millsite State Park

Geological Record

In south-central Utah, unless you are at high elevation, the chances are great that you will be walking on rock or soil derived from rock that was deposited during the Mesozoic Era, the age of the dinosaurs. There are three geologic periods in the Mesozoic: the Triassic, which began about 245 million years ago (ma) and ended 206 ma; the Jurassic (206–144 ma); and the Cretaceous (144–66 ma). The timeframes and names of the periods were developed in Europe, mostly by careful analysis of fossils, and long before radioactive isotope dating methodology emerged. In general, the length and identity of the divisions of geologic time have persisted and remain the standard reference today. The Mesozoic Era itself is bounded on both ends by worldwide mass extinction events that dramatically changed the relative abundance and dominance of life forms.

In the geological record it is usually the case that there are huge gaps of time when there are no rocks to record them. Most often this is because the surface was uplifted and erosion was the dominant factor; less likely is a period of stability with little erosion or deposition. Continental land masses are under constant attack by erosion, with the fastest rates where elevations are highest. The Colorado Plateau is not as high as some of the surrounding mountains, but it does average about a mile above sea level, and it consists of generally very soft rocks. Therefore, the many unconformities that occur in the strata laid down in the past are being repeated right now in the present.

Sedimentary Rock

Clastic sedimentary rocks reflect a process of weathering and erosion of existing rocks somewhere else, the transport of that material by water, ice, or wind, eventual deposition in a basin, and then lithification into rock by a variety of processes. Other sedimentary rocks are the result of evaporation of sea water (gypsum, for example), precipitation of limestone or dolomite directly from water, or the accumulation of marine or lake dwelling animals' calcareous parts (also limestone). Absent significant tectonic forces that tilt or break sedimentary strata, the layers will pile up on each other, with youngest rocks on the top of the pile. The term "layer cake" has probably been overused in describing the Colorado Plateau geology, but it persists because the image is appropriate.

It is interesting to contemplate how several hundred feet, even up to several thousand feet, of sediments of similar type could all be deposited within, say, a dozen yards of sea level. There are two possibilities, both illustrated on the CP. One is that sea level could rise at about the same rate of deposition, and it is clear that sea level has oscillated very significantly over geologic time. Since the periodicity for this ebb and flow (regression and transgression) is fairly short compared to common rates of deposition, it is actually more likely that sea level change will overtake the process and result in different types of environments into which sediment is laid down.

Tectonic Movement

The more important factor is tectonic movement of the earth's crust. When large sections (plates) of the crust move around there is often vertical thickening where the denser ocean plates slide under a continent and drag the crust along until it ripples. The high point of the ripple will be a mountain range, and just in front of that will be a depression, or basin. Just before the Mesozoic, a classic basin formed to the west of the Uncompahgre uplift in western Colorado. Over time, astonishingly thick, recurring deposits of gypsum, dolomite, shale, dolomite, gypsum, and salt were formed as the basin subsided and sea level fluctuated back and forth some thirty or more times. Later, in the Mesozoic, tectonic uplift to the west, in present-day Nevada and western Utah, created a long linear basin just to the east of the emerging mountains.

Tectonic basins are almost always asymmetrical, with a steep side next to the uplift, and a more gradual slope away from it. This was the case with both the earlier Paradox Basin on the east side of the CP, and the Utah-Nevada Trough that developed on the west side during the middle Jurassic Period. The result of the asymmetry is thicker deposits near the uplift. Often, rock units will not only thin as the distance to the uplift increases, but they may grade laterally into an entirely different type. For example, if the basin contains a shallow sea in its deepest part, limestone might be deposited there. On the margin of the sea, rivers could lay down sand, silt, or mud in deltas, and if the climate was arid, as it often was, especially during the Jurassic on the CP, there might be large dune fields on shore between the rivers. Thus, the rock types that result are very diverse, but they are contemporaneous.

The Effect of Climate

The effect of climate on the deposition of materials that will become sedimentary rocks is important. Extreme aridity, in combination with a source of sand, can lead to massive ergs (dune fields). On the other hand, a warm and moist climate, in conjunction with very low terrestrial relief, will produce lush vegetation on the edge of large lakes and swamps. Over the sweep of geologic time, the Colorado Plateau area has seen both of these extremes, along with incursions of inland seas. The major changes in climate over very long timeframes are caused by the movement of the North American plate and the location of other plates. Several times during earth's history, the continental plates have merged into one supercontinent; the last time was during the Pennsylvanian and Permian Periods, just before the Triassic. The huge landmass was called Pangaea, and it extended almost from pole to pole. During the Triassic, the CP was positioned equatorially near the western edge of Pangaea, and there are indications that the climate was monsoonal in nature, with fairly high total precipitation spread over an annual cycle of wet and dry periods.

The break-up of Pangaea began in the Jurassic and the northward movement of

North America carried the CP through many climatic zones. Latitude was an important factor, but orientation to prevailing winds, the presence or absence of upwind mountain ranges, and ocean currents all played a role in determining the paleoenvironment. Just as the Colorado River flows across an arid landscape today, in the past there were times when large rivers flowed from higher ground across the CP. Often, however, the gradients were much lower than at present, and the rivers were agents of deposition rather than erosion.

The Laramide Orogeny

Sedimentary rocks accumulated over hundreds of millions of years on the CP, much of the time when there was low relief and often when at least part of the area was covered by sea water. As noted above, however, the CP is currently about a mile above sea level, and some marine formations are considerably higher than that. The question, then, is how this massive area was lifted many thousands of feet without a great deal of deformation such as folding and faulting. Part of the answer might reside with the onset of the mountain building event that shaped the Intermountain West. The Laramide Orogeny lasted for tens of millions of years centered on the end of the Cretaceous Period. A small Pacific Ocean plate, the Farallon, slipped under (subducted) North America. While the exact mechanism of the uplift is not yet agreed upon, this event elevated the Rocky Mountains some three miles (near the end of the Cretaceous, a large inland sea extended from central Utah to the current Missouri River). It seems very likely that the CP was also elevated at least modestly during this period.

Most of the rise of the Colorado Plateau, however, may be considerably more recent. New ways of looking into the crust and upper mantle have spawned theories about the rise of the CP, but consensus is lacking. Phase changes in the material near the crust/mantle boundary would have resulted in differing specific gravities, and might be responsible for uplift. Alternatively, the low angle subduction of the Farallon Plate could have scraped off some of the bottom of the crust, which was then replaced by hotter and more buoyant material from the mantle. On the other hand, after the compressional Laramide Orogeny concluded, the crust began to stretch under much of the West and all the way east to the Rio Grande rift zone. The Basin and Range Province dropped several thousand feet in comparison to the CP; if the latter was elevated to near its present elevation during the Laramide, perhaps the current situation merely reflects the drop of the Basin and Range.

Erosion

Around the beginning of the period of crustal extension, some 30 ma, magma was able to rise up through the lithosphere. Over much of the Colorado Plateau, the molten material did not break the surface, and solidified in place. These granitic rocks have been subsequently exposed by erosion of the soft sedimentary layers above them, and now stand out as mountains: the La Sals, Abajos, Henrys, and Navajo. When the magmas did reach the surface it was often in the form of explosive eruptions that spread ashflow tuffs over wide areas. Fishlake Hightop, and Thousand Lake and Boulder Mountains are capped by these resistant units. More information on these events is included in the Henry Mountains and Plateaus sections.

The Colorado Plateau is highly unusual in that it was a stable, near sea level, platform for hundreds of millions of years. Unconformities certainly indicate times of erosion, but there were also very long periods of deposition. Now, however, the elevation of the CP and the development of a drainage system to the sea mean that erosion is occurring on a prodigious scale. The Colorado River is the baseline, but its current course is relatively new. Prior to about 6 ma, the drainage pattern in the Grand Canyon area was to the northwest. Sometime in the next 1.5 million years, the river began to flow in its present location, downcutting vigorously through the sedimentary rocks to the crystalline basement rocks more than a billion years old. Many of the spectacular landforms on the Colorado Plateau today owe their existence to the processes of weathering and erosion that were greatly enhanced by the incision of the Colorado River.

More information about geology and specific formations can be found in the descriptions of drives and hikes in this guide, generally at a place where you can see and feel the rock. Given the region's current dry climate and ephemeral watercourses, many of the processes that are preserved in the rock units can be seen in action at the surface. Since the present is indeed the key to the geologic past, it is rewarding to attend to detail occasionally, even when faced with the grandeur of a single vista that reveals 200 million years of earth activity.

Moenkopi Formation

Flora and Fauna

Flora

South-central Utah has an exquisitely diverse spectrum of plants, from showy to mundane, common to very rare. Elevation change does most of the work, but soils derived from an entire suite of sedimentary rocks also matter. Microenvironments and the uncommon presence of perennial streams are significant as well. From the blackbrush desert near Lake Powell to the alpine tundra atop Mount Ellen, this part of the world has plants that are adapted to dry heat all the way to those that can tolerate cold and wind. The differences in elevation give flower lovers an extended period to seek out the blooms; some will appear in March down low, while the peak at 11,000 feet will usually be in July. As a bonus, when the monsoon season brings good summer rain, many species will take advantage and flower again. At all elevations, precipitation is a critical factor, as dry years can be bland and wet years may produce an amazing explosion of color.

In 1889, C. Hart Merriam analyzed the plant communities from the bottom of the Grand Canyon up to the summit of Mt. Humphreys, well above timberline. He then formulated a list of life zones that were mostly dependent on elevation, though he recognized that higher latitudes would result in similar designations. Merriam's life zones are not referenced as much today, but they are useful in providing a framework for thinking about Colorado Plateau flora.

The lowest zone relevant to south-central Utah is the upper Sonoran, generally between 3,500 and 7,000 feet in elevation, and characterized by desert scrub, piñon-juniper forest, grassland, or sagebrush. The transition zone is next, dominated by ponderosa pine and falling at elevations between 6,000 and 9,000 feet. The Canadian zone, 7,500 to 9,500 feet, is recognized by populations of Douglas fir, white fir, aspen, and Gambel oak. From 8,000 to 11,500 feet is the Hudsonian zone, with Engelmann spruce and subalpine fir, and then the Arctic or alpine zone above timberline where lichens, herbs, sedges, grasses, rushes, and mosses dominate. The limitations of Merriam's system are clearly illustrated by the wide variety of ecosystems contained within the upper Sonoran zone, along with the overlapping elevation boundaries. Nonetheless, he reminds us of the impact of precipitation and temperature on the plant communities found on the Plateau.

In the area covered by this guide, it may be more useful to recognize plant zones as follows: desert scrub, piñon-juniper, ponderosa forest, evergreen-aspen forest, subalpine forest, and tundra. A drive from Hanksville up to Bull Creek Pass in the Henry Mountains and then a short walk up Mount Ellen will pass through every one of these zones.

Near Lake Powell, which when full tops out at 3,700 feet in elevation, the plant community is truly desert-like. Summer high temperatures well above 100 degrees are common, and with annual precipitation of about 6 inches, this is tough territory for plants. Characteristic species include prickly pear cactus, blackbrush, mat saltbush, and bunch grasses. During wet springs a profusion of flowers may bloom; if you are fortunate enough to walk the Pedestal Alley Trail, or drive across Big Thompson Mesa (both described in the Clay Point Circuit section) at the right time, it will be an experience to remember. The area around Hanksville, and along Highway 24 to I-70 and on to Green River is desert scrub; near the junction of 24 and I-70 a near monoculture of shadscale exists.

The piñon-juniper zone (often called PJ, and sometimes the pygmy forest) covers a vast territory in south-central Utah. Commonly present between roughly 5,000 and 7,000 feet, PJ illustrates how other factors can extend its range. On the south slope of Mount Ellen in the Henry Mountains, PJ, along with Gambel oak, climbs up from Pennellen Pass to around 10,000 feet on the sunny, south-facing slope. At that elevation there are few, if any, junipers, while at the lowest levels of the PJ zone there are often no piñons. Associated plants are very numerous; a sample includes roundleaf buffaloberry, four wing saltbush, many cacti, rabbitbrush, and forbs such as Utah penstemon, cryptantha, many hard to identify milkvetches, several milkweeds, naked stem sunrays, paintbrush, globemallow, and scorpionweed. The sunrays reflect the impact of soil type, as they like soil that is derived from mudstones with some gypsum present. They are therefore abundant on the Moenkopi and Entrada Formations, and unusual elsewhere. Most of the San Rafael Swell, the lower flanks of the Henrys, the Circle Cliffs area, and Miners Mountain west of Capitol Reef all boast well-developed PJ forest.

Perhaps the best place to see the ponderosa forest is along Highway 12, south of Torrey. Upon en-

Beeplant

Brittle scorpionweed

Evening primrose

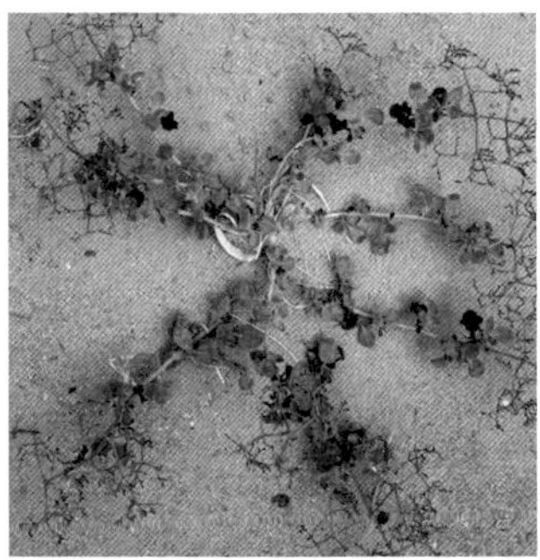

Swett Canyon *Eriogonum*

Fishhook cactus

Gambel oak

Sego lilies

Princes plume

tering the Dixie National Forest, ponderosa pines dominate along the highway until it climbs out of their comfort zone. The ponderosa forest marks a significant change from the scattered small trees of the PJ to large trees that may form a canopy over large areas of ground. Across the Intermountain West, the urban interface that is so vulnerable to fire is often ponderosa forest. The vulnerability has increased over years of fire suppression and now due to the twin forces of warmer temperatures and less moisture, especially in the form of earlier snowmelt. Ponderosas are the home and food of the Abert squirrel, a handsome tassel-eared animal with a long fluffy tail that is white underneath.

With increasing elevation, the ponderosas slowly give way to a mix of aspen and conifers. Douglas fir and white fir may be found at the lower reaches of this zone, though Douglas fir usually prefers wetter areas on north-facing slopes or in canyons. As elevation increases, subalpine fir and Engelmann spruce become more numerous. The stars, of course, are the aspen. Just as the maples of New England attract hordes of leaf peepers in the fall, the brief show of color of aspen in the West is worthy of making a special effort to see. While all four of the mountains described in this book offer wonderful aspen viewing, Fish Lake and Fish Lake Hightop are extra special. Slope aspect is important for aspen; on south-facing slopes they can thrive at high elevations, and are subject to heat and drought-related problems at lower elevation.

When the aspen finally thin out entirely, Engelmann spruce and subalpine fir make up the subalpine forest. Depending on localized conditions, the spruces can be so large and the forest so lush that Utah can feel a little bit like the Pacific Northwest. As the upper limit is reached, the trees are scattered and may be distorted by the severe climate. Small clumps of windblown spruce are called krummholz, from the German words for crooked wood. As of this writing, the spruce in south-central Utah are doing pretty well, but just to the east in the San Juan Mountains of Colorado, the spruce beetle has devastated hundreds of thousands of acres, leaving entire hillsides covered with Engelmann skeletons. Other species of bark beetles affect different trees, and without the cold winters of the past to limit the beetle populations, it is likely that infestations will continue across the West. The plateau of Boulder Mountain is a mix of subalpine forest and meadows, and lovely lakes. The hike to Trail Point is a sublime walk through the subalpine.

The only alpine zone in this region is on the Mount Ellen ridge, where the elevation alone is not quite high enough for tundra without the cold winds that flow over the peak, especially in the winter. Alpine flowers share a couple of qualities: they keep their heads down, and when it comes time to bloom and set seed, they waste absolutely no time. Without competition, brilliant lichens thrive on the summit boulders, while grasses and sedges colonize small pockets of soil among the rocks.

Up through the ponderosa zone, the ability to manage water in an arid environment is a key factor in determining which plants can survive in this part of Utah. There are many strategies. Thick skin that limits water loss works for cacti, in combination with the ability to store water within the plant. Small leaves like those of blackbrush, or the waxy leaves of greasewood help to keep transpiration as low as possible. Roundleaf buffaloberry leaves are light gray and a little shiny on top to reflect light, and fine hairs on the bottom help to cool the leaves. They also curl downward to present less surface area to the sun.

A different approach to water is taken by species that are annuals—those that grow from seed each year. Rather than put a lot of energy into big root systems or foliage, this group sets seed that can persist in a dormant state in the soil for years. When conditions are just right, the seed germinates and the plant quickly goes through its life cycle. The sunflowers so common along the roads in late summer are annuals. Dwarf lupines and annual townsendias are annuals, while others in their genera are perennials. Perhaps the most spectacular display of annuals occurs rarely on the clay flats near Caineville, when yellow beeplant, Eastwoods sundrops, and brittle scorpionweed carpet the gray Mancos Shale. In general, the drier the climate, the higher the percentage of annuals will be. This is largely because the perennials must scatter themselves widely, thereby providing plenty of open soil and sunshine for annuals to grow.

When the rains do come, dry country perennials are ready. Unless there is a nearby subsoil source of water, spending a lot of energy developing a deep taproot is self-defeating. Instead, a wide network of roots, almost always very near the surface, is the strategy that is most effective. Even ponderosa pines have very shallow root systems designed to take advantage of rains that fall short of saturating more than a few inches of soil. An exception to the rule of extensive lateral root systems is found in the bunchgrasses, which focus on creating deep roots below a compact above-ground clump.

Information about specific plants is included in sections of this guide that describe places where the plants can usually be seen. Obviously, in the case of plants that are primarily of interest for their flowers, you will have to be there at the right time during the right year in many cases. When those things come together in spectacular fashion, it is often worth changing a vacation schedule to take advantage of the show.

Fauna

Lizard

Even in dry years, there will be some flowers and shrubs to observe, but animal sightings are obviously more random. Lizards, insects, birds, and antelope ground squirrels are common enough, but the larger, more charismatic species are elusive. Mule deer can almost always be viewed in Fruita in Capitol Reef and alongside Highway 12, especially in late afternoon and early evening, but other ungulates are much less likely to be seen by travelers. Sightings of desert bighorn sheep are not uncommon in Capitol Reef, but rare elsewhere.

There are three large animal species that we see frequently enough to suggest that you might as well, with just a little luck. During the March through October high travel season, elk are in the high country meadows and forest on the plateaus. Highway 12 is the best bet, but Highway 72 and any of the roads that lead up to the higher elevations also are possibilities.

We think that pronghorns are the most handsome of the game species, and they are fairly common in and around the San Rafael Swell, often grazing in alfalfa fields in the Castle Valley. They actually are really fast: one day we were driving at forty miles an hour on a fine gravel road in Buckhorn Flat when we were passed by a single pronghorn running parallel to the road and some 50 yards away from it. Without anthropomorphizing too much, hopefully, it truly appeared that the animal was running for sheer pleasure.

If you have traveled to Yellowstone you have probably seen bison in the wild, or at least as wild as it can be in the midst of motor homes and plaid shorts. A very different experience can be had in the Henrys where the bison herd is truly free-ranging and, because their numbers are kept in check by hunting, they are truly wild. Along with the huge mule deer in the range, the opportunity, even if unlikely, to see bison, certainly adds to the reasons to visit this isolated area and its rough roads.

If birds had twitter accounts, the most likely users would be piñon jays. These bright blue denizens of the PJ forest follow the pine nuts in large flocks, bouncing from tree to tree, chattering loudly as they go. If you are out hiking and a flock passes nearby, it is not something you will forget. The other birdsound that we find memorable is the lovely call of the canyon wren, its descending notes distinctive enough to always remind us that we are back in redrock country. Summer residents such as the spectacular yellow, black, white, and red western tanager and a host of other species are quite common near riparian areas.

Of the several bat species found in Utah, the one most commonly seen is probably the western pipistrelle, for the simple reason that it begins to feed in the early evening when there is still plenty of light. It is the smallest bat in North America, weighing in at less than two-tenths of an ounce. Pipistrelles are often the stars of ranger-led evening programs at Capitol Reef as they zigzag over the amphitheatre feeding on insects attracted by the lights. In the same size range, hummingbirds are common, not only around feeders, but in many canyons as well. The black-chinned is the most likely to be seen.

If you have a special interest in plants or animals, a handy reference is the collection of lists available at the Capitol Reef visitor center. There are handouts describing the common wildflowers, common trees and shrubs, mammals, birds, and reptiles and amphibians. There is also a very useful compendium of all the plants that have been found in the park. Because Capitol Reef contains all but the high elevation life zones, these lists are relevant for most of the areas described in this book.

Mount Ellen mule deer

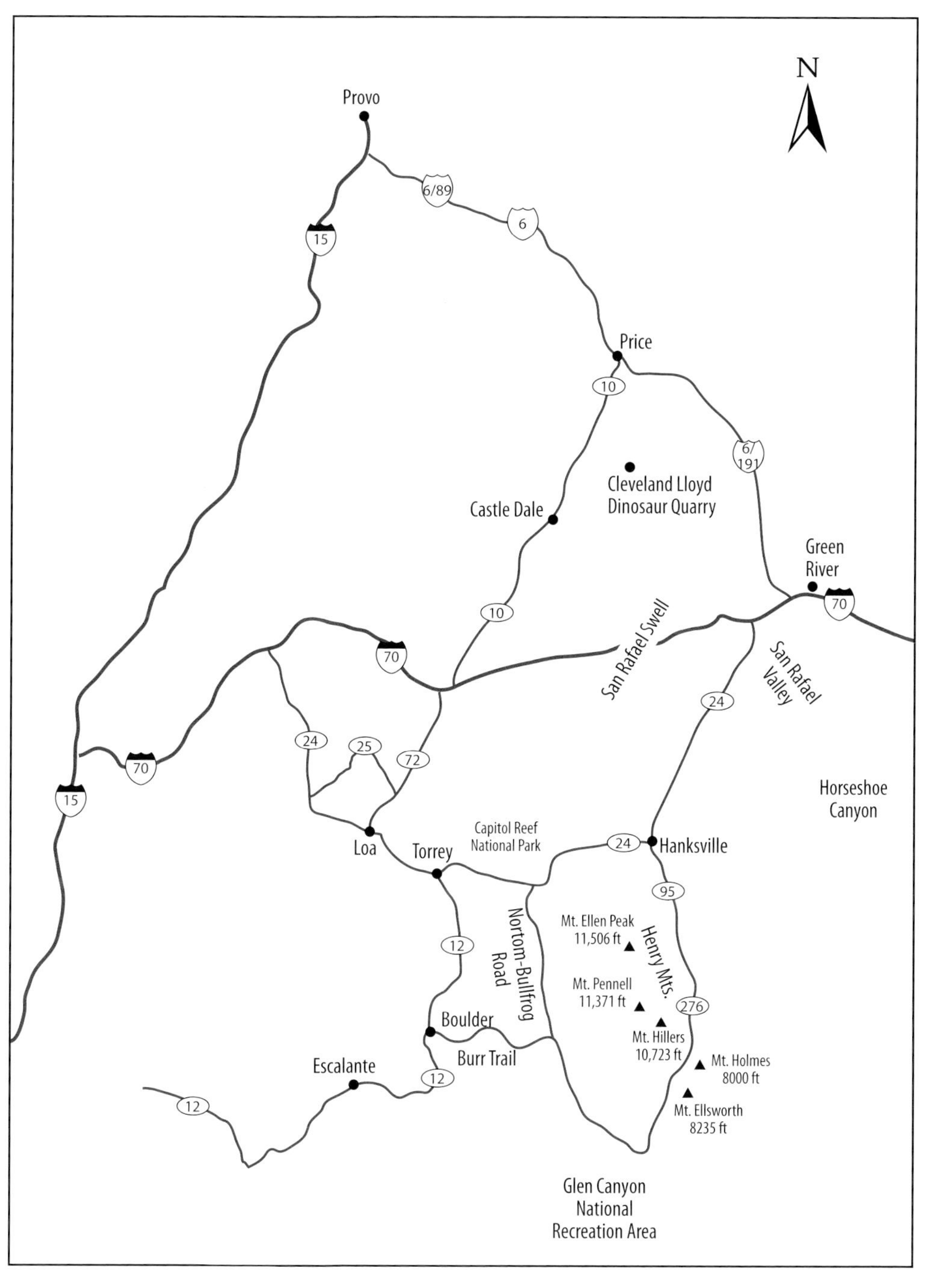
N
Provo
6/89
6
15
Price
10
6/191
Cleveland Lloyd
Dinosaur Quarry
Castle Dale
Green
River
70
10
San Rafael Swell
San Rafael
Valley
70
24
24
25
72
70
15
Horseshoe
Canyon
Capitol Reef
National Park
Loa
Torrey
24
Hanksville
95
Nortom-Bullfrog
Road
Henry Mts.
Mt. Ellen Peak
11,506 ft
12
Mt. Pennell
11,371 ft
276
Boulder
Mt. Hillers
10,723 ft
Burr Trail
Escalante
12
Mt. Holmes
8000 ft
12
Mt. Ellsworth
8235 ft
Glen Canyon
National
Recreation Area

The San Rafael Swell

San Rafael Reef

As the name implies, the San Rafael Swell is a topographic high that rises out of the relatively flat ground between the Wasatch Plateau to the west and the Book Cliffs to the east. Geologically, the Swell bears considerable resemblance to the Waterpocket Fold area of Capitol Reef National Park. Created by an uplift during the Laramide Orogeny, the structure is that of an asymmetrical anticline, with steeply dipping beds on the southeast flank, and less-tilted strata to the northwest.

Along the San Rafael Reef that is prominently exposed along Highway 24 from Hanksville to Interstate 70 just west of Green River, there is a lot of geology displayed over very short distances. A hiker passing all the way through one of the slot canyons along the Reef could begin on the Entrada Sandstone and work back through the rest of the Jurassic Period and, with a little effort beyond the slot portion, cover almost all the Triassic as well. There are few other places where a day hiker can expect to walk on seven different major formations. In the center of the Swell, the arched form of the anticline has been eroded to reveal even older rocks, down to Permian sandstones that are so beautifully cut by Baptist Draw and Upper Chute Canyon.

The Swell is a classic case of a place that means different things to different people. To some, it is empty and forlorn, devoid of occupied houses, dotted with scraggly piñons and junipers, and littered with abandoned dreams and schemes. Others see it as a playground for ATVs and dirt bikes; hunters appreciate the opportunity it offers; and ranchers are happy to have a place to graze their cattle. People with old pickup campers relish the solitude that is easily found. Adventurers travel great distances to work the slots and canyons, and even travelers driving through on I-70 marvel at the sculpted and brilliantly colored rock outcrops. An effort to designate the Swell as a national monument is touted by some, and scoffed at by others. In short, no matter your scenic, travel, or adventure proclivities, there is probably good reason to spend a little or a lot of time discovering its virtues.

The other major draw is one that might surprise the casual observer. The San Rafael Swell is loaded with some of the highest quality rock art sites in the American Southwest, or, indeed, anywhere. What now seems to be a somewhat barren and harsh landscape attracted members of prehistoric cultures from many thousands of years ago up to the people of the Fremont Culture who lived in Utah until roughly 800 years ago. Some of the best panels were painted by people who are now described as members of the Desert Archaic culture. Their artistic style is often called Barrier Canyon, and some of the incredibly well-preserved pictographs may be six thousand years or more old. Over more recent times, a lot of vandalism has diminished many of these beautiful and information-rich sites. The best protection is simply to not publicize locations of panels, so only those that are already well-known and noted on widely used current maps are described here.

Change is already happening, and from our perspective, it would be better to visit sooner rather than later. In the decade that we have been regularly exploring the Swell, the numbers of people and vehicles we encounter have been steadily rising. Little Wild Horse Canyon can be a mass of humanity on almost any nice weekend, and busy much of the rest of the time. New gravel superhighways in the north have made access much easier, and while you might have sunset to yourself at the Wedge Overlook, the chances of that are diminishing. Of course, these things are relative—the Swell is not going to attract visitors at the rate of Zion or Arches, not ever, but the solitude that is currently possible with modest effort is eroding around the edges.

The Swell is neatly divided by I-70, which bisects it on a largely east to west track. The northern half is most easily approached from Highway 10, which links the Interstate to Price, running northeasterly through the Castle Valley. Small towns, flanked by irrigated fields, are dotted along the way. Traffic, including massive coal haulers, increases as you drive toward Price. From Capitol Reef, the easiest way to get to Highway 10 and the Castle Valley is by taking Highways 24 and 72.

Northern San Rafael Swell

Highway 72

Highway 72 is one of the least traveled highways in a state that has plenty of lonely roads, but it is highly scenic and a good alternative for travel from Capitol Reef or scenic Highway 12 to Castle Valley, Price, and the Northern San Rafael Swell along Highway 10. On a clear day the views to the east from Hogan Pass include the San Rafael Swell, Cathedral Valley, Factory Butte, the Abajos, and the Henry Mountains. Our drives on Highway 72 have resulted in more deer sightings than oncoming vehicles almost every time.

From Capitol Reef, travel west on Highway 24 through Torrey and Bicknell to Lyman. Here, the road bends to the west and shoots straight across the Rabbit Valley toward Loa. Less than 2 miles from Lyman, a paved county road, signed for Fremont, heads north (right) and connects in a mile with Highway 72 at a four-way stop. (For those approaching Loa from the west, Highway 72 intersects at a left, or east, turn at Highway 24 on the north edge of town; it is 1.2 miles to the four-way stop with the county road.)

Zero the odometer at the four-way stop, and proceed north (straight if approaching on the county road, and left if already on 72 from Loa). A quick diversion into the village of Fremont at the 3.4-mile mark (turn left, west on Main Street) is worthwhile to see the old Worthen's store, on the right (north), about a block from Highway 72. The store is constructed of red sandstone, gray welded tuff, petrified wood, and, on the front façade, quite a collection of other interesting minerals and rocks. The irrigated alfalfa fields and residences continue for a couple of miles past Fremont, and then there are no more on the entire length of Highway 72 to its terminus at Interstate 70.

The paved road to Mill Meadows Reservoir, Johnson Reservoir, and Fish Lake (described in the Fish Lake section) turns to the left (west) at the cattleguard that also marks the boundary of the Fishlake National Forest at mile 8.6. Just under 2 miles farther on the right (east) is the gravel road that leads to Thousand Lake Mountain (described in its namesake section). Highway 72 drops down to the access road (on the left, west) to Forsyth Reservoir and then begins a gradual climb to Hogan Pass. The country is wide open, mostly high sagebrush meadow with scattered groups of aspen. The pass at mile 16.5 offers several overlooks to the east where expansive views on clear days extend easily to the La Sal Mountains east of Moab.

While deer are the most common large animals (wild ones, that is) along Highway 72, this is also a place where if you are lucky, a herd of elk might be visible almost anywhere along the way. Long lumped together in one species with the red deer of Europe, most references now single out new world elk as the species *Cervus canadensis*. They are the second largest member of the deer family in North America (only moose are larger), and bulls of the largest subspecies, Roosevelt elk, can weigh well over a thousand pounds. In addition to being much larger than mule deer, elk are a darker brown, and have a conspicuous white rump with a tiny tail. The antlers of the males can be very impressive, up to four feet across.

Elk are ruminants, with a four-chamber stomach. Although they do browse like deer, especially in the winter, they prefer to graze whenever possible. Grasses are the mainstay of their diet, but leaves and bark are also consumed. Few sounds, if any, in nature are as spectacular as the bugling of bulls during the rut as they attempt to lure females into their harems. Only the strongest males are able to maintain harems of up to twenty females during the breeding period, which runs from August into late fall. While elk eat almost continuously during the summer, bulls often eat very little during the rut, and may be weakened enough that they are unable to survive a hard winter. During the rest of the year elk tend to congregate in male or female (with calves) groups, sometimes in very large herds. In summer they are usually found at high to very high elevations, especially in meadows that are fringed with dense forest.

The highway descends steeply from the pass and then winds through vast stands of piñons, occasional ponderosas, and meadows. The Last Chance Road goes to the left (west) at mile 23.1. Initially a good gravel road, it eventually becomes high clearance and leads to Red Creek Hole and UM Pass just north of Hilgard Mountain, then descends back to good gravel in Sheep Valley before joining the paved road east of Fish Lake. Highway 72 leaves the national forest at mile 25.8. For the Castle Valley and San Rafael Swell, bear right (northeast) at the junction with Highway 76 at mile 33. Highway 72 then parallels I-70 for almost 2 miles to a stop sign. Turn left (north), pass under the Interstate, and with no fanfare, the road is now designated as Highway 10. Discussion of the northern Swell is in four sections below.

Elk

Cleveland-Lloyd Dinosaur Quarry

Driving distance from Highway 10 near Huntington via Cleveland is 20 miles one way; driving distance via Elmo is 18.2 miles one way.

Cleveland-Lloyd Dinosaur Quarry visitor center

"Remote" means different things to different people, but it is a term that can be employed with confidence when describing the Cleveland-Lloyd Dinosaur Quarry, which is a National Natural Landmark. For the harried traveler this could be a burden, but for others it will be part of the appeal. As the approach road descends the first major hill and begins to wind through an open landscape of scattered junipers and not much else, it can feel like the present is dwindling in the rear-view mirror as the car slips into the Jurassic. The trip might seem long to most in the vehicle, but to an eight year old who not only can name every dinosaur genus but also knows exactly who ate whom, it will no doubt be interminable. Patience will be rewarded.

Getting There

The two approaches from Highway 155 east of Huntington minimize the amount of dirt road driving necessary to get to Cleveland-Lloyd. If coming from the south or southwest, take Highway 10 through Huntington to milepost 49.3, and turn right (east) on Highway 155 to Cleveland. (The trip from Capitol Reef to Highway 10 is covered in the Highway 72 section directly above.) A sign for the quarry, including days and hours of operation, marks the turn. Drive 4.6 miles to a four-way stop in town. A small dinosaur quarry sign marks a right (south) turn at this point. Zero the odometer and go south on the paved road. At 1.5 miles turn left (east) at a T intersection where a sign gives distances to the Cedar Mountain Recreation Area, the dinosaur quarry, and I-70. At the 1.8-mile mark, turn right (south) onto a good graded road where a two-slat sign for the quarry joins the BLM sign that gives distances to the locations above except for a substitution of Buckhorn Wash for I-70. Follow this road south and then east to the 5.3 mark and a major intersection.

The speed limit of 45 miles per hour is reasonable when the road is in good condition, but use caution if there is any washboarding. Turn left (north) at the junction that is signed for the Cedar Mountain Recreation Area straight ahead, the Wedge Overlook and Buckhorn Draw to the right, and the dinosaur quarry to the left. Proceed 4 miles northeast to an odometer reading of 9.3 miles, and turn right (east) on a road signed for the quarry alone, along with the time of operation. The speed limit drops on this last major stretch as the terrain becomes more rolling and junipers begin to appear. At 14.4 miles the quarry entrance road bears left, marked by two signs. It is 1 more mile to the parking lot. Although this sounds complicated, the route is very well signed, except perhaps for the small sign in Cleveland. The 13.6 miles of graded dirt road are generally in good condition, but are no place to be during or after rain or snow.

An alternative for those coming from Price is to turn south (left) on Highway 155 at the northern end of its loop. This turn is marked by a sign for Elmo and Cleveland, one for Highway 155, and another for the quarry (the latter also gives the hours of operation). As is the case for the route described above, the way is clearly signed at every important intersection. Zero the odometer at the junction of Highways 10 and 155 and follow this road log: at 4.2 miles, turn left (east) on a paved road marked by separate signs for Elmo and the quarry; 6.1, bear right (south) at a stop sign at a five-way intersection; 6.2, turn left (east) onto Main Street; 7.2, leave the pavement and turn right (south) onto 800 East; 8.1, enter Desert Lake Wildfowl Management Area and bear left following the sign for the quarry; 10.6, turn right (south); 12.1 turn left (east); 17.2, bear left and reach the quarry at 18.2 miles. This route entails 11.0 miles of travel on gravel and dirt roads, which can become impassable when wet.

Highlights

After the dusty drive across the northern reach of the San Rafael Swell, rounding the final curve to see a modern building is a bit of a surprise. The impressive array of photovoltaic panels on the roof and nearby vault toilet are a tip-off, however, that the Cleveland-Lloyd Dinosaur Quarry (CLDQ) represents a special effort on the part of the Bureau of Land Management. The visitor center presents several well-done exhibits, including a full-scale replica of the skeleton of an allosaur dominating the larger room. The mystery, yet to be fully solved, is why so many of the bones excavated at CLDQ belong to this carnivore, and relatively few to prey species. A second question is why the skeletons are all dis-articulated (broken apart).

Allosaurus replica

The latter question is illustrated within one of two small buildings visible from the visitor center. There are a couple of vantage points inside where the actual quarry can be viewed. Bones yet to be excavated are exposed, but perhaps most interesting is a three-dimensional display of replica bones suspended on thin rods as the originals were found. This technique of 3D mapping will instantly be recognized by those familiar with the way archaeological sites are documented. It also illustrates the complexity of the deposit and the difficulty of interpreting the extraordinary abundance of bones.

There are three walking trails at the CLDQ. Scattered bones may be seen, but these walks are more a way to savor the stark emptiness of the Swell on a nice day. During the summer, temperatures can rise to the point of discomfort, so spring and fall are probably the best times to visit. A lunch in the small picnic area next to the visitor center offers an unusual chance to eat in the shade of large boulders. At this writing the charge for adults to visit the CLDQ is $5 per person, with those under sixteen admitted free.

Replica bones displayed as found

Cedar Mountain Road Trip

Driving distance from Cleveland is 19.7 miles one way; from Highway 10 via Lawrence is 28.6 miles one way.

Cedar Mountain is the high point of the northern part of the San Rafael Swell, and offers expansive views, especially to the south. A unique picnic area has been developed on the southern escarpment, and is a fine place to observe an unusual and interesting conglomerate rock.

Getting There

From the north, the best route is to take Highway 155 off Highway 10 to the town of Cleveland. See the road log in the Cleveland-Lloyd Dinosaur Quarry section above for details on the route. If coming from Price, take 155 south where it is marked for Elmo and Cleveland, but do not turn east on the spur road to Elmo. Instead, continue south on 155 to the town of Cleveland and follow the directions from the four-way stop to the intersection where Cedar Mountain is straight ahead, and the quarry is to the left. Continue east (straight) for 14.4 miles to the boundary of the Cedar Mountain Recreation Area.

If approaching from Capitol Reef on Highways 72 and 10 there are several alternatives. Perhaps the best is to go through the tiny town of Lawrence. Take Highway 10 through Castle Dale, home of the Museum of the San Rafael. The highway bends to the east in town, then curves to the north. Note the junction with Highway 29, which is just over 3 miles from Castle Dale. It is then 0.8 mile to the paved Lawrence road. Set the odometer to zero, turn right (east), and follow this pleasant rural road to the town of Lawrence at 5.1 miles. Turn right (east) on 1800 South. Continue on pavement for 1 mile and turn east (right) yet again at an intersection signed for the San Rafael Swell Recreation Area (SRSRA). In another 0.6 mile bear right (southeast) onto gravel, following the signs to Buckhorn Draw and the SRSRA. Continue straight ahead at 7.1 miles and reach a three-way junction and yield sign at 12.1 miles. Turn left (north) and drive just over 2 more miles to the four-way intersection described in the paragraph above. Follow the sign to Cedar Mountain by turning right (east).

Buckhorn Conglomerate at the Cedar Rim Picnic Site

To this point the gravel roads are generally very good, easily passable to all vehicles. The road up Cedar Mountain is slightly rougher and certainly more winding, but usually passenger cars should have no trouble. As always, excessive moisture means saving the trip for another day. The road winds gradually up the northwest flank of Cedar Mountain, passing by meadows and through increasingly dense piñon-juniper forest. Views are somewhat limited on the ascent, and better on the return trip. At 14.4 miles from the four-way intersection is the boundary of the Cedar Mountain Recreation Area. A short spur road leads to the right (south) to a fine overlook. It is 0.9 mile on the main road to the Cedar Rim Picnic Site, which is worth a stop whether or not it is lunch time.

Highlights

Not many picnic areas need a map, but it is worth taking a minute to look at the signboard map for Cedar Rim at the entrance to the picnic area. The tables are scattered within a labyrinth of narrow cracks in the Buckhorn Conglomerate. Metal stairs are necessary to reach several of them. With careful supervision, this is a place where kids can have a lot of fun exploring and clambering around. The relatively high elevation (about 7,400 feet) and shade from the rocks and piñons make this a reasonable spot to visit even in the summer.

A viewpoint in the picnic area offers a spectacular vista primarily to the south. On the horizon are the La Sal Mountains to the southeast, the Henrys in the south, and the Wasatch Plateau to the west. Far below is Buckhorn Flat, and with the help of a sign, Buckhorn Draw, the Wedge, and Window Blind Peak can be identified. There is little reason to continue east on the road past the picnic area as it soon passes through a large group of communication towers and then deteriorates in condition before dead-ending several miles to the north.

Picnic area map

The Cedar Mountain Formation

Although it was first identified and named in 1944, the Cedar Mountain Formation attracted little interest until the 1990s when dinosaur bones, eggs, and tracks were found in not one, but many locations. Much of the formation looks very similar to the underlying Brushy Basin Member of the Morrison Formation, which has been widely recognized for its fossil assemblages for many years. With the paleontological abundance has come a better understanding of the Cedar Mountain Formation, which turns out to be a complex rock unit, subdivided into five members, not all of which may be present at any one location.

A map of the formation's outcrops at the surface shows a large semicircle around the San Rafael Swell. In the southwest it begins at the northern reach of Capitol Reef National Park, then parallels Highway 10 on the east side, swings around to the southeast near Price, paralleling Highway 6. It then trends generally east to Colorado, but with several sharp changes in direction, most notably where it follows Highway 191 northwest of Moab. Other, less significant, outcrops occur in northeast Utah and in the central Utah valleys, in addition to broad exposures in Colorado.

The Cedar Mountain Formation sediment originated to the west as the result of crustal uplift in central Utah. Early in the Cretaceous Period the San Rafael Swell area was a flood plain with low relief. Rivers flowed across the terrain, sometimes cutting channels into existing sediments and at other times depositing material. Recent research also indicates that large lakes may have existed. As was the case with the Morrison, clay-sized particles often settled in swamps and low relief areas with little oxygen available; the resulting soft claystones can be brightly colored in pinks, maroons, and blue-greens due to minerals that form in reducing environments. The overlying Dakota Sandstone, not always present, marks a deltaic and beach interval at the beginning of inundation of the mid-continental sea that rose and fell (transgressed and regressed) several times over long intervals. The Tununk Member of the Mancos shale overlies the Dakota and is truly marine in character.

Within the Cedar Mountain Formation clays and sandstones, several beds of rather coarse conglomerates are found. The most widespread of these is the Buckhorn Conglomerate, significant enough to be recognized as a member. This is the basal unit of the formation, and where present, it provides an easy marker for casual students of geology to separate the Brushy Basin Member of the Morrison below, from the Ruby Ranch Member of the Cedar Mountain above. The Buckhorn is composed of black, well-rounded, chert pebbles and cobbles in a sandy matrix; the chert can be up to half of the rock. Like the Salt Wash Member of the Morrison, the Buckhorn looks like old cement, but is much darker due to the amount of chert pebbles.

The easiest place to view the Buckhorn is along Highway 24 for several miles just south of its junction with I-70 west of Green River. That outcrop is to the east of Highway 24, atop the colorful clays of the Brushy Basin. While the youngest member of the Cedar Mountain Formation has been dated at about 97 million years old (ma), reliable dating has not been possible on the Buckhorn. Work on other members of the formation does suggest that it might be older than 125 ma.

Buckhorn Conglomerate

View from the Wedge Overlook

Buckhorn Draw and Wedge Overlook Loop Road Trip

Distance: 90 miles

Many noteworthy sites in the northern San Rafael Swell can be visited on this loop tour. Above average clearance may be necessary for a little less than 20 of the roughly 90 miles on the circle that begins and ends in Ferron on Highway 10. Alternatively, an out-and-back drive from Ferron or Castle Dale to the San Rafael River bridge can be done in any passenger car during good weather. The primary points of interest are the Buckhorn Panel of rock art and the Wedge Overlook, but there are many other things to see as well.

Dispersed camping is widely permitted in the Swell, but for those seeking a few more amenities, Millsite State Park just west of Ferron is a good bet. The camping area sits high above the namesake reservoir and offers pull-through hook-ups as well as a loop of sites that offer nice views of the lake and austere Mancos Shale slopes. A boat ramp provides access to the water. Adjacent to the state park is a challenging 18-hole golf course with some of the most interesting holes anywhere; the seventh is truly spectacular. The course is operated by the town of Ferron, and the rates are as amazing as the scenery: at this writing, 18 holes with cart for $34. More information can be found at www.millsitegolfcourse.com. The golf course is 3.6 miles west of Highway 10, and the entrance to the campground is an additional 0.7 mile, all on a paved road that intersects the highway at the south end of Ferron and is well signed for the park.

Millsite State Park

Wedge Overlook

The loop is described in a counterclockwise direction to increase the chances that you will arrive at the Wedge Overlook just before sunset; after the light fades, it is a relatively short and easy drive back to Ferron or Castle Dale. The starting point is at the junction of the access road to Millsite State Park and Highway 10, 26.8 miles north of I-70, and 11.4 miles south of the center of Castle Dale. Zero the odometer and travel south on

Highway 10 for 5.4 miles to milepost 21.7 and turn left on the paved road to Moore. This road runs almost parallel to Highway 10. When it splits at a Y intersection, stay to the left (due south). At 9.1 miles turn left (east) at a T intersection onto the recently paved Moore Cut-off Road and soon leave residences and irrigated fields behind.

The road crosses the eastern margin of the soft Blue Gate Shale Member of the Mancos Shale and then curves through the Ferron Sandstone Member of the Mancos. The sandstone is obviously more resistant, and forms a cliff above the sloping Tununk Shale, which the road soon drops down to enter. The Ferron has abundant coal (the Coal Cliffs are just to the south of the road) and natural gas, mainstays of the Castle Valley economy. The Dry Wash Petroglyph Site is a worthwhile stop at 12.7 miles (milepost 6.6). The paved parking area is on the left (north), but is unmarked.

To the left (west) of the turnout is a big cube of sandstone that has tumbled down from the cliff above and has settled at a 45-degree angle. It is covered with petroglyphs; perhaps most interesting are a couple of snake-like images and a Kokopelli. Behind this block and a little farther to the west is a very large snake on another rock; both panels are very close to the parking area. On the other side of the parking area, to the right (northeast) about 75 yards along and then just to the left (northwest) of what appears to be the old road, is another block with a set of dinosaur tracks along a desert varnished surface. Some of the individual tracks are domed, while others are cupped, and it is easy to determine the stride length of the animal that left them.

Dry Wash petroglyphs

Dry Wash dinosaur tracks

Beyond the Dry Wash site, the Moore Cut-off crosses older and older rocks on the way to I-70. The Dakota Sandstone is at mile 14.3, and a good exposure of the Buckhorn, Ruby Ranch, and Mussentuchit Members of the Cedar Mountain Formation can be seen at mile 14.9. The Morrison, Summerville, Curtis, Entrada, and Carmel Formations follow to the east. The junction with I-70 at exit 116 is at mile 25.9. A short diversion to the Eagle Canyon View Area is worthwhile.

Stay on the north side of the Interstate and follow the paved road 0.4 mile to the viewpoint and rest area. To the east and northeast is the rugged terrain of the Glen Canyon Group of formations bisected by Eagle Canyon far below. The Navajo, Kayenta, and Wingate are the same rock units that form the spectacular scenery on the west side of Capitol Reef. To continue the loop, return to exit 116, cross I-70 and turn left (east) onto the Interstate. Exit 116 is also the beginning of the four-wheel drive trip to the Copper Globe Mine described in the Heart of the San Rafael Swell section.

The highway passes through interesting scenery, including Ghost Rock just to the south of the road; there are rest areas on both sides of the Interstate at this point. I-70 then drops down to a long flat as it passes through the Head of Sinbad area and within sight of the Head of Sinbad pictograph panel (also covered in the Heart of the San Rafael Swell section). Leave the highway at the next exit, 131, turn left under the twin bridges, then stay right (east) on the frontage road, zeroing the odometer. A sign gives distances to Buckhorn Draw 20, and Wedge Overlook 39. The frontage road initially moves away from the highway, but then runs right next to it, and 2.2 miles from exit 131 is an interesting pair of exclosures on the left (north). According to the sign, the Sage Brush Bench demonstration plots were fenced off in 1937 (the west section) and 1961. Perhaps most striking is the difference between both plots and the surrounding ground.

The gravel road bends away from the highway and heads north and northwest to the San Rafael River crossing. It is this stretch that is a little rough, and at times makes clearance an issue. When driving it at time of writing there were two wash crossings that would have been difficult, but perhaps not impossible for the average passenger car. In any event, the going will be slower here than on any other part of the loop. There is a fenced sinkhole on the right (east) at 5.4 miles, and the junction with the Sinkhole Flat Road (also to the right, or east) is a 0.5 mile beyond.

The main road passes through wide valleys and low

San Rafael River and campground

hills separating them for the next several miles before beginning a gentle descent to the San Rafael River. The scenery improves as the topography becomes more severe and the groundcover diminishes. Window Blind Peak, capped by the Wingate Sandstone, and Assembly Hall Peak dominate to the right (east) of the road, and Bottleneck Peak lies even closer to the west. Bottleneck at first appears as a long, almost vertically walled ridge, but as you get closer to the river, the reason for its name becomes more apparent.

The green riparian strip along the San Rafael River is 19.3 miles from the Interstate. The old campground, apparently still in use, is on the right (east) before the bridge, but the BLM has constructed a more attractive one on the north bank where sites are shaded by cottonwoods. The camping fee as of this writing is $6 a night. The latter also is a good spot for a picnic. On the west side of the modern bridge is the old wooden swinging bridge built by the Civilian Conservation Corps in the mid-1930s. Though now closed to vehicles, pedestrians are allowed to walk across this well-built structure that has survived seventy-five years of floods, wear, and tear.

North of the river, the road follows Buckhorn Draw, a pretty canyon with scattered cottonwoods providing contrast to the red rocks. The road condition improves dramatically to fine gravel and a wider surface, though lower Buckhorn Draw is sinuous and there are many curves. At the 23.4-mile mark is the Buckhorn Wash Panel, now restored and developed with a parking area, vault toilet, and interpretive signs. Most of the pictographs here are generally accepted to be Barrier Canyon Style, painted by Desert Archaic people more than two thousand years ago. One section of the panel has been labeled as depicting "rain angels," but rock art defies such easy categorization, and the true meaning of the figures rests with the artists who created them.

Buckhorn Wash Panel

Buckhorn Wash Panel

An interesting feature on many of the anthropomorphic forms is the presence of later "holes" chipped in their chests by more recent people. The Buckhorn Panel suffered a lot of damage over the years due to its obvious location along a heavily traveled route. It is to the great credit of the residents of Emery County, the BLM, and the state of Utah, that a major restoration effort was undertaken as part of the 1996 Centennial Celebration. The work was done by Constance Silver, applying techniques adapted from her work on mural and fresco restoration. Vandalism to rock art remains a serious problem in the Southwest despite heavy fines and increased vigilance by both law enforcement and involved citizens.

At 1.5 miles beyond the Buckhorn Wash Panel, at mile 24.9, is a double pullout on both sides of the road. On the right (northwest), in a small alcove, is the distinct February 17, 1920, inscription of Matt Warner, a notable figure in Utah around the turn of the twentieth century. The nearby cow is probably of later vintage.

Buckhorn Wash Panel

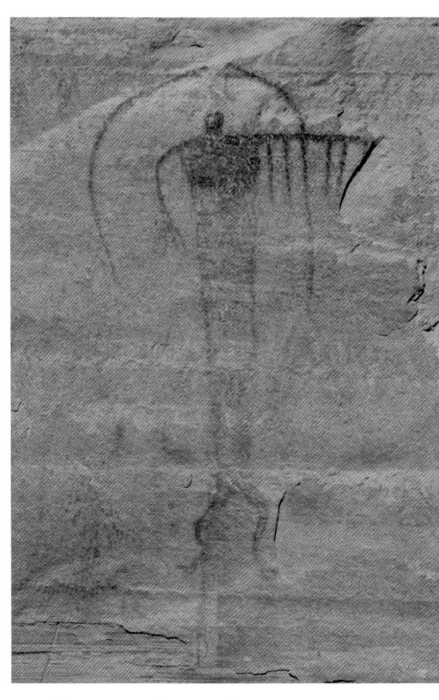
Buckhorn Wash Panel

Matt Warner

The omission of the second "t" in the first name of the inscription might be considered a little unusual, as Warner was educated and motivated enough to leave behind a memoir. He was a rustler, bank robber, inmate, operator of a saloon and brothel in Green River, rancher, family man, and eventually found redemption as elected justice of the peace in Carbon County. The criminal part of his life began when he fled after beating a fellow teenager so badly that Warner thought he had killed him. Real notoriety came when Warner teamed up with Butch Cassidy and the Wild Bunch along the Outlaw Trail that connected Robbers Roost along the Dirty Devil River, Browns Hole on the Green River north of Vernal, and Hole-in-the-Wall in south-central Wyoming.

Warner and Cassidy shared more than assumed names (Warner was born Willard E. Christiansen in Ephraim, Utah, in 1864; Cassidy's actual name was Robert Leroy Parker, born in 1866 in Beaver, Utah). Unlike members of some other infamous gangs, neither Warner nor Cassidy was particularly enamored of violence, and both avoided gratuitous gunplay. Warner was probably more suited to be a rancher than criminal, and both he and Butch were very good with horses.

Warner married for the first time while still on the lam, eventually moving to Washington to run a ranch. Upon his return to Utah he stayed out of trouble until killing two men during a claim-jumping incident. Convicted of manslaughter, he spent three years in prison, and during this time his wife, Rose, died. He later remarried and had two more children in addition to the two with Rose. When he attempted to win elected office for the first time in Carbon County (Price) he used his given name without success. Running as Matt Warner was more effective and his life in law enforcement began. He died at the advanced age of seventy-four in 1938, having led an interesting life.

Another good rock art site is on the right (north) side of the road at mile 26.8. Generally known for years as the Cattleguard Panel, it is a little harder to find now that the actual cattleguard has been removed as part of the upgrade to the road. The pullout is still there, although well below the new road surface. A rough trail leads across a draw and up to the cliff beyond; the panel is not visible from the road as it is behind a mound. Remnants of ill-advised chalking from years ago are still present, but weathering is slowly removing them. The main panel is quite complex, and appears more than most to be telling a geographic story. There are also two chains of figures linked by holding hands.

Cattleguard Panel

Less than 1 mile farther on, at mile 27.6, is a single good dinosaur track atop a low ledge on the right (northeast) side of the road. Park in the pullout on the left (southwest), and walk along the road to the northwest (ahead) until a path appears on the right. Walk up to the bench just above the road, and then walk back southeast to bare slickrock. At this point there is a V-shaped cut in the sand at the base of the cliff above the bench. The track is toward the base of the V, where the slickrock is exposed by rare run-off from above; from the lay of the land it is possible that it could eventually be covered by rock and sand debris. The print is three-toed and more than a foot across, and nicely indented. Please don't love it to death—avoid walking on it and touching it. In the past, some have covered it with a large rock to protect the track. While probably well intentioned, this leads to significant abrasion and should also be avoided.

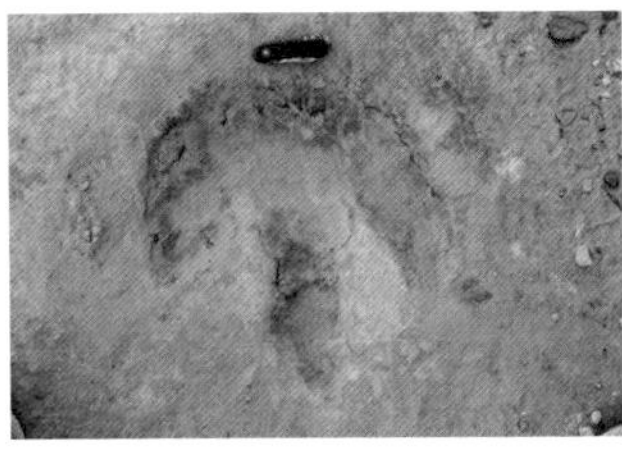

Dinosaur track

The BLM has established an interpretive site for the Morrison Knudson (MK) Tunnels at mile 28.2; the huge pullout is on the left (southwest) side of the road. Information about the project and its ambiguous purpose, along with period photographs, is presented on a signboard. Tunnels are visible across the shallow draw, but the primary site is to the east. It is generally thought that the Defense Department was testing various kinds of rock across the West to determine which would be best for an impregnable underground facility. Apparently, the granite near Pikes Peak in Colorado was a better bet for the North American Aerospace Defense Center (NORAD) than the soft, easily fractured Navajo Sandstone of the San Rafael Swell.

The main location of the project can also be visited with a high-clearance vehicle or a short walk. If you wish to do this, continue on the Buckhorn Road for another mile to the junction with the Green River Road. If daylight is waning and sunset at the Wedge beckons, it might be best to forego the MK Tunnels and turn left (west) here and drive 2.4 miles to the rest area at the Buckhorn Well (see below). If there is time to visit the tunnels, and perhaps the old railroad grade (4WD recommended), turn right onto the Green River Road and keep track of your mileage. In 0.8 mile note a track on the left (north) that heads off to Cedar Mountain; this provides access to the old railroad grade. Continue straight on the primary road that bends down to cross Furniture Draw at the 2.5-mile mark. Climb out of the canyon, pass by one track on the right, and at 3.5 miles take the second road to the right (south). High clearance will become necessary at some point on this road.

At a Y junction 0.9 mile from the Green River Road, stay right (more westerly) and shortly come to the end of the road above the tunnel site. With a 4WD the left leg of the Y can be negotiated (or it can be walked); this approach leads more directly to the information board. There really isn't a lot left to see of the MK Tunnels. In 2009 the BLM and state of Utah filled in the vertical blast holes and gated the tunnel to improve safety due to the shattered rock. Even now, wandering around the area needs to be done with caution as the Navajo Sandstone, ironically, can be very slippery when covered with sand. A visit to the MK Tunnels is really more about contemplating this Cold War project and imagining folks driving from all over to witness the secret 1952 blasts that so clearly indicated how unsuitable it was to build a fortress in the Navajo Sandstone.

While it would be unfair to term the MK Tunnels a boondoggle (after all, it really was at the core a research project), the term certainly fits when applied to the railroad grade just a couple of miles to the north. In 1881 the Denver and Rio Grande Railroad began constructing a railroad grade across the Swell from Green River. The route followed a significant portion of the Old Spanish Trail just below the escarpment of Cedar Mountain, before turning north on the mountain's western flank, and heading into the Castle Valley. After considerable work, including construction of the bed, stone culverts, rock cuts, and stone cabins for the Chinese segment of the work force, a decision was made to route the line along the Book Cliffs (near present day Highway 6) from Green River to Price.

The road along or near the old grade is deteriorating, and our last trip there required 4WD. Major channels were cut across the road, and will only worsen over time unless some maintenance is done. Soft sand in a couple of them compounded the difficulty. The worst problems were on the track leading from the Green River Road to the old railroad grade, and it would be wise to turn around on this stretch if there is any doubt whether your vehicle can make it. Access from the other end is easier, but there were still many cuts and deep ruts. In several drives to and along the old railroad grade, we have never seen another vehicle, so it doesn't make a lot of sense to take chances.

If none of the above deters you (and a certain portion of the populace—you know who you are—will no doubt find the cautions irresistible), return to the Green River Road, turn left (west) back the way you came, and go 2.7 miles to the track on the right (north) mentioned earlier as being 0.8 miles east of the Buckhorn Wash and Green River Roads junction. Turn onto the track (zero the odometer), which initially is on high ground but eventually crosses back and forth through a shallow drainage. It is 1.5 miles to the road along the old railroad grade; where the roads join there is a dam to the right (east) and some vegetation. Turn left (west) and parallel the base of the impressive Cedar Mountain escarpment. At the 1.9-mile mark a track goes off to the right (northwest), providing access to a boulder with good inscriptions from the railroad grade construction period. This rock also has petroglyphs.

Stay on the track past the rock as it returns to the main track at 2.3 miles. From this point to the good gravel of the Lawrence–Tan Seeps Road is another 4.1 miles of slow going. There are other rock art sites not far from the track. These are in the gray area of being described (several sources do provide directions) or being protected by not being included in the discussion. For us, few things are more rewarding than finding rock art, granaries, habitation sites, lithic scatters, and other cultural artifacts that we did not know about beforehand, and thus discovered entirely on our own. Just this once in this book, then, we will let you test your own ability to read the land and do some exploring.

If you have completed the diversion along the old railroad grade, turn left (south) on the Lawrence–Tan Seeps Road. There is a marker for the Old Spanish Trail 2.5 miles to the south, and 0.7 mile beyond that is the four-way junction at Buckhorn Well. As mentioned above, if you elected to skip the MK Tunnels and old railroad grade, bear left (west) when the Buckhorn Draw Road joins the Green River Road, and drive 2.4 miles to the four-way intersection. For decades, the only thing of note at this crossroads was Buckhorn Well, consisting of a pumphouse and holding tank. The original well was drilled in 1945, and saw extensive use during the MK Tunnels work when the water was necessary for drilling. Since then, it has been used for livestock. Now, however, arguably one of the most unexpected rest areas in the entire country has been built on the southeast corner of the intersection. Sited as it is on the stark and featureless Buckhorn Flat, this facility is convenient and, in its own way, impressive.

The road to the Wedge Overlook goes to the south at the rest area. That is a left turn if coming directly from Buckhorn Wash, and straight ahead from the Lawrence–Tan Seeps Road. This road is the same very good fine gravel as the other roads that converge at Buckhorn Well. From the flat it passes the road to Fuller Bottom on the right (southwest) after 0.5 mile; this is the access for floating the San Rafael River through the canyon to the wooden bridge, a trek that is generally reserved only for times of above average flow.

Continuing on to the Wedge Overlook, the road passes a gypsum mine in the Carmel Formation, and then begins to wind up through sparse junipers and piñons. A sign 3.2 miles from the rest area marks the boundary of the Wedge Recreation Area where camping is restricted to ten sites widely scattered in the rolling countryside. The sites are often very large and open with no facilities. A road to the left (east) at the information kiosk at 4.4 miles leads to seven of the camping sites. At 6.7 miles from the rest area a vault toilet is located near the rim of the canyon and the first viewpoint.

Although the good gravel surface ends at this point, the best view by far is to the left (east) in another 0.7 mile on a slightly rougher road. The Little Grand Canyon Overlook extends from a small parking area out onto a point high above the San Rafael River. We worked at Grand Canyon National Park for a couple of years and maintain a healthy skepticism about all the small versions touted by tourism councils. Most of those would better be termed "micro erosional incisions that might qualify as canyons if you live in Iowa." The Wedge, however, overlooks a canyon that does indeed share many characteristics with the big one.

Wedge Overlook

The walls step back and up from a meandering stream and are colorful with little masking vegetation. The 1,000-foot depth is sufficient to provide scale and drama, especially near sunset. This is a fine place to sit and watch the shadows creep down to the river as the color intensifies on the rock walls of the many points that extend out into the canyon. While everyone should visit the original in Arizona, of course, there is something to be said for perhaps having this view all to yourself, with just the whisper of a breeze rather than the whispers of a dozen languages, the clicking of a hundred cameras, and the odor of bus exhaust.

When the shadows take over and the light wanes, return to the intersection at the rest area, and turn left (west) on the good road for 13 miles to Highway 10 just northeast of Castle Dale. To go back to Ferron and Millsite State Park, turn left (south) on Highway 10 for 12.9 miles to the road to the park on the right (west). To do the loop in the opposite direction than described, go east and north of the center of Castle Dale for 1.5 miles to milepost 39.4 and turn right (east) on the Green River Road, which is signed for San Rafael Recreation Access. This would also be the start of an out-and-back 66-mile tour to the Wedge Overlook, Buckhorn Pictograph Panel, and the San Rafael bridge, all on very good gravel roads.

Rochester Panel Rock Art Site Hike

Driving distance from Highway 10 is 4.2 miles one way.
Hiking distance is 0.9 mile round trip.

The petroglyphs of the Rochester Panel alone would make it a prime destination for people interested in rock art, but the sublime location adds immensely to the overall effect. High above the confluence of Muddy Creek and a small, usually dry tributary, the site lies at the end of a high and narrow neck of rock that commands a wide view in all directions.

Rochester Panel site

Getting There

The approach by car doesn't exactly create a burst of anticipation. Access is off Highway 10, just over 16 miles north of I-70. The first town north of the Interstate is Emery, which has few services for travelers. From the post office in the center of town, drive 3.6 miles north to milepost 16.2. Turn right (east) on a paved road signed for the town of Moore, and go 0.5 mile. Turn right (south) onto a good gravel road; there is a sign at that point reading Rochester Panel Rock Art Site. Pass a quarry on the left 1.6 miles from the pavement, followed in quick succession by a gated road to the right and then a communications tower on the left. Another sign for the rock art site confirms that you are on the correct road. From this sign it is just under 2 winding miles to the end of the road at a large circle. It is good to pay attention on this stretch for encroaching ravines to the right (west) and a particularly sharp curve. If approaching from Ferron and the north on Highway 10, do not turn at the first road into Moore, but continue to milepost 16.2 and turn left (east) and follow the directions above from that point.

The trail to the panels begins directly behind the Rochester Panel Rock Art Site sign on the east edge of the parking circle. The path drops down to the left (northeast) for 100 yards before switching back and descending gently into the bottom of the modest canyon at the 0.2-mile mark. After passing through a thicket of big sage, the route begins an up and down contour across a slope covered with huge boulders. While there is nothing really difficult along the way, the tread is rough at times with very short but steep and sometimes loose grades. There are just enough drop-offs to require good supervision of kids, a factor that increases significantly at the rock art site. The first minor glyph is next to the trail just beyond 0.3 mile, and consists of what might be interpreted as a river and perhaps an incomplete animal. Just beyond, the trail emerges onto the narrow rock rib high above Muddy Creek, offering a fine view to the west and down. Less than 0.5 mile from the trailhead, the route ends at the Rochester Panel.

Highlights

The main panel is quite extraordinary, both in terms of the number of individual glyphs and the imagery itself. The cluttered scene is reminiscent of Newspaper Rock on the road to the Needles section of Canyonlands National Park. A dominant feature resembles a rainbow, which is pecked over many of the other figures. While some of the anthropomorphs exhibit Fremont form, others do not, and the presence of several highly unusual zoomorphs adds to the interpretive difficulty. Parallel to, and just to the left (southeast) of the primary panel is another that would be noteworthy by itself if not in the shadow of its more spectacular neighbor. Figures there are less crowded and perhaps a little less creative, but as with the main panel, easy to see and enjoy. Modern graffiti and damage is relatively light at the Rochester site and there is no chalking. The glyphs contrast nicely with the desert varnish and photograph well at midday.

chester Panel

Rochester Panel

Rochester Panels

Ferron Creek Petroglyphs

Another nearby panel west of Ferron is also worth a visit, especially if you are staying at Millsite State Park. Return to Highway 10 and turn right (north) onto the highway. At milepost 26.8, in the larger town of Ferron, watch for a sign to Millsite State Park. Turn left (west) and reset the odometer. Pass the entrance to the golf course at 3.6 miles and the entrance to the park at 4.3. Continue to the end of the pavement and boundary of the Manti La Sal National Forest at 6.3 miles. At 7.3 miles from Highway 10 the graded road passes by a cliff on the left (south) and a long pullout begins on the right. Park at the near end of the pullout, just after leaving the primary road.

The cliff to the south and the one across Ferron Creek to the north form a gateway into the canyon to the west. This kind of feature would have marked an important transition and/or travel route for the Fremont people, and places like it often were favored sites for rock art. Here, the panel is on the face high above the road to the south. A steep and sometimes loose climb is required to attain the level of the petroglyphs, and even then, an outcrop bulges up in front of the bottom portion. A long lens is necessary for close-up photos. The climb is hazardous enough that many people with good binoculars will be satisfied to view the panel from the road.

The panel is not overly large, but is densely packed with images of all kinds. A Fremont anthropomorph above a concave and fringed semicircle (much like the modern map symbol for a cliff) is the dominant figure. Geometrics, including concentric circles and a multi-pointed star, are numerous, along with some zoomorphs. At 1:00 p.m. on a spring day most of the panel, but not quite all, is in the sun, but late in the afternoon it would be shaded.

Eastern San Rafael Reef

The San Rafael Swell's sedimentary rocks are warped into a single, very large anticline, but one where the dip of the beds is considerably steeper on the southeast. The well-exposed and tilted beds form an arc called the San Rafael Reef. The most spectacular (easternmost) part of the Reef can be seen at a distance from Highway 24 and while approaching it from Green River on I-70, but the best way to experience it is to hike through it, or at least drive the dirt road from Highway 24 to the Black Dragon pictograph site.

Conditions along this road can vary dramatically. High clearance is almost always necessary due to rutted sandy sections, and is required on the Uneva Mine and Black Dragon access tracks. The road to Three Fingers Canyon is even rougher and short, steep pitches make 4WD desirable. The above applies when the roads are in good shape, and when they are not, either 4WD is necessary, or they are impassable. Rains can create large mudholes that persist for days, times when it is sensible to be somewhere else. As of this writing these roads are only minimally marked, but the BLM plans to upgrade the signage over the next three years.

Eastern San Rafael Reef

Red Jasper Rock Collecting Site

Driving distance from Highway 24 is 3.7 miles one way.

Jasper

The unsigned road joins Highway 24 on the left (north) at an acute angle at milepost 152.7, which is just over 36 miles from Hanksville and about 7 miles from I-70. Set the odometer to zero. The road passes through the fence over a yellow cattleguard and heads directly west for 1.25 miles to a corral. At 1.7 miles from the highway the road bends to the north (right), with minor tracks leading west and south. At 3.4 miles it crosses a wash, and at 3.7 there is a worthwhile stop for rock collectors.

Here, a large flat area is bounded by a low cliff to the north and west. Park somewhere near the eastern end of the flat where a fairly obvious route to the top can be seen. Small pieces of red jasper should be visible immediately, increasing as you approach the 25-foot high slope. The route to the bench above requires no climbing moves whatsoever as it is a simple and easy way up and around several mid-size blocks. Once on the first bench, much more jasper will appear, and the pieces will be larger as well. In some places the ground is nearly covered with small to fist-size and larger chunks, suitable for tumbling or cutting and polishing. Simply scout the area, and the even more modest rise to the north, and collect only what you will use.

This area is good territory for pronghorn, and it is not uncommon to see a small herd between Highway 24 and I-70. Although pronghorn are often referred to as antelope, they are not. Found only in North America, *Antilocapra americana* is the only surviving member of the Antilocapridae family, which included several species as recently as the last glacial period. Pronghorn are handsome reddish-brown and white animals (males have black cheek markings) that are slightly smaller than mule deer. Their horns (female horns are usually just small bumps) are cored by bone attached to the skull, and covered with a sheath that is shed and replaced annually.

Pronghorn are the fastest mammal in the New World, achieving speeds up to 55 miles per hour, and they can sustain lesser, but still fast, speeds over very long distances. Since this is more than sufficient to outrun any current predator, they must have evolved to escape faster species that are now extinct. In spite of their speed, they are reluctant to jump, making fences a serious obstacle for those herds that undertake long migrations. Pronghorn are flexible herbivores, consuming everything from grasses to cacti, and they get most of the water they need from eating plants. Their numbers were reduced a century ago to just several thousand, but populations are currently healthy enough so that pronghorns are a hunted game species in most western states.

Pronghorns

Three Fingers Canyon Petroglyph Site

Driving distance from Highway 24 is 6.5 miles one way.
Hiking distance behind the reef as described is 4.2 miles round trip.

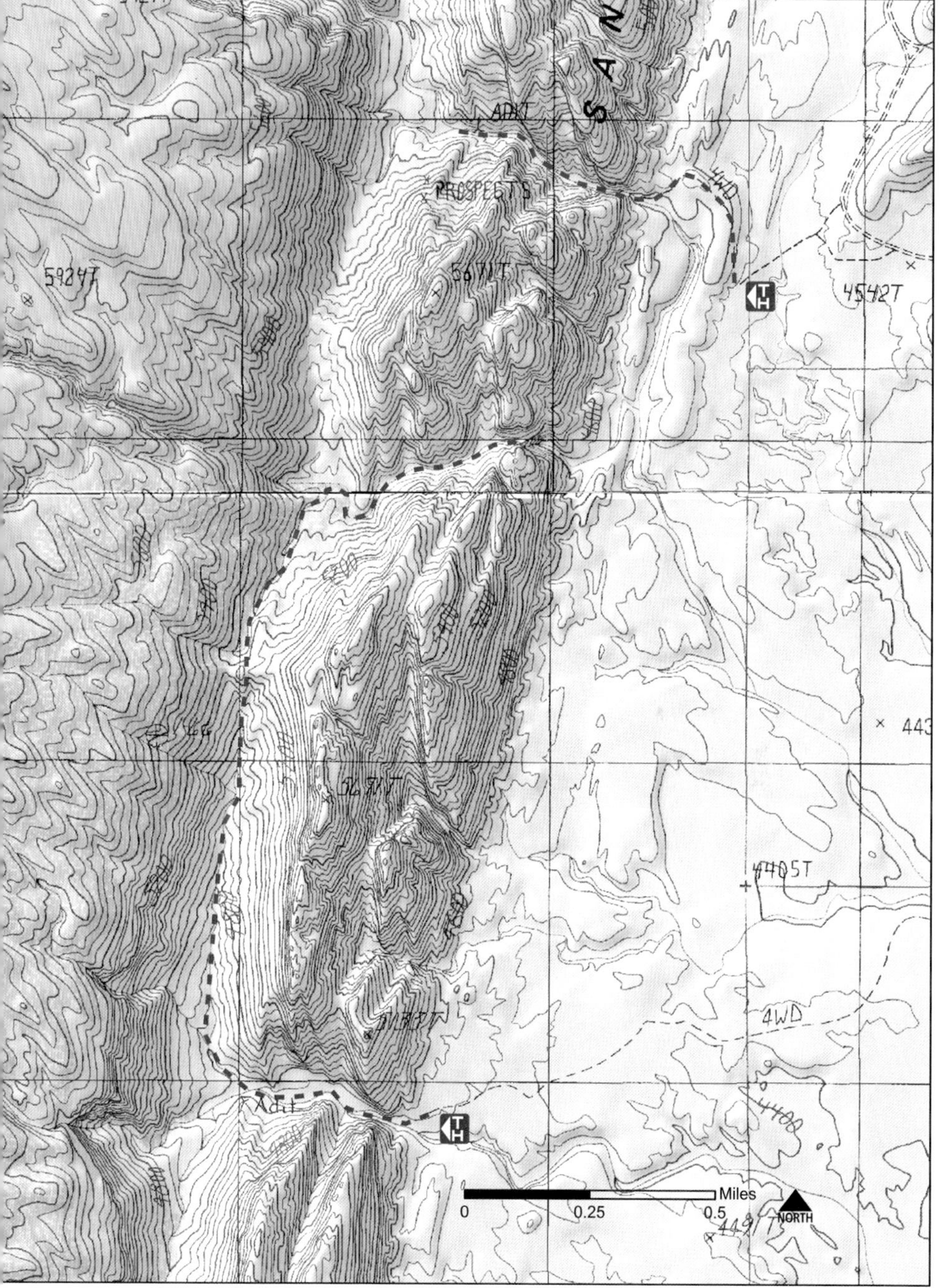

Three Fingers Canyon route (bottom) and Uneva Mine route (top)

The track to Three Fingers Canyon is 0.5 mile from the jasper site, at 4.2 miles from Highway 24. The road heads generally toward the Reef (left or west), and is marked by a designated route sign. It is easy at first as it crosses a flat area, but several wash crossings are steep and rutted. One in particular is very steep, and although it may be possible at times to bull through with a 2WD high-clearance vehicle, it is safer and easier with 4WD. The side road is 2.3 miles long and ends at a small parking area a little more than 100 yards from the entrance to the canyon and the San Rafael Reef Wilderness Study Area (SRRWSA).

To the south and down a steep slope are several tanks, or potholes, naturally cut in the rock. Two of them hold water for long periods after rain or snow, and are almost surely the reason that the petroglyph panel exists at the mouth of Three Fingers. On the other side, the very steeply dipping red and gray beds of the Carmel Formation lap up against the white or light gray Navajo Sandstone which then soars above.

Three Fingers Canyon

To get to the petroglyphs simply walk along the obvious path to the right-hand (north) wall. The images are Fremont, as evidenced by a few broad-shouldered anthropomorphs. More interesting are the connected circles, which could represent the series of tanks just below. The best panel is a triangular grouping on the wall with a series of diamonds above an enigmatic two-pronged and lightly pecked image. A zoomorph with long ears or short horns, connected concentric circles, dots, plant-like features, and an interesting map-like figure are also present. There are many other glyphs on the walls, as well as on the sloped apron that extends down to the wash. The latter have been re-patinated

Three Fingers Petroglyphs

by desert varnish and are harder to discern, and many have therefore been obliterated by careless visitors walking over them unknowingly. Please be very careful to not add to the damage. Photographers should use a long lens to avoid having to step in the areas where faint petroglyphs remain.

Three Fingers Canyon cuts through the Reef with no significant obstructions. Walk down the slickrock ramp from the petroglyph panel and work toward the Swell. The Navajo, Kayenta, Wingate, and Chinle Formations pass by quickly in that order. Directly ahead the hard and resistant Kaibab Limestone rises up steeply, but the softer Moenkopi Formation in front has been eroded to form a kind of trough behind the Reef. This trough is far from flat, however, rising to steep saddles between each canyon that drains through to the east.

Because it is there, and because it is possible, some will want to hike behind the Reef to the north, exit through Uneva Canyon (see below), and walk along the front of the Reef back to their vehicle. This group will probably include many who have walked in the back valley from Ding to Dang, Bell to Little Wild Horse, or Crack to Chute Canyons near Goblin Valley. Those expecting a mellow walk over soft and smooth Chinle clays will be surprised to find that the route from Three Fingers to Uneva is rocky, ledgy, and steep. Two saddles must be climbed and descended on the route. It is about 3 miles between the canyon mouths, and 2 more not altogether easy miles on the east side back to the start.

If you want to experience the back valley, here is an alternative to doing the entire loop hike, which takes longer than one would expect for a relatively short distance. After passing through Three Fingers to the Moenkopi, follow the wash to the right as it turns to the north. The going is fairly easy until the gradient steepens and rocks and small ledges begin to impede progress. The route is largely in the bottom of the drainage, with a couple of easier stretches on the west bench. There are no major obstructions, just a lot of very minor ones. Near the top of the saddle a shallow V-cut leads very steeply up to the sharp crest at 1.1 miles. The views north and south from this probably windy aerie are worth the effort, especially to the north where the dipping beds of the Reef are well exposed.

If this climb is enough, return down to Three Fingers and your vehicle. An intermediate option is to descend north from the saddle, a very steep drop, and continue down to the next canyon in 0.7 mile. This unnamed canyon is **not passable** through the Reef, but is interesting to explore. A resistant bed in the Chinle, standing at about a 70-degree angle, presents a 15-foot high challenge, but can be downclimbed on the right (south). A pothole 200 yards farther on can be passed if the water is not too deep. A narrow cleft then appears in the Navajo Sandstone, signaling the top of an immense vertical pour-off and the turnaround point. The return up to the saddle and on to Three Fingers has less vertical gain as the unnamed canyon is a couple hundred feet higher than the parking area.

Uneva Canyon Hike

Driving distance from Highway 24 is 7 miles one way.
Hiking distance is 1.5 miles round trip.

Whether as part of a loop hike or accessed from a trailhead on the east side, Uneva Canyon is very scenic and should be visited. For vehicle access, return to the main road from Three Fingers Canyon and turn left (north). In 0.9 mile (5.1 miles from Highway 24) a lesser road approaches from the right (east). Stay left, bearing to the northwest for an additional 1.5 miles (6.6 miles from the highway) and bear left (southwest) on another designated route. Shadscale Mesa sits above a good exposure of the banded Summerville Formation to the north. This track, not as rough as the one to Three Fingers Canyon, terminates at a parking area with a sign designating it as a trailhead.

Walk up the old road to the right (north) as it ascends a bench in front of the Reef and enters the SRRWSA. It is an easy hike of just over 0.25 mile to a flat area probably used for parking in the past. The old road drops into the canyon and ends in 100 more yards at a cut in the sandstone. This gap is easily crossed, and the rest of the way through is pleasant.

In addition to its beauty, this passage through the San Rafael Reef is an extraordinary stroll from the middle Jurassic all the way through the Triassic to the Permian in a matter of minutes. From the east, it is .12 mile in the Navajo Sandstone, .09 mile in the Kayenta Formation, .11 in the Wingate Sandstone, and .08 in the Chinle. As the valley is reached the Moenkopi quickly gives way to the Kaibab Limestone that forms the high slope to the west.

A bonus is the well-preserved portal to the Uneva Mine that penetrates the Shinarump Member at the base of the Chinle Formation. The mine was operated for uranium, which in Utah is largely concentrated in the Chinle and Morrison Formations. Only fools enter old mines, and this one is especially dangerous for reasons beyond the typical threat of rock falls within the tunnel, or hard-to-see vertical shafts. As a source of uranium ore, the air in the Uneva contains high enough amounts of radiation to be a peril even during short exposures. The entrance is also deep in mouse droppings, making deadly hantavirus a distinct danger. Stay completely out of the mine and cnjoy thc walk back through thc canyon.

Uneva Mine

Black Dragon Pictograph Site

Driving distance from Interstate 70 is approximately 1.6 miles one way depending on turnaround point.

The trip along the east side of the San Rafael Reef ends with a spectacular pictograph site just north of I-70. From the Uneva Mine trailhead, return to the good dirt road and turn left (northwest). The reef to the left (west) continues to be impressive as the road winds through the Squeeze between it and Shadscale Mesa to the east. A small scattering of jasper is left (west) of the road in 0.8 mile (7.4 miles from Highway 24). Stay to the left just before crossing under the Interstate, noting the track that bears right (east). This road provides access to eastbound lanes of the highway if you are headed toward Green River. The culvert under I-70 is 3.7 miles from the Uneva Mine Road (10.3 miles from Highway 24) and is designed for traffic with approach ramps at both ends.

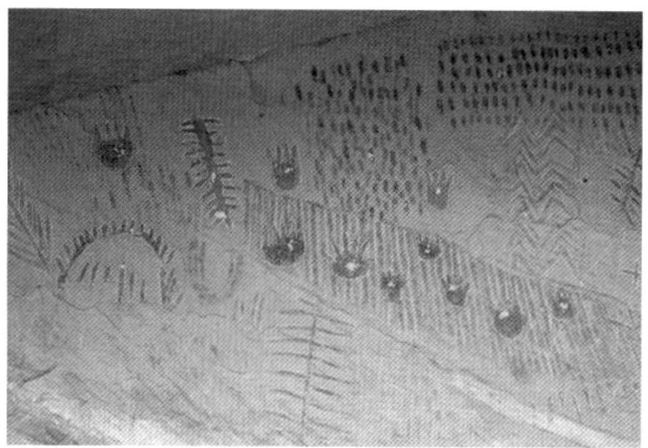
Black Dragon Pictographs

Black Dragon Pictographs

Zero the odometer as you exit the tunnel. About a .01 mile beyond the culvert, an obvious road crosses the sandy wash in which you are driving. (In very dry times, this short stretch in the wash can be quite sandy, making 4WD necessary.) The better road crossing the wash may be preceded by a steep 4WD trail, which should be passed. Turn left (west) up and gently out of the wash. The road quickly makes a sweeping right turn to the north where there is a large parking area used by equestrian tours. After 0.6 mile pass by a track to the left (west), continuing on the more traveled road.

A BLM sign for Black Dragon is a mile along; bear left (northwest) at this point. The route soon divides at a second sign that prohibits camping in the canyon; just to the north is the Mexican Mountain Wilderness Study Area. Both tracks lead into Black Dragon, but at this writing the left hand one (southern) is considerably smoother, and the other leads up the wash. Vehicles with moderate clearance can park along the bench on the left fork, while high clearance vehicles can continue into the canyon itself. As of this writing the road was easily passable for trucks to 1.6 miles, then crossed the wash and became much rougher. With the pictographs only another 250 yards ahead, it makes sense to park rather than degrade the wash any further.

The rock art is protected from wandering cattle by a log fence. A pass-through is located along the fence to the west, directly across from the Black Dragon pictograph on the soaring Navajo wall to the north. A panel of Archaic anthropomorphs brackets the west end of the site, with the so-called dragon to its right (east), and beyond that a leaping zoomorph. The images have been chalked, a practice now considered to be vandalism and illegal. These figures are impressive in their artistry, but the panel farther east in the alcove is both amazing and enigmatic. There are hundreds of short lines that resemble dots in precise patterns. There are red and black marks and it is very difficult to avoid attempting to figure out what they represent. Bird and bear tracks abound, along with geometric figures that include vertically elongated round-topped silo-like images. It will take a long time to absorb this unique panel, and more time to enjoy the desert varnished canyon walls.

This trip can be done from north to south by exiting I-70 at the informal exits barely west of milepost 147. This approach would also be the fastest to just view the Black Dragon pictographs. (Note that the mileposts on I-70 do not coincide with earlier guidebooks printed prior to the great UDOT milepost migration.) From Green River, slow down when milepost 147 comes into view, and turn exceedingly carefully off the highway onto a track that leads to a gate. Pass through the gate, close it behind you, and zero the odometer at this point. Cross the wash at 0.1 mile and follow the description above to drive to Black Dragon Canyon. From the west, look for a road to the right (south) just after crossing over a major wash (and just before milepost 147, which will be visible ahead), pass through and close a similar gate, bear to the right and drive through the culvert under I-70. Zero the odometer here and follow the directions above. To return to I-70 westbound use the track on the north side of the highway, and to go east toward Green River, go under the highway and bear left and around to the north. In either case, extreme caution must be used to re-enter such a high-speed road.

Black Dragon Canyon

Heart of the San Rafael Swell

Head of Sinbad Pictographs

Driving distance from exit 131 on I-70 is 10 miles one way.

There are many wonderful places in the San Rafael Swell, but for many, the Head of Sinbad pictographs are more than wonderful—they are magical. Even with the distant drone of 18-wheelers slipping by on I-70, the setting is special and the rock art sublime. The paintings of red and a little white are Archaic, several thousand years old, and well preserved. There are only two sets of figures, but the detail, artistry, and anthropomorphic ambiguity combine to make this site very distinctive. The larger panels at Horseshoe Canyon and Buckhorn Canyon may be more impressive by virtue of their sheer size, but the Head of Sinbad paintings hold their own, and for some, may be a more satisfying experience.

Getting There

Just because I-70 is visible off to the south does not mean that the Head of Sinbad is an easy place to visit. The quickest access from the east, west, or north is from the Interstate at exit 131, just over 30 miles from the town of Green River. Set the odometer to zero and head south and then almost immediately west. A BLM sign indicates that Highway 24 is 29 miles, Goblin Valley 30 miles, and Temple Mountain is in the same (straight ahead) direction. The dusty gravel road parallels the highway as it heads west before turning south 1.8 miles from the exit. At 3.1 miles is a cattle guard and crossroads intersection (continue straight), and at 3.9 miles turn right (west, then southwest) on a rougher track that is signed for Head of Sinbad 5. This road is rocky in places and high clearance is important (and necessary later). Continue on this cut-off road for just over 1 mile to a T intersection and turn right (northwest) on the road signed for Swasey's Cabin and reset the odometer to zero.

Head of Sinbad cliffs

Head of Sinbad pictographs

Claret Cup

Milkvetch *Astragalus*

Simpsons cactus

From the south the approach requires significantly more time on gravel, but includes a good helping of scenery to offset the dust and bouncing. Leave Highway 24 near milepost 136 between Hanksville and Green River (set odometer to zero) and turn northwest on the well-signed paved road to Goblin Valley State Park. After 5.2 miles, when the good paved road makes a turn to the southwest (left) to Goblin Valley, continue straight ahead on rougher pavement, soon encountering a graded surface. Pass through Temple Wash and by the Behind the Reef Road and a BLM camping area at 7.4 miles. The road ascends up through the Moenkopi Formation, with Temple Mountain to the east. At 16.2 miles from Highway 24 bear right (north) at a junction, following the sign for I-70, and do the same 2.6 miles farther on at a second intersection, again heading for I-70. Pass by the motorcycle trailhead on the right (east), and 23.8 miles from Highway 24 turn left (northwest) at a junction signed Head of Sinbad 5 to the left and I-70 straight ahead. A mile after making the turn is the junction with the cut-off road coming from the northeast, described above. Go straight at this point, but zero the odometer.

Both approaches meet at this location. The road trends to the northwest and is usually in good condition with just a few rocky spots to watch out for, though at times big holes can be a bit of a hazard to anyone not paying attention. Pass by a track to the left (southwest) at 1.8 miles, and bear right (northwest) when a lesser track goes straight at 2.7 miles. At the 3.5-mile mark turn right (north) on a road signed for Dutchman's Arch, and wind through the sagebrush flat for another 0.5 mile to I-70. The passage under the highway is through a box culvert that may be quite sandy.

On the north side of the culvert is a complex network of sandy tracks going in all directions. These roads can be rough, and high clearance is important. During and after precipitation events, the tracks can be impassable. Dutchman's Arch is worth a visit, and directions to it are included at the end of this section. To get to the Head of Sinbad Panel, stay to the right (northeast) at the Y intersection just after the culvert. This is BLM route 644. Follow it for 0.2 mile and then bear right (east) at a T intersection. After just over another 0.5 mile, 644 turns to the right, but stay straight on the track toward the rock outcrops to the north. From this point it is about a 0.3 mile to a sandy circular parking area with a wood fence to the north. This track may be highly eroded and the travel surface both sandy and tilted.

The fence is designed to keep cattle away from the rock art. A pass-through just northeast of the parking area allows people easy access along a sandy path. The panel consists of two small groups of figures. The more easterly section is framed between a pair of juniper trees as the rock wall is approached. The primary figure appears to be blessing its subjects with rain, but such an interpretation is simply conjecture. A secondary figure certainly looks like a dog, and assumes a posture very similar to that of one depicted at the Black Dragon site on the east side of the San Rafael Swell. To the left (west) of this grouping is a second pair of primary anthropomorphs, also painted with consummate artistry. The preservation of the rock art is quite extraordinary, surviving thousands of years of natural weathering and centuries of exposure to later human cultures. One can only wonder, for example, what the Fremont people thought when they first encountered these startling figures. Protection of the Head of Sinbad Panel is really up to all of us from now on.

The location of the pictographs reflects not only the quality of the rock and at least partial shielding from the elements, but also a commanding position overlooking the vast area now called the Head of Sinbad. It is worth pausing a minute to take in the view before leaving the parking area. If your visit is during the spring, there may be an additional stop to make prior to heading over to see Dutchmans Arch. A couple of hundred yards or so from the parking area, look carefully on both sides of the sandy track for small, spherical cacti dotted about the mostly barren ground. In good years sometime around the end of April or beginning of May, *Pediocactus simpsonii* will burst into bloom. Simpson's cactus sometimes blooms with showy pink flowers, but in the Swell the clusters of inch and a half blooms are generally white. The density of individual plants is more apparent on foot than from the car, and it is worthwhile to get out and walk around to view them, especially when they are in flower.

Dutchmans Arch

To drive over to the arch, retrace the route from the parking area of Head of Sinbad: go south on the sandy track for 0.3 mile to join route 644, continuing straight ahead at

Dutchmans Arch

that point, and proceed for 0.6 mile to the point where 644 makes a left turn toward the culvert under the Interstate. Rather than making the left turn, continue straight ahead (west) for 0.1 mile and then go left (south) at a T intersection. After only 100 feet or so, turn right (west) on a track for 0.3 mile to the sign for Dutchmans Arch. The arch is very accessible as it extends out into the flat from the outcrop to the north. Though not huge, it is big enough and sufficiently well situated to be interesting. The track, passable for high-clearance vehicles, continues on past the arch for about 0.5 mile before abruptly changing to a very rough 4WD trail called the Devils Racetrack. To return to the culvert from the arch, go back to the east for 0.3 mile, turn right (south) at the T intersection, and in another 0.3 mile reach the passage under the Interstate. Although the many tracks in the area can seem confusing, the way back from either the rock art or arch is basically line of sight.

Swasey's Cabin

There is one other worthwhile short sidetrip in the area. Swasey's Cabin stands as a reminder of late-nineteenth and early twentieth century life in the San Rafael Swell. The four Swasey brothers—Joe, Sid, Charley, and Rod—grazed cattle over much of the area, beginning in the late 1800s. By most accounts, they were a spirited lot, to the point that some folks living on the margins of the Swell considered them to be less than law abiding. Many interesting landforms on the Swell carry their names: Joe and his Dog, Sid's Mountain, Sid and Charley, and Rod's Valley. In the early days they generally slept wherever nightfall found them, but in 1921 they built the cabin that remains largely intact today.

Swasey cabin and Head of Sinbad

The BLM has constructed a parking lot, interpretive sign, and vault toilet at the site. From the south end of the culvert under I-70, bear right (southwest) and go 0.4 mile, joining the road from the Temple Mountain Road 0.3 mile beyond the original turn to the Head of Sinbad Panel. Continue straight on the primary track, first southwest and then south, for 2.1 more miles, then bear right (southwest), following the sign, for an additional 0.7 mile to the parking lot. The cabin is a very short walk from there.

Baptist Draw and Upper Chute Canyon Hike

Driving distance from Highway 24 is 27.9 miles one way; from exit 131 on I-70 it is 22.2 miles one way.
Hiking distance is 8.3 miles round trip.

These two spectacular slot canyons have been widely known for only a few years, even to the canyoneering community. Today they remain largely off the radar for non-technical hikers, although they are so good that this situation will not last for long. On our hike on a perfect April 30th at the height of the season we did not see another person. Most of the people who come to Baptist Draw and Upper Chute are planning on a loop route that includes a rappel in Baptist Draw, a major rappel down into Chute, and one more to continue south in that canyon. Happily, a lot of the good slot sections can be visited without using technical equipment if the hiker is reasonably agile and fit. Given the length and large upstream catchment basins, only fools would enter either slot when there is any chance at all of rain. The possibility of injury is common to all slots with obstacles, so it is comforting to hike in a small group of perhaps four, so that if something does happen, one person can stay with the injured, and two can go together for help.

Baptist Draw and Upper Chute are located well within the San Rafael Swell, rather than passing through the San Rafael Reef like the slot canyons of Crack, Little Wild Horse, and Ding and Dang. This location means the geology is different as well. The Reef canyons are cut primarily into the Navajo Sandstone in their best slot sections, while Baptist Draw and Upper Chute slice into the even more obviously cross-bedded White Rim/Cedar Mesa Sandstone, undifferentiated here because the intermediate

Baptist Draw

Upper Chute slot canyon

Organ Rock Shale is missing. Because they are more remote and by themselves they have been buffered from heavy visitation, a factor that reinforces the need for good route-finding skills due to the lack of an established trail and the abundance of lightly used hiker-made paths. Note that Chute Canyon continues to the south from its confluence with Baptist Draw and eventually does cut through the San Rafael Reef just west of Crack Canyon. It is pedestrian at that point, but extraordinary in its upper reach as described here.

Getting There

Most of the access roads are quite good, but the last 3.6 miles are rough, requiring high clearance. From Highway 24 northeast of Hanksville, turn left (southwest) on the Goblin Valley Road for 5.2 miles. (Directions from I-70 are included in the following paragraph.) Where the road to the state park turns to the left, continue straight ahead on the Temple Mountain Road directly toward the San Rafael Reef. Pass by large parking and camping areas with vault toilets at 0.5 mile and just over 2 miles, the latter after the pavement ends and the road roughens. Zero the odometer at the entrance to the second camping area (which is on the right, or east). Beyond, the road begins to gain altitude quickly, and exposures of bedrock in the roadbed make for a bit of slow going. A fine view of Temple Mountain occurs at 2.9 miles, and just over 0.5 mile farther is a commanding view of the Henry Mountains over the Wingate cliffs that mark the upper end of all the Reef slots. The first big vista to the north is at 8.6 miles; by this point the road quality has already changed for the better.

Leave the Temple Mountain Road at 9.2 miles by continuing straight ahead (northwest) when the main road bears right (north), marked only by a sign for I-70. A sign on the left (southwest), oriented for oncoming traffic, will confirm that the road directly ahead will lead to Tan Seep and Reds Canyon. Follow this winding, but good, gravel road for just over 2.8 miles, and stay straight (west) at the next intersection where the sign now points toward Reds Canyon and McKay Flat. This junction is also easily reached from I-70 at exit 131. Head south and almost immediately west (paralleling the Interstate) from the exit and stay on the Temple Mountain Road for 9.9 miles. Bear right (southwest) at this point, following the sign to Reds Canyon and Tan Seep. Note the road to Rods Valley 3.1 miles along (which is described at the end of the Driving the Southwest San Rafael section that follows), and continue straight to the junction noted above at 3.8 miles, and turn right (west).

From either direction, zero the odometer and immediately pass over a cattleguard, continuing straight ahead when a heavily used designated route goes to the right. The next junction is at the 0.9-mile mark. Turn left (southwest), following the sign for McKay Flat. This stretch of road is the best of the entire dirt and gravel section. A vast panorama opens up to the southwest at 3.8 miles. The high mountains, from left to right, are Boulder, Thousand Lake, Fishlake, and Marvine. Cross a cattleguard at just over 4.8 miles, and look for an unsigned track 600 feet farther on the left (southeast).

Wild horses on McKay Flat

This 3.6-mile long unsigned track may be heavily rutted, rocky in places, and is no place to be when it is wet (think about how those ruts got there in the first place). On the positive side, McKay Flat is the best place to see the wild horses that live in the Swell. The herd had its genesis when horses escaped from the trading expeditions that frequented the Old Spanish Trail in the early nineteenth century. Over time, excess stock from ranches and other sources augmented the herd to the point where entrepreneurs culled horses for sale. When the Wild Free Roaming Horse and Burro Act was passed in 1971, the animals came under the protection and management of the BLM. In order to keep numbers within the range that can be supported by the land, the BLM periodically rounds up some of the herd and offers the horses to people willing to adopt them. A sighting of the herd along the track is not rare, though also not guaranteed.

The track almost imperceptibly climbs up the wide and open meadow, and when it tops out and passes around the end of a drainage it becomes rocky and ledgy. At 2.9 miles along there is a Y junction, where a less-used track is to the right (southeast), and the route to the trailhead bears left (more easterly). After the Y, the track crosses flat ground, where there are many campsites. It is important to not create new ones, so camp in areas that have already been disturbed. There is really no specific trailhead, so drive on about 0.7 mile beyond the Y and find a good place to camp or park.

The Hike

The routes into both Baptist Draw and Upper Chute are reasonably straightforward for those with good topographic map-reading skills, and the confidence to set out into unknown country. While there are numerous hiker-made trails all over the place, their very number renders them less than helpful. Your route will probably differ from ours, which is given only as a broad brush example. We parked at UTM 0516871mE, 4283039mN. This point is on the flat between points 6739T (to the west) and 6698T (to the east) on the Horse Valley quadrangle. A faint trail leads to the north, and eventually to the rim of the east-west trending canyon below. Continuing along the rim, a slightly higher hill is to the east-northeast. The eastern tip of the hill is about 0.4 mile from the parking point. From this vantage, and indeed from almost anywhere on the canyon rim, a largely conical hill is obvious to the east, and several trails appear below.

The route down is right at the point of the hill and is steep, though not much more than any descent from the rim. A clear trail soon develops, joins with another in 0.1 mile, and then another 0.2 mile ahead. At each junction continue more or less straight ahead on a line that appears to be passing considerably south of the conical hill. The second intersection is at UTM 0517526mE, 4283425mN. Beyond this point the trail swings uphill and closer to the butte, then contours along its south side where there is a tiny bit of exposure.

Conical hill on Baptist Draw and Upper Chute route

The social trail continues on around the butte and descends very steeply down to another use trail below, almost due east of the hill. This descent can be made in other places as well. The lower level trail is on a bench above the wash of Baptist Draw. When you reach it, turn right (south, back the way you came above) to point UTM 0517849mE, 4283499mN, then turn to the east and scramble down the easy slope to the wash. If this route seems hard and you are using climbing moves, you are in the wrong place. It is just over 1 mile from the road to the wash.

Turn right in the wash (southeast). After 0.2 mile there will be six-foot high walls that display the cross-bedding of the White Rim/Cedar Mesa Sandstone to full advantage. A good sinuous slot section begins 0.3 mile from the wash entry point. The first obstacle the day that we did Baptist Draw was a short stem after a boulder choke a little less than 0.4 mile down canyon, and it was followed by two more short problems, neither difficult. Below, the slot deepened considerably for about 100 yards, and then two openings were joined by another good slot. After 0.6 mile, it was a very good slot to the 0.8-mile mark where a high chokestone and walls too close together to stem turned us around. Since this was just above the first rappel, there was little sense in tempting fate. The last section was especially deep and dark. Like most slots, Baptist Draw can be wet or dry (we had just one short pool to stem over), and the obstacles change with every flood.

The slots in Baptist Draw would be enough to justify the time and effort to get there, but there is even better stuff in Upper Chute Canyon that can be accessed without rappelling. Considerable effort and route-finding are necessary, but the payoff is worth it in our opinion. To get over to Chute, return up Baptist Draw to the entry point into the wash, and then continue walking north in the wash for 0.3 mile. At this point there is an obvious side canyon coming in from the right (northeast). Turn into this draw and work up through the trees and rocks, generally staying in or near the bottom. About 600 feet along bear left (more northerly) on slickrock when the way straight ahead consists of broken rock.

At the top of the drainage you should be near UTM point 0518013mE, 4284156mN, and between a low rocky hill on the left (north) and a larger and higher hill to the right (south). The immediate goal is to get into an east-trending wash that is directly east and leads down into Chute Canyon. One point in that wash is about 0.5 mile from Baptist Draw at UTM 0518418mE, 4284246mN. It is more than 0.4 mile farther down this canyon to get to Chute, and it may seem longer than that. The gradient is steep, but there are no major impediments. Generally, a path right down the bottom of the draw may be best. The mile between Baptist Draw and Chute Canyon may take more than 40 minutes to negotiate. For those without GPS units, the drainage that you want to find enters Chute Canyon almost exactly between points 6621T (to the northwest) and 6603T (to the southeast).

Turn downcanyon (right, south) in Chute. It is about 0.25 mile of easy walking in the wash before it begins to slot up in strongly cross-bedded and reddish sandstone. The next 0.5 mile is almost completely very narrow (often shoulder width), deep, often convoluted and sculpted, and dark. The cumulative effect builds as you work down through the several obstacles, with logs often suspended 20 to 40 feet overhead, or just high enough to walk under. Again, it may not be relevant after the next storm, but the obstacles we found were as follows. After a very nice and perfectly straight slot was the hardest: an awkward boulder and very steep wall that was passable on the right and difficult on the return.

For the next 0.4 mile the walking was generally easy on gravel with only minor chokestones and logs, then another large boulder with enough room to pass on the right offered a modest challenge. Just beyond was another awkward boulder choke that can be stemmed. These last two obstacles are in a section that is more open and less spectacular than the stretch above, and if they are a little too formidable, simply turn around, knowing that you haven't missed much. A very large rock with a steeply angled and hard to climb wall will end the trip for almost everyone, especially since the junction with Baptist Draw and subsequent rappel in Chute are just ahead.

While the trek back to your vehicle will no doubt seem longer than it really is, the advantage to visiting these slots without rappelling gear is that you get to do each of them twice. The change in perspective and light on the return makes everything new.

Lichen

Driving the Southwest San Rafael Swell

Driving distance for the Red Canyon/McKay Flat Loop and Hidden Splendor Spur is 50.5 miles.

Probably the most enjoyable way to see Baptist Draw and Upper Chute is to plan on camping both before and after your hike. A fine way to spend the next morning would be to explore the Swell's southwest corner, where the scenery is spectacular and the remnants of the post World War II uranium rush are abundant. The roads, given the topography, are amazingly good, and under normal circumstances a vehicle that can handle the track to the two slots is more than sufficient to drive the tour described below. Since the big views are toward the west, morning is certainly the preferred time, the earlier the better.

Unlike the monoclinal Waterpocket Fold in Capitol Reef National Park, the San Rafael Swell is closer to an anticline in form, albeit with a much more steeply dipping southeast flank. On the southwest side, the dip is less steep, but still significant, and erosion has largely removed the soft Chinle clays. The current surface is therefore what is called a dip slope, where the surface parallels the underlying strata; in this case, close to Muddy Creek, the roads largely descend on the Moenkopi Formation. The west side of the Muddy Creek canyon soars up to Wingate Sandstone cliffs and then higher, and the views are before you during the drive to the Hidden Splendor Mine and Tomsich Butte.

To start the spur and loop drive, return to the McKay Flat Road and turn left (southwest) if you are coming from the Baptist Draw and Upper Chute hikes. If just doing the drive, follow the instructions at the beginning of the preceding section as far as the turnoff onto the high-clearance track that is just after the cattleguard. It is 3.4 miles, much of it across McKay Flat (watch for the wild horses), to the next junction, which is signed to the left for Hidden Splendor 10, and straight for Reds Canyon 6. The out-and-back road to Hidden Splendor is a little rougher than the one to Reds Canyon, but the views are excellent. To go down to the old mining area and Muddy Creek turn left (southeast) at this junction and zero the trip odometer.

The road winds along with good views to the south, eventually descending where the terrain permits. The first good vista down to Muddy Creek is at 3.7 miles, and many more follow. The road has tight turns and is very narrow in places, requiring caution in driving. On the steeper inclines where gravel is easily washed away, the surface can be rough bedrock, but a standard SUV should have little trouble. The carcass of an old car is a reminder of how difficult travel was in the 1940s and 1950s when the Swell was just opening up during the uranium rush. The last several miles down to the information sign at 10.3 miles offer one view after another; photo stops are best on the descent when the panorama is in front of you.

Hidden Splendor Mine

Just beyond the information sign is an airstrip and then a wide open, but flat, camping area from which a track leads down to Muddy Creek. To the south from the sign, the road roughens considerably, but may be passable to very high-clearance vehicles for another 0.5 mile. The remains of the mining operation are scattered over the landscape, and exploration on foot is interesting.

The ore deposit was discovered by Vernon Pick in 1952. His story lends texture to the history of the Hidden Splendor Mine, and, indeed, the Utah uranium boom of the Cold War era. Pick was a self-made man with little education until he began taking extension courses from the University of Minnesota. In the small town of Royalton, Minnesota, he formed a successful business repairing electric motors, but when a fire destroyed his operation, the insurance was insufficient for him to rebuild. Taking the modest proceeds, he embarked with his family on a trip to the West, perhaps with the intent of going to Mexico. An Atomic Energy Commission geologist suggested that he might have some luck finding uranium near Hanksville, and Pick had worked in mining before, so he decided to give it a try. After long days of walking, he found the ore body that he later developed into the quite lucrative Hidden Splendor Mine (originally called the Delta Mine).

When the Atlas Corporation made him an offer he couldn't refuse, Pick sold out for $9 million, and moved to an 800-acre spread in the Santa Cruz Mountains of California. There he developed a laboratory with a staff of scientists researching electronics and geology. Pick read widely, and admired Henry Thoreau, whose lifestyle he followed even after he became wealthy, and for whom he named his California operation Walden West, and a subsequent lab in British Columbia, Walden North. Pick died in 1986. The postscript is that Atlas mined for three years and produced only about $2 million in ore. Thus, the local name for the mine changed to the "Hidden Blunder."

Road to Hidden Splendor Mine

Reds Canyon Loop Tour

To continue with the loop tour, return to the intersection with the McKay Flat Road and turn left (northwest), again zeroing the odometer. The road descends to the creek in 6 miles, with the first good views just 0.7 mile along. The road condition is generally quite good, with only a few short rough spots. At 5.1 miles is a Y junction, signed for Hondu Arch to the left, and Reds Canyon to the right. Bear left (west), and keep an eye out to the right for the many remains of the Tomsich Butte mines that dot the slopes to the north. The first view of Hondu Arch occurs at the 5.5-mile mark. It is high on the horizon to the southwest and across Muddy Creek, and is impressive for its size and unusual configuration. A signboard is at 5.9 miles, and the road soon devolves into tracks that lead into a popular camping area for tours and individuals. Scattered cottonwoods dot the area, and one track leads to the edge of Muddy Creek, flowing crystal clear at the time of our visit.

Hondu Arch

Hondu Arch

As with the Hidden Splendor, it is a little difficult to imagine the activity that occurred at Tomsich Butte during its mining heyday. Perhaps as many as 450 people lived here, including enough families that a school was necessary. The lode was developed by John Tomsich and WJ Hannert, but under unusual circumstances. Apparently, they filed claims adjacent to, and alternate with, each other, and worked them separately, thereby failing to achieve economies of scale. When Tomsich's claims played out, he reportedly committed suicide. The old mines are very dangerous and obviously should never be entered, and the slopes leading up to them are also hazardous.

The loop is completed by returning to the Y junction (actually a triangle) and bearing to the left (northeast) after resetting the trip odometer. The road climbs up to eventually contour along the northwest side of Reds Canyon. The cab of an old truck is good foreground for the rugged cliffs beyond. After 3.7 miles the road first enters the wash, and for the next 8 miles is either

Tomsich Butte mines

right in the gravel or cutting across sandy meanders of the almost always dry drainage. The gravel was very firm during our trip and the going was easy in two-wheel drive, though conditions can certainly change. A sharp climb at 11.9 miles takes the road onto higher and harder ground, with glimpses of well-named Family Butte on the left (north). Continue straight ahead at an unsigned junction at 14.8 miles. It is another mile to the intersection with the McKay Flat Road and the end of the loop.

Rods Valley

From this point you can retrace your route back to Highway 24 or go up to I-70, or take the "shortcut" through Rods Valley (not to be confused with Reds Canyon) up to the Swasey Cabin and the Head of Sinbad Pictograph Panel. The Rods Valley road is generally easy for 4.5 miles, but then has a very steep and very rough pitch that will challenge standard SUVs and for which low-range 4WD is handy. The cabin and rock art panel are much more easily accessed from the Temple Mountain Road as described in the Head of Sinbad section, so Rods Valley is only for those with robust vehicles.

From the end of the Reds Canyon loop as described above, return 0.9 mile to the junction just beyond (east of) the cattleguard. Turn left (northeast) and drive 0.7 mile to the intersection with the Rods Valley road. Turn left (north) and zero the odometer. This track is a little rough at the start and then winds along the margin of a wide draw, mostly with a packed sandy surface. At 3.8 miles it leaves the sagebrush and the canyon begins to tighten. A pour-off in the canyon requires the road to climb very steeply on a rough, rocky ascent at 4.5 miles, by far the most difficult bit of driving in this entire section. A left (west) turn at 5.9 miles leads in another 0.8 mile to the parking lot for Swasey's Cabin, or you can continue straight ahead for the Head of Sinbad rock art panel (see the Head of Sinbad section for directions and also for the description of the Swasey Cabin).

Copper Globe Mine

Driving distance from exit 116 on I-70 is 6.7 miles one way.

Sometimes it is difficult to imagine the period context of historical sites when their immediate surroundings have undergone so much change that everything around them speaks to modern times. In spite of its location near I-70, this is decidedly not the case with the Copper Globe Mine. The shafts and adits, buildings and machinery, all sit in splendid isolation in the San Rafael Swell, and the rough 4WD drive necessary to see them only adds to the sense of privation and toil that the Fugate family must have endured as they tried to turn a profit on a low-grade copper deposit.

Getting There

The drive to the mine from the I-70 is less than 7 miles, but takes about an hour. Head east from Highway 10 or west from Green River on I-70, and take exit 116, which is signed for Moore. Reset the odometer to zero on the south side of the exit, where the eastbound exit and entrance ramps join the road that passes beneath the highway. Go south for a few feet and then east (left) on a paved road that parallels the entrance ramp and then the Interstate. After 0.2 mile the road turns sharply to the south (right) and crosses a cattleguard, beyond which the surface turns to gravel. The large Justensen Flat OHV parking area is on the left (north) at 1.4 miles after a long descent. A BLM sign points straight ahead to the Copper Globe Mine Road and Devils Canyon. To the right (south) is the boundary of the Devils Canyon Wilderness Study Area (DCWSA).

After the parking area, the quality of the road decreases, with minor ledges slowing progress. Navigation is made more difficult by virtue of the maze of ATV trails that cross the flat. The route to follow is the one that maintains the straightest possible path, especially after about 2 miles. A sign at the 2.3-mile mark is reassuring. It points right (south) for the Copper Globe Road and Devils Canyon. The ATV tracks end when the long and sometimes steep descent into Devils Canyon begins. Several pitches on this segment will require low range for the return trip. The wash of Devils Canyon is entered after a short drop (watch for a rock on the left) at 3.7 miles.

Traveling upstream (left) in the wash is easy, but a ledge where the road begins to ascend out of it was the hardest obstacle when we drove to the mine. Previous drivers had placed several rocks to help, but the sand had swallowed most of them and also made traction a bit of an issue. Impediments like this have a way of worsening or, conversely, disappearing over time, so it pays to be prepared for anything. If by chance the ledge is too imposing (and it shouldn't be unless it gets considerably more difficult), then it would be reasonable to park out of the way and hike the remaining 2.6 miles to the mine.

Above the wash the road makes an ascending traverse along the west side of a deepening drainage. There are several places where a big storm could potentially cause serious erosion problems, but on our trip the going, though slow, was easy. At the 5-mile mark a pillar of Navajo Sandstone is just to the east, and 0.5 mile farther on is a good view of the high point of the Swell, the San Rafael Knob, also to the east. When the road finally reaches a sagebrush flat 1 mile from the Copper Globe, it is nice to be able to look around for a change. This area of the Swell is the home of a herd of wild horses and we did see a group of six from the junction of the roads to the mine and Kimball Wash. This intersection is 6.4 miles from I-70 and is signed for Kimball Wash and Muddy River straight ahead and Copper Globe Mine to the right. The distance given for the mine is 1 mile, but the actual distance is only about 0.3 mile.

A few hundred feet beyond the junction is a short loop road to the right (north) that goes to a marker commemorating the death of a sheepherder in the early winter of 1890. The memorial suggests that the Robbers Roost gang may have borne responsibility for killing Henry Jensen. The rest of the way to the mine is sandy and easy, and the road ends at a parking area with a marker noting that many local agencies and volunteers worked at the site in 1999.

Jensen memorial

Highlights

The Copper Globe Mine dates from 1900 when a father/son team by the name of Fugate began to extract copper. The primary ore mineral appears to be azurite, which can be seen in place in the Navajo Sandstone in the form of nodules, much like the far more abundant iron-rich Moki marbles common to the formation.

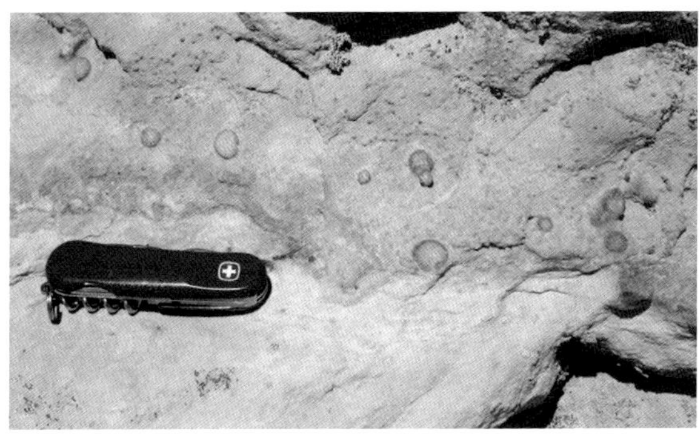
Azurite at Copper Globe Mine

The mines and structures are located in two areas. The larger can be seen from the parking area and includes a horizontal tunnel, an inclined shaft with the framework for a winch, a small cabin, a much larger building that is losing its metal roofing, and, most impressive, a huge pile of cordwood that was to be used to fire the smelter. A miscalculation regarding the brick used for the latter led to its premature failure, so the wood remains in a long and high stack after more than a hundred years of exposure to the elements.

The second area of interest is to the west. A fairly obvious social trail hugs the base of the Navajo cliff beyond the woodpile and adjacent building. It is along this path that the azurite nodules can be seen in a line in the sandstone. After passing around the outcrop, a small cabin comes into view to the northwest, next to a chain link fence. The latter surrounds a square vertical shaft. A little farther on is an interesting cabin partially embedded into the hillside, with an exterior shelf exhibiting a collection of eclectic items associated with the operation. The interior can be easily viewed from the windows. Both preservation of the cabin and the threat of hantavirus make it inappropriate to enter. Below the cabin a partial rock wall is all that is left of the water capture system devised by the miners.

It is a rare opportunity to explore a place like the Copper Globe. As long as this privilege is not abused by taking historical artifacts, entering or harming the buildings or equipment, defacing anything, or suffering injury by failing to take necessary care around shafts and adits, it is an experience that should by enjoyed for years by those taking the time and effort to visit.

Copper Globe Mine woodpile

Goblin Valley and Nearby San Rafael Reef Slot Canyons

Goblin Valley and the slot canyons close by are the most popular destinations in the San Rafael Swell. The state park and Little Wild Horse Canyon attract the bulk of visitors, so a bit of solitude may be achieved in the other canyons, at least outside of high-use times. The slots pass through the steeply tilted Navajo Sandstone and successively older rock units before emerging into the interior of the Swell. They entail different degrees of difficulty, but share relatively easy access. Often the slots are dry, or nearly so, but after rain or snow standing water can make them less pleasant, especially when it is cold. Flash flood danger can be extreme, especially during the monsoon season of July through September. When the weather is good, this small region is a good place to spend a week exploring the Reef.

Goblin Valley

Goblin Valley State Park

Driving distance from Highway 24 is 11.7 miles one way.

Goblin Valley State Park Campground

Whether the approach is from Hanksville or Green River, it is abundantly apparent that this is austere country. The smattering of cattle suggests that there must be something out there to eat, but exactly what may not be clear. There is a lot of sand and, at least in the distance, rock. As the same mile seems to pass by again and again, it might be hard to believe that just a few miles off Highway 24 lies Kid Central. Together, Goblin Valley State Park and Little Wild Horse Canyon attract large extended-family gatherings, especially in the spring, but during all the warm months. If you have children, a couple of days in the desert will be memorable for them and for you, and if you don't, the goblins and the slot are still worth a visit. With other canyons through the San Rafael Reef nearby, which are much less crowded, there is opportunity to enjoy a bit of relative quiet as well.

Goblin Valley State Park is quite remarkable, merely for its geological and human presence. The campground, visitor/entrance center, and housing are all solar powered, and the campground even has showers. In addition to the twenty-four campsites, there are two yurts, each sleeping five people, and equipped with swamp coolers to make the summer heat bearable. The campground is very popular and reservations are highly recommended. As of this writing, sites are $16 per night, and the yurts $60, costs that seem more than reasonable given the constraints of the park's location. While it is often the case that state parks in general do not get the attention and visitation they deserve, Goblin Valley is the exception. People from all over the world are drawn to the hoodoos.

Getting There

The turn off Highway 24 to the park is at milepost 136, a little less than halfway from Hanksville to I-70. Set the odometer to zero then turn west onto the good paved road and travel toward the San Rafael Reef for 5.2 miles. Although a paved road continues straight at this point, follow the sign, turn left (southwest), and travel another 6.1 miles to the turn for Little Wild Horse. The Goblin Valley entrance station and visitor center is visible a short distance straight ahead. Presently, the entrance fee is $7 per car. The developed section of the park is small. From the entrance station it is 0.5 mile to a T intersection; the campground is less than 0.25 mile to the right, and the valley of goblins is 0.7 mile to the left. There are three short hiking trails in the park, lightly used because the main event is simply rambling through the three connected areas of hoodoos.

Highlights

At the end of the road is a large parking area with a vault toilet and several good interpretive signs. The view of the hoodoos is impressive from this elevated position, and it will be hard keeping the kids from rushing down the stepped ramp to get into them. The hoodoos are mostly short compared to those at Bryce Canyon National Park. They range from about three feet to ten feet tall in the basin to the south of the parking area, with taller ones closer to the encircling cliffs, which afford some protection. The park advises against climbing on them; this is very good advice indeed. There is more than enough room for kids to run around and play whatever variation of hide and seek that they choose.

The hoodoos of Goblin Valley are fine examples of the impact of slightly different resistance to erosion in a sedimentary rock layer. At Bryce, the harder limestone layers are easy to pick out, but at Goblin the difference is hard to see simply by looking closely at the rock—and easy to discern by taking in the entire hoodoo. The rock unit here is Entrada Sandstone, the same formation into which the arches of Arches National Park are cut, along with the 400-foot high drip castle–like temples of Capitol Reef. If you are traveling Highway 95 from Hanksville to Blanding and don't have time for Goblin Valley, the kids will be almost as happy at Little Egypt, described in the Henry Mountains section.

Entrada Sandstone at the Red Desert

Entrada Sandstone and Curtis Formation

The Entrada Sandstone is widespread, extending to the east well beyond the Colorado Plateau. Over this vast extent it exhibits slightly different lithologies and thus varied paleoenvironments of deposition, but in general it was laid down by winds coming from the shoreline of the Sundance Sea to the north and west. In places the Entrada stands tall and straight, as with the Slick Rock Member that forms the arches in Arches National Park. Where the formation is less durable, as in Cathedral Valley in Capitol Reef National Park, weathering and erosion have produced spectacular soaring monoliths. Here in Goblin Valley is an intermediate type of erosional feature—hoodoos, or short pillars.

The landforms associated with the Entrada reflect the influence of faulting and/or jointing on weathering and erosion. Whether it is vertical movement on fractures due to the movement of salt at depth (at Arches NP), or response to large-scale faulting and jointing as in Cathedral Valley, or small-scale jointing at Goblin Valley, in each case weathering was enhanced by the zones of weakness that resulted. Surface water, slightly acidic, is able to penetrate the joints or fractures and more effectively dissolve the calcite that bonds the sand grains into sandstone. Where the dominant fractures are parallel, fins can form, leading to arches. When the joints cross each other, the stage is set for hoodoos to form. Very minor changes in the rock layers can make one slightly more resistant to erosion, thus forming the cap across many adjacent hoodoos.

The Entrada Sandstone reflects small changes in sea level, where some windblown deposits were subsequently reworked by wave action. To the east, farther away from the inland sea, the formation is more consistently eolian in nature. The overlying Curtis Formation, separated from the Entrada by an unconformity, was deposited in shallow marine conditions as sea level rose. Thin layers of mudstone, sandstone, and limestone were laid down during the middle Jurassic Period, about 163 ma. The Curtis is light gray in color, in contrast to the chocolate brown of the Entrada. It is also more resistant, often capping Entrada landforms. Just to the north of the campground, Wild Horse Butte nicely displays the Entrada-Curtis sequence. When the sea receded to the north for the final time, the thin beds of the Summerville Formation were deposited from the west, and the Summerville is also well exposed at the top of Wild Horse Butte.

North Temple Wash Drive

Driving distance from the paved Goblin Valley Road to the mining area turnaround is 4.2 miles one way.

After looking at all of Goblin Valley's hoodoos, it might seem a bit much to go out of your way to see another one, but the short side trip into North Temple Wash is worth the short time it will take. On the way back to Highway 24, stop at the information kiosk at the ninety-degree turn that is 6.5 miles from the park entrance station. To negotiate the North Temple Wash Road all the way to the mining area on the east side of Temple Mountain you will need a good high-clearance vehicle. Although a fair amount of travel is in the wash itself, the gravel seems pretty firm and it would be unusual, though not impossible, to need four-wheel drive.

North Temple Wash hoodoo

The best way to access North Temple Wash is to take the road that goes out of the information kiosk parking lot and after just less than 0.1 mile turn left (northeast) at a four-way intersection. Stay straight ahead when other tracks enter on the left (north). A mile from the pavement is a junction; turn left into the wash and follow it as it curves left and then right before trending largely northwest. At the 1.5-mile mark look to the right (northeast) to spot quite an amazing pillar with an outsized top. The Navajo Sandstone is a little less uniform here, and the jointing that resulted from the folding of the San Rafael Reef is pronounced, causing a variety of sharp features nearby.

The wash passes through the Navajo at 2.2 miles, and the road becomes considerably rougher as it crosses ledges in the Kayenta Formation. The Wingate Sandstone passes by quickly, and the rest of the trip to the mining shack is on rusty Chinle Formation claystone. The old cabin at 4.2 miles is a good place to turn around, keeping in mind that all the ground in the area is under active claim. The very good view of the east side of convoluted Temple Mountain is especially fine in the morning.

Temple Mountain and miner's cabin

Little Wild Horse and Bell Canyons Hike

Driving distance from Highway 24 is 16.8 miles one way.
Hiking distance is 9 miles round trip.

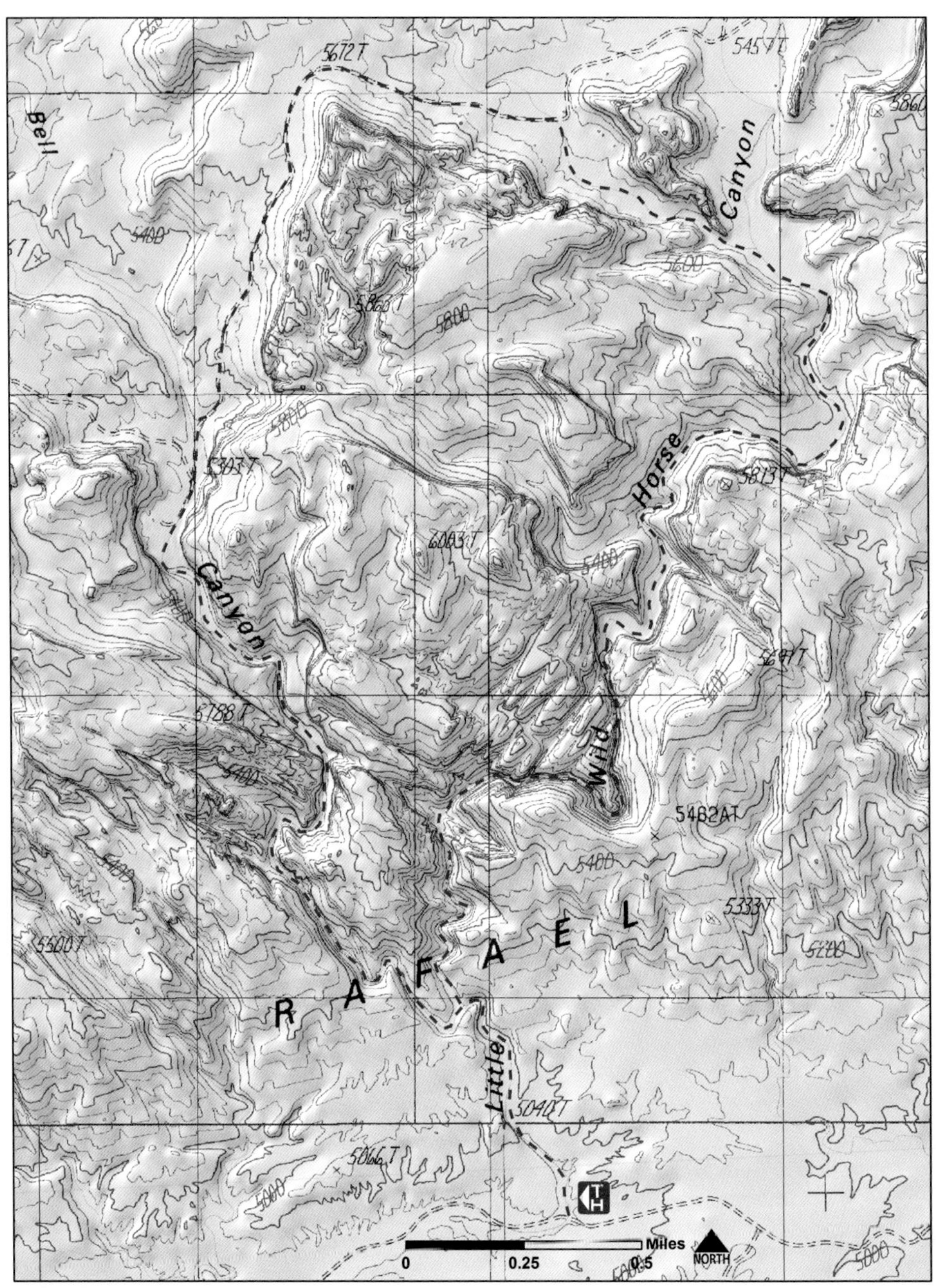

Little Wild Horse/Bell route

Little Wild Horse Canyon near Goblin Valley State Park is probably the most visited slot canyon in Utah. On a nice Easter weekend the number of vehicles strewn about at and near the trailhead is truly impressive, and the sounds of enthusiastic children echo through the narrows without cease. All this is due to the fortuitous merging of three factors: ease of access by car, lack of major obstacles in the slot, and legitimately spectacular canyon scenery. If sharing your commune with nature with two hundred other people is not your cup of tea, there are options that promise much more solitude and leisurely enjoyment of this fine canyon system. Most obvious, of course, is to avoid holiday weekends, and weekends in general in the spring. Additionally, making a loop of Bell and Little Wild Horse avoids a lot of the foot traffic due to the length of the hike, which is just under 9 miles. As with any slot canyon, even the prospect of rain is enough to warrant choosing some other activity rather than being at risk for a flash flood.

Getting There

The drive to the trailhead is on a paved road. From Highway 24 between Hanksville and Green River, turn west (left if coming from Hanksville) onto the Goblin Valley State Park road at milepost 136. Go 5.2 miles to a well-signed left turn and proceed southwest toward the park. At 11.3 miles from Highway 24, when the Goblin Valley entrance station is visible ahead, look for a three-way junction and turn right (west) on a recently paved road. A sign soon indicates that it is 5.3 miles to Little Wild Horse Canyon. The trailhead is well marked and includes a substantial parking area, with overflow parking just beyond. There is a vault toilet and information board with a map at the trailhead. To give an idea of the popularity of this hike, we last visited Little Wild Horse mid-week on a sunny April day after Easter and spring breaks, and there were fifteen vehicles in the parking lot, representing eleven different states.

The Hike

There are two quite different ways to hike the narrows. For those seeking a little solitude and a much longer hike, making a circuit of Bell and Little Wild Horse fits the bill nicely. Most, however, simply do a much shorter out and back in Little Wild Horse where the best slot sections are. We think the loop hike is very worthwhile, and that is described here, but if you are short on time, a quick visit to Little Wild Horse alone would still be rewarding. For the loop, a clockwise hike (Bell Canyon first) is our choice, unless recent rains have left pools in the upper part of Little Wild Horse. There are often long periods when both canyons are mostly dry, but after rain or snow there can be substantial water in them. In the spring that water, even though almost always less than waist deep, can be cold enough and the pools long enough to make hypothermia a possibility, and discomfort a certainty. The staff at Goblin Valley may be able to provide current information on the amount of water, if any, in the canyons.

From the parking area, follow a short trail that quickly drops into the wide Little Wild Horse wash; simply stay in the main drainage as it slowly narrows and deepens, and enters the Crack Canyon Wilderness Study Area (CCWSA). About 0.4 mile from the trailhead, the easy walking is interrupted by an eight-foot high pour-off that will be difficult for some. Either climb it directly or backtrack to an ascending ledge on the left (west), looking upstream. The bypass goes high above the canyon floor and is a little exposed, and the descent back to the wash above the dryfall is steep. The bypass returns to the wash almost directly across from the junction of Bell and Little Wild Horse Canyons. There is a sign marking the confluence. As you finish the descent, Bell is to the left (northwest) at this point, while Little Wild Horse goes straight (northeast). To do the circuit described, stay in Bell, and soon enter a narrows section in the Navajo Sandstone.

While its near neighbor is certainly more glitzy, outside of its shadow, Bell would stand alone nicely as a fine canyon ramble. There are several minor obstacles in the forms of pour-offs and chokestones, and a 0.5-mile section of narrows that are quite good. The canyon opens after about 1 mile and before the wash leaves the Navajo. In the overlying Kayenta Formation, the more resistant layers form dryfalls, even in the wide gorge. The two most significant obstacles are passed on the left (west) on easy slickrock ramps. When Bell and Little Wild Horse cut through the Wingate, instead of narrows, the drainages are wide and sandy. The hike in the upper reaches of both is very easy and pleasant.

When Bell widens even further and the wash becomes broad and sandy, there is enough room for piñons and junipers to thrive and provide shade for a lunch or rest stop. The wash trends straight ahead for several hundred yards, and a road is visible on the mauve-colored hill just to the right (east) of the wash. This track actually enters the wash for a short distance. Hikers on the loop will encounter it first coming in from the west (left), perhaps follow wheel tracks for a short way if recent rain or wind hasn't obscured them, and then exit the wash on the road when it goes to the right (east) and begins to climb a long slope. There may be signs to help negotiate this spot, but remember that the hike is clockwise, so stay right and head east, parallel to the Wingate wall to the south. The GPS coordinates for the point where the road leaves the wash are UTM 0515997mE, 4272874mN.

The walk along the road is an interesting interlude between the two canyons. This area is the interior of the San Rafael Swell, while the canyons slice through the San Rafael Reef. The interior of the Swell is rugged, but much less imposing than the Reef. Here, the road traverses the Chinle Formation, consisting of clays and volcanic ash deposited largely in a massive swamp environment. It is about 1.5 miles of walking on the road, basically up and over a single hill in wide open country.

When the track eventually descends into a significant drainage, leave the road and walk down the wash to the right (southeast). There may be a sign to Little Wild Horse at this point (UTM 0517232mE, 4273097mN). In about 0.5 mile this small wash joins the much larger Little Wild Horse wash. Head downstream (right, south) at this point (UTM 0517912mE, 4273496mN), which may have a sign oriented for those headed in the opposite direction. Navigation for the rest of the hike simply entails staying in the obvious main canyon in the downstream direction.

At first, Little Wild Horse in the upper reaches is very similar to Bell, with a wide, sandy wash floor and Wingate walls. In the ledgy Kayenta the canyon begins to narrow but the going remains easy for most of the way through the formation. Eventually, however, the walls close in and there are several minor pour-offs to negotiate. A more significant obstacle can be passed on the left (south) with a steep downclimb back to the wash. The next dryfall can be descended by staying in the channel. After passing underneath a huge rock in a dark slot section, the wash widens broadly for a last time, with a long open stretch with thick birchleaf mountain mahogany on the benches.

When Little Wild Horse cuts into the Navajo Sandstone, the result is an astonishingly long series of narrows and slots that are very impressive. The depth is more than sufficient to impart a cave-like feel for much of the way. The walls close to within three feet for long periods, and in places are almost tight enough to require sideways movement. In the lower part, the canyon becomes very sinuous as well. The highly scenic part of the canyon goes on for about 1.5 miles, and lasts almost to the junction with Bell. Our second trip around the loop was difficult due to considerable water in the upper part of Little Wild Horse; it is hard to describe just how cold one's feet can get after

Little Wild Horse Canyon

Little Wild Horse Canyon

Little Wild Horse Canyon sandstone

sloshing carefully through many long pools. However, when we did a short in and out after a good rain to confirm the presence of pools for this book, we found that gravel had filled in all the depressions and the walk all the way through the best slot sections was delightful. This was just another indication of how quickly conditions in slot canyons can change, and reinforces the principle that hikers always need to be willing and able to adjust, or come back at a different time.

When the narrows gradually recede, the walk back to the confluence with Bell Canyon is short, and after the junction just another 0.5 mile is left to the trailhead. If you have done the loop it might be enough for the day, but if not, there is an option to continue canyoneering nearby, either in Crack Canyon or Ding and part of Dang Canyons. The Bell/Little Wild Horse loop will take longer than a trail hike of similar distance; if you allow time to savor these beautiful clefts, the circuit might take six hours or even more.

Little Wild Horse Canyon

Crack Canyon Hike

Driving distance from Highway 24 is 11.6 miles one way (2WD) or 12.3 miles (4WD) one way.
Hiking distance is 4.25 miles round trip from the 4WD trailhead.

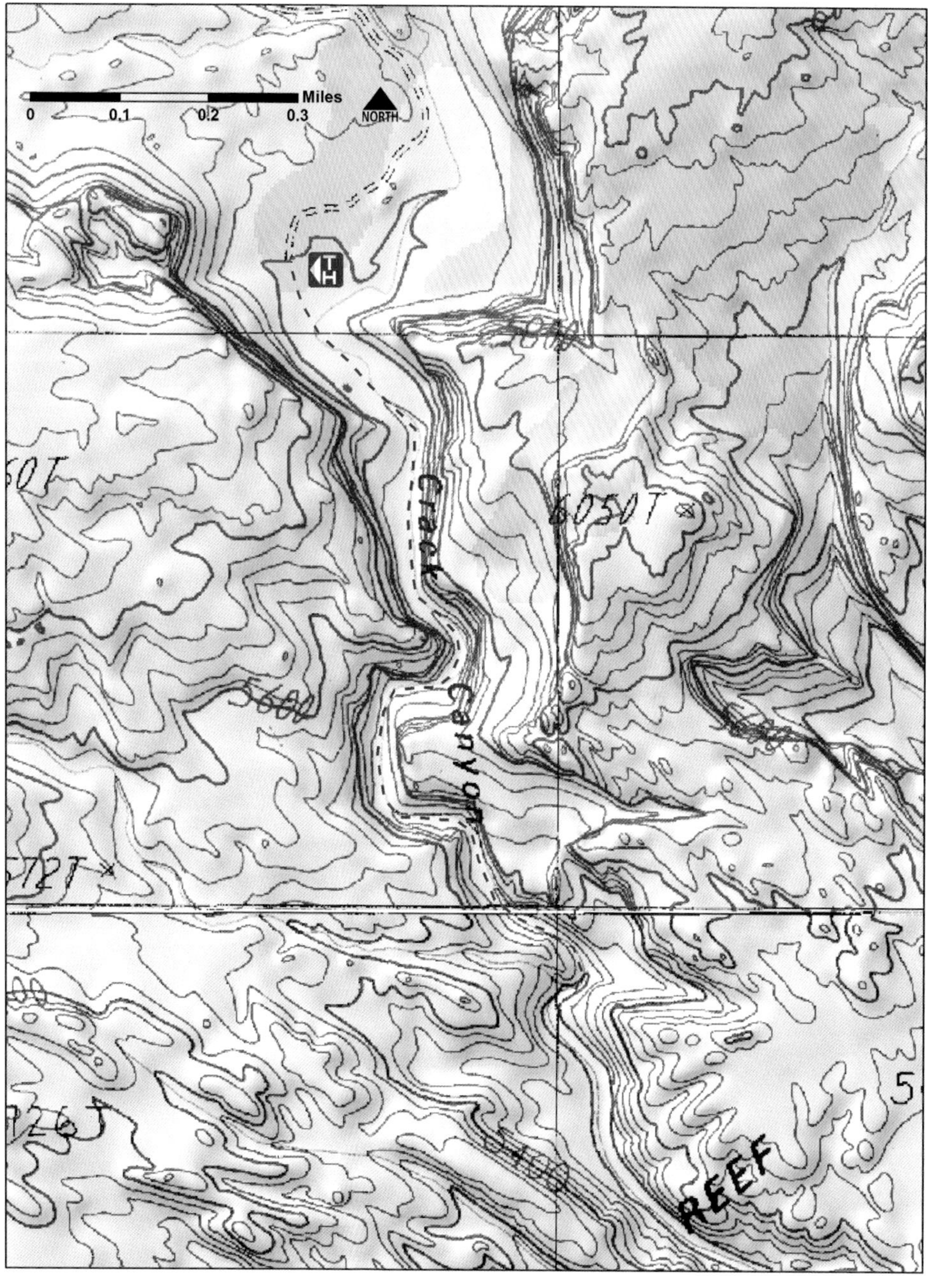

Crack Canyon route

Of the seven major breaches through the San Rafael Swell near Goblin Valley State Park, Crack Canyon is the second most difficult (behind Dang) to traverse. In just over 0.25 mile there are a number of obstacles that are nicely challenging for people who have a little experience in negotiating slot canyons. The level of skill and confidence necessary for Crack is just about at the limit for canyons described in this book. Should you find Crack to be so easy as to approach boring, it is time to move up to one of the many guides that cover more difficult canyons. The upper section of Crack is very interesting in its own right, and accessible to almost any hiker.

Getting There

To get to the trailhead, go 20 miles northeast of Hanksville on Highway 24 and turn off at milepost 136 onto the signed Goblin Valley State Park road. Zero the odometer and drive west. Continue straight ahead at 5.2 miles when the route to Goblin Valley turns to the left. At 0.5 mile farther on is a very large RV parking area with pit toilets. The pavement ends as the road passes through the reef. The unsigned Behind the Reef Road turns off to the left (west) 7.3 miles from Highway 24, and just after a second very large parking area. This road has rough spots, but should generally be passable to carefully driven passenger cars with good clearance. The track into Wild Horse Canyon is at the 9-mile mark, and the one to Crack Canyon is at 11.6.

There is a signed trailhead on the left side of the Behind the Reef Road just beyond the track. Passenger cars will have to park here. As of this writing it appears that the BLM is permitting vehicles to drive down the rough track 0.75 mile to the boundary of the CC WSA. The status of this road can change; check with the BLM if there is any question about whether it is open to travel. Good clearance is required to get to the WSA fence. There are several popular dispersed camping sites near the end of the track.

The Hike

Trail distances start at the fence and WSA boundary. Add 1.5 miles round trip if you start at the passenger car trailhead on the Behind the Reef Road. The first 0.85 mile is easy going and very scenic, making it a nice hike for almost anyone. The canyon is wide at first, with high Wingate Sandstone walls and a wide sandy floor. After 0.25 mile there is a series of small bedrock drops, often with a pool at the bottom of the lowest. These can easily be passed on either side. At 0.2 beyond, the route passes through a narrow cleft with overhanging walls that create a tunnel effect.

Crack Canyon

Crack Canyon

Crack Canyon solution cavities

Freshly exposed solution cavities in Crack Canyon

The walls of the canyon here and for the next 0.3 mile are pock-marked with thousands of holes, large and small. It takes only a little imagination to see all sorts of ghoulish Halloween figures peering mournfully out of the rock. In fact, "Canyon of Ghouls" would perhaps be a better name for this cut through the Reef. The holes are more formally known as solution cavities or sometimes tafoni. If you look carefully, they are usually arranged in linear fashion reflecting bedding planes in the host rock. Sandstone consists of small grains of sand that are cemented together, often by the mineral calcite. When slightly acidic groundwater percolates through the porous rock, it dissolves a bit of the cement where it emerges. Over time this creates small cavities that are then enlarged by rain water that may be made more acidic by windblown organic matter. When the lines and ages of the holes are just right, ghoulish figures appear. The wall about 0.7 mile from the fence is one of the best expressions of this phenomenon.

Less than 200 yards after this spectacular wall is the first significant obstacle, one that definitively ends the easy hiking. Here, a log has performed the job usually done by a chokestone, and created a drop of about nine feet that is one of the more difficult problems in moving down canyon. Of course, this may be gone tomorrow, or last a decade. As long as the log remains in place, it will be a good test. A few steps lead to the next drop, much easier, and then it is 150 yards to a short, 20-foot deep slot. Beyond that the canyon is easy for 0.1 mile to a steep pour-off that is easier to climb than it looks.

Another stretch of mellow canyon precedes a couple of problems that rival or exceed the first in difficulty. The first is a chokestone that overhangs an eight-foot drop, but the walls are close enough to stem through. Just beyond is a similar obstacle, a little less high, but also requiring some thought. As mentioned at the outset, experienced canyoneers may view these drops as very easy, and novices may not get past the first one. The important thing is to stay within your comfort zone and be safe. The entire section of chokestones and pour-offs is quite narrow and scenic, and, viewed from above, nice and dark as well.

The final chokestone described above is the last of significance, and the reward is just 0.25 mile farther down canyon. This slot is about 400 feet long, aesthetic, deep, and dark. After passing through, a nice slope of slickrock is a good place to take a break before returning up to the trailhead. If you have time, however, there is more pretty canyon beyond, and easy walking. This open stretch extends for 0.25 mile to a good view of a turtle-like rock on the left (east) side, and then 0.3 mile to the first point where the flat ground in front of the San Rafael Reef can be seen. If you hike on to this point, the overall distance round trip to the fence is about 4.25 miles, and to the 2WD trailhead, about 5.75 miles. As usual, however, in slots, distance is less important than time, which in turn depends primarily on how long it takes to negotiate the obstacles. Larger groups can slow progress significantly.

We have done Crack in a wet time, and when it was completely dry. The latter is better as you might surmise. If there are pools and the water cold, it can be quite a chore unless the temperature in the shade is very warm. Since this is likely to be during the summer monsoon season and hence a dangerous time to be in any slot, Crack is best during a dry spring or fall.

Crack Canyon

Crack Canyon

Ding and Dang Canyons Hike

Driving distance from Highway 24 is 18.1 miles one way.
Hiking distance as described (up and back through Ding, over to Dang and part way up and back) is 6.2 miles round trip.

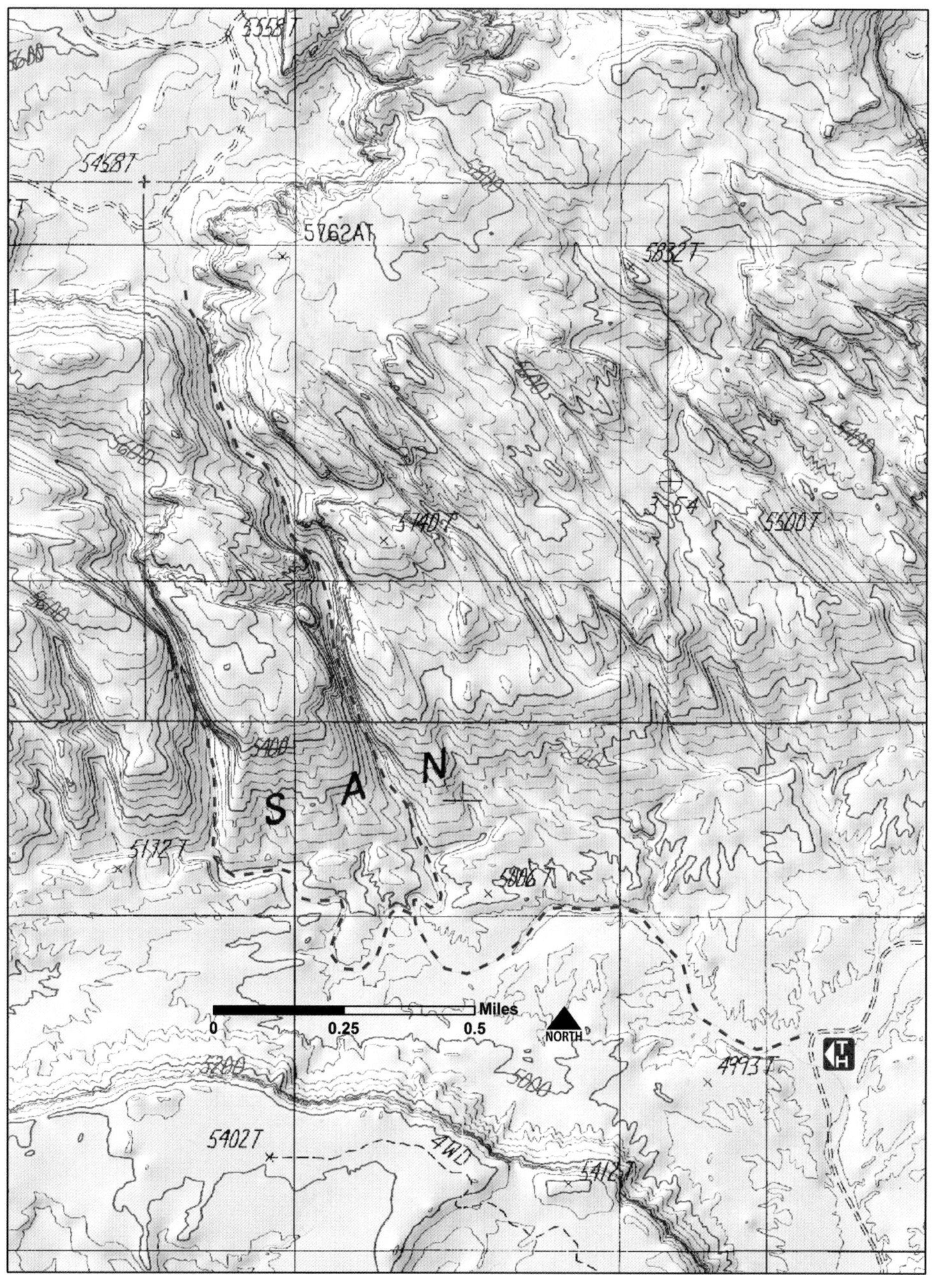

Ding route (to the east) and Dang route (to the west)

Perhaps it is a nice spring day and you have decided to hike the Bell/Little Wild Horse loop. With an early start, you arrive at the trailhead only to find a small community already there. RVs are parked in every available spot not already taken by a flotilla of SUVs, pickups, and, now that the road is paved, even low-slung cars. Kids and harried adults are roaming around, all apparently getting ready for the journey into Little Wild Horse. The opportunity to enjoy the canyons in peace and quiet seems a distant possibility. It might be time to continue on down the road a bit and savor the relative solitude of Ding and Dang Canyons.

Getting There

From the Little Wild Horse trailhead, continue west for 1.3 miles to the point where the road makes a sweeping curve to the south (left). Here, a broad wash continues straight ahead and a large informal parking area is marked by a sign and several cottonwood trees, one of which is multi-stemmed. Unless storms have created problems, this stretch of road should be passable to high-clearance vehicles. Around the parking area there are sandy places where 4WD is handy; if there is any chance of rain, neither you nor your vehicle should be near this wash.

Ding and Dang are yet another pair of narrow canyons cut through the Navajo, Kayenta, and Wingate Formations that form the San Rafael Reef, here contained within the CC WSA. Skilled and intrepid canyoneers can make a loop of the hike (sections of Dang are beyond the scope of this book), but many others will be satisfied by negotiating Ding as an out-and-back walk and scramble. Ding has a nice slot section cut in the Navajo, but does not rival Little Wild Horse in terms of the quality, and certainly the length, of its narrows. It does offer an array of obstacles that makes it a good training ground for reasonably agile people who are just getting familiar with Utah's fabulous suite of canyons.

Ding Canyon

Dang Canyon

The Carmel Formation

At the confluence of the Ding and Dang washes, the distinctive Carmel Formation envelops both drainages. Its uniqueness lies in the many different rock types that often occur in relatively thin beds right above and below each other, and in the frequently convoluted appearance of those layers. While the overlying Entrada Sandstone and the underlying Page and/or Navajo Sandstones are generally consistent in composition and color, the Carmel can be red, brown, gray, green, and white. It is middle Jurassic in age, and where the Page Sandstone is absent, it is the earliest formation in the San Rafael Group.

The effect of sea level changes is quite apparent in the relationship between the underlying Page Sandstone and the Carmel. A brief description of the Page is in order here. It is a windblown sandstone that was laid down along the eastern shore of the southern extension of the ancient Sundance Sea. Named after the type locality at Page, Arizona, this unit has only recently been recognized and given formation status. It rests on the Navajo Sandstone and looks very much like it aside from its characteristic vertical weathering habit, which is most spectacularly exposed on the top of the Golden Throne in Capitol Reef. Eventually sea level rose sufficiently to end the deposition of dune sand, and a fine sequence of mostly marine sediments were laid down.

The Carmel consists of mudstones, limestones, and gypsum. The type of material depended on the depth of the sea and whether it was increasing (transgressing) or lowering (regressing). Especially near the top of the formation, there are extensive deposits of gypsum, a component used in the manufacture of sheetrock, or wallboard. As of this writing there is at least one active mine in the northern San Rafael Swell for this material. Gypsum is an evaporite, left behind as sea water evaporates in a closed basin or embayment. As the Sundance Sea retreated to the north, large pools were cut off and gypsum was deposited. When the water was gone, another period of dune formation occurred, and the Entrada Sandstone succeeded the Carmel Formation.

Carmel Formation in Dang Canyon

The Hike

From the parking area, walk west in the wash, which is about as easy-going as it gets. The drainage is largely cut in the soft brown Entrada Sandstone, though it does wander into the gray and red Carmel Formation at one point. The well-layered Summerville Formation forms the distant wall off to the south, while the white Navajo soars above to the north. It is just under 1 mile to a confluence where two washes join in a narrow Y. The drainage to the right (more northerly) leads to Ding, while the lower entrance to Dang is the left (more westerly) fork. A large and solitary juniper tree is the marker for Ding. Head toward it and continue in the wash as it bends to the east just beyond the tree, and passes by young cottonwoods in the Carmel Formation. Shortly the wash bends back to the north and heads straight for the Reef. At 0.25 mile from the juniper the wash again curves more easterly, and a slickrock ramp rises straight ahead. The ramp is the entrance to Ding Canyon.

Approach to Ding and Dang Canyons – Ding to the right, Dang to the left

An easy friction climb up the ramp leads to more slickrock slopes, and in another 0.25 mile directly into the best and most narrow part of the cut through the Navajo Sandstone. Just after noon in late April the sun lights up this section very nicely. There are some chokestones to navigate, but the path through the Navajo is generally more scenic than difficult, and can be negotiated in fifteen or twenty minutes.

The Kayenta is a bit of a different story. Because it consists of alternating beds of resistant sandstone and much more easily eroded soft shale, the Kayenta tends to form cliffbands of various thicknesses. These can than become significant impediments in narrow canyons. In Ding the beds tilt (dip) steeply down to the southeast at an angle similar to the gradient of the canyon floor. The result is many steep slickrock stretches and a number of minor pour-offs that cumulatively slow progress. An interesting line of potholes identifies the beginning of the Kayenta. None of the obstacles are very difficult once the best route is determined.

When the gradient flattens into a sandy wash, the canyon is cut in the Wingate. Vegetation increases and the typical solution cavities begin to appear, especially on the left (west). When a sharp, pointed pyramid appears on the left (west), the hiker-made trail over to Dang can be seen on the slope in the middle distance. Continue straight up a small wash as the primary drainage bends to the right (east). The trail will emerge and there are many cairns to mark the way. Dang has obstacles that are difficult enough to restrict through-hiking to experienced canyoneers, and should not be attempted if there is any uncertainty about the competence of anyone in the group. Even then, aid will likely be necessary. If you do decide to explore the upper part of Dang, be prepared to turn around if it is beyond your skill level.

Several small narrowleaf cottonwoods have taken root at the wash confluence. *Populus augustifolia* is much less common in south-central Utah than Fremont cottonwood, but shares the need for reliable water and is therefore found in riparian areas or along usually dry washes where water is not far from the surface. As its common name implies, the leaves are indeed narrow, pointed, and up to four inches long with a short leaf stalk. Young trees have smooth gray bark like Fremont cottonwoods, but the difference in leaf shape is immediately apparent. Narrowleaf cottonwoods often provide a welcome touch of green in Utah's red rock canyons.

Ding Canyon

Twinpod

In the event that the prospect of heading down Dang seems a little uncertain, its lower reaches can be explored by returning through Ding and then heading west in the dry wash at the junction 1 mile from the parking lot. The wash remains easy to walk and is perhaps a little more interesting between the two canyons. A lot of the way it is cut into the Carmel Formation. The wash trends along the strike of the beds, so when it does curve toward the Reef, the angle that the rocks are tilted (the dip) is very apparent at roughly thirty degrees.

After just over 0.75 mile there are two minor slickrock ramps, white in color, followed by a third tan ramp in less than 200 yards. Almost exactly 1 mile from the wash junction the Navajo slots up after a sinuous sandy stretch. Whether you intend to attempt to go all the way through Dang or just sample the lower, and arguably most scenic, part, the initial 200 yards are very good. Experienced canyoneers will zip through, while novices can test their abilities and judgment.

The canyons that cut through the San Rafael Reef from (big) Wild Horse Canyon on the northeast to Dang on the southwest have a common response to rain or snow. When moisture is moderate, they have many depressions that fill with water. During the prime seasons of spring and fall, the water can be very cold, and evaporation is slow. In any given year, however, it is also likely that the pools will have a chance to dry up at some point, making for more enjoyable hiking for many (and less exciting fun for a select few). During wetter times, Dang (and Ding) will have water right from the start.

The first three pools can be stemmed without much trouble, since the walls of the slot are so close together. For first-timers, this technique, which becomes simple and routine with practice, is perhaps a little intimidating. The east (right going up-canyon) side of the slot is nearly vertical, while the west is more angled. By putting one's back against the vertical wall and feet slightly lower on the other, a very stable position is created when the distance between the walls is comfortable. Good clean tread on boots is obviously important, and often somewhat difficult to obtain when there is a lot of mud. Once a good position is established, it is surprisingly easy to move both laterally and vertically within the slot. If there is water, the first section is a perfect place to practice, since the chokestone at the upper end is relatively low.

Dang Canyon

Dang Canyon

The second chokestone requires stemming even when the canyon is dry as it is too high to climb by other means (unless, of course, a flood eliminates it or fills in below). In wet times a third long pool can be stemmed, but the next is too wide and must be waded in order to get to a very large arrow-shaped chokestone. It is easy to proceed under this obstacle to gain a few more feet of slot, but the next impediment is high and the walls wider, requiring higher levels of skill than are assumed in this book. If you do not feel safe attempting this chokestone, simply reverse field and return to your vehicle.

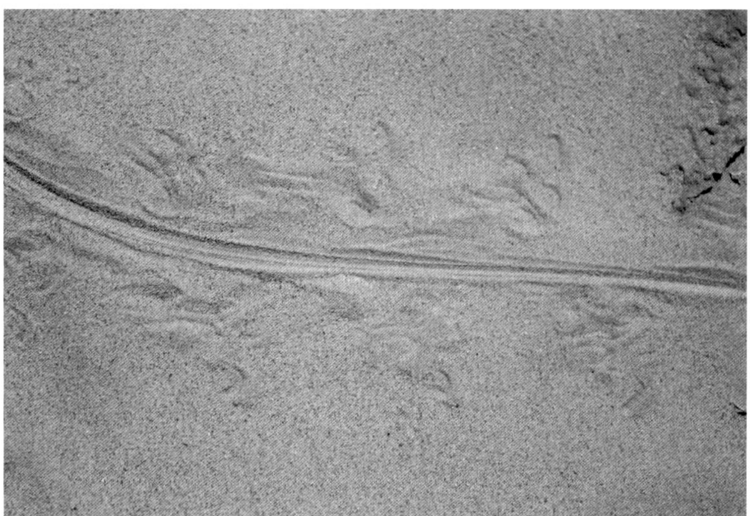

Lizard tracks

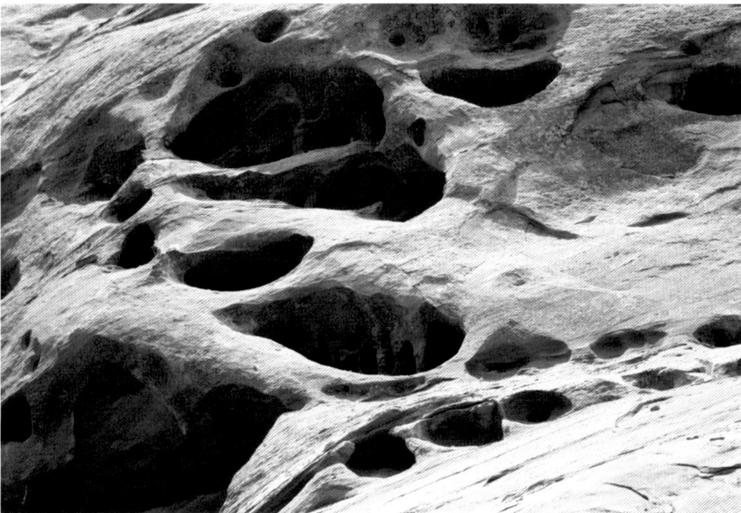

Ding Canyon solution cavities

Wild Horse Canyon Hike

Driving distance from Highway 24 to the lower end of the canyon is 6.4 miles one way.
Hiking distance is 6 to 7 miles round trip.

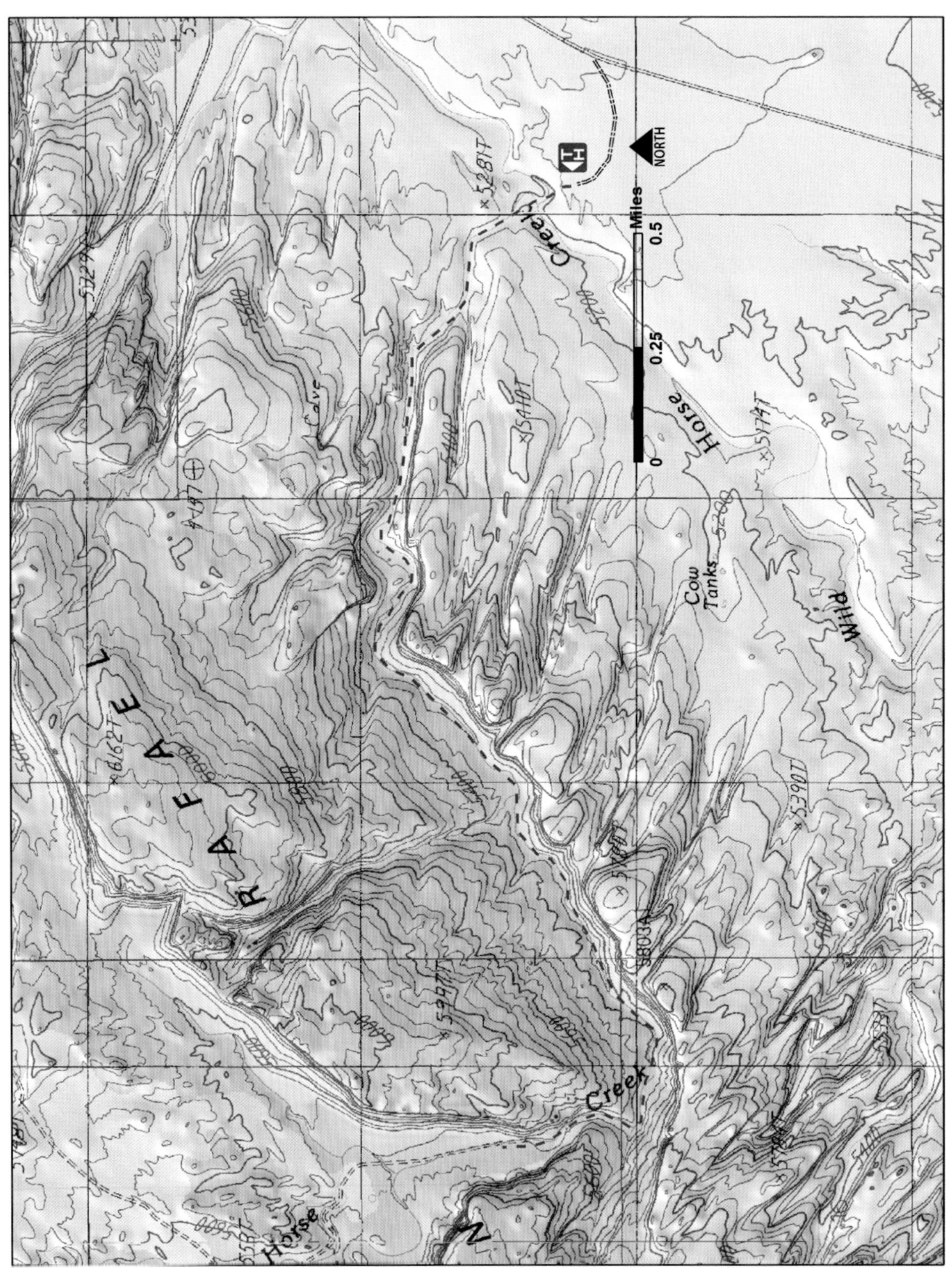

Wild Horse Canyon route

Wild Horse Butte—from the bottom: Entrada, Curtis, and Summerville Formations

Nomenclature of features north and west of Goblin Valley State Park can be confusing. Little Wild Horse is well known as one of Utah's premier family slot canyons, while nearby Wild Horse Creek and its canyon are far less notorious. The two drainages do not merge in spite of the implications of their names. Wild Horse Creek, which is dry most of the time over most of its course, begins northeast of Goblin Valley not far from the South Temple Wash. The drainage begins inside the San Rafael Reef, and trends to the south, cutting through the Wingate and Kayenta Formations before turning northeast along the Navajo until breaking through and turning back southwest along the front of the Reef.

Wild Horse Canyon is an easy and enjoyable stroll through varied surroundings, and is a good alternative for those seeking a little solitude, though the days of seeing no one are largely past, at least during the prime hiking seasons. It is especially suited for groups that have more than one vehicle and can do a through-hike.

Getting There

During dry weather, vehicular access is straightforward. The southeast (down-canyon) trailhead is just off the paved road that leads from Highway 24 to Goblin Valley. If coming from Capitol Reef and Hanksville, turn left (west) on the newly reconstructed road to Goblin Valley State Park. After 5.2 miles, turn left (southwest), following the sign to the park. Proceed another 0.8 mile and turn right (northwest) on a prominent track. Note that the BLM has closed several other tracks to travel in the area, at least three in the 0.8 mile before the correct turn-off. Drive down the track, which is normally passable to carefully driven cars, for 0.4 mile and then turn right (east) and go 100 yards to an informal parking area on the edge of a steep slope that leads down into the Wild Horse drainage. A track continues beyond the parking area, but it is closed despite the absence of a sign on this end.

For out and back hikers we recommend starting from the down-canyon end, but those who have two vehicles might want to leave one here, and start from the top. The upper trailhead is reached by returning to the paved road and retracing the route back to the intersection that is 0.8 mile to the northeast. At the stop sign turn left (northwest) on a chip-sealed road that leads through the Reef. After 0.5 mile the BLM has constructed a huge parking area, largely for recreational vehicles to camp. At times of high usage, the community there can be very impressive. There are two vault toilets available. The road surface turns to graded dirt a short way beyond the camp area, and has some rocks, but cars should be able to proceed without too much difficulty. At 1.5 miles beyond the first camping area is another one, also basically a large parking area with a vault toilet. This one may be less crowded, and has a nice view of Temple Mountain. Turn left (west) onto the Behind the Reef Road just after the camping area and 2.1 miles from the stop sign. As of this writing, this junction is unsigned.

Those in passenger cars will have to pay more attention to the road and drive with caution. The road climbs a long hill (near the top is a fine view back toward Temple Mountain), and then descends into the Wild Horse drainage. After 1.7 miles on this road, turn left (south) on a sandy track and go 0.2 mile to a signed parking area that is the upper trailhead for Wild Horse Canyon. If this track is a concern, leave the car along the Behind the Reef Road and walk the short distance to the trailhead. If hiking from the trailhead, simply walk down the wash, which will probably show signs of vehicle passage for up to 0.5 mile. Eventually all vehicles are stopped by obstacles as the canyon starts to narrow; this is also roughly the boundary of the Crack Canyon Wilderness Study Area. The hiking description below does not start here; it begins at the lower end of the canyon.

The Hike

Out and back hikers starting from the down-canyon trailhead can see the best of Wild Horse in a round trip walk of between 6 and 7 miles. The gradient is so slight (just over 100 feet per mile) that the vertical gain seems almost negligible. Before leaving the lofty parking area, look over the scene to the northwest, directly toward the San Rafael Reef. Below, in the foreground, two shallow canyons converge, and beyond, a distinctive sinuous slot canyon can be seen cutting into the white sandstone of the Navajo Formation. This is the entrance to Wild Horse Canyon.

From the southwest side of the parking area (left, looking at the Reef), locate a faint trail that drops steeply down into the wide canyon. Cross the first wash just above the confluence, enter the second wash and go up-canyon (right, northeast). The drainage

Wild Horse Canyon

will quickly bend to the left (northwest) and enter the slot, only about 250 yards from the parking lot. The narrow section is a few hundred feet long and not very deep, but does give a sense of confinement. There can be water in a handful of pools in the slot, even though the rest of the canyon is usually dry. If this is the case, the narrows can be avoided by climbing the slickrock on either side. The bypass is shorter and easier on the right (east), with enough steepness and exposure to warrant keeping an eye on the kids.

After the slot, the canyon bends gently west, and then sharply to the right (northwest) at the 0.4-mile mark. At this point a cluttered tributary canyon continues straight ahead to the southwest. It is narrow and often choked with vegetation, but is fun to explore. The main canyon cuts through the rest of the Navajo Sandstone and turns southwest to run roughly along the contact between it and the overlying Kayenta Formation. Walking is generally very easy on the sand or gravel surface. Just over 1 mile along, a great sweep of Navajo forms the left wall, with long blacks streaks of desert varnish for embellishment. At 1.3 miles the bottom of the canyon narrows to a slot about 150 feet long and 12 to 15 feet deep. The boulder choke at the end is a difficult climb, and it is easier to backtrack to an easy bypass on the left looking up-canyon (southeast). At 0.25 mile farther on, the sandstone is riddled with iron mineralization in numerous shapes that stand out on the gentle slickrock on the right (northeast).

The canyon continues along the Navajo-Kayenta contact for more than 1 mile farther, with the monolithic wall of the former on the left (southeast), and the stepped slope of the latter on the right. Excellent solution cavities occur in exposures adjacent to the wash, and at 2.4-miles there is another small cut in the bedrock in the floor of the wash. The six or seven foot high groove at the end is an interesting challenge to climb, but most hikers will simply stay on the slickrock to the right of the narrows to bypass it. At 2.9 miles from the parking area Wild Horse Canyon swings to the right (north) at a 90-degree angle and cuts quickly through the Kayenta to enter the red-stained Wingate Sandstone. More solution cavities appear, and some of the eroded blocks have weathered to the extent that the cavities have been sliced open to form mini-arches. The canyon widens over a short distance and the turnaround point is up to the hiker. The up-canyon parking area is 3.9 miles from the southeast trailhead.

Wild Horse Canyon sandstone

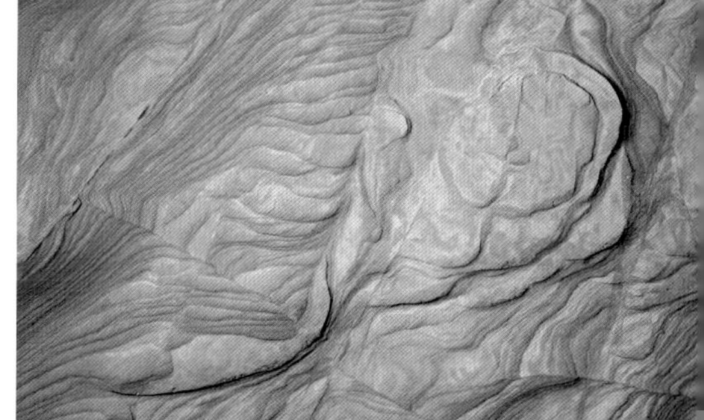

Henry Mountains above the Fremont River Valley

Below the Henry Mountains

Of all the areas described in this book, this section is the least well-defined. An alternative title would be "The Desert," but Muddy Creek, the Dirty Devil River, and Lake Powell all come into play. On the map, the region forms a reverse C around the Henry Mountains, beginning in the north, and extending east and then south and west around the range. Relatively low elevations make this area very, very hot in the summer. Prime visitation periods are therefore April into May, and late September and October. Summer thunderstorms can be dangerous for hikers, and more than vexing for drivers. Aside, perhaps, from Horseshoe Canyon, the hikes and drives in this section offer good opportunities for solitude and exploration, even during the best times to visit.

The Northwestern Region Below the Henry Mountains

Last Chance Desert Loop Road Trip

Driving distance from and to exit 91 on I-70, including the East Cedar Mountain side trip is 63.2 miles.

Maybe you have been visiting all the wonderful parks in Utah, along with all the other people, and now it is time to get away. With a full tank of gas, plenty of food and water, a robust vehicle in fine mechanical condition and with good tires, a good map and pristine clear skies, the area around the Last Chance Desert might be just the place. The exception would be during holiday weekends and sometimes other weekends as well, when the Mussentuchit Sand Dune attracts a few Utahns, although that impact is localized within a tiny part of a huge area.

The Last Chance Desert, Blue Flats, Mussentuchit Flat, and East Cedar Mountain are located south of Interstate 70, just east of Highway 72 and Thousand Lake Mountain, and north of Captiol Reef National Park's Cathedral Valley section. Access is possible from Cathedral Valley or the east slope of Thousand Lake Mountain, or from I-70. Three of the four primary access roads are described below, while the Baker Ranch route is discussed in the Thousand Lake Mountain section. As always in the backcountry, be

Last Chance Desert

prepared for rough roads, the condition of which can vary dramatically from one trip to another. This is the land of clay as well, so wet weather stops everything.

The first route discussed here is a stem and loop, with an out and back side trip. There are many other combinations of routes possible, as shown on the *Benchmark Utah Road and Recreation Atlas.* Allow a lot of time to drive these roads and enjoy the scenery and walks—at least a day for the loop and side trip described. Begin at exit 91 on I-70 on the west side of the San Raphael Swell, where Highway 10 heads northeast to Castle Dale and on to Price. (Alternative access from exit 99 is described two paragraphs below.) On the south side of the exit take the gravel road that goes south for a short distance before bending east to parallel the highway. The road is quite good for a couple of miles to a large gravel pit on the left (north) and a Y intersection. Stay right (basically straight) here, set the odometer to zero, and follow a lesser quality, but still quite good, road as it swings back to the south and then quickly to the southwest. Pass by a track to the left (east) at 0.9 mile, and another at 1.8 miles. At 2.5 miles the road narrows and drops sharply into North Hollow, passing a coal seam on the right (southwest). An old cabin is on the left (northeast) at 3.3, and another coal seam appears on the right (southwest) at 4.4 miles. A junction is at 5.5 miles, just beyond the crossing of Willow Springs Wash.

A sign at this intersection lists Last Chance, Cathedral Valley, and Highway 24 all straight ahead, and Mussentuchit Sand Dunes to the left (east), 10 miles away. Turn left and head generally east amidst expansive scenery. Mesa Butte is to the north (left), and then at 10.2 miles the road descends, with several igneous dikes visible to the south (right). These linear features were intruded into the sedimentary rocks in quite recent

Last Chance Desert

geologic time, and the ground is littered with debris from them. When the road crosses a wash at 10.9 miles, the exposed bedrock is the Summerville Formation, a Jurassic unit derived from sediments carried from the west where uplifts were occurring. When the road goes along a fence and wash on the left (north) 1 mile later, the Summerville is on the right (south) side. Another intersection is at 12.2 miles. The sign here is for traffic coming from the Interstate on rough roads from exits 99 and 107. To continue on to the dunes or East Cedar Mountain, skip the next paragraph.

When conditions are dry, the clay road from exit 99 (Emery) is the shortest route from pavement to this point, and is a good option for those coming from the north or east. From the Castle Valley along Highway 10, head southwest on the highway and turn left (south) on 300 East at milepost 12.9 on the east edge of the town of Emery. Zero the odometer and stay on the pavement (left) at 0.8 mile, following the sign to Millers Canyon and I-70. A sign on a fence to the right (west) at 3.2 miles marks the route of the Old Spanish Trail, and the road quickly drops into pleasant Millers Canyon. Cross the Interstate at 9.4 miles, and bear left (southeast) as the road turns to clay, following the sign for Mussentuchit Flat and Middle Desert Road. If coming from the east on I-70 take the Emery exit (99), turn left (south), cross the highway, and continue on the clay road. Initially this track is on Mancos Formation clay with interesting sandstone blocks scattered about. The road then winds through the desert with enough ledges and holes to require the attention of the driver, though much of the way it can be fairly

Agate

Townsendia

Cryptantha

smooth. At 8.5 miles from the end of the pavement there is a T intersection; turn right (west), cross a wash, and in just 0.2 mile come to another T with an old sign to Mussentuchit 4, and Cedar Mountain 9, both to the left, and U-10 14, to the right.

From the exit 91 route continue straight ahead (south), and from exit 99 turn left, zero the odometer, pass a corral on the right (west), and quickly cross a cattle guard. The road is now a graded path across the Morrison and Cedar Mountain Formations, and it doesn't take a lot of imagination to figure out what would happen to the clay if it rained. Vegetation is minimal on the clay due to its propensity to expand when wet, thereby expelling any seeds right out of the ground. A track leads to Mussentuchit Wash on the right (west) at 1.3 miles, perhaps worth a brief detour. In 0.5 mile this secondary track divides at a Y. The right (more westerly) arm climbs sharply to a flat in 0.4 mile; agate is plentiful along the road and at the top. The left (more southerly) branch at the Y leads to the end of the road at 0.4 mile. A short walk to the west in the canyon accesses Sand Cove Spring, where a trickle of flow feeds a pool that is an important water source in this barren area. Several sills in the canyon walls are interesting as well.

To do the loop, visit the sand dunes, and/or climb East Cedar Mountain, continue straight ahead at the junction with the Mussentuchit Wash track for another mile to a T intersection. The entrance track to the dune area is 1.5 miles straight ahead, but an interesting side trip begins with a left (east) turn, and is described here.

Side Trip to East Cedar Mountain

Driving distance from the primary loop to the starting point for the East Cedar Mountain climb is 8.2 miles one way.

For even more solitude, a good climb, and some fine scenery, turn left (east) at the T intersection, zero the trip odometer, and follow the sign arrows to Cedar Mountain 8 and the Moroni Slopes 11. At first, the road across the northern tip of Mussentuchit Flat is very straight and very flat, but at 1.4 miles it curves to the south and heads toward the twin peaks of Cedar Mountain. Beyond the 4-mile mark prominent sills protect a cliff of Entrada Sandstone on the right (west). Sills are, like dikes, intrusive igneous rock, but where dikes cut across the sedimentary layers, sills find their way between the strata, so if the latter are flat-lying, the sill is horizontal as well. Wash crossings precede a track to the east (left) at 5.8 miles. The main road is straight ahead (south).

For the next 1.5 miles the road winds between East Cedar Mountain on the left, and the larger, but only very slightly higher main block of Cedar Mountain to the right (west). At 7.5 miles cross a cattleguard with a view of the Henry Mountains directly ahead. At a Y junction at 8.1 miles bear left (southeast), following the sign to Segers Hole (Carlyle Wash is to the right). To climb East Cedar Mountain go another 0.1 mile and note the terrain to the left (north), then drive up the hill to a wide point in the road and park.

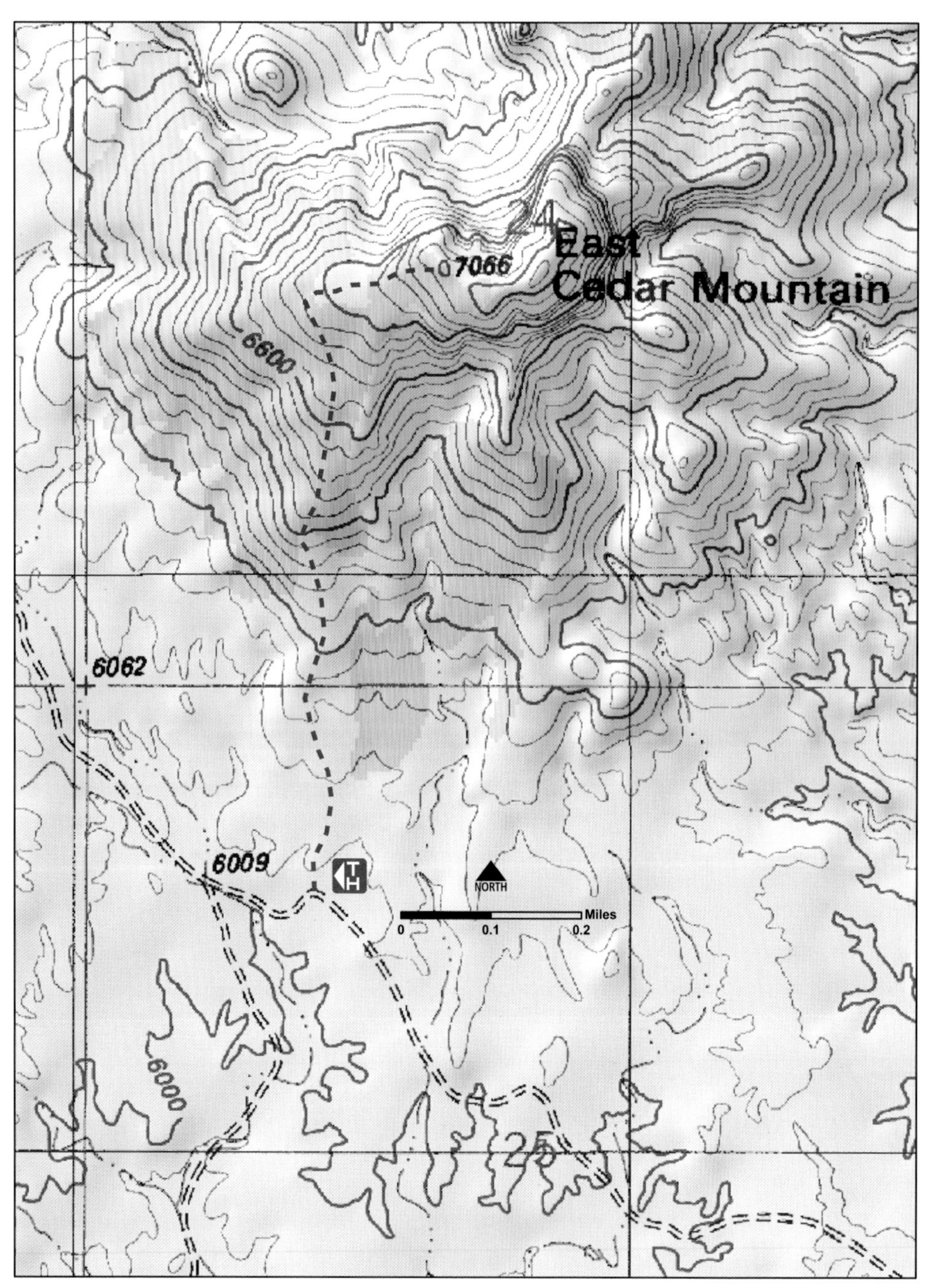

East Cedar Mountain route

East Cedar Mountain

East Cedar Mountain Hike

Hiking distance is 2 miles round trip.

The hike is not for the faint of heart or fitness, and if anything bad happens, you will be a long, long, long way from help. The day we climbed, we did not meet, or even see, another vehicle from the time we left the Interstate until we returned to it. The route is very steep, there is no trail whatsoever, and much of the way is over loose pieces of angular basalt. This is one to do with companions, in cool weather. Any time you gain 1,000 feet of elevation in just a mile, it is obvious that the climb will be a workout.

The general route should be obvious from the road, although your path will no doubt differ at least a little from ours. We left the road at the bottom of the hill and followed an eroding dike to the north, aiming to the right (east) of a small "smile" of brown Entrada Sandstone. A narrowing grassy slope climbs at an increasing grade up to a small flat, then the ridge bends a little to the right (northeast). Work up the boulder-strewn slopes to another flat, then simply follow the spine of the ridge as it bends around to the east and the first of three knobs. Unless you are highly experienced, stop here, as we did. There are two more knobs, slightly higher, but the route is exposed and dangerous and we do not recommend it. The view from the western knob is very good, southeast over the Moroni slopes, north down to interesting dikes, west to the main block of Cedar Mountain with Thousand Lake Mountain beyond, and south to the Henrys.

Mussentuchit Dunes and the Rest of the Last Chance Loop

As mentioned above, there are several options in driving back from East Cedar Mountain, but the dunes are worth a stop, so the description now returns to the T intersection that is 8.2 miles back the way you came. Turn left (south) here; if you are just doing the loop, stay straight, in either case following the sign to Last Chance Wash (the dunes are not mentioned on this sign). Zero the odometer and go south for 1.5 miles to the most obvious track to the right (west) that leads to Mussentuchit Dune—plainly visible just 0.3 mile away. The sand is plastered up against an Entrada cliff and is very steep. The climb to the top isn't easy, but it is fun and the kids will have a ball. Once up, the views are huge in all directions.

Mussentuchit Dunes

Once everyone has enough sand in their clothes, you can either backtrack to I-70 or complete the loop. For the latter, return to the road and turn right (south). Check the trip odometer at the cattleguard where we were at 5.6 miles, including the out and back to the base of the dunes. Red Point looms to the right (west) before the next junction at mile 7.1. Turn right (west) and follow the Last Chance Wash Cutoff Road as it twists through dissected terrain. Cross a cattleguard at 9.8, and the main wash farther on. At the time we were there Last Chance Wash was flowing right along, and the crossing did not appear inviting, but we had no trouble. Just make sure of the conditions should there be active flow; it is, after all, a long way to anywhere. Eventually, the road climbs out of the drainage and heads due west across the Last Chance Desert. At a T intersection at mile 15.6, turn right (north) on the (relatively) more traveled Cathedral Valley Road.

A cattleguard is at mile 17.8 and marks a sudden change as the road winds sharply up through broken country. At 18.5 a rusted iron sign on the left (west) side of the road reads "S COUNTY E," marking the boundary between Sevier and Emery Counties. Just 0.1 mile beyond the sign is a swale to the right (east) with ample room to pull off and park. The flat is littered with colorful agate and a few scattered balls of barite, which is both unobtrusive and not attractive. The agate, however, is very good, and in some places almost completely covers the ground. Chunks big enough to cut cabochon slabs are plentiful. Even if you are not a rockhound, this is a fine place to pick up a multicolored souvenir of the Last Chance Desert Loop.

Beyond the agate area, the road passes by another swale that in wet periods may hold a considerable amount of water, enough to form a pretty pond. As the route drops back down to the Blue Flats, a north-facing slope hosts a beautiful wet-spring garden of wildflowers, especially rimrock paintbrush and townsendias. At 23 miles the loop closes at Willow Springs Wash. To return to I-70, continue straight ahead, bearing slightly left and retrace the stem of the loop for 7.4 miles to exit 91.

Intrusive sills

Last Chance Desert Access from Highway 24

Driving distance from Highway 24 to connect with the Last Chance Loop is 36.7 miles one way.

A longer, but highly scenic (if you like desert) approach to the Last Chance Desert can be made by driving the Caineville Wash Road from Highway 24 just west of Caineville. This road is mostly on BLM land, but crosses through a corner of Capitol Reef National Park. A short side trip in the park to the Temples of the Sun and Moon is more than worthwhile. The Capitol Reef visitor center is a good place to get current information about road conditions; it is not uncommon for the Caineville Wash Road to be washed out, and a brief downpour can render it impassible at any time. High clearance is necessary for this trip.

If you are heading east from Capitol Reef on Highway 24, the Caineville Wash Road is on the left (north) at milepost 97.9, which is 9.7 miles east of the east entrance to the park. The junction is unmarked on the highway, but there is a street sign that reads 490W in large characters, and 'Cathedral' below in smaller letters. Just off the pavement, a sign confirms distances to the Gypsum Sinkhole and Cathedral Valley, both 26 miles, and also notes that the road (0082) accesses Thousand Lake Mountain. Zero the odometer at the highway. In 0.3 mile, road 0089 branches off to the left (northwest); continue straight ahead, as the road follows the base of the North Caineville Reef to the right (east). At 2.5 miles the reef angles to the northeast, and a side track (the North Caineville Mesa Road, #0090) veers off parallel to it. Continue straight ahead on the much more traveled Caineville Wash Road as it soon leaves the flat and climbs sharply through colorful Brushy Basin clay and siltstones.

The going can be a little rough as the track passes over the basal Salt Wash Member of the Morrison Formation (just below the Brushy Basin), dropping into and climbing out of small drainages cutting into the resistant rock. Huge pink, gray, and mauve rounded

Caineville Wash Road entering Cathedral Valley

What is a Reef?

The term "reef" is widespread in south-central Utah. Capitol Reef and the San Rafael Reef are probably the best known and most obvious. Each is the erosional expression of a steep limb of a fold; resistant rock layers dip so precipitously that they appear to dive into the earth. Other features that carry the term, such as Molen Reef, North Caineville Reef, Sweetwater Reef, and Red Reef are less spectacular. None of them represent ancient coral reefs; the resistant eolian (wind-blown) Navajo Sandstone that is the dominant component of Capitol Reef and San Rafael Reef was laid down in a vast terrestrial desert.

In south-central Utah, "reef" generally refers to a ridge or escarpment that is at least a modest barrier to travel. Apparently, some of the early explorers and prospectors who passed through the area in the 1870s had been at sea as mariners long enough to adopt the seafaring reference to any barrier as being a reef. Elsewhere, as in southwest Utah and Montana, the term reflects the assumed appearance of a reef, or refers to heavily mineralized strata. Much as visitors are confused by northern cultures' many words for snow, travelers from the East or abroad are often amused by the fact that very similar appearing features might be called benches, ridges, points, breaks, cliffs, terraces, mesas, buttes, plateaus, and reefs.

hills rise north of the road, one topped by a pair of incongruous boulders. Willow Seep is on the left (southwest) at 7 miles, and road 0146 is on the left at 9.5. A signed, but very modest, Caineville Wash crossing follows at 10.6 miles, and the first distant view of the Temple of the Sun is 0.8 mile farther on. At the top of a small rise is a sign that reads Entering Cathedral Valley. Off to the southwest in the middle distance is a good sequence of Entrada Sandstone, Curtis Formation, and Summerville Formation (bottom to top). From this point all the way to a short distance up the Baker Ranch Road, the Caineville Wash Road lies on the soft Entrada Sandstone.

A mile beyond the Cathedral Valley sign, 12.7 miles from Highway 24, the road crosses a lightly vegetated flat. To the south about 150 yards there are a couple of very low mounds and a hard-to-see post. When the sun is low and at the right angle, the ground near and on the mounds (which are about 18 inches high) sparkles like the surface of a lake in a gentle breeze. The flashes are from hundreds of selenite (gypsum) crystals that have weathered out of the Entrada. Given how soft the mineral is, it is quite amazing that they persist as the sandstone is eroded or abraded away. A necessary factor in the crystal longevity is the very arid climate in the lee of the high mountains to the west. Individual crystals up to three inches are not uncommon, and some are almost clear, and are well formed, including terminations. Large groups, fragile as they are, can also be found.

If you have trouble locating the spot described above, just continue to mile 15.0 and turn right (north) on a weak track (road 8211) that soon bends to the left (west). When it curves to the right 0.3 mile from the Caineville Wash Road, the hill just to the east (right) is littered with selenites quite similar to the first locality. An interesting and different selenite occurrence is just another 0.2 mile beyond this hill, and the track runs right by it. Once deposited and covered by other sediments, gypsum can become

Selenite

bile, sometimes settling into a wavy appearance that also affects the overlying beds, sometimes recrystallizing in bedding planes or joints, and sometimes forming good single crystals and groups. Rarely, huge interlocking crystals of selenite form large masses. This is the case here, 0.5 mile from the Caine-ville Wash Road. Although most of the crystals have been removed or damaged, this remains an interesting site.

A better example is nearby Glass Mountain, in Capitol Reef National Park (see below).

Back on the Caineville Wash Road, it is just 0.7 mile west to a spur road that leads into Capitol Reef and to the Temples of the Sun and Moon. These monoliths are a major goal for many visitors to the national park, including a surprising number of Europeans. To visit them, turn left (southwest) on the signed road that winds through a wash, and soon crosses a cattleguard that marks the park boundary. At 1.2 miles along, a road to the right (north) goes to Glass Mountain, a fairly well-preserved stack of huge selenite crystals. Straight ahead, the road drops down to the floor of Lower Cathedral Valley, passes right by the Temple of the Sun, and ends behind the Temple of the Moon. The temples are erosional remnants of Entrada Sandstone, looking like drip castles that soar 400 feet up from the flat valley floor. No collecting of any kind is permitted in the park, and there is no charge to visit the temples.

To continue to the Last Chance Desert (or up onto Thousand Lake Mountain), return to the Caineville Wash Road, reset the odometer to zero, and turn left (northwest). The road is often quite sandy during dry periods, as it is back to the east. The route winds along Middle Desert Wash, with good views of the Little Black Mountains ahead and to the right, and Entrada cliffs topped with the more resistant Curtis Formation to the left (southwest). Dikes and sills of basalt cut across, or, especially in the case of the Little Black Mountains, lie parallel to the rock layers. The igneous rock is considerably harder than the soft sandstone that it intrudes, so the dikes project up above the ground, and the sills protect the underlying material from erosion.

The road enters the national park at 5.3 miles after crossing to the northeast side of Middle Desert Wash. Stay left (more westerly) at an unsigned junction with the cut-off to the Oil Well Bench Road immediately after entering Capitol Reef. The road to the Gypsum Sinkhole (the ultimate fate of Glass Mountain) is on the left (south) at 9.5 miles; it is 1 mile to the sinkhole on this dead end spur road. The turn north to the Last Chance Desert is on top of a small hill at 9.6 miles. A sign on the right identifies the intersection as Cathedral Valley Junction, and gives distances to Baker Ranch 7, and

Interstate 70, 27. On the left (south) side of the road is another sign giving distances to points along and beyond the Caineville Wash Road in both directions. If you have the time, a short detour into Upper Cathedral Valley is worthwhile.

Otherwise, turn right (north), heading for Baker Ranch and the Interstate. Immediately on the left (west) after the turn is a swarm of nearly vertical dikes standing well above the surrounding sandstone. The road ascends a very steep slope and then flattens out before leaving the park at 11.9 miles. The Oil Well Bench Road approaches from the right (east) at 13.3 as the Baker Ranch Road swings to the west.

To continue to the Last Chance Desert, stay on the main track as it curves slightly to the west and then runs straight across an almost level surface. A major junction occurs at 14.3 miles; it is a triangle, and the sign is placed facing north for traffic coming from I-70. This intersection is a decision point. For the Last Chance Desert, swing around to the right (north). If you have had enough desert for the day, or if it has turned hot, or if thunderclouds are looming, an alternative trip straight ahead up to Thousand Lake Mountain might be in order. This route is described in the Baker Ranch Access part of the Thousand Lake Mountain section.

The road to the north turns back to the east and quickly drops through an interesting wetland area, usually with a fringe of evaporated salts. Back down on a relatively flat Entrada Sandstone surface, the road bends to the northeast. Just off to the east is Solomons Temple, a stepped butte with a craggy top. Entrada cliffs, topped with Curtis Formation limey sandstone, approach the road on the left (west) before it tops a small rise on the south edge of the Last Chance Desert. Terminology, including road names, is variable around here, and the Last Chance name is variously applied to the relatively small area extending a few miles north and east of this point, or to a considerably larger region extending to the rim above Muddy Creek.

A short diversion is possible by turning sharply right (east) at mile 19, and following a side track for 0.4 mile out to a viewpoint and expansive vista. This road has a very steep and possibly rough section before topping out on a bench at an exceedingly lightly used "parking area." The view is to the east, south, and west, and includes the northern Henry Mountains, Solomons Temple, Boulder Mountain, and Thousand Lake Mountain. To join the Last Chance Loop, return to the primary road, turn right (north) and continue for 2 miles to the 21-mile mark. The unsigned track to the right (east) joins the loop in the opposite direction as described above, and leads to the Mussentuchit Dunes. Straight ahead follows the loop in the clockwise direction; exit 91 on I-70 is 14.8 miles to the north.

Solomons Temple

Highway 24 from Capitol Reef to Hanksville Road Trip

Distance: 28 miles

Brushy Basin Member of the Morrison Formation

The 28 miles from the east entrance of Capitol Reef National Park to Hanksville along Highway 24 affect people in vastly different ways. Some are struck by the "emptiness," some by the contrast between the narrow Fremont River corridor and everything else, some are simply astonished by the beauty of the desert, and some are intrigued by the geology so clearly exposed. The combination of riparian green and shale gray is unusual for Utah, and many travelers will find this landscape intriguing.

This road log begins at the east entrance of Capitol Reef National Park where Highway 24 is joined by the Notom-Bullfrog Road from the south. (Highway 24 through the park is described in *Capitol Reef National Park, The Complete Hiking and Touring Guide*.) The cliff face just south of the highway and east of the Notom Road is a good exposure of the banded Summerville Formation on the bottom with the resistant Salt Wash Member of the Morrison Formation above. The Fremont valley narrows for the next couple of miles as the river cuts through the harder sandstone.

At 1.7 miles from the park's east entrance is a parking area on the right (south). Nestled in a small alcove to the right (southwest) of the short entrance road is what remains of a small granary made of stones mudded together. Granaries were used by people of the Fremont Culture to store grain and seeds, often in pottery vessels or their unique one-rod-and-bundle style baskets. Frequently these small structures are well hidden and even less accessible than this one, but all were carefully sealed to prevent rodents from entering.

The hard Salt Wash sandstone that protects the granary soon gives way to the soft clay of the Brushy Basin Member of the Morrison Formation. This multi-hued rock was laid down in swamps and low relief coastal plains. Both parts of the Morrison contain many fossils, including dinosaurs (see the section on the Cleveland Lloyd Dinosaur Quarry for more information). At 2.6 miles Highway 24 passes over the easily missed Pleasant Creek, and just beyond and right at milepost 91 is the signed turnoff for the river ford and road into Cathedral Valley, also described in the *Capitol Reef* guide. This road always requires high clearance and often four-wheel drive, and should not be attempted without getting the latest information from the Capitol Reef National Park visitor center. Dry Wash Canyon and the Red Desert rim, described in the following sections, are a short distance north of the ford.

Beyond milepost 91 the highway ascends a hill, curves to the right (southeast) and descends. At 3.6 miles from Capitol Reef and just before milepost 92 a dirt road enters from the right (southwest). The stop sign for the Old Notom Road is easily visible to eastbound travelers on Highway 24. If there are fossil lovers in the car (surely no family would have fewer than two), turn right on the dirt road and drive a little more than 0.1 mile to a flat parking place on the right (north). If the Old Notom Road is wet, pull off safely on Highway 24 and walk. The hills north of the dirt road are covered with fossil oysters. These invertebrates may be collected for personal use, and there are thousands from which to choose.

Locally called devils' toenails, these one-inch oysters are *Pychodonte newberryi*, and they mark the top of the Dakota Formation and the bottom of the Tununk Member of the Mancos Shale. They lived in a low-energy shallow sea, moving with the currents along the bottom. The Dakota is a near-shore formation, often consisting of sandy reefs, while the Tununk is a deeper marine clay. Since the Tununk lies above the Dakota, the inference is that sea level rose, and the oysters were no longer able to survive in this area.

Brittle scorpionweed

Beyond the Old Notom Road the highway crosses a bleak Mancos flat. On the left (north) side of the road is a usually reliable stand of scorpionweed. *Phacelia crenulata* gets its common name from the curvature of the flower spike that resembles a scorpion's tail. Blooming from late April into June, this plant has pretty, small, purple flowers that are bell shaped with prominent stamens extending beyond the five fused petals. Scorpionweed produces a set of basal leaves in its first year, and then flowers during the second. The stem and leaves are covered with stiff hairs and touching the plant can cause a toxic reaction in some people. In this area scorpionweed often grows next to black andesite boulders, and sometimes in proximity to orange globemallow; either combination is handsome.

After the flat, Highway 24 ascends a long hill and drops sharply down to cross the Fremont River. Beyond the bridge, a gap to the right (southeast) offers a glimpse of the Henry Mountains. Around milepost 96 the gray clay sparkles in the sun where shards of selenite (gypsum) weather out to the surface. At the top of a double hill the road is arrow-straight with a spectacular view. North Caineville Reef and Mesa are directly ahead, while to the left (north) is a colorful sequence of the Brushy Basin Member of the Morrison Formation topped by the equally showy Cedar Mountain Formation. Both are the result of deposition of clays and volcanic ash in very low relief, sometimes swampy, environments. Much of the pink color is due to the breakdown of the ash into clay minerals. The presence of the darker and rockier Buckhorn Conglomerate, the basal member of the Cedar Mountain, is the only easy way to distinguish the two formations.

The east entrance to the rough Cathedral Valley loop is 9.7 miles from the park's east entrance at milepost 97.9. It is marked by a street sign that reads 490 W in larger print, and "Cathedral" in smaller print below. This is the Caineville Wash Road, which is especially susceptible to becoming impassable during rain or snow, and, once again, should only be driven in a high-clearance vehicle, and only after getting a condition report from the Capitol Reef visitor center. This route is described in the Last Chance Desert section above.

Caineville is a shadow of its former status as one of the larger villages downriver from Fruita and Torrey. Modern travelers, especially those low on gas, are often surprised by the lack of services. On the other hand, eastbounders may be pleased to see verdant green alfalfa fields to the south of the highway, with soaring South Caineville Mesa as backdrop.

Mancos Shale

The flats and slopes of the Mancos Shale are riddled with selenium and are largely impervious to standing water (although when the water does evaporate, huge mud cracks follow). This is not a welcoming environment for plants. Rarely, however, the spring rains fall heavily and in timely fashion, and this stark landscape explodes into purple and gold. It is best to withhold high expectations since the profusion of beeplant, brittle scorpionweed, and Eastwood's sundrops happens at best once every few years. These plants are discussed in detail in the section describing the Factory Butte Road.

After a long straight stretch of road, the highway curves up a gentle hill, and at the top, 17.4 miles east of Capitol Reef (milepost 105.5) the unmarked road to Factory Butte heads north (left), and a lesser road goes south (right). The latter makes a short and interesting side trip. About 0.2 mile from 24 and at the top of an intermediate rise you can park and walk along a fairly flat swale to the left (east) and look for well-formed selenite crystals in a small, two- or three-foot deep gully that runs down to the northeast. This is not a prolific locality, and the amount and quality of crystals, if any, depends on recent precipitation to exhume them.

From this point it is another 0.2 mile to a Y intersection. The road to the right (west) dead ends at a radio facility, so bear left and after a short distance stay right (basically straight ahead) as the more used track goes left into a borrow pit at another Y. The road is now a two track that leads after an additional 0.4 mile (0.8 mile from the highway) to a poignant cemetery, and in another 0.1 to a prominent viewpoint high above the Fremont River. Off to the east is the easily recognizable silhouette of the steamship (a Mancos Shale promontory), which can also be seen from Highway 24 farther east. A pleasant sense of solitude is easily obtained in this quiet place.

Back on the highway it is only 1.2 miles to the turnoff for the old town site of Giles. Recent activity near the highway and at the town site and cemetery has attempted to keep memories of Giles alive, and is succeeding to some extent. Where Caineville is only a fraction of what it was, Giles, Elephant, Aldrich, Clifton, and Mesa are no longer inhabited at all. The settlement of these communities was in response to encouragement from the LDS Church, and for a while in the late nineteenth century things went passably well, with pioneers settling along the Fremont. The river that made irrigation, and thus life, possible, was also the undoing of these small towns. Routine floods ranged from annoyances to serious threats as diversion dams and ditches would have to be repaired and cleaned out after each one. It was the big floods, however, that truly sapped the strength and spirit of the hardy people living here, and the final straw was a massive event in 1909. After this flood people were not only allowed but encouraged by the Church to move to more benign locations.

Access to the original town requires at least a high-clearance vehicle, and if you want to drive all the way to the cemetery, 4WD is required for the last 0.3 mile. After turning right (south) just after the sign for Giles, follow the road through thick riparian vegetation to the ford of the Fremont River. When water levels are low, this crossing is easy, and when they are high, impossible. A concrete slab is very helpful, as long as you can safely determine where it is and thus be able to stay on it. At times of flood, either postpone a visit to Giles, or, if the rains are upstream and not local, approach from Hanksville by back roads.

After the ford, the occasionally graded clay road bends to the east and heads for the bow of the steamship. At 1.6 miles from Highway 24 the Henry Mountain Road bears

Ford to Giles townsite

Giles townsite

Giles Cemetery

off to the right (southeast); take the lesser track that continues straight ahead. A sign announces the Old Giles Townsite, and in 200 yards another track bears left (north). This road tops a tiny ridge and leads to the gridded remains of the town. Several foundations remain, and the perfectly cut sandstone blocks that formed the town's buildings are scattered about, or still stand in walls up to four or five feet high.

To reach the cemetery, return to the track running to the east and turn left. Continue straight ahead when two tracks signed for water go off to the north (left), and proceed 0.6 mile to a large cross with 28 names on it. The cemetery is across the deep wash farther east, and near the cross is a good place to park unless you have a robust four-wheel drive vehicle. The track leads easily down into the wash, but the sandy climb out on the other side is very steep, and may be deeply rutted. Since the walk across the wash is only 0.3 mile, if you have any doubt about driving, don't. The cemetery is a stark reminder of the isolation of the residents of Giles, and indeed all the communities along the Fremont, until after the Second World War.

After visiting Giles, return to the Henry Mountain Road and back to the highway. After again fording the Fremont and regaining the secure pavement, head east (right) toward Hanksville. In 1.6 miles (20.2 miles from Capitol Reef) pass by an old stone building now protected within a chain link fence. This apparently served as a roadhouse during the early years, but not a lot is known about it. A long and flat stretch of road follows.

If (and decidedly only if) the weather and roads are dry, a side trip on the unmarked clay road that heads north (left) at milepost 112.8 might be in order. This turn is at the 24.7-mile mark. The track climbs quickly away from the highway, and passes through a fence on a cattleguard in 300 yards. Just beyond, at the bottom of the steep hill, is parking for an agate collecting site. The best material is on both sides of the fence to the west (left), and both red and white pieces may be found. The road beyond is starkly beautiful, with the banded Brushy Basin sediments looming gently over a largely flat gray plain.

At 3.3 miles from the highway a track, signed as route 1103, bears to the left. After a short distance it rounds a corner to reveal a quite startling sight: the Mars Desert Research Station. This facility, off the power grid, is operated by the Mars Society and sits in splendid isolation in this deserted place. Back on the main track it is just 0.7 mile farther to a place where the clay is covered by small rocks scattered along both sides of the road. This material is black and brown and shiny, and seems to hold together better than obsidian, which it resembles. Though the pieces are in the one- to two-inch range, they might cut or tumble into interesting cabochons or stones.

After returning to Highway 24, turn left (east) for the remaining 3.8 miles to the junction of Highways 24 and 95 in Hanksville. Along the way, beginning in just over 0.5 mile, the Summerville Formation is next to, or a little distance from, the road to the north (left). Hanksville is now largely a town defined by service to travelers, though many of those doing the traveling may be somewhat bemused by that fact. On 100 West is the Henry Mountains Field Station. This BLM office is a good source of information not only for the desert that surrounds, and during windy spring days threatens to engulf, the town, but also for the Henry Mountains. After a difficult history of flood-ravaged agriculture (hope now attaches to a new diversion dam south of the junction of the road to the Mars Station), spent mining booms, passing outlaws, and isolation, the town is perfectly situated just far enough from Lake Powell, Capitol Reef, and I-70 so as to have cemented its place as a travel stop. Still, in February, Hanksville is a far piece from Salt Lake City in every regard.

Steamboat Rock from Highway 24

Dry Wash Canyon Hike

Driving distance from Highway 24 is 2.7 miles one way.
Hiking distance is 5 miles round trip.

Summerville Formation

Dry Wash Canyon offers an unusual opportunity to hike for an extended period within the interesting Summerville Formation, which will appeal to those with a geological affinity. It also is a place to find solitude while walking down the sinuous wash under high vertical walls, and almost everyone will find it impossible to resist taking home at least one brightly colored chunk of agate, or perhaps even a piece of selenite (gypsum).

Access to the canyon is from the Hartnet Road, not far north of the river ford that is the initial nail biter for many first time visitors to the Cathedral Valley part of Capitol Reef National Park. The entire hike, however, is on land administered by the Bureau of Land Management (BLM). The first step is to stop at the Capitol Reef visitor center to get information on the Fremont River ford. At times the crossing is rated for two-wheel drive high-clearance vehicles, but it is not infrequent that four-wheel drive is necessary to negotiate the sand leading into or out of the river, and especially the long sandy stretch after the ford. It should not be attempted at any time in passenger cars. Big storms, such as those in September 2013, can render the crossing impassable for all vehicles, so it really is important to get up-to-date information.

Getting There

Assuming that the ford is in a condition that your vehicle can handle, travel east from the junction of Highway 24 and the Notom-Bullfrog Road (at the east entrance to Capitol Reef NP) for 2.7 miles to milepost 91. Just as the eastbound highway begins to ascend for the first time after the visitor center, a sandy road, signed for the river ford, drops down to the left (east). Turn here and stay straight for 0.5 mile, then bear left (north) through willows to the bank of the river. If you come to a corral you have missed the turn to the ford. For many years the best way to cross the river has been to drive into it, and turn right (downstream), following a course near the right bank before

Fremont river ford to Dry Wash Canyon and Red Desert

turning across the rest of the river, but after September of 2013, it is even more crucial to get good advice from the Capitol Reef visitor center. The obvious exit is on the left (north), only about 50 yards down river. Often, the biggest problem is not with the ford itself, but with the 0.3 mile of sand track on the north (far) side of it. Good information, including the river depth (often a foot or less), can prevent serious difficulties. Even then, the river can look forbidding, but rest assured that those of us familiar with the ford do not even hesitate to drive right in when conditions are all right. First timers would do very well to have 4WD for assurance.

Reset the odometer to zero just before crossing the river. After the ford and sandy stretch, the road is simply hard and rough during dry weather, easily traveled in small SUVs. (Significant rain brings everyone to a halt.) A mile from the Fremont, the road enters an intensely colorful exposure of the Brushy Basin Member of the Morrison Formation and then winds up and down with good views to the east. At 2.2 miles from the south bank of the river, pull over to the side of the road and look carefully for two thin white posts off to the right (east), and down from the road about 100 yards. Mark the spot and drive ahead to a place where you can pull off the road safely. The starting point is at UTM 0493243mE, 4237891mN.

The Hike

There are no obvious and easy routes down into Dry Wash Canyon (see map on page 122). This one may be the best of the limited possibilities, but it still requires good route-finding skills, and the ability to climb down a short cliff band and then descend a long and very steep slope. If finding or negotiating the first eight-foot cliff band is a problem, it would be better to simply look into the canyon from the rim. From the road, descend east through the white posts (they won't be there forever) and bear slightly left (northeast) toward the tallest juniper tree on the edge of the rim. There might be a black boulder cairn just southeast of the tree to mark the route down; it is at UTM 0493338mE, 4237961mN. Just below the rim a small skunkbush shrub marks the way and it should be fairly easy to get down through the small opening. Once on the slope below, angle down and left (northeast), eventually walking near the rim of the canyon to the north (left). Continue to the east where another possible black boulder cairn at UTM 0493537mE, 4238061mN marks the top of the steep descent into the canyon.

This point is directly on the rim of the main canyon. If you are in the right place, the rib that leads down should be clear. The first few feet are protected by a heavily weathered piece of rock; step down and to the right, and onto the rib. If the rock is missing or loose, this route should not be attempted. This is a place to be exceedingly careful and it cannot be emphasized enough that if it doesn't look good to you, it would be best to move on, perhaps to the Red Desert rim, described in the next section. The ridge may be soft enough to allow heels to be dug in, and there are several swales between the rounded knobs that provide a chance to consider the next descent. The vertical drop is less than 200 feet, and even a very slow and careful descent will not take long. As with the slot canyons considered in this guide, *stay within your ability and confidence levels, and be prepared to turn around any time they are exceeded.*

View from the Dry Wash cairn hike

In stark contrast to the descent into the canyon, once down, the walking is so easy that it is far more like strolling than hiking. The wash channel is like sidewalk—to 20 feet in unobstructed width, generally smooth, and usually very firm due to the gravel that weathers out from the coarse sandstone and conglomerate that is the rim rock. There is good canyon in either direction from the entry point described above. To the left (generally west, though at first southwest) it is just over 0.5 mile to a small group of cottonwood trees and slightly farther to the high pour-off that definitively marks the end of the canyon. (The Hartnet Road passes near the edge of this dryfall just north of the parking for the hike, and it is worth walking up the road to look down into the canyon from there.) Given how easy and pleasant the walking is, it makes sense to see it all by first walking to the pour-off, then retracing steps to the entry point.

In both directions the walls are about 150 feet high, and except for the very top layer, they consist entirely of the mudstone, siltstone, sandstone, and gypsum of the Summerville Formation. Occasionally there are thicker beds, but often they vary from less than an inch to four inches thick. The effect is that of horizontal stripes that make for an unusually attractive rock at the scale present in Dry Wash Canyon. The Summerville was laid down during middle Jurassic time (about 160 million years ago) on the western edge of a retreating inland sea. Sediments were introduced by streams flowing from the mountains to the west, often vigorously. The climate was very warm and very dry in the lee of the mountains, and near the top of the formation a very thick layer of gypsum is often found. Gypsum accumulates as saline water confined in closed basins evaporates, leaving behind a variety of salts. In Dry Wash Canyon there are huge chunks of this material that have fallen from near the top of the canyon wall.

To see the rest of the canyon walk back past the entry rib and follow the winding wash floor another 1.7 miles to the confluence with the Fremont River. Along the way the walls stay high for almost the entire distance before lowering near the river as the wash widens. From the dryfall to the river in the canyon bottom is about 2.25 miles; from the entry to the river is about 1.75 miles. At a bend about 0.5 mile from the river a group of cottonwoods and tamarisk marks a point where the various types of gypsum are exposed in several thin beds on the north wall. Fibrous, platy, crystalline, and rounded orange masses are forms that are exposed there or very nearby. Big pieces of rim rock, the Salt Wash Member of the Morrison Formation, litter the canyon floor, looking just like old concrete. Red, yellow, white, and other colors of agate generally decrease in size near the Fremont, and in fact are more impressive above the rim on both sides of the canyon where they are abundant.

Massive gypsum in Dry Wash Canyon

The confluence with the Fremont is pretty mundane, and it is a good idea to watch out for a bit of quicksand here; the wet sand quivered when we disturbed it. The walk back to the entry rib seemed just as flat as it was in the opposite direction as the wash drops only about 50 feet in more than 2 miles. Tracks of desert bighorn sheep entering and leaving Dry Wash Canyon were recent, but the only large animals we saw were longhorn cattle that had wandered in from across the river.

On the way back to the river ford you might notice a large figure atop a prominence to the left (east). While it is really just a cairn that looks bigger than it is, the hill on which it sits offers very nice views down into Dry Wash Canyon, east to the Caineville Mesas, south to Thompson Mesa and the Henrys, and west to the Waterpocket Fold. In the fall when the cottonwoods turn gold, the Fremont River valley to the east and south gleams across the gray expanse of Mancos Shale. The climb up and walk over to the cairn is short and easy. Drive 0.6 mile back south toward the ford from the point above the white posts, and park. Pick any of several easy routes up the slope to the southeast, and once on top, enjoy the easy stroll to the small saddle that separates the main body of the hill from the knob that hosts the cairn. Scramble down and up, watching out for loose rocks, and enjoy the view down into the canyon, and indeed, all around the 360-degree panorama. The walk to the knob (identified as point 5118T on the Caineville quadrangle) is 0.5 mile each way.

Red Desert Rim Hike

Driving distance from Highway 24 is 3.5 miles one way.
Hiking distance is 4.5 miles round trip.

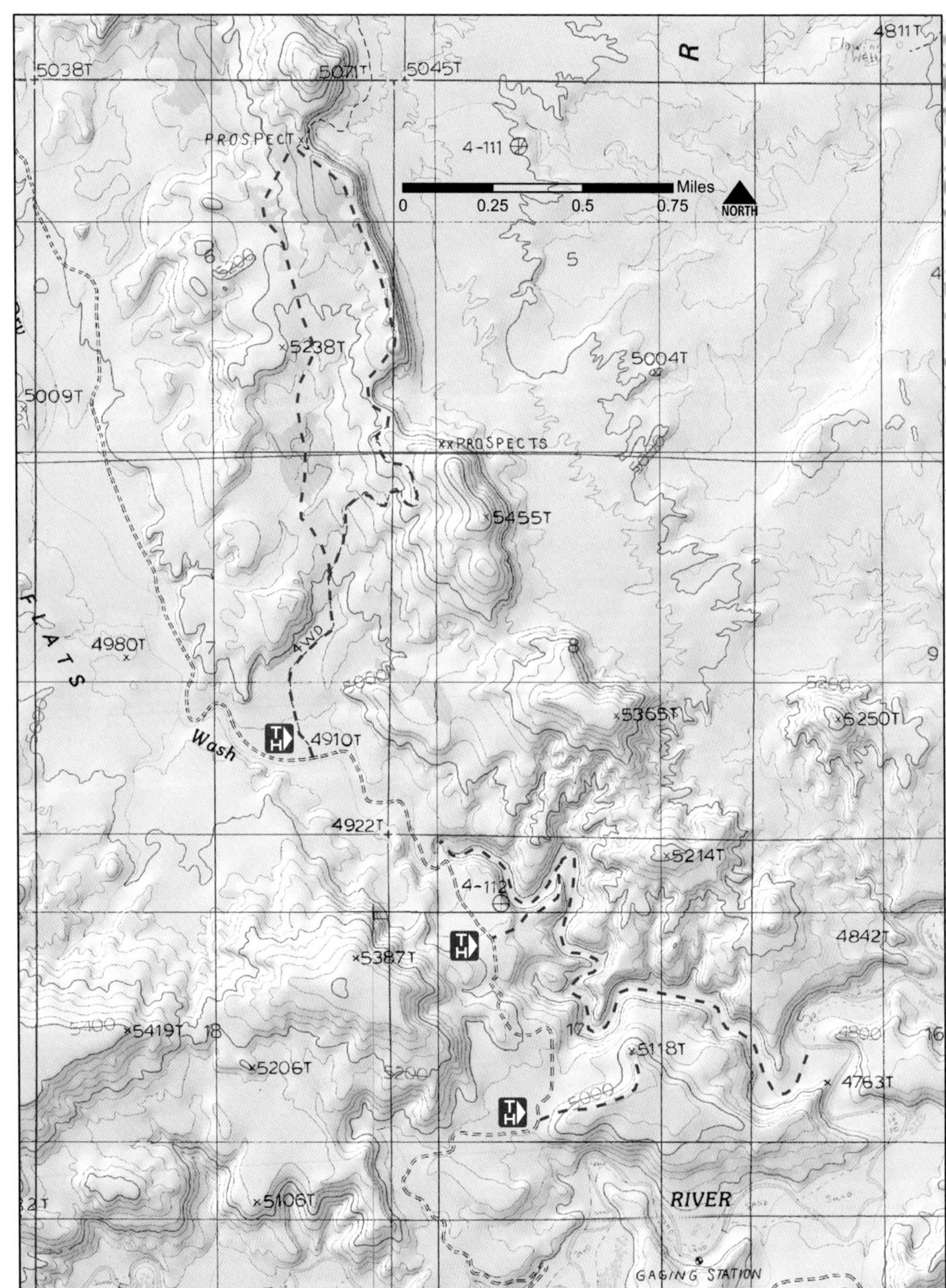

Dry Wash Canyon and cairn routes at bottom; Red Desert Rim loop route at top

Red Desert

Though they begin less than a mile apart, the hikes into Dry Wash Canyon and up to the rim of the Red Desert are completely different. Strong hikers could do both in a day and thereby enjoy a brace of desert walks in what would likely be complete solitude just a few miles from Highway 24. It surely needs to be said here that this sort of country isn't for everyone, or even for many. Rather, the desert rambles are for those who prefer sparse to fulsome, detail to grandeur, and peace to crowds. The area around the Henry Mountains is perfect for exploration—huge tracts of public BLM land where a person with a topographic map and well-defined sense of direction can spend a lifetime leaving footprints that will likely blow or wash away long before anyone else sees them. The descriptions here are really just a taste; the main course is when you simply study a map, find something that might be interesting, and go there.

Getting There

To get to the start of the walk to the west rim of the Red Desert, follow the directions to Dry Wash Canyon from Highway 24 in the section above. From the point on the road above the two white posts, continue driving north for 0.8 mile. Here, where the road is trending to the west, look for a BLM route sign for road 0827, which is a track to the right (north). While it might be possible to drive up this old mining road a short distance, we think it is better to park just off the Hartnet Road and walk.

The Hike

Initially the going is easy, and soon soft, smooth slopes of colorful Brushy Basin clays flank the road on the left (northwest). Dark petrified wood hints at things to come, and

Brushy Basin Member of the Morrison Formation

old bedsprings on the left and then right speak to the past. A post just before the 0.6-mile mark signals the beginning of a steady climb up the resistant Salt Wash Member of the Morrison Formation, here dipping back to the west.

The old road, still easy to follow, swings back and forth, and claim markers can be spotted in several places. A turn to the west at 1.15 miles seems like the wrong direction, but it soon bends back and reaches the rim of the Red Desert at 1.4 miles from the Hartnet Road. The view here to the east is good, but not nearly as fine as it is farther north along the edge on higher ground. Because the old road crosses the saddle and turns back to the southeast to old uranium prospects, the best views require cross-country hiking. From the saddle, strike out to the north (left when looking out over the Red Desert), and head for the obvious high point. The best routes will be well away from the rim for this stretch. Top out just over a 0.25 mile from the saddle; the view is now better, but not the best. The next high point to the north is 1.8 miles from the start, and offers a full view of the jagged Entrada cliffs surrounding the hummocky terrain of the Red Desert with the stark Mancos slopes and mesas beyond. The route is just back from the lip of the cliff, and various holes in the rock indicate a lack of stability, so stay well away from the edge.

Agate on the Red Desert Rim

This is a good place to turn around and retrace your steps, unless you are seeking agate or perhaps a route-finding adventure. For the former, continue along the rim to just before the 2-mile mark where there is abundant, very pretty yellow agate (some might call it jasper) with good red accents. Large pieces of slightly less attractive material are also scattered about. Pay attention to the edge and stay well away from it, and be as careful as you can to not crush the biological soil crust that surrounds a lot of the agate. Good material continues for nearly 0.25 mile to the north.

The terrain to the west of the western Red Desert rim allows for cross-country travel back to your vehicle. This assumes that you have the Caineville topographic map and

Geologic Origin of the Red Desert and North Blue Flats

The Red Desert is a topographic depression rimmed by Entrada Sandstone walls of varying height. To the west, easily visible from the rim, is another topographic low, North Blue Flats, which front the Waterpocket Fold farther to the west. The Caineville quadrangle shows both very clearly. The floors of both basins are roughly 5,000 feet above sea level, but the rock units (Entrada Sandstone and Mancos Shale) are of very different ages and more than 1,000 vertical feet separate them in the Colorado Plateau stratigraphic column.

The topography reflects the underlying geologic structure. East and west of the two low areas are monoclines that dip (tilt) to the east. These folds in the sedimentary rock occurred during the Laramide Orogeny, a mountain-building event that elevated the Rocky Mountains over millions of years, centered about 65 ma. Between the monoclines are a syncline (North Blue Flats) and an anticline (Red Desert). These folds have two dipping sides, with a syncline looking like a bowl in cross-section, and an anticline like a hump. The spines of these features trend nearly north and south, parallel to one another and to the bordering monoclines, which have only one significantly dipping leg.

On the map, both North Blue Flats and the Red Desert are oval or egg-shaped, rather than long linear troughs. This is because the axis of the Red Desert fold plunges away to the north and south, and the North Blue Flats fold axis plunges from both ends in toward the center of the basin. Erosion has significantly leveled the landscape, and the geological structure is then revealed, leaving the late Cretaceous Mancos Shale in North Blue Flats at the same elevation as the mid-Jurassic Entrada Sandstone in the Red Desert.

have paid attention to the landscape during the hike to and along the rim. Vegetation is limited and the Hartnet Road is usually visible on the flat off to the west, which should help in navigation. While your route will no doubt be different, we found it best to continue north from the agate area, quickly dropping down into the saddle where the obvious road that crosses the Red Desert climbs up to the rim. To the west, the road becomes an ATV trail down the slickrock to the southwest. The track becomes more obvious below the slickrock where it crosses a shallow wash, turns northwest and then west.

While the track appears to eventually connect with the Hartnet Road, we struck off to the south just after crossing the wash and followed gentle terrain up and then down into a south-trending drainage. When that wash bends to the right (west) we exited on the east side and continued south, soon joining the old mining road. The trick is to stay east of, and fairly close to, the hills of colorful Brushy Basin clays to the west (if you have a compass, the route is almost due south) until intersecting with the old road. Our loop was just under 4.5 miles. Obviously, you should attempt cross-country travel only if you are confident that you can find your way; otherwise retrace your steps along familiar ground.

Skunkbush

Bloody Hands Gap Hike

Driving distance from Highway 24 is 10.1 miles one way. Hiking distance is 4 miles round trip.

Bloody Hands Gap prints

Of all the hikes described in this book, the walk to Bloody Hands Gap is the one that will reveal whether you have real desert rat blood in your veins. The bleakness factor increases as you hike, culminating in more than 0.5 mile crossing of flat Mancos Shale that is nearly devoid of plant life except for invasive Russian thistle. The account ends just beyond the gap, but there is (literally) nothing to stop you should the visible trail up distant Blue Notch be irresistible. The hike is essentially flat except for the drop into and climb out of Blind Trail Wash, but good route-finding skills are necessary along with comfort in this austere place. It should go without saying that high summer is a terrible time to undertake this walk. Don't even think about it when it is anything warmer than cool. Nope. If it is above 70 degrees, calm, and sunny, why would you choose the frying pan when there is all that high country to be explored?

Getting There

The route to Bloody Hands Gap is off the Notom-Bullfrog Road. Turn south from Highway 24 at the east entrance to Capitol Reef National Park, and drive 7.4 miles on the pavement and turn left (east) on a dirt track with a street sign for 6710 South, which is Burro Wash Road. On our visit this road (BLM route 0089) had been recently graded and was fine for any vehicle, but there are no doubt times when rains would greatly reduce the road quality. From the pavement to the end of the road is 2.7 miles; a corral about halfway along is the only marker of note. The cliff to the left (northeast) is predominantly the thin-banded Summerville Formation, described above in the Dry Wash Canyon section. Although the Notom quadrangle shows the road continuing beyond Sandy Creek, all vehicles must stop at the 2.7-mile mark.

The Hike

As of this writing, a situation that may well change, the best approach to begin is to simply walk down the channel of Burro Wash that is directly adjacent to the small parking area at road's end. Proceed generally east on a winding path through the willows for

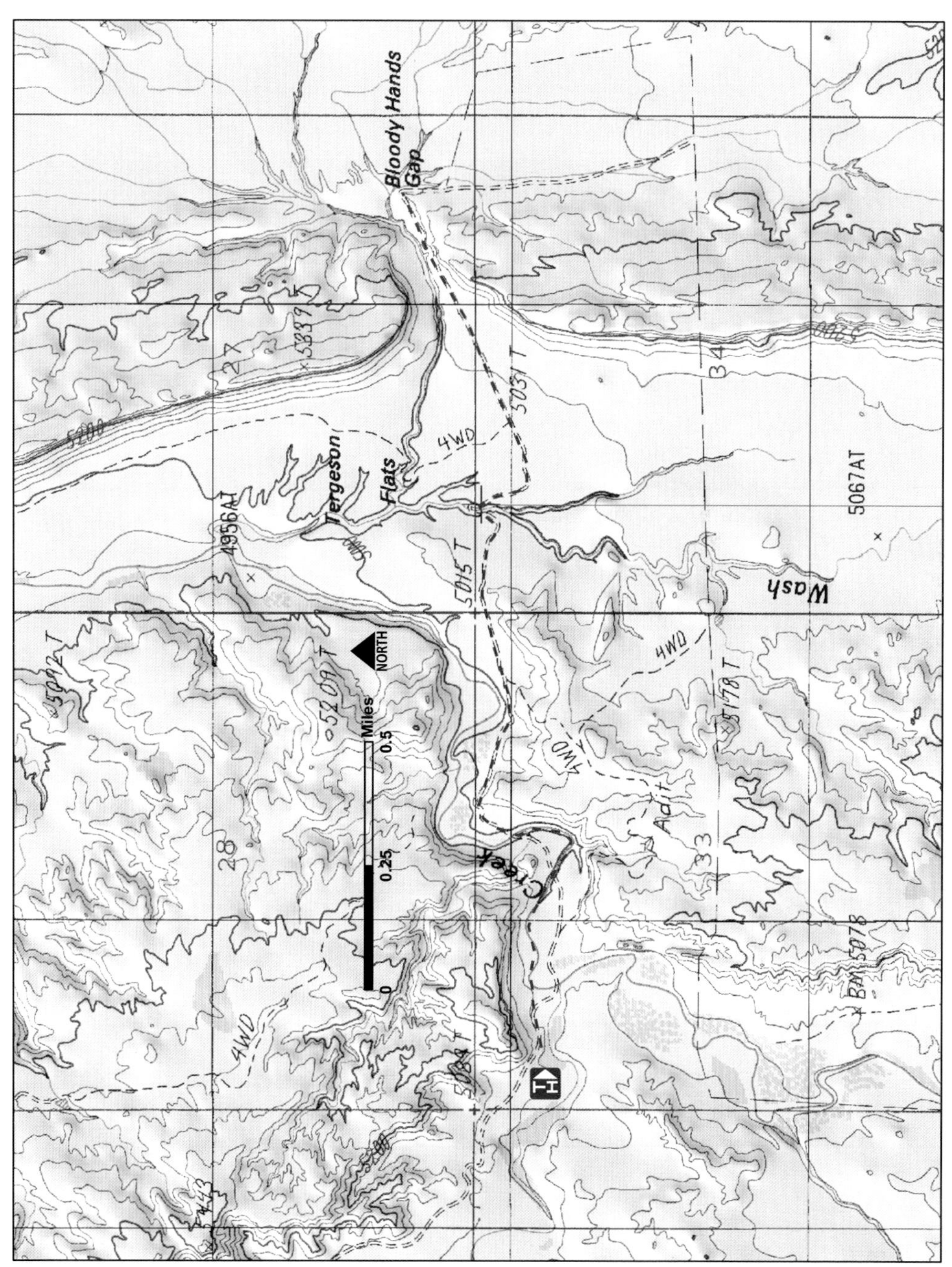

Bloody Hands Gap route

Bloody Hands Gap

0.25 mile to the confluence of Burro Wash and the much larger Sandy Creek wash. This part of the hike will be easy if recent floods have scoured out some of the vegetation, but if not, take the easterly path of least resistance to Sandy Creek. The GPS coordinates for the confluence are 0494928mE, 4223849mN.

We found the best way to proceed from this point was to stay in the Sandy Creek wash (downstream, bearing slightly left, generally east, at the confluence with Burro Wash) for 0.3 mile. The crux of the route finding is to then locate the remnants of the old road as it climbs out of the wash onto a bench to the right (east) at GPS point 0495292mE, 4224032mN. The old track actually crosses the wash at this point, but has been obscured by flooding to the west. To the east, however, it is possible to catch a glimpse through the vegetation of the road as it curves up onto the much less vegetated bench. If you miss the road, the wash soon becomes much more deeply incised with vertical walls about 30 feet high. It is about 500 feet from the wash to the bench on its right (east) side. Near the top of the small hill there is an outcrop of the Salt Wash Member of the Morrison Formation. Dark seam agate is abundant here, but do not try to collect any under the unstable overhang. Good-sized loose pieces are scattered about, making any work with tools unnecessary.

Once on the bench, the way forward is clear for the next 0.5 mile as the old track is pinched between the vertically walled canyon on the north and rising ground to the south. Just over 1 mile from the parking area the last tongue of the Brushy Basin Member of the Morrison is passed; while most of the Brushy Basin is soft, colorful claystone, there are gravelly beds such as this one included within it. Bloody Hands Gap is now

Mancos Shale

During the Cretaceous Period (144 ma to 66 ma), the earth was considerably warmer than it is today, and sea levels were correspondingly higher. Beginning roughly 100 ma there is a clear record of oscillations in sea level across much of the western United States. While the reasons for generally higher sea levels are quite well established—no planetary ice, warmer ocean temperatures, and accelerated sea floor spreading—it is much less clear why there were at least four sequences of 300-foot changes during the deposition of the Mancos Shale alone. Whatever the cause(s), the sedimentary record near Capitol Reef could hardly be more obvious in recording the results.

As the Mancos sediments were laid down, Utah was near the western coast of the Cretaceous Inland Sea that stretched east about to present-day Omaha. The Dakota Sandstone, preceding the Mancos, reflects a shoreline environment of deltas and beaches, often reworked by ocean currents. Huge masses of fossil oysters in Capitol Reef are good examples of the coastal environment. At this time, sea level was relatively low, but it soon began to rise. The term for the period when sea level increases is transgression; when it falls it is called regression.

As the Cretaceous sea transgressed to the west, the Capitol Reef area was submerged and the first shale layer of the Mancos was deposited. Fine clays piled up in prodigious amounts, along with considerable organic matter (which gives the shale exposed today its dark, black when wet, appearance). Eventually, the ocean regressed, to the point that the region was again close to the margin, and a sandy layer was emplaced. This kind of transgressive-regressive sequence occurred several times during the Mancos, and continued on through the overlying Mesa Verde Formation and Lewis Shale.

The hike to Bloody Hands Gap illustrates the fluctuating ocean levels very well. After the last vestiges of the Morrison Formation pass by, the flat gray wasteland ahead is the basal member of the Mancos; it is called the Tununk Shale, and it is a marine deposit laid down when sea level was high. The ridge ahead, cut by Bloody Hands Gap, is a shoreline deposit named the Ferron Sandstone. To the east is another clay layer, the Blue Gate Shale, which fronts the Muley Canyon Sandstone. The sandstones are obviously more resistant than the shales, and form some of the "reefs" that make travel so difficult in parts of south-central Utah.

There is an interesting side note about the Mancos between the Waterpocket Fold of Capitol Reef to the west, and the Henry Mountains to the east. As you walk toward Bloody Hands Gap, you pass through the first sequence quickly, given its thickness. This is because the strata are tilted (dip) down to the east. If they were flat, as they are a bit to the south and east, the sandstones would cap large mesas. Farther east, on the flank of the Henrys, the Mancos beds actually dip to the west, having been thrust up by the injection of the igneous rock that cores the range.

Mudball in Sandy Creek wash

Lichen

clearly visible ahead. Past the resistant rock the old road may be less distinct. Continue generally toward the gap (due east) until you encounter a very deep cut in the clay. This is Blind Trail Wash, and it would be very difficult to cross without the old dugway that remains very passable. The west side of the dugway is at 0496290mE, 4224059mN, but if you don't have a GPS and have missed it, simply walk the edge in either direction until you find it. Back on the bench on the other side of the wash, the route goes southeast for 0.2 mile, then bends to the east-northeast, bearing straight for the gap. The southeast trending stretch is important in order to bypass other sharp cuts in the clay; if you are having to cross many small washes, walk a little farther to the southeast (to the right of the gap) and then turn more directly toward Bloody Hands Gap.

Once you make the turn, it is a 0.5 mile to the gap across a featureless flat. The long ridge formed by the more resistant Ferron Sandstone is breached by a deeply incised channel that drains the area to the east in a classic dendritic pattern that resembles a live oak tree on the Notom topographic map. At the gap the old road is forced to the base of the unstable cliff, a good place to be careful of falling rock to the right (south), and crumbling clay to the left. In the gap is a small panel of seven red handprints, along with some faint inscriptions that date at least as far back as 1908. Beyond the handprints (which are large and somewhat crude), it is just over another 0.1 mile east to the final exposure of Ferron Sandstone and a good view across the clay to the Henry Mountains.

Factory Butte Road to Goblin Valley Road Trip

Driving distance from Highway 24 to the Goblin Valley Road is 30.2 miles.

Sometimes, even in the relatively untraveled reaches of south-central Utah, it is nice to take a drive in the desert backcountry and have a good chance of achieving automotive solitude. Twice we have driven the dusty road from Highway 24 west of Hanksville to Goblin Valley State Park and not even seen another vehicle. One of those trips was in late April when the bleak Mancos clay flats were carpeted with flowers, or, in other words, a time which should have been the busiest of the year.

Although this route may not require 4WD, high clearance is most definitely necessary, and 4WD makes the ford of Muddy Creek a more relaxed (or possible) venture. The middle stretch of the ride, where the road is the worst, is most likely the spot where some random and undesirable event would occur, so the standard cautions apply: make sure your vehicle is in good shape, and be prepared to spend a night or two in the desert. Rain or significant snow brings all forward progress to a halt; drying out may be a matter of hours or days. The crossing of Muddy Creek is frequently easy, even unglamorous, but during and after periods of high flow it can be impassable. Upstream storms can raise levels quickly. A predictable time when the ford might be impossible is at spring melt during those years of heavy snow in the mountains. May would be the usual month of highest flow, but in any case check with the BLM offices in Hanksville or Price for an update before setting out.

Factory Butte Road

The southern end of the drive connects with Highway 24 halfway between mileposts 105 and 106, just over 10 miles west of Hanksville and about 26 miles east of the Capitol Reef National Park visitor center. From the highway the road is marked only by a street sign that reads 6650 East. Turn north, zero the odometer, and head for distinctive Factory Butte on a good graded road. Immediately there is a turnout on the right (east) with a signboard that describes the limited use area through which the road passes. Travel is restricted to roads and designated routes, and cross-country travel is prohibited with the exception of the Swing Arm City OHV Area. Access to the latter is on the left, 0.8 mile from Highway 24 (or directly off Highway 24 to the west of the Factory Butte Road intersection). The staging area is marked by a wooden fence, signboard and map, and vault toilet. Farther on, at 4.5 miles, is a sign at the boundary of a second proposed OHV area, but one that is not yet open, pending the completion of studies that will determine its potential impact on an endangered cactus. Continue straight ahead at 6.1 miles when a lesser track goes off to the right (east).

Once every few years, winter and early spring moisture are sufficient to paint the normally austere flats near Factory Butte purple and gold. The Mancos Shale in this area consists of gray marine shale layered with more resistant sandstone layers. Factory Butte, named for its resemblance to an early woolen mill in Provo, clearly illustrates how the harder sandstone protects the underlying soft shale to the point where the butte can stand high above the surrounding gray flats.

In those few years when conditions are right, the drab clay explodes into bloom with yellow beeplant (*Cleome lutea*) and brittle scorpionweed (*Phacelia demissa*). Beeplant can grow as tall as four feet, but on the arid and hostile flats is lucky to attain four inches in height. The plants are easy to identify by virtue of their palmate leaves and the profusion of stamens protruding from the flower. Brittle scorpionweed does not really resemble other *Phacelias*. When they appear along the Factory Butte road they are usually small (four inches), but due to their abundance, mighty in effect. Oval leaves are supported by stems that are distinctly reddish, and the purple flowers are pretty five-petalled cups sitting upright. The stamens are subdued and do not extend beyond the petals. Some large expanses are covered by beeplant, some by scorpionweed, and some by both growing together.

Soon after Factory Butte passes by on the west, observant travel-

Sundrops and brittle scorpionweed

ers during good flower years might notice that the shade of yellow seems to be subtly changing from slightly golden to canary. Flowers close to the road seem less fuzzy as well, though still diminutive in size. From this point almost to Muddy Creek a different species assumes the yellow role. It is Eastwood's sundrops (*Camissonia Eastwoodiae*), which up close is nothing like the beeplant. Leaves are oval and tend to hug the ground, and the blooms have four bright yellow petals adorned with red dots. The show, if it is to appear at all, is most likely to peak in April; call the BLM office in Hanksville or Capitol Reef National Park for information.

At 8.8 miles from the highway the road crosses Coal Mine Wash and a track goes off to the left (west). Soon, at 9.6 miles, is a Y junction. At this point the good graded road bears off to the right (northeast) and the easy driving ends. Continue straight ahead on the unsigned and clearly less-maintained and traveled road. At 10.2 miles a High Clearance Vehicles Only sign confirms that you are on the correct route. Shortly beyond is a BLM sign on the right and a county line sign on the left, and the road surface becomes rocky. An interesting boulder-strewn slope follows quickly, and at 11.1 miles the road tops a rise and drops to a T intersection. The view over broad Salt Wash to the Moroni Slopes and San Rafael Reef is impressive. Turn right (northeast) and proceed down to the Muddy River ford at 14 miles from the highway.

Crossing the Muddy is sometimes fairly routine. As of this writing the approach from the Factory Butte side is obvious. The south side of the ford is more gentle, while the river flow is concentrated on the north bank, rendering it a little steeper. The stream bottom seems to be firm. During a fall crossing when the water was clear, the channel could be seen to be covered with small rocks, but during a ford just at the beginning of the high water period in the spring the bottom was obscured and seemed to be softer. In both cases it may not have been necessary to use 4WD, but it is a very long walk in either direction if you get stuck. If in doubt, thoroughly investigate the situation; this means a walk across the river.

Muddy Creek ford

After crossing the Muddy, bear left when the tracks divide, and in 150 yards pass by the back of a signboard. (If driving in the opposite direction, stay left (east) of the sign for the ford. Tracks come and go in this area, but at this writing the route described was the best option.) The road passes through sandy bottomland before emerging onto harder ground. At 15.2 miles is the driveway to an old two-story cabin. Just beyond, the largely plant-free ground on the north (left) is covered with small fossil oyster shells up to a couple of inches long.

Geyer onion and oyster shells

The road follows a circuitous path through the Brushy Basin Member of the Morrison Formation. Sharp gullies are cut into the soft and colorful clay and the San Rafael Reef looms over the scene to the north with long vistas, including the Henry Mountains off to the south. The roughest section of road, including many minor, but bumpy, ledges is next. Harder layers of rock provide niches for plants, and spring can bring many species to bloom. A steep descent into Little Wild Horse Canyon is complete at 21.1 miles and the slow going is finished. The canyon is easy driving, and at 21.7 miles the torte-like Summerville Formation appears on the right (east).

The most likely spot to see another vehicle is at the parking area for the Ding and Dang slot canyon hike at 23.6 miles. In another 1.3 miles the likelihood increases of encountering not a few, but many, vehicles at the trailhead for Little Wild Horse and Bell Canyons. On a nice spring weekend dozens of cars, trucks, motorhomes, and ATVs will be parked here. The road is now paved from this trailhead back to Highway 24. Imposing Wild Horse Butte stands over the wide flat that leads north to the Reef and Swell. Several tracks lead off to the south to dispersed camping areas, which are often occupied by small RV villages.

Factory Butte

The Eastern Region Below the Henry Mountains

Horseshoe Canyon Hike

Driving distance from Highway 24 is 32.1 miles one way.
Hiking distance is 8 miles round trip.

Horseshoe Canyon contains such magnificent rock art that it has been set aside as an outlier in Canyonlands National Park for protection. The Barrier Canyon style Archaic Culture pictographs in the Great Gallery are spectacular. The setting and the intensity of the rock art combine to make this a special place, and for many, a spiritual one as well. At the very least, it is a marvel that painted figures more than two thousand years old, exposed to direct sun and only partially protected from rain and wind storms, are vitally present today.

The Great Gallery

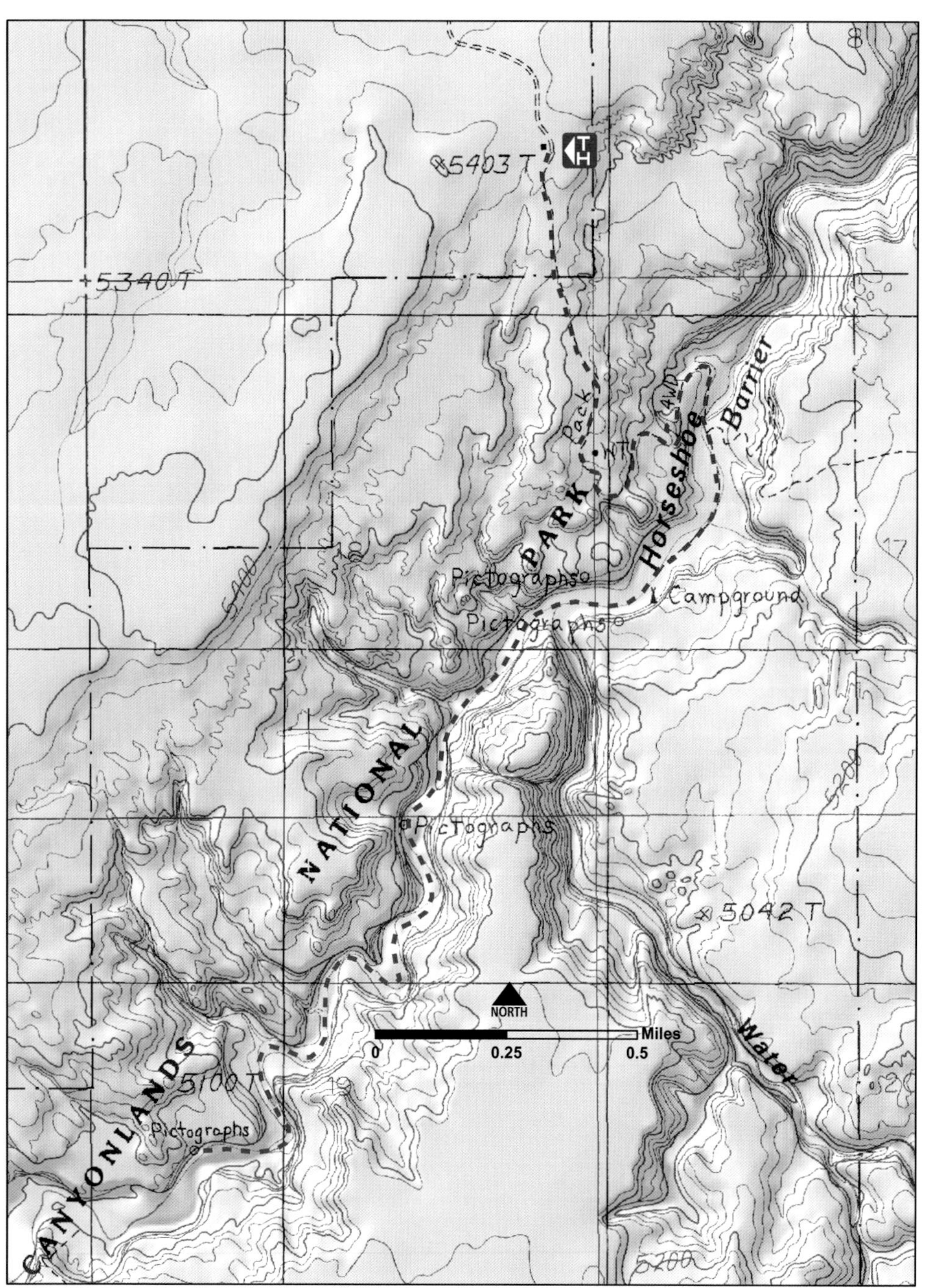

Horseshoe Canyon route

Getting There

Access to Horseshoe Canyon, by vehicle and then by foot, is just difficult enough to keep crowding to a minimum. Probably the best way to drive to the trailhead from anywhere is to proceed to milepost 135.5 on Highway 24 between Hanksville and Green River, and turn south (right if coming from Hanksville) onto the graded road that the *Benchmark Utah Road and Recreation Atlas* labels the Hans Flat Road. This intersection is about 0.5 mile southwest of the road into Goblin Valley State Park. An alternate route, requiring more travel on graded dirt, leaves the Airport Road just southwest of I-70 in Green River and winds south; the condition of this road is often not as good as the Hans Flat Road.

From Highway 24 near the Goblin Valley road, proceed south across the San Rafael Desert for 6.7 miles to a corral and a sharp turn to the left (east). The road heads directly for a saddle between Little Flat Top on the north and the main Flat Tops mesa on the south. Just before the cattleguard at the crest is a good view to the left (north) of the layered Summerville Formation that forms most of Little Flat Top, with small Entrada hoodoos in the foreground. From the cattleguard simply stay on the main road for 18.5 more miles to a three-way junction atop a low rise. Along the way the road climbs to a bench above the flat San Rafael Desert floor, and at times runs right along the edge of the escarpment with good views. It also passes through a dune field that wages an ongoing battle with the road crews.

At the well-signed junction, bear left, continuing on to the east. The road to the right goes to the Hans Flat Ranger Station, and beyond that to the 4WD Flint Trail and tracks into the Maze District of Canyonlands National Park. (See the section on the Hite to Hans Flat Road Trip that follows for a description of this route.) The quality of the road may diminish slightly after the intersection, but should remain passable to cars except during and after storms. Dirt roads in south-central Utah are never a good place to be when they are wet. From the junction to the lesser track to the trailhead is a distance of 5.2 miles. The track is marked by a small sign that is parallel to the main road and easy to miss. Cars with above average clearance should generally have little trouble negotiating the track, including the ledgy part very near the trailhead, but low-slung cars will have difficulty, especially when conditions are less than ideal. From the main road (labeled as the Lower San Rafael Road in the *Benchmark Atlas*) to the spacious trailhead parking area is 1.7 miles. There is a pit toilet on the north side of the parking lot and an information board on the south side near the rim and the trail itself.

The Hike

The round trip hike to the Great Gallery from the rim is almost certainly more than the distances given on the signboard and in most publications. It is common to see the distance listed as 6.5 miles. On a direct route to the Great Gallery, avoiding detours to the other panels along the way, our GPS unit recorded a one-way distance of just under 4 miles. Including those side trips, the total distance is at least 8 miles, and that's not all. Usually the walk up Horseshoe Canyon itself is in very soft sand, which significantly increases the exertion expended during the hike. (We have slogged through the dry sand, and also walked in the day after a good rain had perfectly firmed up the tread; the latter is way better, and if you are in redrock country for an extended period, waiting until after a rain has a lot of merit.) Then, of course, there is the climb out of the canyon at the very end of the hike to add to the difficulty. Put this together and throw in some summer heat, and the hike becomes not only hard, but perhaps hazardous for those whose fitness levels fall short of very good. There is no water at the trailhead or anywhere along the walk, making it imperative to arrive prepared. As with many relatively low-altitude hikes in this area, fall and spring are far better times than summer to walk to the Great Gallery.

Approaching the Great Gallery

There are four major galleries along the walk in Horseshoe Canyon. From our observation, most people stop on the way in at each of the three that precede the Great Gallery, spend some time at the latter and then hike straight out and up to their vehicles. We prefer a different strategy: we walk directly to the Great Gallery, focusing on the beauty of the canyon itself. During the last half of October when the cottonwoods are at the height of their fall color, a late morning start down the trail leads to good backlighting of the pure yellow foliage within the red walls. We arrive at the Great Gallery fresh and with the other three panels to break up the hike back. Photographers might want to check out lighting at the second and third panels in both directions, however, especially the Alcove Panel that becomes fully shaded early in the afternoon.

The trail begins to the right (west) of the information board, and descends on sand and slickrock down an old oil exploration road originally built in the 1920s to cross the canyon. The trail is usually easy to follow, though the roadbed is not necessarily obvious at all times. Usually there are cairns marking the places where the route might not be entirely clear. The elevation drop from the rim to the canyon floor is about 650 feet over a distance of 1.3 miles. Much of the initial descent is quite gentle down to a gate 0.2 mile from the rim. Just beyond the 0.5 mile mark is a large tank and trough system where the trail bends to the right (southwest). The pipe from the tank can be seen from the canyon floor on the way to the Great Gallery. After the trail crosses that pipe it is about 250 feet to where the route makes a sharp right (west) and drops down sharply. Cows are kept out of the canyon by a pass-through that is just over 1 mile from the top. From this point it is a little less than 0.3 mile, mostly on a sandy track, to the canyon floor.

Don't Touch!

A sign at the cattle exclosure reads, "Please don't touch the rock art," and appended to it is an addendum: NOT EVEN ONCE. The vast majority of people making the effort to see Horseshoe Canyon are experienced rock art viewers and know that images literally thousands of years old can be damaged in a few seconds by even well-meaning visitors. When the rock art is in the form of painted pictographs, the dangers are even greater. First is simple abrasion, where the gentlest of touches can cause a chip of brittle paint to fall away. While the Archaic Culture seems to have figured out how to make paint last a lot longer than modern science, it is still subject to flaking due to deterioration as well as by the slow dissolution of the calcite cement holding the sandstone together behind the image. Secondly, the oils that are naturally present on our skin, along with all those we administer in the name of softness, cause direct chemical damage to the paint. In places like Horseshoe Canyon, where over a year there are a lot of visitors, the cumulative result of many touches would be disastrous.

Perhaps less obvious is that the residue left by modern fingers renders it exceedingly difficult or even impossible to obtain accurate dates for the paint. A common pigment used to color Archaic paint red, brown, or maroon, is iron oxide, often in the form of the mineral hematite. Six thousand years ago it was known that something had to be added to the pigment to make it adhere to a surface and endure in place. These fixatives were usually organic, derived from plants, animals, or human urine. Because of their organic content, the paints can be radiocarbon dated. Adding oils from the twenty-first century obviously skews the results of any test.

Horseshoe Canyon is cut into the Navajo Sandstone. The walls are widely spaced and the flat, sandy floor is dotted with Fremont cottonwood trees, and even occasionally with horsetails and willows where moisture is near the surface. If you elect to walk directly to the Great Gallery as we do, it still makes sense to note the locations of the three panels on the way. From the point where the trail from the rim reaches the canyon floor, it is 0.4 mile to a possible cairn on the left (southeast) side of the primary wash, and a loop path to the base of the steep slope up to the High Gallery. The very good panel in Horseshoe Shelter is another 0.1mile along, but on the other (northwest) side of the wide canyon. There is usually a good hiker-made trail from one to the other, but there is considerable vegetation that can occasionally make the easiest route a little unclear.

Another 0.1 mile from Horseshoe Shelter is a major fork in the canyon, and footprints often follow both branches. To stay in Horseshoe Canyon continue in the right canyon (southwest) and into the younger trees. From the confluence it is almost exactly another mile to a huge amphitheater on the right (northwest) that is the site of the Alcove Panel. Another mile of sandy walking is required to reach the Great Gallery, which is also on the right (northwest) side.

The pictographs at the Great Gallery are so large and contrast so clearly with the light-colored sandstone on which they are painted that they can be seen from quite some distance while approaching them. The Park Service has thankfully taken a minimalist stance in providing amenities at the site. There might be a couple of boxes with binoculars and some interpretive information, along with a handful of very informal benches. Unobtrusive chain marks off areas that are off limits to foot traffic, including the rock leading up to the wall. Appreciation of the images comes down to personal preferences, but for many the best way is to sit far enough away so that the entire football field–length of the panel can be absorbed at once. Photographers seeking to capture some of the spectacular detail in the figures will need to have a long lens; our 55-250 mm digital lens was sufficient. During periods of even modest visitation there may be a ranger available at the site to answer questions.

Plan on spending considerable time at the Great Gallery. The so-called Holy Ghost and Attendants group toward the left (west) end of the panel is especially impressive, but so are the heavily decorated anthropomorphs concentrated in the middle. Smaller figures also are worthy of inspection. If you are fortunate enough to have the site to yourself, its impact may be quite profound. Imagine a group of people passing through the canyon, say six thousand years ago, and encountering the Great Gallery. Perhaps they would have known about it, or perhaps not, but surely the impact would have been profound. Then, of course, the simple realization that these images have persisted for thousands of years is tribute to those who painted them and humbling to our modern sensibilities.

On the return to the Alcove Panel keep an eye on the left (northwest) wall for faint figures high above the canyon floor—almost everyone misses them. The Alcove Panel is in a huge amphitheater with an elevated floor well above the wash. In order to prevent unnecessary damage to the site, the Park Service has established a single entry, located toward the west side of the alcove, up onto the bench. The rock art here is of uneven quality, and the main panel, off to the right (east) is faded. The amphitheater itself, however, is very impressive, both exceedingly high and wide, with a nice canyon view.

The artwork at Horseshoe Shelter is more impressive, with a long string of interesting images, including two that are much darker than the rest. To the right (east) of the primary panel, a path leads around some rubble to a very different kind of hunting

Horseshoe Canyon pictographs

Barrier Canyon Style Rock Art

The Archaic Culture was one of hunters and gatherers, mobile people who followed game and wild food sources through the seasons. Some evidence suggests that Archaic people may have lived in Utah as long as eight thousand years ago or perhaps even longer. Their nomadic lifestyle and the great span of time have left little to study, primarily figurines and rock art. The Great Gallery is widely considered to be the best of the latter, although there are at least two hundred sites with similar imagery.

Horseshoe Canyon was originally called Barrier Canyon, and the rock art there and elsewhere is now labeled as Barrier Canyon Style. It is dominated by larger than life red figures that often are without legs or arms, and are probably spirit or shamanic representations. Because they do have heads and are in the basic configuration of a shrouded human body, they are called anthropomorphs. Other kinds of images are also commonly present, including usually smaller figures with proportional appendages, and a variety of animals, frequently bighorn sheep. A circle of small animals is an interesting feature at the Great Gallery. Many of the larger anthropomorphs are heavily decorated, sometimes with white lines or dots. Various interpretations have been offered for the symbolism, but these are just educated guesses, leaving it up to you to come up with your own.

An interesting sidelight to the galleries in Horseshoe Canyon is that the panels are all painted along curving alcove walls that apparently have unusual acoustic characteristics. A person speaking at normal volume can stand, perhaps even out of sight, at one end of the alcove and to another person standing in the middle of the curve, the voice will appear to come directly out of the wall. If there is a heroic-sized spirit figure painted in that spot, the implications for shamanic affect and perhaps power, are intriguing.

scene done in a style that varies significantly from other images in the shelter, and may be much more recent. Just beyond, the High Panel—the only one facing north—exhibits many interesting figures, including some that are also unlike most of the other Horseshoe Canyon motifs. It is a steep climb up to a point approaching the base of the wall, and the panel itself is still higher on the cliff. From the High Panel back to the rim is about 1.75 miles, followed by a long and somewhat tedious drive back to pavement (unless you are camping on nearby BLM land), so it is important to plan accordingly by leaving appropriate refreshments in your vehicle.

Hite to Hans Flat 4WD Road Trip

Driving distance from Highway 95 to Highway 24 is 78 miles one way.

With two exceptions, the backcountry drive from Highway 95 near the Colorado River to the Hans Flat Ranger Station and on to Highway 24 near the entrance to Goblin Valley is an easy venture through open and desolate country. The crux is the Flint Trail, an amazing piece of road that ascends a series of stepped cliffs in the Wingate Sandstone. The track is very steep, the rounded dirt waterbars high, and the switchbacks so sharp that most vehicles will have to back up to negotiate them. Experienced drivers operating short wheelbase 4WDs will not be intimidated by the Flint Trail, but it absolutely is no place for neophytes driving standard SUVs.

Much of the route is at what serves as low elevation in southern Utah, which means very hot temperatures in the summer. Since summer is also the prime time for monsoonal thunderstorms in the afternoon, it is decidedly not the time for this drive. Far better to do it on a mild day in the spring or fall. There is even a caveat to these times: make sure that there is no chance of any ice remaining on the Flint Trail switchbacks; they are carved into a north-facing wall that retains ice for long periods, just like the trails leading into the Grand Canyon from the South Rim. Rain also renders parts of the route entirely impassable, so due diligence is necessary in determining conditions prior to setting out.

This account follows a south to north direction, which requires ascending the Flint Trail. With a good low-range transmission option, the grade up the switchbacks is tem-

Desert near Hite backed by Henry Mountains

pered by a surface that is good and hard all the way. The backing up that will probably be necessary to get around the switchbacks must be done toward the edge, however, which could make drivers and passengers a little anxious.

To begin the trip, drive south from Hanksville on Highway 95 to milepost 46.3, between the bridges over the Dirty Devil and Colorado Rivers. The unmarked dirt road joins Highway 95 from the left (east) 1.1 miles south of the center of the so-called Steel Bridge over the Dirty Devil. At 0.4 mile from the highway there is a signboard with useful information and maps. While the route is easy to follow, it is important to have a good map along to keep track of progress and to know what you are seeing. We have found the *Benchmark Maps Utah Road and Recreation Atlas* to be accurate and detailed.

The Dirty Devil River

The Dirty Devil River is one of the wildest waterways in the continental United States. Born at the confluence of Muddy Creek and the Fremont River within sight of the Highway 24 bridge just north of Hanksville, the Dirty Devil flows briefly near irrigated fields before plunging into a deep canyon. Between this point and its end at the Colorado River, the stream is accessible by vehicle only at the ford on the rough Poison Spring Canyon Road (see the section on Happy Canyon). The remoteness of the Dirty Devil naturally attracted folks who might need occasionally to leave civilization behind; Butch Cassidy and his band were the most notorious of this breed, being particularly fond of the complex Robbers Roost Canyon system. In its lower reaches the canyon is deep and handsomely stepped, with abundant side canyons. The river itself, however, is less comely, living up to its name that was first applied by a member of John Wesley Powell's expedition down the Green and Colorado Rivers.

The road begins as an easy high clearance 2WD route that follows the contact between the hard underlying Cedar Mesa Sandstone and the softer brown Organ Rock Formation above. The route contours around the head of several interesting canyons in the Cedar Mesa that invite exploration. Most of the travel surface is graded dirt with intervening rougher bedrock stretches. After about 6 miles the road veers south and then back north to pass by a thin fin of Organ Rock capped with resistant White Rim Sandstone; another quite amazing set of broken fins is bisected by the track at the 13.7-mile mark. A little more than 1.5 miles later the road goes north of a hoodoo that looks like a candle in a holder, only one of many erosional remnants that call out for naming along the way. There should be good light for photographing the candleholder from one side or the other.

After passing through a broad and open flat, there is an unmarked Y junction at 19.6 miles. The route to the left (northwest) follows a drainage, passes a heavily used campsite, and then gets increasingly rougher and more narrow as the streambed constricts and becomes rocky. The main route continues to the right (northeast) at the Y, passing easily along the bench below Wingate cliffs to the northwest. A lesser track turns off to the right (east) at 24 miles, with a good view of the La Sal Mountains to the northeast. Another track angles off to the right (southeast) at 29.4 miles.

The route remains easy to a major intersection at 30.7 miles. To the right (initially southeast, then shortly northeast) is the increasingly rough track to the Land of Standing Rocks and ultimately, after 20 miles, the Dollhouse. Make sure to get complete information on this difficult road before setting out. To the left (northwest), a 4WD road crosses Sunset Pass, descends Hatch Canyon to a ford of the Dirty Devil River, and ascends up Poison Spring Canyon to Highway 95, 17 miles south of Hanksville. (See the section on Happy Canyon for information on the upper end of the Poison Spring Canyon Road.) Continue straight through the crossroads to continue to the Flint Trail.

Along the Hite to Hans Flat drive

After several more easy miles, the complexion of the route changes dramatically. Visible ahead for quite some distance, the road begins a very steep climb up to a resistant bed in the Chinle Formation. The Chinle is largely clay, and even a minor amount of rain will render this ascent impossible for any vehicle. Once on top of the western rim of the Red Cove, views to the east are substantial over the Standing Rocks and on to the Abajo Mountains. Some short sections along the rim are a little exposed. At 37.6 miles is a second signed intersection, where a road goes right (northeast) to the Maze Overlook. The Flint Trail continues straight ahead.

The famous Flint Trail switchbacks are only 1.5 miles farther on. The amount of trepidation they engender will depend upon the driver's (and passengers') experience and the vehicle. Usually the Wingate Sandstone forms a sheer cliff for its entire thickness of 300 to 400 feet, but here it steps up in big lifts with intervening slopes sufficient to permit the construction of the road. The hill is very steep, but the surface is good, generally providing excellent traction. In our pickup we had to back up on three switchbacks; the last (upper) one several times in a constricted and exposed spot. Very high and rounded waterbars require better than average clearance and short to medium wheelbase. The climb is 1.2 miles long.

From the top of the Flint Trail to the ranger station at Hans Flat is 12.4 miles. Along the way are both sandy and rough slickrock conditions, but the going is easy. The route remains close to the Orange Cliffs at first, with good views at the Flint Trail Overlook, and again at 43.7 miles at the Bagpipe Butte viewpoint. Side roads to the left (southwest) lead to the Happy Canyon tent site and Big Ridge at mile 40.5, and to the Flint Seep camp at mile 41.5. At mile 50.5 the North Point Road goes to the right (east), eventually branching off to Cleopatra's Chair and Panorama Point. Our driving time to Hans Flat was just about five hours.

The Hans Flat Ranger Station is one of the more remote National Park Service outposts in the lower 48 states. It is 46 miles from the nearest paved road. Drinking water must be trucked in, and a large photovoltaic array is the source of electricity. The vast patrol area served by the station consists of broken and convoluted country, accessed mostly by roads worse than the route described here; most patrols must negotiate the Flint Trail switchbacks in both directions. Rangers live on site during their work schedules, and then have a long, dusty drive just to get groceries.

The flavor of that dusty drive can be tasted on the way to Highway 24 between Hanksville and Green River or via a longer dirt road directly to Green River. From Hans Flat continue straight ahead at the visitor service building. The road improves, but still requires attention in negotiating sand and unexpected rocky sections. It is 13.8 miles to the Ekker Ranch junction to the left (west) and another sometimes rough 7.1 miles to a three-way intersection. To the right (east) it is a short distance to Horseshoe Canyon (described above) and to the left it is 25 miles to Highway 24. This last dirt road stretch is generally in considerably better condition than the rest of the drive. Even if the destination is Green River, it is usually easier and quicker to take the route to Highway 24 as described rather than proceeding past Horseshoe Canyon and on to Green River on the Lower San Rafael Road.

Sego lilies

Happy Canyon 4WD Road Trip and Hike

4WD driving distance from Highway 24 is approximately 16 miles one way depending on where you stop.
Hiking distance is 9 miles round trip.

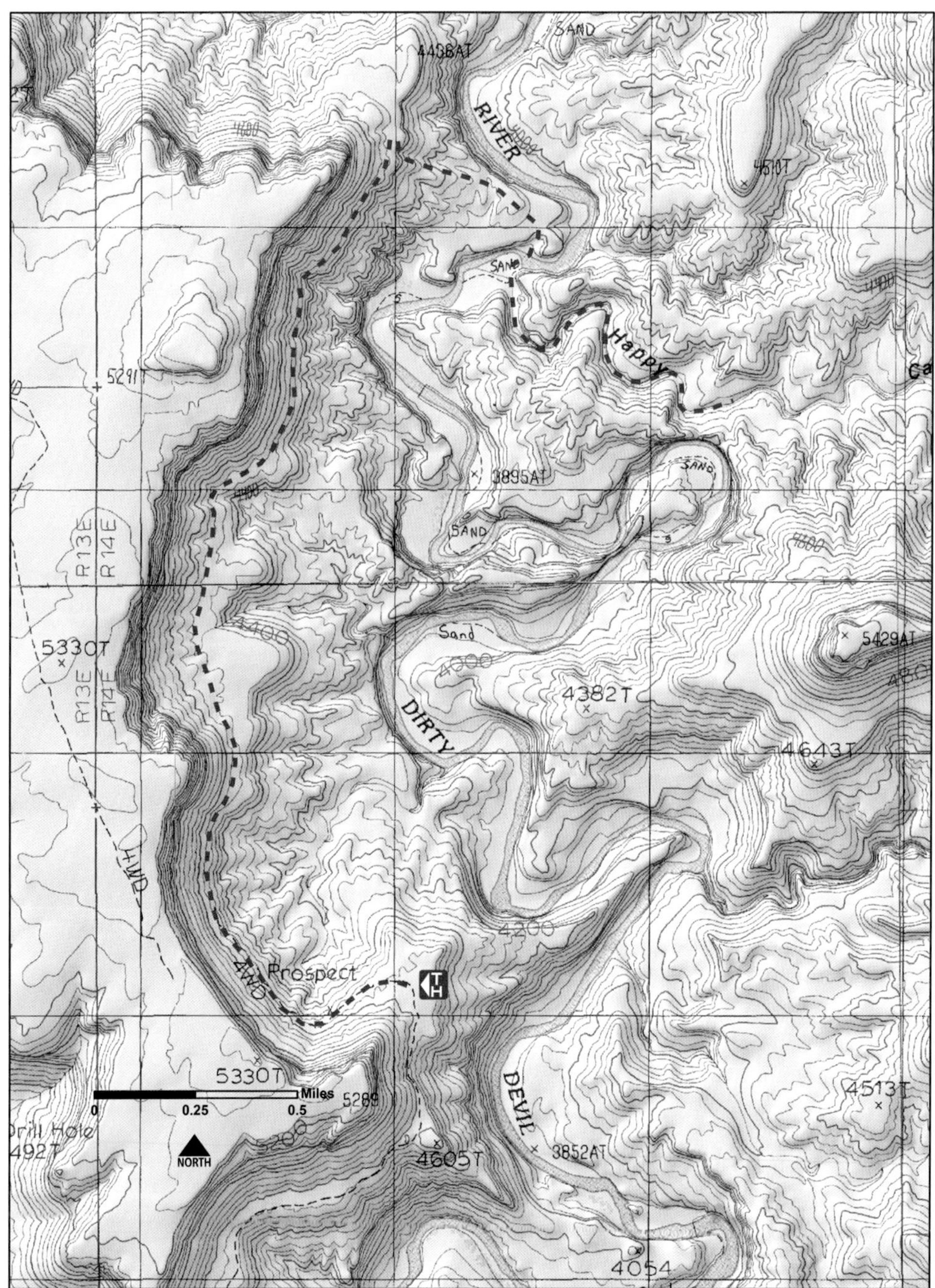

Happy Canyon route

Dirty Devil River ford near the mouth of Happy Canyon

Happy Canyon, southeast of Hanksville, is a tributary of the Dirty Devil River. Aesthetically, it ranks in the top handful of Utah canyons. Narrow, convoluted, cross-bedded, and reasonably colorful, Happy would attract thousands of visitors were it even somewhat accessible, but the difficulty in getting there allows a measure of solitude not only foreign to, say, Antelope Canyon, but indeed any of the many narrows along the Escalante River.

The long trek to Happy Canyon is a combination of a couple of hours of sometimes very rough four-wheel driving, another two hours of hiking, wading the river, an hour to enjoy walking up the canyon, and then repeating the entire sequence in reverse. A good 4WD vehicle with above average clearance is necessary. Standard SUVs, especially long ones, will have considerable difficulty if in fact they are able to make the trip at all. Given the isolation of Happy Canyon and the high possibility that no other people will be encountered, comfort would be increased for many if they were part of at least a two-vehicle group. While it is possible to complete the drive and hike in a long day, consider camping at the end of the 4WD road before or after the hike.

Getting There

From the junction of Highways 24 and 95 in Hanksville, drive south on Highway 95 to milepost 17 (Hanksville is milepost 0 for Highway 95). Turn left (east) on the Poison Spring Canyon Road, which is unmarked on Highway 95. Shortly a sign indicates a number of destinations, including the Dirty Devil River, which is 16 miles. At first, the going is easy as the road leaves the wash and crosses gently rolling terrain. Near the first cattleguard is a BLM notice board that presents important information for anyone continuing on. By the second cattleguard at 3.2 miles the "road" simply follows the path of least resistance in the wash, only occasionally crossing meanders on higher benches. For the most part sand is the only obstacle for the first 7.5 miles, and its difficulty is dependent upon recent weather, especially wind. Generally 4WD may be necessary briefly, if at all.

The crux of negotiating the Poison Spring Canyon Road comes abruptly. The gravel and sand give way to a series of ledges and, usually, flowing water. The first drop is the most significant and should be scouted. At this writing, the best line is to the far right (south). Previous travelers may have left some helpful rocks for driver-side wheels. The next 100 yards are very rough and the water makes it difficult to determine the best line. High clearance is mandatory, and with it, the passage will be bumpy, but not breathtaking. Beyond, the going eases, and a few benchland stretches are a relief.

An old uranium prospecting track branches off to the left (northeast) 10.8 miles from Highway 95. The track can be spotted on the high ground across the wash, but the connection to it may change with any serious flood. Often the junction and route across the Poison Spring wash are obvious, but if you find yourself descending over the prominent cliff that is called the Black Jump, you have missed them. Even when conditions are good the climb out of the wash will likely be steep and possibly difficult.

The mining track is no picnic and could wash out at any time as it did during the flood of 2011, which also rendered the Poison Spring Canyon Road impassible for a long period. It is often passable only due to the work of those going to Happy Canyon as well as the claim holders who have staked out the Shinarump, a uranium-bearing member of the Chinle Formation. (In this location the Shinarump may also be called the Moss Back.) Much of the route rests on the clay of the Chinle, leading to interesting potholes many feet deep, along with small erosion channels cut across the track. Other sections consist of clay ramps barely wide enough for small pickups. Rain renders the entire miners road impassable. After bouncing along for 5.8 miles it is a relief to come to a large boulder that prevents further progress. It is best to stop on one of two broad benches at 5.1 or 5.4 miles, where there is also ample space for camping, and hike from here.

The Hike

Much of the walk to Happy Canyon continues on what remains of the mining track beyond the big boulder. Hiking along the track is easy, with only modest grades. At one point the old road is covered with a debris flow that is easily crossed as of this writing, but which may become problematic in the future. From the rock to the route that descends to the river is 2.5 miles. All along the way the impressive canyon of the Dirty Devil stretches expansively to the east. The rim cliffs are formed in the Wingate Sandstone that sits atop the Chinle and Moenkopi Formations. The stream cuts through the White Rim Sandstone, into which the spectacular narrows of Happy Canyon are incised. Halfway along the road walk is a broad, flat bench, followed by a smaller one that has a segmented petrified log resting in a bed of biological soil crust. Pieces of petrified wood dot the path, and can also be seen along the mining track 3.3 miles from the Poison Spring Canyon Road.

Dirty Devil River canyon

Petrified wood

After a little less than 2 miles of hiking, the mouth of Happy Canyon is visible on the far side of the river, fronted by a large expanse of sand and willows. Most of the route down to the Dirty Devil is also in view and worth studying, especially the semi-circular slope that is cut into the White Rim bench leading to the riverbank. The mining track eventually descends gradually to the tip of a prominent Wingate headland on the left (west) and a steep but negotiable slope on the right (east). There may be a large cairn to mark the way down, along with smaller cairns on at least the top portion of the descent. The GPS coordinates for this point are UTM 0551958mE, 4221259mN.

The route immediately below the road is steep and sometimes loose, with short pieces of hiker-made path. The route winds southeast through a small cliff band and then bears more easterly to proceed down the spine of the now easy-going ridge. When a south-trending drainage almost cuts through the crest, drop down to the point where it can easily be crossed and then contour southeast above it, heading directly toward the semi-circular break in the bench right above the river and just upstream from the mouth of Happy Canyon. Pick a way down the rocky and loose slope, and work through a band of tamarisk and a second and thicker line of willows to the sandy riverbank. The crossing is usually easy, perhaps a little slippery, but less than knee deep with a fairly gentle current. Obviously, the flow in the Dirty Devil can change quickly. Spring is generally not a good time for the hike as snowmelt from the mountains to the northwest swells the river and renders it uncomfortably cold. Summer is very hot at this low elevation and also brings the thunderstorms of the monsoon season, leaving fall as probably the best time to attempt Happy Canyon.

The first ten minutes of walking in the canyon are pleasant and easy, but not impressive. When the walls close in, they do so quickly, and the entrance into the narrows is marked by an hourglass-shaped rock portal. About 1 mile of continuously interesting passage follows, with, as of this writing, no serious impediments at all. There are a couple of rocky sections, but much of the walking is on sandy gravel, making it easy to appreciate the surroundings. The canyon walls are vertically sinuous, swelling and receding from the floor up to the rim some 50 feet overhead. In many places the narrows appear to be pear-shaped, wider at the bottom than the top, creating almost a tunnel effect. Prominent cross-bedding in the sandstone adds significantly to the beauty of the narrows with sweeping, angled lines and forms.

Happy Canyon

Happy Canyon

As with many very tight canyons, photography is best in Happy during the middle of the day when sunlight can penetrate into the depths. This is especially true during October, which might be the best time to make the trip. At that time, light may reach the bottom of the narrows only for one short stretch during a two-hour visit. In spite of this limitation, and even with high clouds, good pictures with a little yellow or orange color can be captured. The turnaround point in the narrows is at the choosing of the hiker as the canyon walls slowly lower and Happy begins to fade from spectacular to pretty good. After rainy periods a pool in the upper end may make this an easy decision.

The glow of Happy Canyon lasts well beyond being there. That is certainly a good thing when staring up at the 500-foot climb in 0.75 mile back to the mining track, the hike to the truck, and especially the journey back to Highway 95. If you are attempting this all in one day, may you be fortunate enough to arrive back in Hanksville before all the restaurants close for the evening.

Happy Canyon

Hog Canyon Hike

Hiking distance is 2.2 miles round trip.

Not every hike needs to be a day-long affair. Sometimes a couple of hours out of the car can be the perfect therapy for driver and passengers alike. From Hanksville to just south of Blanding, Highway 95 is a scenic buffet, but canyon country is a tactile place, where all the senses long to be engaged, not solely the eyes. The short walk up Hog Canyon to an unexpected watery grotto fills the bill nicely on a trip from Capitol Reef to, say, Monument Valley.

Hog Springs pool

Getting There

The Hog Spring Rest Area is located at milepost 33.2 on Highway 95, or 7.1 miles south of the junction with Highway 276. It is well signed and has a very large parking area with a vault toilet directly adjacent to the road. Even if there isn't time for the hike, the rest area has two covered picnic table areas that are very nice, and lunch in the red Wingate canyon, here accented with cottonwood trees and away from the traffic, would be a good break.

The Hike

To find the beginning of the trail that proceeds up canyon, cross the footbridge from the parking lot and walk along the cement sidewalk past the first covered picnic tables.

Before reaching the second set look down and to the right (northwest) for a plastic flexible sign that identifies the trail. The footpath descends quickly to the bottom of the drainage where, depending upon conditions, there may be water filtering slowly through the grassy vegetation. From this point the route alternately tracks along banks above the tiny waterway, or winds along the bottom of the canyon floor. There may be many crossings of openly flowing water, or wet spots in the grass, but none more than a trickle.

The rock layers in North Wash (through which Highway 95 descends to Lake Powell) dip down to the lake less steeply than the gradient of the wash. Thus, while travelers heading to Hite are losing altitude, the rocks are getting older even faster. The trail in Hog Canyon lies mostly in the Wingate Sandstone, an early Jurassic dune sand now often colored red by iron staining derived from shales in the overlying Kayenta Formation. The Wingate is especially susceptible to the development of solution cavities, and early in the hike the north (right) wall is pockmarked by them.

The canyon is sparsely dotted with Fremont cottonwood trees that add warm color from April almost to the end of October, then flame out in bright yellow for a brief, but memorable, period that often falls between October 20 and early November. Once new growth pushes up through last year's residue, the grasses and reeds similarly provide contrast to the red canyon walls. Several varieties of cactus are best recognized during the late spring blooming time, and there is plenty of rabbitbrush to color the fall along with the cottonwoods and skunkbush.

From the picnic area to the falls and grotto is just over 1 mile. At 0.3 mile along, the path becomes a little rough and edges along a steep slope above the stream. A large, reed-lined pool is nearby downstream. While the first crossings are marked by more flexible posts in the initial 0.6 mile, as of this writing the trail, especially early in the year before increased use, can be a little hard to follow when they stop. At this point the canyon floor is wide and flat, covered by a thick mat of vegetation. A large cairn on a rock on the south side of the drainage is a good target, and once there, the path again becomes clear. At the 0.8-mile point the trail cuts a meander by climbing across a sandy saddle. From this feature it is only 0.3 mile to the falls, with the walking easygoing like the rest of the hike. The trail divides near the falls, but just stay to the right (north) to reach a gravel bar that extends along the wall to the pool.

Highlights

The small stream is spring-fed farther up the canyon. It drops over a small ledge at the bottom of the Kayenta Formation and into a pool some 50 feet across. A tangle of willows fronts the pool on the east and southeast, with low rock walls surrounding the rest. Especially on the north side, the rock is severely undercut,

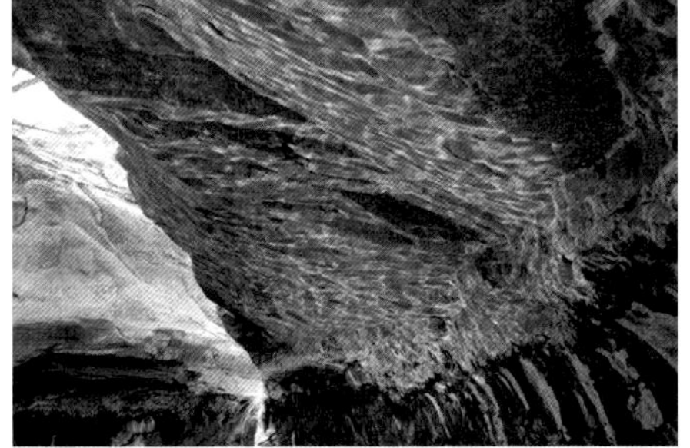
Reflections

which leads to the grotto-like feel of the place. If the light is favorable, the small ripples created by the falls will be reflected on the roof of the chamber, shimmering in undulating patterns. The wall also has a seep layer, and to the left (south) of the falls it supports a nice maidenhair fern population. The grotto would be of interest anywhere, but its appeal is enhanced by its unexpected presence within the wide canyon.

Above the falls the canyon becomes less interesting, but it can be traversed all the way to the spring. The route upstream continues from the south side of the pool, near the densest collection of maidenhair ferns. A sandy route goes along the end of the rock wall and quickly climbs above the falls. The ledgy Kayenta surrounds the drainage beyond.

Desert star jasmine along Highway 95

Burr Point Road Trip

Driving distance from Highway 24 is 10.7 miles one way.

The Dirty Devil River is not one of Utah's most sought after tourist destinations. Surely, more than 99 percent of those who see the Dirty Devil do so at the Highway 24 bridge near Hanksville or the Highway 95 bridge near Hite. In the former case the stream is wide, shallow, sluggish, and non-descript, and in the latter it is either submerged in Lake Powell or overshadowed by the Colorado during periods when the lake is low. In between these points, however, there is a canyon that is deep, colorful, and well worth the effort necessary to see it.

The Dirty Devil name originally applied to the Fremont River as well, but later sensibilities reduced the use of "Dirty Devil" to only that portion downstream from the confluence of the Fremont and Muddy Creek, within sight of the Highway 24 bridge. The straight-line distance from Hanksville to Lake Powell is about 40 miles, but the river flows east or west about as much as it trends to the south. The Fremont is reservoir controlled and much of its flow, along with Muddy Creek's, is used for irrigation. The Dirty Devil for most of the year therefore meanders back and forth across the canyon floor, easy to ford and difficult, often impossible, to paddle.

It is the Colorado River that is responsible for the deep side canyons of the San Juan, Green, Escalante, Virgin, and Dirty Devil Rivers. Its speedy down-cutting increased the gradient of its tributary streams, enabling them in turn to erode more forcefully. Many of the rock units of the Colorado Plateau are very soft and are easily removed both from above and below the harder sandstones and limestones. The resulting canyon landform is that of mirroring stair-step profiles on either side of the river. Much of the Dirty Devil canyon has walls of Navajo Sandstone at or near the rim, and a major cliff of Wingate Sandstone halfway down. Near or at the bottom are the soft Triassic Chinle and Moenkopi Formations that form slopes, although a couple of members of the Chinle are resistant enough to form benches. Approaching Lake Powell the river cuts down through the resistant White Rim and Cedar Mesa Sandstones, and smaller tributaries such as Happy Canyon may form narrows and slots.

The easiest way to see the canyon of the Dirty Devil is to drive south from Hanksville on Highway 95 to milepost 15.7, not coincidentally the exact distance from the junction of Highways 95 and 24. Although there is no sign on the pavement, immediately after turning east (left) onto the graded dirt

Dirty Devil River canyon from Burr Point

road a BLM sign for road 0107 gives distances to Dell Seeps 5, Adobe Swale 8, and Burr Point 11. Zero the odometer after making the turn. The road is maintained, but it doesn't take a lot of weather to cause it to drop from passable to passenger cars down to carefully driven cars with above average clearance and then down to high-clearance vehicles. A little more weather can render it impassable to all. During long dry and windy periods enough sand can blow over the road to even make four-wheel drive necessary. When we drove it, high clearance was required, with the worst stretch about halfway to Burr Point.

Much of the route is on sand derived from the Entrada Sandstone. The resulting soil, aridity, and largely flat and exposed terrain make for hard growing conditions. Sagebrush, Mormon tea, and blackbrush shrubs dominate the landscape. Stay straight at 0.2 mile when a lesser track goes off to the right (south). At the 1.4-mile mark low dunes are being stabilized by very short Gambel oaks, an unexpected phenomenon. Once established, they form their own little soil production facility, capturing organic matter amidst the stems, and piling up sand to prevent evaporation of soil moisture.

Continue straight again at 1.8 when a track bends off to the left (north) and cross a cattleguard at 2.7. The road soon enters and leaves a wash, then quickly passes by a picturesque corral at 3.4. The next side track is also to the left (northeast) and the main road curves to the right. The following 1.5 miles may be a little rough, especially dropping into and climbing out of washes. There are also some large rocks to be avoided. A vast sea of sagebrush in a wide and gentle swale follows and the road gets a little better. The most used side road branches off to the left (north) at 7.9 miles and is signed as route 0101. Continue straight ahead and soon cross a small dam that may impound a cattle pond during wet times.

A sense that the scenery may get more interesting begins at 9.5 miles when views open up to the south (right), and it is just 1.2 miles farther on to a large iron drill pipe marked Richfield Oil Corp, and the first viewpoint into the canyon of the Dirty Devil. The river winds along far below, coursing across the soft Chinle and Moenkopi Formations. The white rock in the foreground and just below the viewpoint is Navajo Sandstone, and the red cliffs below are Wingate. Directly east is Sams Mesa, with a couple of small buttes rising above its largely featureless expanse. Northeast lies Sams Mesa Box Canyon, and to the southeast upper Happy Canyon extends almost all the way to the Hans Flat Ranger Station. From the end of the improved road a high-clearance track continues to the south. An intermediate viewpoint is 0.4 mile along, and the track terminates at Burr Point itself at 0.7 mile.

Highlights

Here, views open to the south over Bert Mesa to Cedar Point, and the best downstream look at the Dirty Devil occurs. Below, the Navajo forms slickrock cones and domes, and just beyond where the river turns to the south and disappears around a bend is the mouth of Happy Canyon. The return to Highway 95 offers unobstructed views of Mount Ellen in the Henry Mountains almost the entire way.

The Southern Region Below the Henry Mountains

Swett Canyon Hike

Hiking distance as described is approximately 8 miles round trip.

Mount Hillers, looking north from Highway 276

Even with hundreds of canyons to explore in Utah, it can sometimes seem that entire busloads of tourists have been deposited in the one that you are visiting. The narrower the cleft, the more people are likely to be drawn in. Spooky or Little Wild Horse lose much of their considerable charm when they are wall to wall with people. There may come a time when a hiker is more than willing to trade a little of the thrill of a tight slot for the solitude of a lightly visited, but nonetheless handsome canyon that is merely narrow.

Swett Canyon is such a place. Its many attributes include paved road access, which would usually suggest popularity, but its location on Highway 276 is sufficiently off the beaten track to buffer visitation. The presence of several other interesting drainages in the area tends to spread out the few who do come. It's just a guess, but each hiker traveling Highway 276 is probably outnumbered a hundred to one by boaters headed for Lake Powell.

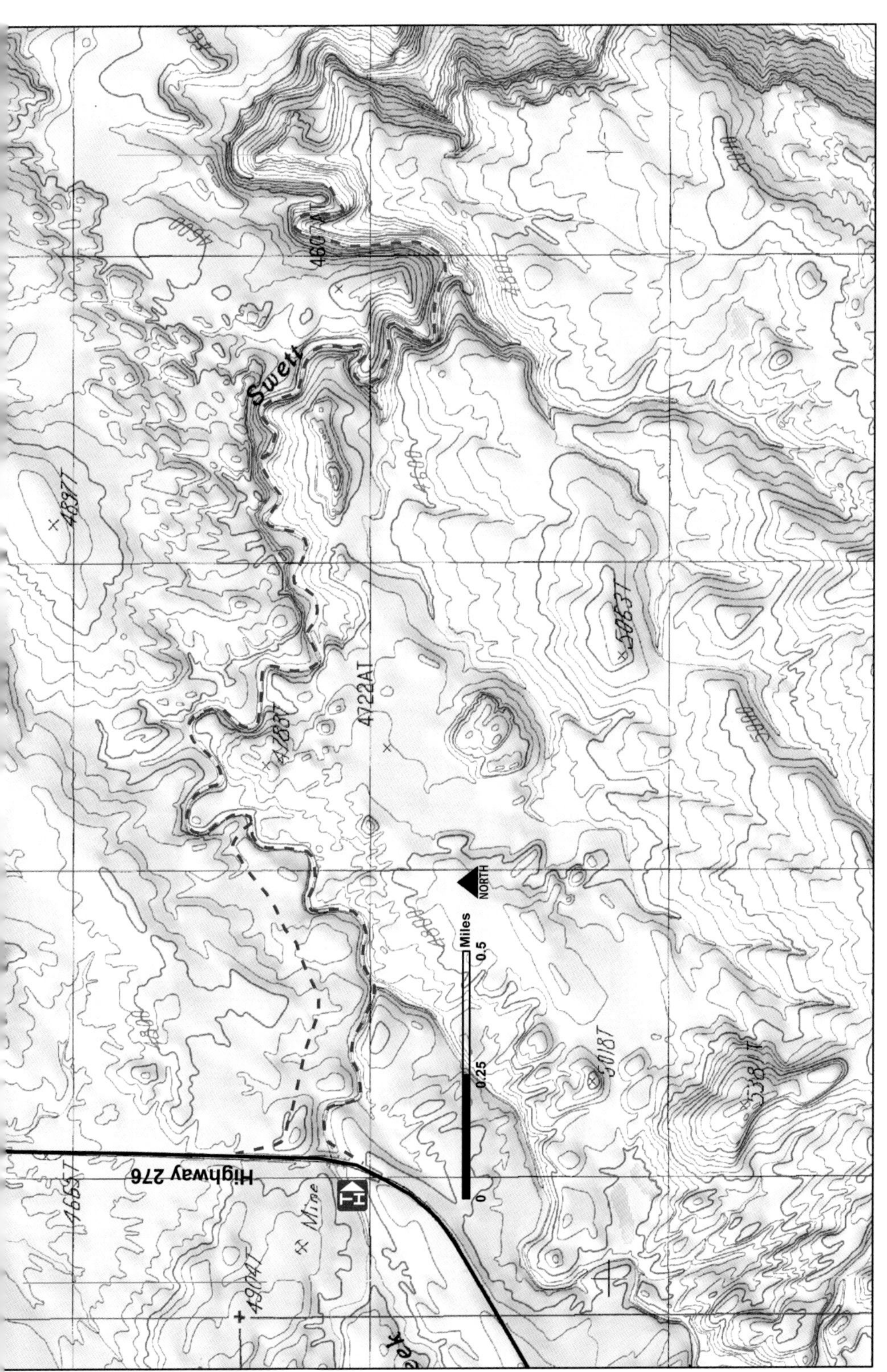

Swett Canyon route

Getting There

To enter Swett, drive south out of Hanksville on Highway 95 for 26 miles, and turn right (southwest) on Highway 276 to Bullfrog and the lake. Since the mileposts on 276 start at this junction, you can do an odometer check by resetting to zero and comparing the reading to the mileposts as you go along. At 13.5 miles from Highway 95, Highway 276 crosses Swett Canyon on a high road fill. The best parking in terms of getting well off the road is on the left (southeast) side, and just beyond (southwest of) the canyon. It takes a long distance for a truck pulling a fifth-wheel trailer pulling a large boat to stop, so exercise extreme caution here. It is best to continue on, find a safe place to turn around and come back to park off the shoulder and outside the reflector posts.

The Hike

From your vehicle, walk southeast across a shallow drainage, turn more easterly (toward the canyon below), work down the blackbrush-covered slope to the bottom, and turn right (south). A large piñon makes a good target for the descent, and a marker for the return. This approach to Swett is less than 200 yards, and once in the canyon, the narrows begin immediately and continue for 4 miles with only one short open stretch. The canyon may be dry for most of the hike, but the drainage does flow for fairly long periods after rain, and since it is quite narrow in places, even modest current means choosing a different hike (two possibilities are described at the end of this section). Obviously, Swett is no place to be if there is any threat of rain since it will flash flood.

In south-central Utah erosion occurs at rates that seem too fast to be measured in geologic time. The reasons are twofold: exceedingly steep stream gradients and relatively soft rock. It also helps that vegetation is minimal, and that a significant proportion of annual precipitation comes during thunderstorms that cause flash floods. The latter are quite capable of sweeping along vast amounts of sand, gravel, and even boulders, all of which act as grit to aid in down-cutting. Interesting recent studies of terraces in Capitol Reef indicate that the Fremont River has been incising its channel at a rate of about a foot per one thousand years. The Fremont has nice hard andesite basalt boulders and cobbles with which to work, while Swett Canyon also has an igneous rock sediment load that is much harder than the sandstones through which it cuts.

Swett Canyon

That rock is the granodiorite porphyry that makes up the high peaks of the Henry Mountains, including Mount Hillers directly to the north. It all makes for an unusual scene: a light gray canyon floor snaking between red sandstone walls. The diorite is also porphyritic, with larger feldspar crystals embedded in the fine-grained rock, along with occasional chunks of a black mineral, probably pyroxene.

The narrows start in the Navajo Sandstone, with walls rising straight up from the canyon floor, which varies from six feet wide to more than fifteen. In Capitol Reef and Zion National Parks the Navajo has undergone leaching that has removed much of the iron originally deposited with the dune sand, and is therefore white. Here, however, and in most of the Glen Canyon area, the Navajo is red, and often difficult to differentiate from the older Wingate Sandstone. There are two clues that help, and they are both exhibited in Swett Canyon. The Navajo has more fully developed crossbeds that are most obvious on weathered surfaces above the inner canyon walls. It also tends to erode into more rounded forms than the Wingate, again especially high above the wash. Both formations are shown to fine advantage in Swett Canyon.

Once in the wash, a couple of minutes of walking leads to an interesting series of bolts that are drilled into the walls on both sides. Walking is easy, with only a couple of small chokestones, but things can change and the passage is sufficiently narrow that a storm could create a more significant obstacle. Just under 0.5 mile from the road a major side canyon (Milk Creek) enters from the right (west), and it is a good idea to make a mental note of this junction for the return hike, since the tributary appears to be the better route when headed up canyon. At 1 mile from the highway there is a slope on the left (north) wall with a good crack with some vegetation in it. This can serve as an emergency exit, and also offers an interesting way to return to your vehicle on the hike back. That route is described five paragraphs below. The narrows continue unabated to the 1.3-mile mark where the canyon walls constrict a little more and deepen for the next 0.3 mile.

Just under 2 miles from the highway the ledgy Kayenta Formation appears ahead and there is a wide open area. A leaning rock tower rests against the cliff on the left (north). The typical plant assemblage of single leaf ash, piñon, juniper, big sage, Mormon tea, and evening primrose is present, the latter sometimes growing right out of the cliffs. For the next 0.5 mile the gradient of the wash increases slightly and becomes a little rockier. A ledge walkway leads around a huge boulder in the stream way, and it is at this point that in mid-April you might see the first of many redbud trees gracing the canyon with a burst of purplish-pink blossoms.

Western redbud, also called California redbud, is unusual in Utah, generally restricted to the very southwestern corner of the state, and the drainages that flow into Lake Powell. The flowers generally cover the entire tree, and bloom before or just as the leaves unfold. The plant is a member of the pea family, and the blossoms are characteristic. Leaves are kidney-shaped. *Cercis occidentalis* (also listed as *Cercis orbiculata*) is likely to be in bloom in mid-April in southern Utah. Hikers familiar with the Grand Canyon may easily recognize western redbud, especially if they have passed through Indian Gardens in the spring. From the first encounter in the Kayenta Formation, there are numerous trees all the way to the turnaround point for the Swett Canyon hike.

Western redbud

A high, undercut cliff is passed at 2.7 miles, followed by a rock jam easily passed on the left (north). From this point the wash cuts through the Wingate Sandstone, which often displays long streaks of desert varnish. The narrows reappear 3 miles from Highway 276 at a sharp right-hand bend where a 100-yard stretch of sand is a nice walking respite. Just beyond, the canyon curves back to the left where there may be a considerable pool. The water can be bypassed on slickrock to the left (northeast) where a short steep down-climb is necessary. At 0.25 mile farther on, the walls soar ahead over a large undercut that has a hanging garden well above the wash.

Swett Canyon slickrock

After a canyon junction ornamented by numerous redbuds at 3.6 miles, water begins to emerge from the canyon floor, creating a series of small pools. One might be large enough to suggest a bypass to the right (south) on slickrock. Another nice stretch of narrows follows, until, at the beginning of a long straight, the far wall dead ahead is more stratified, while a rounded, thirty-foot high wall with nice desert varnish curtains is on the right (east). This makes a good turnaround point unless you are intent to continue on to Lake Powell, a long round-trip day hike.

As noted above, there is an alternative to retracing your steps for the last mile to your car. The landmarks of Mt. Holmes and Mt. Hillers make it possible to do this cross-county walk without a GPS, but it is nonetheless comforting to have one and to have taken a waypoint at your vehicle. The route is circuitous, but overall heads southwest and then west, never far from the rim of the canyon. If you aim to the right of jagged and lower Mt. Holmes and to the left of Mt. Hillers (which dominates the scene to the northwest of Highway 276) there may be a little backtracking and guesswork, but eventually the highway will come into view. At the least you should have the Mt. Holmes quadrangle topographic map. On the map Swett Creek reaches its most northerly point east of Highway 276 in the form of two lobes that look like rabbit ears. The exit point is at the bottom of the west "ear." Swett Canyon will keep you from veering too far south, and trending left of Mt. Hillers will keep you from going too far north.

One mile beyond the opening and leaning rock tower at the midway point of the hike (when heading back) is the slope and crack described previously. The coordinates for this point are 0538184mE, 4188415mN. The ribbing in the sandstone helps in climbing. At the top there are good views down into Swett Canyon to the west (left) by walking out to the rim. Drop quickly down into the red sand and walk 0.25 mile in the easy going wash. When a less developed wash comes in from the left (west), take it and come to a great old juniper 0.4 mile from Swett Canyon. Avoid potholes easily by staying to the left, and at 0.5 mile pass by a pothole pour-off on a moderately steep slickrock slope to its right (north). Above the pour-off bear left (southwest) and then right (northwest) on slickrock, cross a swale and aim for a small, old juniper on a low cliff band ahead. This point is 0537625mE, 4188148mN.

Climb up right behind the tree and then up the ribbed slickrock beyond. At the top of the rise you might be able to spot the highway and your vehicle, still quite a ways to the west. Drop gently down to the top of a modest pour-off, now a little more than 0.8 mile from the canyon exit point. Walk up the slope directly toward Mt. Hillers, and repeat with the next ridge. Stay to the right (northeast) of the highest hill, and traverse slightly uphill, still aiming at Mt. Hillers. When you reach the roadcut for the highway, turn right and drop down to the road in less than 100 yards. A short road walk to the left (south) will lead back to your vehicle.

Optional Hikes

Hiking distance for both walks is variable, perhaps 1 mile round trip.

If it sadly turns out that Swett Creek is flowing too much to walk in the canyon, there are a couple interesting things to do to pass some time. For both, drive back toward Highway 95 (northeast). Go down the hill to the Sweet Canyon crossing, and up the other side to just over the crest of the hill at milepost 13 and find a place to park. To the southeast (right, headed toward Highway 95) of the road an easy slope leads southwest up to undulating high ground above Swett and a good view down into the first narrows.

It is a fine ramble to continue south and southeast well above the canyon, simply picking what seems to be the most interesting route. The farther you stay to the left (east) the more likely it is that you will be on the Carmel Formation, with its more apparent bedding, while closer to Swett the bare Navajo slickrock dominates. Pay attention to what you are doing if you walk more than a short distance, especially if you get far afield from Swett Canyon. This is confusing country, with plenty of steep pitches that can lead to circuitous routes. If you do get lost, heading toward Mount Hillers to the north will at least get you back to the highway, and if you have a GPS you can find a waypoint in the text just above and follow the route described.

This hike is notable for its early floral display. Before most flowers at higher elevations are in bloom, the south-facing terrain near Lake Powell is usually dotted with flowers, often in small areas of sand on the Navajo, or in tiny drainages in the Carmel. Mid to late April is the best bet, though precipitation and temperature may move the peak bloom two weeks in either direction. On May 10, during a very cool spring, a short hike yielded a palette of cryptantha, scorpionweed, evening primrose, sand verbena, Colorado four o'clocks, princes plume, globemallow, pepperbush, blackbrush, cliffrose, greenthread, Utah daisy, paintbrush, and fishhook cactus.

A different kind of hike is possible from the same parking spot by crossing to the northwest side of Highway 276 at the northeast end of the roadcut and walking west (back toward Swett Canyon) up a slope that parallels the highway. At the top of the slope cross a flat area and enter a shallow wash (not Swett Canyon) and turn upstream toward Mt Hillers. Good colorful agate is fairly abundant in the wash, sometimes in fist-size pieces. The remains of a mining operation are along the west side of the wash and the ground is probably still under claim and should be avoided. This short walk takes less than half an hour round trip, not including time to collect agate and enjoy the surroundings.

Swett Canyon

Clay Point Circuit Road Trip and Hike

Driving distance (not including the Big Thompson Mesa Loop) is 63.6 miles.

The baseline for topography covered in this book is the Colorado River, or, in modern times, the current water level in Lake Powell. Full pool for the reservoir is 3,700 feet in elevation, though it has been many years since that has been reached. The country around Lake Powell, by virtue of its relatively low elevation, is generally very warm, with high rates of evaporation. Summer days are often above 100 degrees at Bullfrog, and although that is a popular time for boating, it really isn't the best for land travelers and hikers. April, especially during moist periods, is perhaps optimal, with the twin caveats that it can be windy, and when the gnats and biting flies emerge sometime around the end of the month or in May, it might be good to go elsewhere. Fall, notably October, is also a good choice, largely bug-free, but with possibly cool, and definitely longer nights.

The loop drive described in this section is a combination of good and fair pavement, a short section of gravel, about 10 miles of rough track, and around 23 miles of occasionally graded clay. The high-clearance loop across Big Thompson Mesa past Halls Creek Overlook can be bypassed on the paved Notom-Bullfrog Road. The rest of the circuit can sometimes be driven in passenger cars with normal clearance, but the accurately named Clay Point Road is the crux. If it has been recently graded and remained dry, it can be adequate for cars; if it is rutted after rains, but has dried out, high clearance is probably necessary; and if it is wet it will most definitely be impassable to any and all vehicles. Road condition reports may be available from the BLM office in Hanksville or from the Glen Canyon National Recreation Area (GCNRA) visitor center in Bullfrog.

Because this section generally describes a loop through diverse scenery on dramatically different kinds of road surfaces, it is unlikely that more than a few people will drive the circuit in its entirety in one trip. The most traveled part of the circle by far is the section of Highway 276 from the Starr Springs access road on down to Bullfrog on

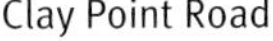
Clay Point Road

Lake Powell. Fewer visitors will drive the Notom-Bullfrog Road (sometimes identified as the Burr Trail on maps) from Highway 276 to the junction with the Clay Point Road and beyond. Note: while the Notom-Bullfrog Road is paved to the Clay Point Road, there is an at-grade crossing of Bullfrog Creek 5.2 miles north of Highway 276. This short section often requires high clearance, sometimes 4WD, and may be impassable during and after storms. A tiny fraction of drivers will attempt the Clay Point Road itself, and even fewer will negotiate the high-clearance (sometimes 4WD) track that traverses Big Thompson Mesa.

Big Thompson Mesa Track Loop

Driving distance is 17.2 miles.

The easiest way to find the Big Thompson Mesa track is to begin at the northern end of the paved part of the Notom-Bullfrog Road that begins at Highway 276 near Bullfrog. From Capitol Reef National Park this point can be accessed by traveling south from Highway 24, 9 miles east of the visitor center, on the Notom-Bullfrog Road. It is paved for the first 10 miles south of the highway, and is then graded dirt and clay to the junction with the Burr Trail, 31 miles from Highway 24.

This point can also be reached by taking the Burr Trail for 36 miles east from its junction with Highway 12 in the town of Boulder. The first 30.5 miles of the Burr Trail are paved. From the intersection of the Notom-Bullfrog Road and the Burr Trail in Capitol Reef National Park, proceed southeast on the graded surface (signed for Bullfrog Basin 33, and Starr Springs 32) for 11 miles, to the junction with Clay Point Road, which continues straight ahead (east), and the beginning of the paved southern portion of the Notom-Bullfrog Road that goes to the right (south). The unpaved roads can be impassable in wet weather. If coming from Highway 276, simply take the Notom-Bullfrog Road north 19.5 miles to the T intersection where the pavement ends.

From the point described above, travel south on the paved Notom-Bullfrog Road for 0.9 mile to a track on the right (west), identified by a small sign for Halls Creek Overlook. The Big Thomson Mesa track condition varies significantly over the year, but high clearance is always necessary to drive to the overlook, and then down and across the mesa. If the road is wet, save the trip for another day. Once on the track, stay left when a secondary track branches off to a popular dispersed camping spot. The road climbs sharply up a small hill, and eventually emerges onto the top of Big Thompson Mesa. At 2.6 miles from the pavement, a signed side track to Halls Creek Overlook leads to the west (right). It is just 0.3 mile to the viewpoint where there is a signboard and picnic table. The last couple of hundred yards of this road are very ledgy, and some may want to walk this distance. The view from the overlook is impressive, down into Utah's "other" Grand Gulch, south to the massive Red Slide, and directly across to the distant Brimhall Bridge, a double arch. The backpack to spectacular Halls Creek Narrows begins here; it is described in detail in *Capitol Reef National Park, The Complete Hiking and Touring Guide.*

After taking in the view, return to the Big Thompson Mesa track and turn right (south). High clearance is usually necessary to negotiate deep ruts. The mesa is an interesting topographical pause between the Waterpocket Fold to the west and the Little Rockies to the east. Because it retains a sandy soil, this broad flat area sustains a denser plant community than most of the surrounding area. Grasses and blackbrush dominate, but in those springs when conditions are good, Big Thompson Mesa turns purple with locoweed in flower. The vast sweep of color, generally at the end of April or beginning of May if it occurs, is truly amazing. Additionally, if the locoweed is good, chances are that many other species will be as well. During an early May visit one year there were fine stands of Utah penstemon, townsendia, cryptantha (cats paws), paintbrush, scorpion-weed, and evening primrose to complement the purple haze.

Two tracks lead west off the primary route and are worth driving out to the edge of Grand Gulch. The first is 2.3 miles south of the Halls Creek Overlook spur, or 4.9 miles

Locoweed

Fishhook cactus

Globemallow

from the Notom-Bullfrog Road. It extends 0.4 mile to the rim of the drainage, which is far below. A good view of the Red Slide is just to the northwest. The slide is a prodigious, and geologically recent, earth movement. Its escarpment is plainly seen in the Wingate Sandstone high on the fold, and the material that flowed down to the east spreads out laterally for more than a mile on the floor of Grand Gulch.

The second track intersects the main track just 0.1 mile south of the one described above. It is then 0.9 mile through the locoweed to the rim. A break in the upper rock strata offers a good view down into Halls Creek, and a 0.25 mile stroll up the rim to the north is worthwhile as well. At the westernmost high point there is a fine view of the Fountain Tanks across the valley. The string of depressions, several of which often have water, extends deep into the Waterpocket Fold.

Return to the main track (reset the odometer to zero), turn right (southeast) and soon switchback twice down a moderately steep dugway. In the flat below, again if it is a good flower year, orange globemallow and white evening primrose are a nice combination. A long climb follows, much of it on the Brushy Basin Member of the Morrison Formation. Deep ruts are often present, a useful reminder of the effect of just a little precipitation on the clay surface. The top of the rise is 2.7 miles from the second track to the rim, and the flower contingent expands to include large amounts of white pepperbush, fragrant sand verbena, and dusty maiden.

The track crosses a sandy wash at 3 miles, and a more difficult one at 3.5 miles. Eastbound travelers may want, or need, four-wheel drive to climb out of this one. The track ends a little less than 1 mile farther on at the Notom-Bullfrog Road. Broad views to the south toward Lake Powell highlight the last part of the track. Turn left (north) on the pavement to go to the Clay Point Road, 7 miles away (described below), or right to Highway 276 and Bullfrog.

Clay Point Road and Starr Springs

Driving distance from the Notom-Bullfrog Road to Highway 276 is 26.6 miles one way.

The Clay Point Road is similar in some respects to the Factory Butte Road: it traverses Mancos Shale–derived clay, and is thus empty, stark, low on vegetation, and, to many, bleak. On the other hand, for those of us whose inner desert rat yearns to be free, the drive may just do the trick. Of course, if the weather is wet, nothing will be set free, most notably any and all vehicles.

We think it is best to travel from west to east on the Clay Point Road, preferably in the late afternoon when the light will be most favorable, especially as you approach Mount Hillers. Follow the directions above for the Big Thompson Mesa track to locate the start of the Clay Point Road at its west end terminus at the Notom-Bullfrog Road. A sign at this junction indicates that Starr Springs is 23 miles to the east.

Set the odometer to zero and head east across a long flat, and then northeast, aiming directly between Mount Pennell and Mount Hillers, as the road descends down to

Bullfrog Creek in 4.2 miles. Just before the road passes through the drainage a track to the right (southwest) leads to an incongruous dwelling, located in, or at least close to, the middle of proverbial nowhere. The Bullfrog Creek crossing may be wet, and is usually easy, but subject to becoming entirely impassable due to rain or snowmelt in the Henry Mountains.

The next drainage is Saleratus Wash, which is also likely to be wet, but the crossing is often easy in good weather. The climb out of the wash on the east side is steep. The true nature of the Clay Point Road now becomes obvious, with barren clay flats and slopes fronting Coal Bed Mesa in the middle ground and the Henrys beyond to the north and east, and steep canyons down to the south and Lake Powell. At the 9.6-mile mark the road passes close to the edge of Four Mile Canyon with its overhanging rock slabs along the rim. The lesser track to Clay Point itself, along with Saleratus Point, goes to the right (south) at 10.4 miles. After this junction, the Clay Point Road swings around to the northeast and trends toward Mount Hillers.

Good views of the upturned sedimentary rocks that flank the mountain begin 3 miles farther on. The igneous intrusions that eventually weathered to form the Henry range were injected into the largely flat-lying beds of the Colorado Plateau about twenty-eight million years ago. In the process, the older strata were pushed up all around the stocks and laccoliths. The southwest slopes of Mount Hillers display this phenomenon to its best advantage, and it will become even more obvious as the road approaches the peak.

A track that accesses Hansen Creek and a shortcut to Shitamaring Creek (also called Shootering Creek) turns off to the right (south) at mile 16.3. Hansen Creek is an old agate collecting area, though we found little of interest here. The side road is in fair condition for the first 0.3 mile until it leaves Hansen Creek and climbs sharply over the Copper Creek benches and then down into the Shitamaring Creek drainage. To explore Hansen Creek, bear right (south) at that 0.3-mile mark and proceed on what is more an ATV track than a road in places. Cross a large wash 1 mile from the Clay Point Road, and search the gully on the right (west) at 1.1 miles for a fairly non-descript, generally white seam agate.

The color in this area during good springs will be provided by the many golden sego (mariposa) lilies that dot the ground. *Calochortus aureus* is a lovely flower with three bright yellow petals, each accented by a maroon slash near the base. As with its far more numerous relative, the white sego lily, the foliage consists of long, very thin basal leaves that appear more like grass until they wither. Golden sego lilies grow in sandy areas at relatively low elevations. They emerge from bulbs during favorably wet springs, and occasionally burst forth in yellow sweeps of color when conditions are perfect. *C. aureus* naturally occurs only in the Four Corners states.

Golden Sego lily

Back on the Clay Point Road, it is 2.5 miles to another junction, this one signed for Shootering Canyon. This route bears generally south and passes through the Ticaboo Mining District, with significant uranium reserves. In the early 1980s a mill was constructed, the town of Ticaboo built, and ore was processed for a few months. The price of uranium was insufficient to justify continuing to mine and mill, and the facility has been mothballed since then. A recent change in ownership and increases in the price of uranium have generated some activity, but the operation remains shuttered at this writing.

The intersection of the Stanton Pass Road on the left (north) and the Clay Point Road is 21.3 miles from the Notom-Bullfrog Road. The Stanton Pass Road (also known as the Hoskinini Freight Road) winds past the southwest face of Mount Hillers, then turns northeast to eventually join the road from Pennellen Pass to Trachyte Creek. This route is described in the Henry Mountains section. To continue on to Starr Springs, stay straight and proceed 1.9 miles to the entrance to the ranch house foundation and campground. The latter has 12 small sites scattered within a gambel oak grove with 30-foot high trees. This unexpected mini-forest is made possible by the water from the spring, and is a fine respite from the heat of summer on the south-facing slope. Depending on conditions, it usually opens in April and doesn't close until November. A very modest fee ($4 at this writing) is charged for camping.

Starr Springs makes an excellent base of operations for exploring the southern part of the Henrys, the Little Rockies, Swett Canyon, and the circuit described here. From the campground a good gravel road descends to Highway 276, 3.4 miles from the entrance. Fine views of Mount Holmes are dead ahead much of the way, with Mount Ellsworth farther to the right (south). To continue on the loop, turn right (southwest) on the highway and drive past Ticaboo and boat storage facilities to a point just short of milepost 35.

Mount Hillers

Notom-Bullfrog Road from Highway 276 to Clay Point Road

Driving distance from Highway 276 to the Clay Point Road is 19.3 miles one way.

The Notom-Bullfrog Road (also called the Burr Trail) branches off Highway 276 just under 35 miles from Highway 95, and 3.1 miles north of the Glen Canyon National

Recreation Area (GCNRA) entrance station. Turn west (right when headed south) and zero the odometer. The chip-sealed road winds across eroded Entrada Sandstone, and there are a few places where sand accumulates on the pavement during windy periods. There are side roads to the left (southwest) that lead to camping areas on Lake Powell's Bullfrog Bay, but they are only open when the lake is at or near capacity. At 4.8 miles the modest parking area for the Pedestal Alley Trail is on the left (south). The hike is described below.

Pedestal Alley Trail Hike

Distance: 3 miles round trip

Pedestal Alley Trail

In temperate weather the lightly traveled Pedestal Alley Trail in Glen Canyon National Recreation Area is a pleasant and very easy walk, and during periods of peak flower blooms, it can border on spectacular as well. From the parking area, the trailhead is on the other side of the road, and back to the east (toward Highway 276) about 100 yards, where there is a sign.

Pedestal Alley is a desert hike of 3 miles round trip. It is generally flat and easy to walk, aside from some soft sand. There are numbered flexible signposts along the way that are helpful in staying on track since a windstorm can obliterate the route at any time. While the hoodoos for which the trail is named are modestly interesting, especially those at the end, the scenery along the way is generally not the kind that inspires awe.

When conditions are right, however, the variety of forbs in bloom can be reason enough to hike here. On average, the height of color might be in late April, though it could be as late as early May. Keep in mind that the flower show in desert regions can vary from non-existent one year to beautiful the next, and that the timing of good years can also vary, sometimes by several weeks. Pedestal Alley is more notable for variety than swaths of solid color, making it a fine place to perhaps see and learn a new plant or two.

Prickly pear cactus

From the sign, the trail trends in a northerly direction, staying on the east (right) edge of a small gully cut into the sand. The path may be fairly easy to follow at first, but if not, aim for a signpost with the number 2 on it, about 300 yards from the road. After this point stay to the right of the wash, following the most conspicuous and direct use trails to another post (#3) at the 0.5-mile mark. In this stretch there are several large purple sage shrubs that can be covered with lavender and white flowers arranged along the upper branches. *Poliomintha incana* also occurs near the end of the trail in similar sandy habitat. The plants along the trail are quite large, more than three feet high and wide. Scattered individual plants of spectacle pod (*Dithyrea wislizenii*), a member of the mustard family, also dot the area with their four-petaled white blooms.

Spectacle pod

At 0.1 mile beyond the #3 post, the route crosses the wash and is marked with obvious cairns. Head for a narrow cut through the Entrada Sandstone walls, and follow the cairns through it and down the other side, bending to the left (west). Interesting weathering of the rock is exposed on a small block on the left (south) side of the trail. A few very short hoodoos dot the landscape as the path heads slightly downhill on hard-packed sand. After the #4 sign, leave the wash on the right (continue west), eventually curving around back to the north. At the 1.1-mile mark, near sign #6, there is a pillar off to the west. Three more signs follow in quick succession, and then the trail becomes faint. A good target from this point is to locate the next sign (#7) on high ground ahead, with one tall pillar to its right (east). The route turns more easterly, drops down to a wash, and then rises to end at sign #8 on a small pass that leads into a broad flat area.

Hopi blanketflower

The best hoodoos and pillars are visible ahead and to the

Sand lily

right (southeast) from this point, and it is an easy and short walk to them. The tallest are reasonably impressive amid the many shorter ones and their fallen comrades. The basin beyond, and the last 0.25 mile of the trail proved to have the best flower variety during our visit. The prickly pear cacti were numerous enough and in full bloom to create bright pink pools of color, and there were several competing eye-catching tufts of Hopi blanketflower as well. *Gaillardias* are popular in gardens, but it is nice to see them in their natural habitat. The bright yellow ray flowers contrast with disk flowers that are purple, making for an especially pleasing composite.

Other species to look for include Kanab prairie clover (*Dalea flavescens*), sand lily (*Eremocrinum albomarginatum*), and telegraph flower (*Hymenopappus filifolius*). Kanab prairie clover presents its rocket-like flower spikes at the end of tall stems more than a foot tall. Leaves are finely divided with linear lobes that do not resemble typical lawn clovers. Sand lilies also develop on spikes, with the white blooms irregularly scattered along the flower stalk. The petals may have green highlights, and the leaves are very thin and grass-like. This particular sand lily is found only on the Colorado Plateau. Telegraph flowers are small, bright yellow collections of disk flowers only a quarter inch or so across, but atop plants up to a couple of feet tall. Leaves are highly dissected, with basal leaves larger than stem leaves. Many other more common flowers can be seen along the Pedestal Alley Trail as well. Allow about two hours for a leisurely hike.

Notom-Bullfrog Road—Continued

From the parking area to the Bullfrog Creek crossing is just another 0.3 mile. This very short, unpaved section can be passable to almost all passenger vehicles to high-clearance units, or to none at all depending on whether the creek is flowing or has recently had water. Coming from the south the short distance back to Highway 276 renders the uncertainty a minor nuisance, but from the north it can be a major inconvenience. Get good information before setting out from Capitol Reef or Boulder.

After the crossing, the road approaches a high cliff on the left (west) with an excellent exposure of three of the San Rafael Group formations. The Entrada Sandstone, honey-combed with solution cavities, is at the base of the cliff; small dunes often lap up against it. The gray layer is the Curtis Formation, a marine unit that is more resistant than the Entrada. The upper bands are a fine example of the Summerville Formation, deposited when tectonic forces elevated land to the west. The Notom-Bullfrog Road switchbacks up to the top, exits the GCNRA at mile 7.7, and continues to climb up Middle Point.

At 9.9 miles there is a good view back to the south that includes Lake Powell and Bullfrog. The track from Big Thompson Mesa, described at the start of this section, connects with the pavement at mile 12.3 (it is on the left, or west, side of the road). A couple miles later, Clay Canyon parallels the road on the right (east); it is an impressive dissection. The pavement ends at the T intersection with the Clay Point Road, 19.3 miles from Highway 276. A left (west) turn leads to Boulder via the Burr Trail, or Capitol Reef on the Notom-Bullfrog Road.

Henry Mountains

Aspen near Lonesome Beaver Campground

Despite the fact that the Henrys are visible from a great distance in all directions, they are not exactly overrun by visitors. One reason is simple: the network of roads that provides access to the high country is not suitable for passenger cars, and during and after significant precipitation events every approach road can become impassible to all vehicles. Look at most popular road atlases and there is no welcoming green shading that signifies national forest land; the Henrys are managed by the Bureau of Land Management, which many associate with sagebrush and cattle, if not outright desert. Without a signature scenic highlight, tumbling mountain stream, or spectacular system of hiking trails, and thus no real glamour, the range serves most travelers by providing a nice western backdrop as they drive along Highway 95 between Hanksville and Lake Powell.

The lack of glamour aside, the Henrys have always called to us. Like the sky island mountains of southern Arizona, the immense difference in flora, fauna, and climate between, say, Mount Ellen and the Dirty Devil canyon just 20 air miles away is remarkable. At the higher elevations aspen provide good fall color, and often fringe huge meadows. The feeling on the summit of Mount Ellen is truly top of the world, with vast vistas in every direction. A surprising number of interesting old structures are dotted around the fringes of the Henrys, along with vestiges of a modest mining industry. The cool and quiet of the high country are siren songs during the hot summer.

There is one time when the Henrys aren't quite so quiet. That is during the various hunting seasons when a few lucky hunters have drawn tags for the trophy mule deer or bison that live in the range. The Utah Division of Wildlife Resources manages both deer and bison hunting in the Henrys to produce huge bucks and to maintain the free-ranging bison herd population at a level that is sustainable. Generally, the bison seasons begin around the beginning of November and extend well into December, times when casual visitation to the mountains is minimal. The general deer season is often in late October, and in 2012 the limited entry hunt in the Henrys was during the same time. A shorter season to hunt smaller bucks in the unit follows the general hunt.

Archery and muzzleloader seasons precede the general hunt, and it is a good idea to wear blaze orange if you are going to hike anytime after mid-August. Check with the DWR for specific dates if you plan to visit the Henrys in the fall and hunting is a concern. After the aspen drop their leaves, usually in early October, the mountains are less scenic, and temperatures down in redrock country are more amenable anyway, so we tend to spend our Octobers there.

Bison in the Henrys

The bison herd in the Henry Mountains is wild and somewhat elusive. Sightings are usually a surprise, and fleeting. Spread out over some two million acres, it stands to reason that seeing any of the four hundred or so free ranging bison would be unusual. Nonetheless, especially around Pennellen Pass, it is possible, and those sightings mean more to us than the traffic jam–inducing encounters in Yellowstone National Park or Custer State Park.

Bison were brought to the area in 1941 from Yellowstone, and have maintained a genetically pure status in the intervening years (most herds in North America have some level of cattle genes). Although they were first located in the austere Dirty Devil River region, they quickly moved to the flanks of the mountains, and then onto higher ground in the 1960s. The Henrys are well suited to bison, with extensive grasslands interspersed with forested areas, and very short migrations necessary during winter—they simply move to lower elevations.

North American bison are divided into two subspecies, the larger wood bison (*Bison bison athabascae*) in Canada, and the plains bison (*Bison bison bison*) in the United States. Together, they are the largest land animals on the continent, with bulls often weighing in at over a ton. Although bison were nearly extirpated in North America during the twentieth century, they once ranged from the Rockies almost to the Atlantic Ocean. Their diet consists mostly of grasses and sedges, with the latter more prominent for bison living in mountainous terrain. In the wild, a lifespan of some fifteen years is typical. Calves are born after a gestation period of just over nine months, and the population rebound of the plains bison in the last several decades indicates the species can do well if left alone (or, more likely, if given enough protected territory).

In the Henrys, bison are managed to keep the herd size in line with available forage, not only enough to maintain the bison herd, but also to sustain the trophy mule deer that inhabit the range. The primary method of control is hunting. Licenses are awarded through a lottery, and there are so many applicants that a hunter may draw a license only once in a lifetime. The state has set a target herd of 325 animals, and adjusts the number of tags that are available each year. A newer control tool has been the capture and relocation of bison to the Book Cliffs area north of Green River, Utah, where a new herd is being established.

Bison south of Mount Ellen

Travel in the Henrys is rewarding, but also requires good preparation and equipment, along with a level of comfort in a very isolated place. In the best of times, the roads are rough and suitable only for high-clearance vehicles, and grades are so steep that four-wheel drive reduces tire spinning and bouncing. In anything less than the best of times things can get dicey in a hurry. Rain or snow can make every approach road impassible, and in a thunderstorm this can happen in a matter of minutes. When the washes flow anywhere on the flanks of the mountains, gullies can be cut that also stop travel. Some roads are graded across diorite (see below), which is sharp and hard on tires. It is also possible to get lost, although good maps and a general sense of how the land lies should reduce this possibility. The kicker is that if something does go wrong, the chances of another vehicle happening by are slim. We have spent many days in the Henrys and, except during or just before hunting season, on perhaps half of them have not seen anyone else. Prior to embarking on even the simplest trip into or across the Henrys, get up-to-date information on road conditions from the BLM office in Hanksville (a half mile south of Highway 24 on 100 West) or call 435-542-3461.

Before setting out, take the time to get oriented to the region. The Henrys are circled by Highways 24, 95, and 276, and, on the west, by the largely graded-dirt Notom-Bullfrog Road. The mountain range consists of four primary summits. They are, from north to south, Mount Ellen, the highpoint, south Mount Ellen, Mount Pennell, and Mt. Hillers. (The so-called Little Rockies to the south of Highway 276 are much lower.) The Ellens and Pennell are well above 11,000 feet in elevation, and Mt. Hillers a little less. There are passes with roads between each pair of neighboring peaks. Campgrounds at Lonesome Beaver, McMillan Springs, and Starr Springs all make good base camps for extended visits to the Henrys.

The following descriptions are arranged to cover the majority of the roads in the Henrys that are more than Jeep trails. The three routes each cross the mountains, and together cover the five primary access points. The Sandy Ranch–Little Egypt and Sandy Ranch–Trachyte Creek sections are west to east routes, while Hanksville–Starr Springs is north to south. Any number of combinations is possible, and these alternatives, as well as several cut-offs, are cross-referenced in the text. Good maps are critical. The Hanksville BLM office has a one-sheet map that is helpful, and we have found the *Benchmark Utah Road and Recreation Atlas* to be reasonably reliable.

Mount Ellen and Mount Ellen Peak

Geology

In 1876, eminent American geologist Grove Karl Gilbert looked to the east from the Waterpocket Fold and saw before him "… a vast dissection that laid bare the very anatomy of the earth." Here, the tributaries to the Colorado River have indeed cut through the many layers of sedimentary rock that characterize the Colorado Plateau, but the Henry Mountains were not so much cut by those waters as revealed by them. The durable intrusive igneous rocks that core the Henrys are entirely different than the strata on their flanks. The result is a fine freestanding range that towers a mile and a half above the surrounding country.

The Henry Mountains are quite different than the other highlands covered in this book. Their uniqueness begins with the geology. The mountains to the west of Capitol Reef are all covered by sheets of andesitic tuffs, resulting in broad plateau-like summits. The Henrys also are of igneous origin, but in their case the molten material was injected into the overlying sedimentary rocks rather than extruded onto the surface. The fine-grained granitic rock that also contains larger crystals is a granodiorite porphyry, and the lenticular form that it sometimes takes is called a laccolith. In fact, this term was coined by G. K. Gilbert during his work in this area in the 1870s. More recent work suggests that the Henrys were more likely formed by stocks (intrusive bodies that extend downward without narrowing to a feeder column) and other intrusive forms. Similar features form the nearby La Sals, Abajos, and Navajo Mountain.

As the magma was forced into the surrounding rocks, the flat-lying strata were tipped upward, so that a kind of dome was created. Over roughly the last 28 million years erosion has stripped off the soft formations around the igneous cores, leaving a sharply peaked range surrounded by steeply tilted sedimentary beds. While it is likely that the intrusions were emplaced over a relatively short time, dating of the event is from 31 ma to 23 ma, so the 28 ma figure is simply shorthand for this activity. It is very interesting that not only are the LaSals, Abajos, and Navajo Mountain about the same age, but the explosive igneous rocks in the San Juan Mountains to the east of the Colorado Plateau and the ashflow tuffs that form the plateau mountains on the west side are also of similar age. This extent of volcanism is rare deep within the margins of continents and probably reflects an unusually low angle subduction of the Farallon Plate and subsequent rise of magma along with melting of the bottom of the crust. Perhaps the relative thickness and durability of the Colorado Plateau prevented the magma from surfacing in the middle of the province, while faulting permitted explosive eruptions on its edges.

An additional important geological feature of the Henrys is that the diorite is highly mineralized, as are some of the beds on its flanks. This has resulted in a rich human history in the range, and contributed significantly to the network of roads that covers the mountains like a spiderweb.

Sandy Ranch to Little Egypt Road Trip

Distance: 43.7 miles

This trip is the shortest of the three, but is very interesting, beautiful, and geologically diverse. The access point, Sandy Ranch Junction, is 13.5 miles south of Highway 24 on the Notom-Bullfrog Road. The latter intersects with Highway 24 at the east boundary of Capitol Reef National Park, which in turn is about 9 miles east of the visitor center. The first 10 miles of the Notom-Bullfrog Road are paved, and then the surface is good gravel. In the event that this portion is wet and your tires are kicking up a constant chatter of small stones, turn around and try again after things dry out. The chances are that the approach road to the Henrys will be much worse, and likely impassable.

BLM sign near Sandy Ranch

Approaching Sandy Ranch Junction from the north a BLM sign indicates the distances to important destinations in the Henrys. They are Sweetwater Junction 9, Birch Spring 17, McMillan Spring 19, and the Horn 23. Just beyond, at the turn-off, is a small Sandy Ranch Junction sign. Turn left (east), zero the odometer, and leave the traffic behind (that is, if you have met a single vehicle on the Notom-Bullfrog Road). The lush riparian environment along Oak Creek quickly passes by on the right (south), and the route begins slicing across Upper Jurassic sedimentary rocks on a speedy journey to Cretaceous strata. After 0.8 mile stay left (east) when a track goes off to the right. When the road leaves the alluvium of the Oak Creek valley it very briefly crosses a bit of brown Entrada Sandstone, then as it tops a small rise just before dropping to cross Sandy Creek, traverses the Curtis Formation.

As the road climbs the east bank of the wash through a dense stand of greasewood at 1.4 miles, it passes through the Summerville Formation and the Salt Wash and Brushy Basin Members of the Morrison Formation in rapid succession. In less than 0.4 mile, the soft gray Brushy Basin is capped by a thin layer of the Dakota Sandstone. The Dakota is the basal unit of the Cretaceous in this area, and is a near-shore deposit. It often contains abundant oysters, but they appear to be absent in the area where the road passes through and then swings south to parallel the exposure of the Dakota.

The southerly trend continues for a couple of miles along Blind Trail Wash to the left (east). The gray slopes of the basal member of the vast Mancos Shale are on the far side of the wash. This is the Tununk Shale, which is protected by the Ferron Sandstone. The track crosses the wash and turns to the east, quickly passing through these two units and then crossing a brief flat on the next Mancos member, the Blue Gate Shale. At 5 miles the road enters the mouth of a pretty little canyon, crosses a cattleguard at 5.3, and then winds up through the next resistant layer, the Muley Canyon Sandstone. A highpoint at 7.3 miles is a good viewpoint to gaze at the bulk of Mount Ellen and consider the road building necessary to climb it. In the foreground is the drainage of Sweetwater Creek and a denser juniper woodland.

Immediately after the Sweetwater crossing at 9.3 miles is a junction. Facing eastbound drivers is a sign with left arrows for Stevens Mesa Junction 3, Birch Spring 8, McMillan Spring 10, and Bull Creek Pass 15. There is also an information board with a map of the entire Henry Mountains region. To find out where the right fork goes, turn around and on the southwest side of the intersection is another sign for travelers coming the other way. It shows the distances to Tarantula Mesa and the Horn to the left, and those to Sandy Ranch and Highway U-24 to the right. The arrangement of the signs reflects that this junction is the westernmost point of the Bull Creek Pass Scenic Backway, which begins at Highway 95 near Little Egypt and terminates at Trachyte Creek on Highway 276. This is also where the roads diverge for the Sandy Ranch–Little Egypt and Sandy Ranch–Trachyte Creek routes. For the latter see the next section, but for now, bear left (northeast) for Bull Creek Pass.

After a little more than another mile the road climbs up onto a broad mesa covered with grasses and sage. Continue straight ahead when a track leads to dead-end roads to Cedar Creek Bench and Stevens Mesa (signed) at 12.0 miles. The next junction is at 13.4, and the sign is for westbounders: left to King Ranch and right to Sandy Ranch and Highway U-24. Go straight ahead here and cross a cattleguard at 14.2 miles and signed South Creek at 15.3. Another intersection comes up at 16.7 miles. The sign introduces a new destination, Nasty Flat, which is 5 miles to the left, while Bull Creek Pass 8, and another new destination, Copper Creek Ridge 13, both also to the left. Birch Spring 1, and the Horn 9 are to the right. Stay to the left (northeast) and begin climbing in earnest.

Piñons begin to take over from the junipers as elevation increases, and at the 18.7-mile mark the first ponderosa pines appear. At 0.4 mile farther on are two signs, one pointing left to Dugout Creek and Cedar Creek, and one to the right to Willow Spring 0.4, Nasty Flat 3.8, and Bull Creek Pass 6.8. Interestingly, with the increased precision of mileages to the tenth, accuracy decreases: it is only 5.2 miles to the pass. It is only after a left turn at the pair of signs that it is clear that they are also at the entrance of the McMillan Springs Campground. Ten campsites are arranged in a large circle in the pines. They are numbered in a counterclockwise direction. Sites 7 and 8 are very nice. Camping is $4 per night; if the water is on, a sign indicates that it is unsafe for drinking, so bring plenty of your own. One pit toilet near sites 7 and 8 serves the campground. This is a great place for stargazing and watching the blinking lights of jets containing more people in each one than there are in a 25-mile radius of McMillan Springs.

To continue up to Mount Ellen, leave the campground and turn left (east) back onto the road from Sandy Ranch. The fenced Willow Spring supports heavy vegetation, and a private cabin is nearby. At 21.2 miles, or a couple of miles beyond the campground, the first aspen appear after a large meadow. The broad west-facing slopes of Mount Ellen are a beautiful mix of aspen and sweeps of open grassland, and nearer the summits, subalpine forests. Views to the west over the Waterpocket Fold of Capitol Reef and beyond to the high plateaus are quite spectacular.

The next junction is at Nasty Flat, 21.8 miles from the Notom-Bullfrog Road. A post provides directions for travelers on the Barton's Peak Loop, partially an ATV trail, but there is no standard road sign. The road to the right (east) is marked as number 14400, and is described in the Hanksville–Starr Springs section. Continue straight ahead at this intersection. At 0.3 mile farther on is another unmarked junction, where route 14670 goes to the left (northeast), and a sign proclaims the main road as narrow with no turnouts. Again, stay on the main track, bearing a little to the right (east). In another 0.5 mile the first subalpine forest begins, with Engelmann spruce and subalpine fir dominant, and aspen dotted among them. The road is cut into the side of the mountain, becoming what is called a shelf road. While it is narrow, there are many places where two vehicles could pass, in the unlikely event that such a thing would occur. The forest is not continuous, so the views, now largely to the northwest, continue.

Bull Creek Pass is 5.2 miles from McMillan Springs and 24.3 miles from Sandy Ranch Junction. A fenced parking area with room for several vehicles is on the left (north). This is the trailhead for the trail to the summit of Mount Ellen, the highpoint of the Henrys, and the ramble up to south Mount Ellen. The hike to the summit is described at the end of this chapter. Views from the pass now expand, especially to the north and northeast. The bulk of Bull Mountain dominates the near scene to the northeast, with the vista beyond extending well into the San Rafael Swell. To the east the relatively flat plain leads to the canyon of the Dirty Devil River fronting the mesas and ridges that are the western edge of the Maze section of Canyonlands National Park. On clear days, the La Sal Mountains east of Moab are easily visible in afternoon light.

Beyond the pass, the road stays high, passing through lovely copses of subalpine forest interspersed with meadows. When the descent to Wickiup Pass begins in earnest the road enters areas of standing dead evergreens, burned in the Lonesome Beaver Fire in 2003. This is a fine example of forest succession at the very beginning of a new cycle. Aspen almost always reproduce clonally, as they are doing in this location in great abundance. In the long term, however, the evergreens will win the succession battle until they are culled by fire, insect infestation, or avalanches. When that happens, the aspen roots in the area are signaled to sprout, which they do with great energy. On the east and northeast sides of Bull Creek Pass, the 10-foot high aspen stems are in vigorous competition with each other for light and nutrients. After another two or three decades, the individual trees will have grown to the point where they provide enough shade for the spruce seedlings that will eventually take over. Given enough time without major disturbances, the spruce and fir will eventually squeeze the aspen out and become the climax forest.

East of Wickiup Pass

In addition to the spruce and fir, there are scattered occurrences of limber pine, a five-needled white pine. These trees are usually in rough, open areas such as the flat at the 25.8-mile mark, which people have used as a camping spot. *Pinus flexilus* lives up to its name, with branches so flexible that they can be tied in knots. When limber pine are solitary and not in a dense forest, they can look very much like piñon from a distance, as they can be as wide as they are tall. Some North American limber pine stands are severely threatened by white pine blister rust, which is especially virulent in whitebark pines, but this disease does not yet seem to have reached the Henrys.

The road continues to wind down, sometimes steeply, to Wickiup Pass where there is a three-way junction. The road to the left, which trends to the north, leads to Hanksville and is described in the Hanksville–Starr Springs section. There is no sign for travelers headed north, but there are signs with many destinations for those going west or east and south. The road to Little Egypt bears to the right (southeast) and is signed for Granite Creek 0.6, Crescent Creek 3.3, and several other points south, but not east.

As the road approaches the Granite Creek drainage there are fine views ahead, especially in the fall. A small sign identifies the creek, and 0.3 mile beyond it the track crosses a cattleguard after a long uphill stretch. The diorite is nicely exposed around mile 29.3, including in the roadbed where it is a bit of a hazard for tires in poor condition. The shelf road descends directly into the Crescent Creek drainage, reached at 30.3 miles. There is a four-way junction here, and the route to Little Egypt is a very sharp left (east) turn that will require backing up for almost all vehicles. The sign at this intersection is for travelers going in the opposite direction, and it gives distances to Wickiup Pass 3, Sawmill Basin 6, and Hanksville 26.

Initially the drive down Crescent Creek is a good illustration of the effect of slope aspect on vegetation. To the left, the south-facing hillside supports a typical piñon-juniper woodland, but the canyon bottom and north-facing slope to the right has a mix of aspen and Douglas fir that would normally have to be either at higher elevation or in a wetter environment. The road bears left (east) at the junction with a track to the right (south) that is numbered 14156, and a short distance beyond at mile 31.5 is the gate to an active mining operation. The vegetation gets more sparse as the road continues to descend. A cattleguard is at 33.0, and the Eagle Bend FAA Airstrip, complete with windsocks, is 1 mile farther on. In another mile, the Entrada Sandstone is exposed to the south (right), with the Summerville Formation topped by a cliff of the Salt Wash Member of the Morrison Formation ahead.

A picturesque log cabin on the bank of Crescent Creek is on the right (east at this point) at mile 35.7, and after two creek crossings, a well-preserved stone cabin is on the

Stone cabin near Crescent Creek

left (north) in another 0.7 mile. The rock here is the soft Brushy Basin Member of the Morrison, deposited in very low relief lakes and swamps which produce a chemically reducing environment in which the iron minerals that form tend to have a greenish-gray hue. This area was one of several where placer mining for gold from the Bromide Basin has occurred in the past.

The route leaves the Crescent Creek drainage after the second cabin and bends to the south. Mount Hillers is straight ahead, with Mount Pennell to its right. At 38.5 miles from the Notom-Bullfrog Road several adits, or mine tunnels, can be seen in the Salt Wash to the right (southwest). Although not much uranium ore was taken from this area, it wasn't for lack of trying; there are many such short tunnels and exploration holes impaling the Salt Wash where it outcrops around the Henrys. Only to the southwest of Mount Hillers has there been significant investment in uranium, and even there, the future of the venture is unclear.

A sign facing those driving west is at 39.2 miles, and an information board is 0.6 mile beyond on the right (south). The map identifies the four wilderness study areas in the Henry Mountains and is helpful in giving a general idea of the roads and terrain. At 200 yards farther on is a Y junction with a sign indicating that Highway U-95 is 3 miles to the left (north), or 4 miles to the right (south). Little Egypt is 2.4 miles to the left where an easily missed sign on the left (west) marks the standard parking place. See the section on the Little Egypt Geological Area for details on this interesting erosional remnant. The smooth and quiet macadam of Highway 95 is a little less than 1.5 miles away, completing this 43.7-mile transect of the Henrys.

Little Egypt with snow covered Mount Hillers

Sandy Ranch to Trachyte Creek Road Trip

Driving distance from the Notom-Bullfrog Road to Highway 276 is 45.1 miles one way.

This route also begins at Sandy Ranch, and diverges from the one described above at Sweetwater Junction. It then meanders through lower elevations to upper Bullfrog Creek before climbing steeply to Pennellen Pass, and traversing around the Horn. Along the north and then east flanks of Mount Pennell the route goes up and down long grades to the Straight Creek Junction before the long descent over the Coyote Benches down to the creek and on to Highway 276 a little less than 5 miles south of Highway 95. There are many very rocky stretches, and on the west side numerous wash crossings. High clearance is required, as it is everywhere in the Henrys, and four-wheel drive helps reduce chatter on the steep climbs.

Mancos Shale east of Sandy Ranch

Sandy Creek crossing

It bears repeating that wet weather stops travel on the lower reaches of the mountains. We crossed Sandy Creek two weeks apart one October. The first time the wash was well graded and there was just a trickle of water. The second time the banks had been severely cut, the flow was high, and it was only because someone had done considerable work that we were able to cross in 4WD. Be prepared, and be prepared to turn around if conditions warrant.

To begin this trip, follow the description above in the Sandy Ranch to Little Egypt section to Sweetwater Junction, a distance of 9.3 miles. The relevant sign will be on your right (southwest), facing east, and gives distances to Tarantula Mesa 11 and the Horn 14, both in the direction you will be driving, and Sandy Ranch 12 and Highway U-24 26, both back the way you came. If you are traveling westbound, the latter two distances are about 3 miles too long. The sign facing west only gives destinations to the left, including McMillan Spring and Bull Creek Pass. This sounds more complicated than it is. Simply stay to the right and zero the odometer. If there are recent tracks, most will probably go left, an indication that the route you are embarking upon is even less traveled than the road over Bull Creek Pass.

The general direction of travel to the Horn will be to the southeast, but the route has many twists and turns. The crossing of the South Creek wash in 0.6 mile can be either very rocky or muddy after recent precipitation. The route curves to the right (south) at mile 1 where there is a junction with road 14210, which goes straight ahead. The country here along South Creek is typical Mancos Shale derived soil that supports a limited vegetative cover dominated by Utah junipers and smaller shrubs. In the fall the slightly orange-tinted yellow of Utah serviceberry brightens the otherwise somewhat drab vistas. To the southwest a jagged ridge provides interest as well. Another junction, this time with road 14200 that connects with the Bull Creek Pass route, occurs at 3.7 miles. Again, stay to the right (south), leaving the South Creek drainage, but remaining in similar terrain.

The Horn

The Henrys are largely public land, mostly BLM with many square-mile sections of Utah state land scattered about. There are a few ranches and several mining claims, however, and it is important to respect these private lands. Some are well marked, and others, such as the ground near the intersection with road 14200, are not. At 5.5 miles a sign indicating that hunting is by written permission only marks one such piece of private property.

Diorite from the peaks begins to show up in abundance in the road and creekbeds at mile 6.5. Just beyond, on the left (north) is a group of four hoodoos fronting an impressive cliff of banded Mancos sediments that are flat lying. Less than 1 mile farther on, at 7.4, is a slope that is steeply dipping to the west and covered with interesting and brightly colored iron-stained lumps and bumps. The Mancos Shale units (and the underlying older rocks as well) on the west side of the mountains have been elevated and tilted by the intrusive igneous rocks that core the peaks.

The road passes through the resistant, iron-rich layer at Stevens Narrows. When road 14240 bears off to the right (west) for Tarantula Mesa at 10.9 miles, continue straight ahead. Minor washouts in the roadbed may reveal black pipes formerly used by ranchers to move water to cattle. The next intersection is not far at the 11.7-mile mark. It is signed for Airplane Springs 3, and Horn Mountain 4, both straight ahead, and Cave Flat 6 to the right on road 14250. The latter is clearly a lesser track, and bears only slightly to the right in a tight Y junction. Stay left, drop quickly into the Bullfrog Creek drainage, and begin the steep to very steep climb up to Airplane Spring. This pitch is also very rocky in several places.

Airplane Spring memorial

The 1961 Airplane Spring Seeding Demonstration Plot at mile 14.4 is marked by a sign; the experiment must have worked, since at the time of our visit several cows were grazing inside the fence. Just beyond and off to the left (north) is a plaque surrounded by a metal enclosure under an old ponderosa pine tree. It is a memorial to two airmen, Colonel Lorin Lavar Johnson and Staff Sergeant Billy J Nash, who were killed in a military aircraft crash nearby in 1950. Airplane Spring is just to the east. A fence surrounds the large seep, which supports a thick stand of wild rose.

At mile 15.2 road 14500 bears to the right and winds up to the top of the Horn, while the main road goes straight. Views open back to the west over Mancos Shale beds in the foreground, the Waterpocket Fold of Capitol Reef National Park, and up to Boulder Mountain farther to the west. Pennellen Pass is reached 15.6 miles from Sweetwater Creek. The two signs here are positioned for drivers coming from the north (Mount Ellen), and each lists seven destinations. To the east the distances for places on the route described here, Dark Canyon 3.3, Gibbon Springs 5.0, Straight Creek Junction 8.5, and Trachyte Ranch 18.0, are right on the money. The distances to the west, such as Airplane Spring, are largely accurate as well. There is only a small Pennellen Pass sign for those heading north toward Mount Ellen.

Continue straight at this three-way intersection. Thriving piñon-juniper forest continues on the left side for a short distance, and then the road fully enters the massive burn area of the Bulldog Fire of 2003. In spite of the passage of more than a decade, the skeletons of thousands of trees remain standing with most branches, even small ones, still intact. This area is considerably lower than that burned by the Lonesome Beaver Fire of the same year on the northeast slopes of Mount Ellen, and there was no aspen presence at the time of the fire. Thus, it is left to the Gambel oaks to begin the next succession pattern, and they are indeed busy at the task. In many places, however, it is predominantly grasses that are thriving.

In addition to the abundant browse for ruminants, the burn scar also opens views up to the Horn and Mount Pennell, over to Mount Ellen, and out over the Dirty Devil River to the Block and Gunsight Butte. The Horn protrudes to the north from the main body of Mount Pennell and has high cliffs to the north and especially to the east. The road contours along and then away from the Horn, and as it approaches Dark Canyon, Mount Pennell rises up directly ahead. A small aspen clone has a toehold in the bottom of the drainage just above the road crossing. A long climb leads in 1.5 miles to fenced

Gibbon Spring and a pleasant grove of ponderosas that survived the fire, probably due to the moisture from the seep.

Mount Pennell from the north

At 21 miles the road tops out at a high point near a second group of ponderosas. This is a popular dispersed camping spot. This part of the Henrys is a long way (in terms of driving time) from any of the three developed campgrounds. The principles of dispersed camping (also called at-large camping) remain important even when there is little camping pressure. It is best to select a site that has already been disturbed so that the amount of new resource damage is minimized. Once at such a site, select tent or parking areas with a careful eye to prevent any significant impact. If others who have preceded you have been careless or unthinking, clean up their mess when you leave. In short, treat the area as you would treat your own property, which, in fact, it is.

View west from near Pennellen Pass

The views to the east and northeast are panoramic from just beyond the trees. Mount Hillers, the southernmost major summit in the Henrys is directly ahead to the southeast, and to its left in sequence are the Abajo Mountains on the horizon, Gunsight Butte over North Canyon, the La Sal Mountains, the distant Book Cliffs, and the San Rafael Swell. The road, rough at times, descends steeply, and then regains the lost elevation on the way to Straight Creek Junction at 24.1 miles. Turn left (east) here, following road 14000 and the sign that shows Coyote Benches 2, Trachyte Ranch 9, and Highway 276 14. The latter distance is about 2.5 miles too long. The Coyote Benches fan out far below and the initial descent is steep. Once on the bench, the gradient becomes more moderate, and abundant dispersed campsites may have quite a variety of trailers on them during hunting season.

At 28.5 miles the road drops off the bench and down into the Straight Creek drainage. The next junction is signed for westbound traffic (the sign faces east), indicating

Straight Creek

Quaking Aspen Spring 4 and Stanton Pass 5 to the left, and Coyote Benches 2 to the right. At the 31-mile mark a gentle slope leads down to Straight Creek that at this point cascades lightly over a series of small ledges. In the fall, scattered cottonwoods provide slashes of color to complement the red and yellow shrubs that take advantage of the water and the protection afforded by the canyon.

At 0.4 mile farther on a series of mine tunnels can be seen in the Salt Wash Member of the Morrison Formation across the stream to the south. The scene is very much like that 7 or 8 miles to the north along the Sandy Ranch–Little Egypt route. A network of old roads can also be seen. The Morrison produced about three-fourths of the uranium mined in Utah during the cold war, with most of the rest in the lower members of the older Chinle Formation. There is no reason to enter the mines, and two major ones to stay out: they are susceptible to cave-ins and they are concentrated sources of radiation. Additionally, most are on legitimate claims and are thus private property.

The entrance to the Trachyte Ranch is just before a cattleguard at 33.4 miles, and from here it is 2.4 miles to the pavement of Highway 276. The junction of 276 and 95 is 4.7 miles to the north (left), and because the mileposts begin at that intersection, the turn-off for travelers doing the Trachyte Ranch to Sandy Ranch route east to west will find its start at milepost 4.7 where there is a sign for the Bull Creek Pass National Back Country Byway. The byway goes from here to the Sweetwater Creek junction where it turns right and heads back east to Bull Creek Pass and Little Egypt as described in the section above. Hardy drivers and passengers can drive the entire byway in a day from either terminus. The total mileage of this byway is just over 70 miles, but it will be a dawn to dusk trip with all the photo and other stops. It might be better to simply drive part of the way and stay at McMillan Springs Campground or disperse camp for a night or two.

After the rain

Hanksville to Starr Springs Road Trip

Distance: 60 miles

At just over 60 miles, this is the longest of the three routes through the Henrys that are described in this guide. Running from Hanksville south along the east sides of Mts. Ellen and Pennell, and west of Mt. Hillers, the trek is, after the first 15 miles or so, interesting, beautiful, or both. The road surface, like all Henry Mountains roads, is rough to very rough, requiring high clearance and driver fortitude. There are very steep grades up to Wickiup Pass and down to the Hoskinini Freight Road. This route includes a little more than 3 miles of the Sandy Ranch to Little Egypt crossing, and 8.5 miles of the Sandy Ranch to Trachyte Creek tour.

An advantage to starting at Hanksville is that it is easy to visit the BLM office there to get the latest information on road conditions and other topics such as camping and hunting seasons. The office is open on weekdays, usually until 4:30 p.m. with a closure during the lunch hour. In addition to general maps, USGS topographic maps are available. Another reason to stop by the office is to take a look at the old Wolverton Mill, the waterwheel of which was helicoptered to Hanksville from its original location on the southeast flank of Mt. Pennell. The mill was built in the early 1920s by Edwin T. Wolverton, originally from Maine, who came to the Henrys in search of gold. After considerable effort, he was eventually able to establish several mining claims on Mt. Pennell. He was more successful at constructing the rather elaborate mill (it crushed the ore and then pulverized it with an arrastra, and also operated a saw to cut timber into useful dimension lumber) than he was at finding and extracting gold. While much of the mill was reconstructed at Hanksville by 1988, the overshot wheel is original.

Reconstructed Wolverton Mill

There are two alternative routes to the Fairview Ranch, a notable marker on the Henry Mountains Access Road. In Hanksville, the shortest path is to go west on Highway 24 for 0.3 mile from its junction with Highway 95. Turn south on 100 East and reset the odometer to zero. The pavement ends in 0.3 mile and the road becomes graded dirt, the condition of which can vary from newly graded to heavily washboarded. At 6.2 miles when a road bears to the right (west) continue straight ahead. At 10.8 miles from Highway 24 there is a cabin to the east with a nearby corral. Past this point the road surface is considerably rockier. A cattleguard and sign at 11.4 miles indicates entry onto private land, and at 12.3 miles is a junction just west of the Fairview Ranch. A BLM sign here points straight ahead to Lonesome Beaver Campground, 10 miles south, and left (east) to Highway 95, 7 miles away.

The second alternative route is by traveling 9.9 miles south of the 24/95 junction on Highway 95, and then turning right (west) on 3150 E, the Fairview Ranch Road. Once on this road, a sign gives a 7-mile distance to the ranch, and 16 miles to the Sawmill Basin. The road is very good for 0.8 mile to a junction. Continue straight at this point as the better road bears right (northwest) to an industrial facility. At the 2.8-mile mark from the highway is a Y, signed to the left for the Granite Ranch and to the right for the Fairview Ranch and Lonesome Beaver Campground. Stay to the right (west) and follow the main route to the Fairview Ranch and T intersection with the Henry Mountains Access Road at 6.3 miles. Turn left (south), joining the route described in the paragraph above at the 12.3-mile mark.

Lonesome Beaver Campground

The cobble-based road runs straight toward the mountains for more than 1 mile until a left bend puts squat Bull Mountain dead ahead. In dry times a noticeable band of green vegetation can be spotted to the right (west), running across a uniform slope; its cause becomes apparent at 13.8 miles where a pipe carries water to the ditch below. An information kiosk and map is on the right at 15 miles and the climb steepens almost imperceptibly. Piñons and junipers rapidly cover the terrain soon after.

Piñon pines in this part of Utah are the species *Pinus edulis*, and are the source of the pine nuts so prized by contemporary chefs. Sadly, this is a masting species that sets copious amounts of seed only every few years. When they are producing, however, the abundance is almost daunting. At just the right time, it is possible to spread a sheet or tarp under a tree and gently shake the branches with a broomstick and watch the seeds pour out of the cones like rain. The nuts can be eaten raw for a decidedly piney taste, or carefully roasted (watch them like a hawk to prevent burning) to bring out their true flavor. Since shelling piñon nuts is very time-consuming, the temptation to eat

Piñon nuts

too many of these calorie-packed nuggets is diminished. Silvery roundleaf buffaloberry bushes begin to appear in abundance at 17.5 miles, adding interest to the piñon-juniper woodland.

A cattleguard and sign announce the boundary with Garfield County. The tread gets a little rockier until it tops out on a long flat. After a significant descent, the road settles into the Bull Creek drainage, aspen appear alongside for the first time, and the small stream is crossed at the 20.3-mile mark. A second, and final, crossing is not far beyond, and there have been times when we found both to be difficult after storms, although generally they are not an issue compared to other spots. A sign marks the Sawmill Basin, and the very pleasant Dandelion Picnic Area with shaded tables and a vault toilet is at 21.2 miles.

The Lonesome Beaver Campground, with five sites, is less than 0.5 mile south of the picnic area. The three BLM campgrounds in the Henrys have distinctly different feels. Lonesome Beaver lies in the bottom of a deep and steep valley and is densely shaded by spruce trees, with a few aspen for a change of color and texture. Bull Creek passes by just to the west, and each site has its own water spigot, fire ring, and charcoal grill. The high walls to the east and west block both evening and morning sun, a possible virtue in summer, and not so much in the fall when shadows creep into the deep valley a good hour and a half or more before sunset.

Beyond the campground the road begins to steepen, especially as it switchbacks up to Wickiup Pass at mile 23.3. The sense of being at higher elevation becomes clear at this saddle and beyond as openings begin to expose views of Mount Ellen to the west and vistas to the east over the Dirty Devil canyon. A sign at the three-way junction lists many destinations; they include Bull Creek Pass and the Sandy Ranch to the west (right) and Crescent Creek and Pennellen Pass to the left (southeast)—bear left. The road drops into the Granite Creek drainage at 23.9, and then ascends very steeply to Granite Ridge. The route becomes a shelf road with huge views to the east as it descends to Crescent Creek at mile 26.6.

West slope of Mount Ellen

A very sharp left-hand turn at the four-way junction leads to Highway 95 near Little Egypt (described above in the Sandy Ranch–Little Egypt section) and offers a shorter (though not really short) way back to pavement in the event of bad weather or driver fatigue. The road to the right (west) leads up into the Bromide Basin, an often active mining district. To continue on to Starr Springs, stay straight, and almost

Gambel oak on east flank of Mount Pennell

immediately cross the small brook. A sign just ahead confirms the correct route, giving distances to Copper Ridge Junction, Pennellen Pass, and the Horn. Bear right (southwest) at a Y junction with road 15050 at 26.8, and eventually climb up to Copper Creek Ridge at the 29-mile mark.

The view from the ridge opens to the south and southwest, providing a good look at the rest of the Henrys and the southern part of the Waterpocket Fold. Just east of south is Mount Hillers, and to its right is Ragged Mountain, almost due south. Between it and Copper Creek Ridge are the well-named Raggy Draws. To the right (west) of Ragged Mountain, and farther away, is Mount Pennell, with the prominent Horn fronting it. Continuing west, the southern part of Capitol Reef National Park is evidenced by the linear exposure of the steeply dipping strata of the Waterpocket Fold.

Conical Ragged Mountain in front of Mount Hillers, with Mount Pennell to the right

Side Trip: Circle Route around South Mount Ellen

Driving distance for this loop back to Copper Creek Ridge is 17.5 miles.

From Copper Creek Ridge you can continue straight ahead to Pennellen Pass and on to Starr Springs (covered below), or make a sharp right (northwest) turn onto road 14400. The latter traverses along the south and west flanks of Mount Ellen's south summit ridge to connect with the Sandy Ranch–Little Egypt route at Nasty Flat. From there it is a short drive up to Bull Creek Pass and on down to Wickiup Pass to complete a circuit around the mountain. If you have just one full day to spend in the Henrys it would be hard to beat driving this loop and hiking Mount Ellen (described below) from a base camp at Lonesome Beaver.

Road 14400 ascends sharply from Copper Creek Ridge, switchbacking up to a junction with road 14410 that goes to the right (north) into Bromide Basin. Continue straight ahead through a short open area and then largely Gambel oak forest at about 9,500 feet in elevation. A saddle just under 3 miles from Copper Creek Ridge offers another good view of Mounts Pennell and Hillers, and Ragged Mountain. The track then drops 300 vertical feet into a deeply cut drainage before climbing out and then traversing to South Creek Ridge where it turns to the north.

Views from this point are spectacular to the west with Boulder Mountain over Capitol Reef. The next 2 miles to Nasty Flat pass through largely open ground, so the views are maintained. Small aspen groves along the way provide interest along with a golden glow in the fall. The distance from Copper Creek Ridge to Nasty Flat is 6.6 miles, and the road is generally in about the same condition as others in the Henrys. From the three-way junction at Nasty Flat it is 2.5 miles to the right to Bull Creek Pass and the Mount Ellen trailhead, and another 2.7 down to Wickiup Pass.

Continuing South on the Hanksville–Starr Springs Route

From the Y junction on Copper Creek Ridge (at mile 29) the road to Pennellen Pass is a pleasant stretch of views to the south, with long flats and moderate descents. The south-facing slope is covered by a mix of piñon and oak, with one anomalous cascade of aspen in a draw at mile 31.7. An intersection at 33.4 offers another chance to circle Mount Ellen, but about 1,500 feet lower and with considerably more distance. The only sign here is for northbound drivers. A turn to the right (west) on to road 14007 leads to Birch Spring and then to the Sandy Ranch–Little Egypt route, 6.7 miles to the northwest; a right turn there leads up to Nasty Flat in another 5.4 miles of steep climbing. Although the views are generally better on the circle route described above, this route does offer a very good stretch where the Waterpocket Fold and Boulder Mountain rise above a foreground of interesting, sharply cut, Mancos Shale canyons.

From the junction with 14007, road 14500 drops down to broad Pennellen Pass in just under 1.5 miles. A side road to Box Spring branches off with an acute left (north-east) turn, and the three-way junction with road 14000 is at 34.9 miles. Turn left (east) at this point. For the next 8.5 miles the route is the same as the Sandy Ranch–Trachyte Creek trip described above; see that account for details of the interesting, and often rough, drive to Straight Creek Junction T intersection at mile 43.4.

The T intersection above Straight Creek is another decision point. The drive to pavement from here is considerably shorter (less than 12 miles) and easier by staying on road 14000 and turning left (east) to Trachyte Creek and Highway 276. If this is the preferred option, continue to follow the description in the Sandy Ranch–Trachyte Creek section above. If you are eager to get to Starr Springs and complete this north-south tour of the Henrys, turn right and descend to the crossing of Straight Creek, usually only a trickle of water. The road surface is rocky and rough all the way to the Hoskinini Freight Road just southwest of Stanton Pass.

The first time we traveled this track was in the summer, and the views of Mount Hillers, back to Mount Pennell, and off to the east were the clear highlights. The second time, however, was in very early October, and the vast blankets of Gambel oak that were pretty tame in green, were an explosion of color in the fall. Since brown is their usual autumn and winter hue, the red, orange, and yellow patches that covered the slopes along which the road wanders were an unexpected dividend.

Gambel oak

Gambel oaks are often considered a nuisance in the West, especially when they impinge on desired species such as ponderosa pine. For the many animal species that depend upon them for food and cover, however, they are essential. Oaks, the genus

Quercus, are divided largely into two groups, red and white (a third group, golden cup, is much less common, found mostly along the Pacific Coast and in Arizona), and Gambel oaks have the round-lobed leaves of the white oak group. In the Four Corners states *Quercus gambelii* is by far the most common oak species, and it is comparatively easy to identify because its leaves are deeply lobed, in contrast to other southwestern oaks. Thick-capped acorns up to an inch long sustain many animals through winter, and are a favorite pre-hibernation calorie source for bears. Gambel oaks are a hardy species, able to thrive in hot, low elevation canyons all the way up to and above 10,000 feet. In the Henrys they opportunistically sprout in abundance after fires, covering entire landscapes as they do here on the east flank of Mount Pennell.

At 46.8 miles the road rounds Bulldog Ridge, the southeastern extension of Mount Pennell, and turns briefly to the southwest. A fine view in that direction includes the southern end of the Waterpocket Fold and a bit of Lake Powell. Navajo Mountain is prominent and directly over the gray Mancos Shale of Clay Point. At 0.5 mile beyond is Mud Spring Junction, where road 13610 bears to the right (west) near a tower. Stay to the left (southeast) at this point. The most difficult section of road described in the Henrys in this book begins at mile 48.8. A set of very steep and sharp switchbacks descends through a burn area toward the Pennell Creek crossing. Vehicles with a wide turning radius might have to back up on one or two of the switchbacks, and there is enough exposure to warrant considerable caution, though experienced backcountry drivers will take them in stride.

Mount Hillers from the north

A triangle junction with the Hoskinini Freight Road, also called the Stanton Pass Road, is at mile 49.6. A sign gives distances to Cow Flat Road, Squaw Spring, and Starr Springs, all to the right (southwest), which is the route. At 52.6 miles continue straight into Saleratus Wash when road 13040 bears to the right (southwest). The route to Starr Springs turns to the east and climbs up to a high point at 55.1 and the first view of nearly vertical sedimentary strata on the southwest side of Mount Hillers. An even better view is at mile 56.1. This is a classic case of older sedimentary rocks being pushed up during the introduction of granitic material from a magma chamber, and no doubt informed G. K. Gilbert as he attempted to understand not only the genesis of the Henrys, but other laccolithic bodies as well. Erosion has sculpted the harder Navajo Sandstone into impressive flatirons that resemble those along the Front Range of Colorado as well as some along the Waterpocket Fold. In the latter two instances, however, the rocks were tilted by regional and local folding rather than by forcible igneous intrusions.

As the road winds in and out of numerous drainages toward Starr Springs, there are many views to the south and east of the Little Rockies, which consist of Mount Holmes to the left (northeast) and Mount Ellsworth to the right (southwest). These rugged peaks are also of igneous origin. A triangle junction with the Clay Point Road is at mile 58.6 and is unsigned for southbound traffic (there is a sign for those coming from Starr Springs). Turn left (northeast) for the remaining 2 miles to the entrance to the Starr Springs Recreation Area and campground on the left (east). The very pleasant campground is described in the Clay Point Circuit section. From the entrance to the recreation area, a good gravel road descends southeast 3.4 miles to Highway 276.

Sedimentary rocks tilted by Mount Hillers intrusion

Little Egypt Geological Area

Driving distance from Highway 24 is 1.5 miles one way.

A short and worthwhile diversion on the trip around the Henry Mountains, especially for families with children, is the Little Egypt Geological Area. The site is south of Hanksville just off Highway 95 at milepost 20.3. A brown Scenic Backway sign marks the turnoff, which is downhill to the right (west). Once on the dirt road there are several additional signs, the last of which announces the Bull Creek Pass National Back Country Byway. The dirt road is usually passable to standard passenger cars except during and just after wet periods when it may be impassable to all vehicles. Occasionally it may also be somewhat rutted, but careful driving should usually suffice if the surface has dried out. Follow the road to the west and then south for a total of 1.5 miles. At that point a brown sign reads Little Egypt Geological Site, and a track leads off to the right (west), quickly terminating in a rough circle. Passenger cars with low clearance can be left on the side of the main road.

From the "parking" circle the hoodoos of Little Egypt are plainly visible to the west and south. They distinctly resemble those in Goblin Valley State Park, which is reasonable given that both are in the Entrada Sandstone. Little Egypt has far fewer than Goblin Valley, but also far fewer people. The best of the hoodoos are to the south, in front of imposing Mount Hillers. To get to them walk down the slope to the south and then cross-country for about 100 yards. The ten-foot high forms surround a barren flat and are very accessible. The hoodoos are the result of the presence in the Entrada of layers that are slightly more resistant to erosion than the rest of the sandstone, and thereby protect the latter for a short time (geologically speaking). If Goblin Valley is not on the itinerary, Little Egypt makes a good substitute. Avoid climbing on the hoodoos as they may be unstable.

Little Egypt and Mount Hillers

Mount Ellen Hike

Hiking distance is 3.7 miles round trip.

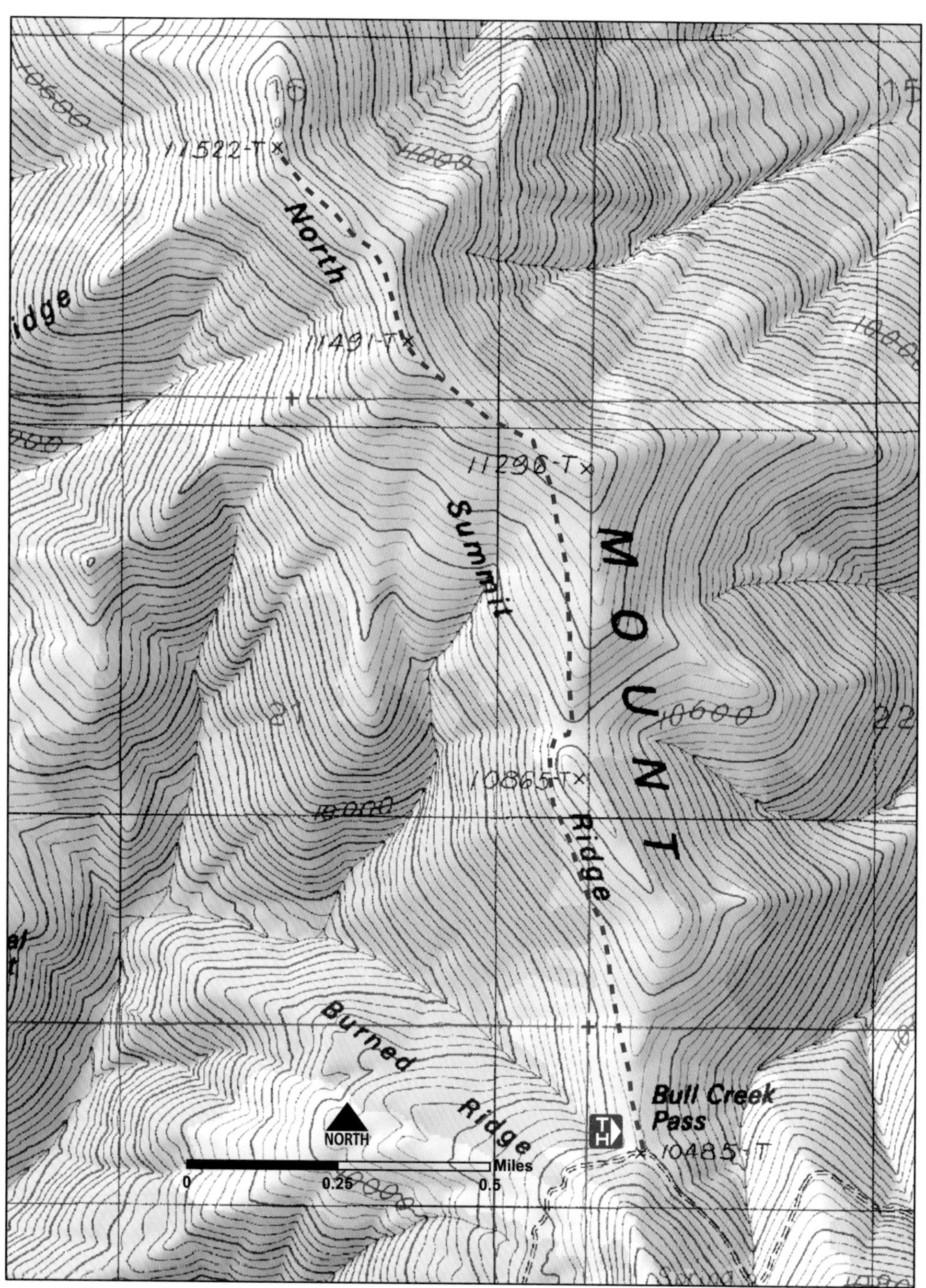

Mount Ellen route

There are views, and then there are vistas: grand panoramas offering diverse and beautiful scenery. There are several described in this guide, but it is Mount Ellen that tops them all, both in elevation and sheer holy cowness. The peak would be very popular if a nice paved road crossed Bull Creek Pass, but since that is not the case, weekdays are pretty quiet on top. Weekends during the summer and early fall can be a little busier, to the point where you might meet a local family group or a stray from the Grand Circle tour crowd.

For experienced and fit high-altitude hikers, the trail up to the highest point on the summit ridge will be a walk in the park, but for others it can be difficult or impossible. The gradient is moderate or less, about 1,000 vertical feet in just under 2 miles. It is the altitude, of course, that will be limiting for many. Bull Creek Pass is just below 10,500 feet in elevation, a level where altitude sickness can be a real issue for those not acclimated to the thin air. When the exertion of climbing a steady grade is added, a high percentage of casual hikers will experience some sort of altitude-related symptoms. Pay attention, and turn around if you have problems.

Getting There

The trailhead is a large parking area and wooden fence right at Bull Creek Pass. Follow the directions in either the Sandy Ranch–Little Egypt or Hanksville–Starr Springs sections to get to the trailhead. The hike could be done as a nice break on the Sandy Ranch–Little Egypt drive, or, better yet, from a base camp at McMillan Springs or Lonesome Beaver campgrounds. In summer, when the sun is high in the sky, an early morning or late afternoon hike is best (assuming there is no lightning risk), but perhaps the best time is the early fall with lower sun angles and the chance of less monsoonal moisture in the air. Even when air quality is good, the views are so vast that the La Sals east of Moab (85 miles away) may not appear crystal clear, though they will almost certainly be more than just a faint outline.

The Hike

From the west side of the parking area take a look north to the ridge. Just barely visible, and appearing to be lower, is a rounded peak to the left (west from this vantage) of what seems to be the obvious high point. It turns out that the latter is a false summit, but due to the gentle terrain on top of the ridge, reaching the actual summit beyond is not difficult. To begin the hike, sign the register and pass through the opening in the fence to the obvious trail. The first part of the hike is a gentle ascending traverse mostly along the west-facing slope. The diorite along the trail contains many large phenocrysts of black pyroxene crystals embedded in the white groundmass of the rock. After 0.5 mile of walking, the path goes through a grove of limber pines and then crosses a talus slope where a small aspen clone has a toehold at 10,800 feet above sea level. At the 0.7-mile mark the route jogs to the right (east) through a pretty spruce and limber pine group and emerges onto an open saddle.

Mount Ellen, looking south

Mount Ellen, looking north

Mule deer on Mount Ellen

The way ahead is clear, and the huge cairn on top of the false summit is obvious. The trail tread remains strong as it climbs a steeper slope, then fades at 1.2 miles as the grade decreases near a cairn almost on the ridgeline. There is another cairn ahead on top of the nearest hump, and the tread again appears. If you don't find this one, simply head up the ridge. At 1.4 miles there is no trail across the expanse of steep, but fairly stable rocks. Pick your way up to the top of the knob, and marvel at the giant cairn. A trench cut in the solid rock offers protection in the event that the usual wind crossing the ridge is strong. Views are spectacular in all directions.

The actual summit is less than 0.4 mile ahead. Drop down from the knob and pass the next one on the left (west) side where a hard-to-see cairn marks the route, or simply walk up and across the very minor hill. Go right over the next hump, and then straight to the high point at just under 1.9 miles, where a mailbox contains the summit register. Directly to the north is Mount Ellen Peak, a nice pyramid that often appears to be the high point when the range is viewed from the north. It is just under 1 mile of walking along the ridge to the peak; there is a clear trail near the top. The drop to the intervening saddle is 400 feet, so there is a fair amount of climbing involved in hiking over to it.

The vista from the high point is worth savoring. Just to the right of Mount Ellen Peak are the green fields around Hanksville, with the San Rafael Reef and Swell farther to the north and northeast. The Fairview Ranch is barely visible just over the ridge that connects the peak and Bull Mountain to the northeast. The La Sal Mountains are on the horizon over Bull Mountain, and almost directly east is Gunsight Butte. Continuing to the south, the view includes the Abajo Mountains, then just the summit of Mount Hillers peaking up to the left of the radio tower and building on top of South Mount Ellen. To the right of the tower is Mount Pennell, with Navajo Mountain on the horizon slightly farther west (right).

Continuing in the clockwise direction, the long, flat Straight Cliffs narrow south to Navajo Point, then Powell Point shows in the southwest at the tip of the Aquarius Plateau. Directly west it may be possible to locate the irrigated fields of the Sandy Ranch, right below the southern point of Boulder Mountain. The ranch is at the base of the Waterpocket Fold, which can be seen for almost its entire length. A little farther north is Notom, with the Golden Throne and other prominences in the fold just under Fishlake Hightop in the distance. In the northwest, Thousand Lake Mountain rises over the Caineville Mesas and Cathedral Valley to complete the panorama.

On the return hike the knob with the huge cairn can be bypassed on the right (west). At the saddle just below it, look for a fairly obvious stretch of trail that goes around the hump; it is marked by a few cairns. Eventually, the trail disappears on the southwest side of the knob, and a rough contour across the rocks back to the ridgeline is necessary to regain the rest of the route. In some ways it may be easier to simply go back over the hump, but then the rocks will still have to be descended.

Aspen regeneration after fire on the east flank of Mount Ellen

Circle Cliffs and Slickrock

Hells Backbone

The designation of the Grand Staircase–Escalante National Monument has markedly increased visitation to the slot canyons south and east of the town of Escalante. They are certainly worthy, but the portion of the national monument east and north of the Escalante River is pretty special as well, and with much less hiking pressure. There are two quite distinct areas covered below: the Circle Cliffs and the slickrock expanse to the west, on both sides of the town of Boulder.

The Circle Cliffs are the erosional expression of another Laramide uplift. Red Wingate Sandstone walls nearly surround a large area bisected by the Burr Trail, just to the west of Capitol Reef National Park. Where canyons have been carved in the Wingate, the results are highly scenic. The slickrock that nearly surrounds Boulder is the dazzling white Navajo Sandstone, not only beautiful, but enticing to those who like to ramble on their own itineraries. Scenic Highway 12 and the Burr Trail provide good access across the region, and there are more adventurous roads to travel as well.

Burr Trail Road Trip

Driving distance from Boulder to the Notom-Bullfrog Road in Capitol Reef National Park is 36 miles one way.

The Burr Trail traverses some of the most spectacular terrain in North America. For many visitors to south-central Utah it is a destination in itself, and rightfully so. Combined with the Notom-Bullfrog Road on the east side of Capitol Reef National Park, and Highways 12 and 24, the Burr Trail is also part of a 125-mile loop that goes from 5,000 feet above sea level to 9,600 feet, from claret cups to aspen, and from 26 million-year-old rock to 200 million-year-old layers.

The nomenclature for the Burr Trail and Notom-Bullfrog Road can be confusing. There is no uncertainty regarding the Burr Trail from Boulder to its intersection with the Notom-Bullfrog Road in Capitol Reef, nor for the latter to the north from this junction. To the southeast, however, various maps and publications differ. The *Benchmark Utah Road and Recreation Atlas* covers all the bases by labeling the route from the park southeast to Highway 276 near Bullfrog as the Notom-Bullfrog Road and the Burr Trail Scenic Backway. This section describes the portion that is clearly the Burr Trail, from Boulder to the switchbacks in Capitol Reef, and then briefly touches upon the section beyond to the Clay Point Road.

From Boulder, the first 30.5 miles of the Burr Trail are chip-sealed, and though speeds are limited by sharp curves, at least this part is an all-weather road except for the rare snowstorm. The Notom-Bullfrog Road south of the Clay Point Road is also chip-sealed **except** for the at-grade crossing of the Bullfrog Creek wash, which can range from accessible to cars with good clearance to impassable to all. In between are 16.6 miles of graded dirt or clay road that under good conditions can be driven in passenger cars, but precipitation can change that in a hurry. In general it is nice to have a vehicle with good

Burr Trail switchbacks

clearance and certainly good tires if you are going to leave the pavement. Road condition information and weather forecasts may be obtained at Anasazi State Park in Boulder, the Capitol Reel National Park visitor center on Highway 24, the BLM office in Hanksville, or in Bullfrog at the visitor center for Glen Canyon National Recreation Area or other facilities there.

It seems that more travelers begin their drive on the Burr Trail from Boulder, and because that end is paved and accessible to all, that is where this description begins. The Burr Trail heads due east from Highway 12 at milepost 86.3 in the village of Boulder. At that point the highway makes a sweeping right angle turn west and north. Zero the odometer at this point, and proceed east (straight if coming from Escalante, left if coming from Torrey). The scene is very pastoral and pretty at first, with pastures fronting Boulder Mountain to the north and Navajo Sandstone slickrock hills to the south. It is just 1.5 miles to the Grand Staircase–Escalante National Monument (GSENM) boundary.

Regulations for visitors in the monument differ significantly from those in the Dixie National Forest or Capitol Reef National Park. Some important provisions: GSENM requires a permit for overnight camping, but does allow campers to use dispersed camping guidelines; dogs under close control are allowed in the backcountry; rock, mineral, and fossil collecting are prohibited. Regulations change from time to time, however, and it is the responsibility of the visitor to know and follow them in each jurisdiction. If there is any doubt, stop in at the interagency visitor center on the west edge of the town of Escalante where all three agencies are represented, or at Anasazi State Park.

After entering the monument, the Burr Trail passes through an interesting area where there is sufficient surface water on the northeast (left) side of the road to support a lush riparian ecosystem. Across the road the sand and moisture host tall ponderosa pines at the base of spectacular slickrock slopes of heavily jointed Navajo Sandstone. Over time, weathering has accentuated the joints, which are often described as a checkerboard. Visitors coming from Zion National Park will be familiar with this pattern. The large, unsigned, and informal parking area for the Deer Creek loop hike is at 5.4 miles, and a mile later, the road crosses perennial Deer Creek, a pleasant little stream typical of several similar waterways that course down from Boulder Mountain. A sign marks the entrance to Deer Creek Campground, which is small, with seven sites. The creek is pleasant, camping (as of this writing) is just $4 per night, and there is water along with a vault toilet. Sites are very small, however. At the end of the campground road, a track enters the stream on private property.

The Burr Trail leaves the Deer Creek drainage to cross interesting ground with good views north to Boulder Mountain before plunging down into the Gulch. The descent is very steep, the road narrow, and there are no guardrails. Be extremely careful if you pull off the road to take in the view up Long Canyon to the east. Near the bottom of the grade is the turnoff on the right (west) to parking for overnight hikers in the Gulch. The short road to the parking area is pretty rough. The Burr Trail makes a sweeping left-hand bend down into the Gulch drainage where Fremont cottonwoods add a swath of green in the spring and summer, and a beautiful yellow late in October. Hikers can go either up or downstream in the Gulch, following hiker-made trails.

After crossing the bridge over the Gulch (which may or may not be flowing) at 10.4 miles, the Burr Trail begins a spectacular ascent of Long Canyon. The 350-foot high red walls are cut into the Wingate Sandstone, which at this location is dipping down to the southwest at almost the same gradient as the road. The red cliffs (red due to iron staining; the sandstone is actually tan when fresh) are heavily jointed, and weathering on the joints has created huge vertical slabs that eventually fall to leave scattered blocks on the underlying Chinle Formation slopes.

Beyond the bridge over the Gulch the road winds along the bottom of Long Canyon as it begins to narrow. At 0.9 mile after the bridge is a small pull-out on the left (northwest) where a short hiker-made trail leads down into the bottom of the drainage. Directly across the wide channel (which is usually dry) is a deep cleft in the Wingate that is easy to walk into on the sandy floor. The path ends abruptly at a high pour-off, but not before going in far enough to give a good sense of walking right into the rock. In the fall, this area is especially pretty when the cottonwoods at the mouth of the narrows are dressed in yellow. This part of Long Canyon is the point where the road is nearly at the contact between the Wingate and the underlying Chinle Formation. As noted above, the Wingate tends to erode to vertical faces, while the much softer Chinle clays erode to slopes. The more Chinle that is exposed, the wider the canyon will be; at the cleft there is little Chinle, leading to less distance between the Wingate cliff walls on either side of the road. As the Burr Trail winds up the canyon, the walls recede as the road cuts more deeply into the clay.

Long Canyon on the Burr Trail (above and below)

In this part of the Southwest, almost every canyon and drainage that hosts a perennial stream or has permanent subsurface water is lined or dotted with Fremont cottonwoods. *Populus fremontii* grows to prodigious size, with trunks up to ten feet in diameter supporting huge canopies of large, triangular, deep green, waxy leaves that turn bright yellow in the fall. In the spring, Fremont cottonwoods flower before leafing out, and green (female) and red (male) catkins soon litter the ground, to be followed by a snowfall of seeds embracing the breeze with snow-white plumes.

Cottonwoods do a great deal of good ecological work. They stabilize stream and wash banks—it is not uncommon to see flood debris wrapped around them many feet above a wash bottom—and their persistent leaf duff is a good soil builder. Although there are some indications that the invasive tamarisk onslaught that has negatively affected cottonwood populations may be on the wane, the loss of the big trees has been significant. A different kind of scourge that people notice is the explosion of western tent caterpillars soon after the trees leaf out. The web-like nests are made even more obvious as the caterpillars consume the emerging foliage, leading many to believe that the trees will die. The two species are adapted to each other, however, and healthy cottonwoods are able to refoliate after the caterpillars have left to pupate.

It is almost 5.5 miles farther on to the top of Long Canyon, and the drive is both slow and very scenic. You will know when you top out. There is a very large viewpoint parking area on the right (southeast), a cattleguard, and the road begins a steep descent. It is certainly worth the time to pull off at the top. The vista to the east includes the peaks of the Henry Mountains, and closer, the eastern arm of the Circle Cliffs. Directly down and to the east from the viewpoint is a quite spectacular exposure of barren Chinle slopes exhibiting a wide range of rusty and pinkish hues.

Chinle Formation

The road plunges down the Chinle after the viewpoint (small mudflows can close the road during and after storms) and then passes onto the brown Moenkopi Formation. Near the base of the hill there may be a stand of Palmers penstemons in the summer. This species (*Penstemon palmeri*) sends a flower spike up to three feet in height that is covered with big white blooms well marked with maroon lines to draw in pollinators. At mile 18.4, the signed Wolverine Loop Road goes off to the south (right). This high-clearance, sometimes 4WD track leads to popular slot canyons and a fine petrified wood area. It is described in detail in the Little Death Hollow/Wolverine Loop section. After this intersection the Burr Trail winds through typical piñon-juniper forest, along with open sagebrush meadows, all the way to Capitol Reef. Almost everyone will want to simply stay on the pavement, but a select few might be interested in exploring the area encompassed by the Circle Cliffs to the north, which is described below.

The Chinle Formation

The Chinle Formation is widespread across the Colorado Plateau. It may be best known for the petrified wood logs that erode from it at Petrified Forest National Park near Holbrook, Arizona. It is named for its type locality near Chinle, Arizona, the gateway town for Canyon de Chelly National Monument. Almost always, where the Chinle is exposed, it is protected by high cliffs of the overlying red Wingate Sandstone. This is especially clear along the north side of Highway 24 from west of Torrey down to Capitol Reef National Park, and then south along the park's Scenic Drive. Long Canyon, here on the Burr Trail, is another good sequence.

When Chinle deposition began in the late Triassic, the paleoenvironment changed significantly. The climate, instead of being extremely arid as it was both before and after the Chinle, was warm and wet, with a monsoonal summer rain pattern. Given that there was little change in latitude, the difference is attributed to a shallow sea to the west that during summer provided sufficient moisture over the flat Chinle plain to generate wetting rains. Whatever the cause, it is abundantly clear that the climate and surface water availability was able to support lush forests with huge trees, many of which are preserved today in the form of petrified wood. (See the Cooks and Meeks Mesas hike section for details on how petrified wood forms.) The same sea level rise shut down erosion, with the result that sluggish rivers originating in what is now to the southeast (Texas and Oklahoma) flowed onto the plain where there were numerous lakes and swamps.

The low energy streams were able to carry only tiny, clay-size material for the most part (except during flood events). An additional source of sediment lay to the west, where a volcanic arc developed offshore. Eruptions threw enormous amounts of ash into the atmosphere, where wind currents carried it east. The modern Chinle is mostly a mudstone, with bands of bentonite clay that formed as an alteration product of the volcanic ash. The bentonite weathers into a popcorn-like, very soft and crumbly surface which is easily swept away, and which is inhospitable to plant root systems. Bare Chinle slopes are therefore largely barren of vegetation.

In an area where rocks are often bright white or dark colors, the Chinle stands with its later cousins, the Brushy Basin Member of the Morrison Formation and parts of the Cedar Mountain Formation, as largely a palette of pastels. Hues range from greenish or bluish gray to mauve, pink, lavender, and light maroon. Just as the reds, oranges, yellows, and browns of other rocks indicate the presence of oxidized iron, the Chinle colors reflect an environment where oxygen was in short supply. The iron minerals that formed did so under reducing conditions like those found in swamps where decaying organic matter depletes the oxygen content of the water.

Side Trip to the Lampstand and Upper Trailhead for the Gulch

Driving distance from the Burr Trail to the Gulch is approximately 11 miles one way.

Upper end of the Gulch

Any guidebook presents a range of things to do, and a range implies that some are spectacular and some less so, and by definition there has to be one that makes all the others look good. Of course, that one will probably differ from traveler to traveler, and may depend upon weather, the quality of lunch that was packed, the mood(s) in the car or on the trail, and several hundred other factors. Thus we have this side trip to and possibly beyond, the Lampstand. The appeal is solitude and exploration with a modicum of scenery, but the track may be rough or turbulent, impassable when wet or cut by flash floods, dusty if dry, high clearance all the time, and when we made it to the Gulch, 4WD low range was helpful in climbing back out. With the possible exception of hunting season, or an unlikely meeting with a rancher, the chances of seeing anyone else are slim. It is a long walk back to the Burr Trail if things go south.

There are two access points on the Burr Trail for the Lampstand Road: the western one at mile 21.8, and the east leg at mile 24.2. If the intent is to visit the Lampstand area or the upper Gulch and then continue east to Capitol Reef, it would make sense to take the west approach and exit the eastern one; there is little that would be missed on the Burr Trail between them. The sign for the first track (for those headed east) indicates that the Lampstand is 5 miles to the left, and for some reason, points to the right reading Burr Trail 13. Perhaps the 13 miles refers to the distance to the switchbacks in

Lampstand

Capitol Reef, but worry not—you are on the Burr Trail pavement at this intersection!

For the Lampstand Road, zero the odometer and bear left (northeast) on the dirt track. The road to the eastern route is generally fairly easy except for the stretch where it traverses a usually dry streambed. This portion can be very rocky. At 1.9 miles is a triangular junction, signed in each direction. Bear left (north) here for the Lampstand or Upper Gulch. At 3.1 a track goes to the right (east) across a large grassy flat. Stay left (northwest) as the road crosses a meadow. The Circle Cliffs surround this area. As the track approaches a couple of broad mesas of brown Moenkopi topped by lighter Shinarump, there is a saddle between them. In the middle of the saddle is a raised area that is flat and which must have resembled a lampstand to someone. This is not the scenic equivalent of, say, the Golden Throne in Capitol Reef. Still, it may be enough, since better scenery is 5 miles farther on, and the track through that stretch is likely to be much worse.

If you can't bear turning around when there is more to explore (or if you want to get to the Gulch "trailhead"), continue on as the track crosses mostly flat ground dissected by shallow washes. There is a track to the right (northeast) at 5.1, stay straight here. The flora is typical big sage, piñon-juniper, four-wing saltbush, and a fair amount of Fremont mahonia (barberry). The next significant junction is at 7.7 miles where there is a cattleguard and a corral. Bear right (northwest) and pass a small earthen dam at 8.5. The terrain begins to get more interesting, and at 10.2 miles there is a Dixie National Forest boundary sign, which means you are leaving the GSENM.

The undulating descent into the Gulch was very rough when we drove it. Flooding had washed out most or all of the fines, and there were some sharp cuts as well. Had others not blazed the way, it would have required a lot of tedious shovel work to proceed. The almost invisible hiker-made path into the upper Gulch is on the left (south) at 11.1 miles. The road continues, but a big hole in the Chinle roadbed at 11.5 suggests that it is wise to turn around. The area around and just beyond the trailhead is quite scenic, with the wall of the Circle Cliffs soaring above to the west, and scattered cottonwood trees in the drainage below. The return trip out of the Gulch was made much more comfortable by using low-range 4WD. To return to the Burr Trail to the east, go back to the signed triangular junction, bear left (east) and go 2.4 miles to the welcoming pavement.

Burr Trail Road Trip—Continued

If you have elected to stay on the Burr Trail, the unsigned track at 24.2 miles is the eastern access point for the Lampstand. This junction is in a broad, open flat. Good views back to the Circle Cliffs and Boulder Mountain are at 26.4 miles as the road attains high ground before the long descent into Capitol Reef and the Muley Twist drainage. The east end of the Wolverine Loop comes in from the right (south) at 28.8 miles, and the pavement ends at the Capitol Reef National Park boundary 30.5 miles from Highway 12. At 0.5 mile into the park the view of the Henry Mountains is very good, and this is a fine place to take it in and get oriented to the country ahead. From the left (northeast), the broad ridge is Mount Ellen, and to its south are Mount Pennell, Mount Hillers, and the two Little Rockies summits of Mounts Holmes and Ellsworth.

The Burr Trail drops steadily down to the Waterpocket Fold, which dominates the foreground views. The high clearance, possibly 4WD, side road to Strike Valley Overlook and the Upper Muley Twist trailhead is on the left (northeast) at 32.8 miles, and directly to the east is a good look at Peek-a-boo Arch, which resembles the old comic strip character Calvin. Detailed descriptions of the Strike Valley Overlook Road, and the Upper and Lower Muley Twist, Surprise, and Headquarters hiking routes can be found in *Capitol Reef National Park, The Complete Hiking and Touring Guide* available at the park visitor center. The Burr Trail crosses the Muley Twist wash and ascends briefly to the small pullout on the right (south) for Lower Muley Twist hikers at 33.9 miles. At 0.1 mile beyond is a short but rough track to the right (south) that leads to a picnic table in very scenic surroundings. The track to the table is right at the top of the famous Burr Trail switchbacks.

There is ample room and reason to carefully pull off before negotiating the descent. The Henrys now seem much closer, and the Mancos Shale slopes that fringe Swap Mesa in front of the mountains are impressive as well. The road at the bottom seems very far below as it winds out Burr Canyon to join the Notom-Bullfrog Road. The switchbacks are formidable to some drivers and perfectly routine to others, though they really are not for big RVs and vehicles towing long trailers. The road is certainly steep, but it is quite wide, usually enough so that vehicles can easily pass when they meet. The corners are sharp, but nowhere near the point that would require backing up for cars, SUVs, and pickups. Often the most significant problem is the washboarded surface that can impact control if speeds are too high. Slow and easy is the safe way to handle the mile of switchbacks, though the complete lack of guardrails may be disconcerting to some. At the bottom the road passes through the short canyon and joins the Notom-Bullfrog Road at 36 miles.

The intersection here is a triangle. Bear right (east, then southeast) to continue down to Bullfrog on Highway 276, or to the Clay Point Road east to the Henrys. The road follows the Halls Creek drainage for about 2.5 miles, with the impressive Navajo Sandstone flanking the Waterpocket Fold soaring up to the southwest. The red chevrons at the base of the Fold are erosional remnants of the Carmel Formation. Trailheads for

Surprise and Headquarters Canyons are 1.8 and 2.3 miles, respectively, from the intersection. The latter is also at the side road to a second trailhead for Lower Muley Twist Canyon, a fine two- or three-day backpack. The road then leaves Halls Creek and winds through a small drainage to the eastern Capitol Reef boundary at 39.3 miles.

Palmers penstemon

From the flat beyond the boundary there are fine views of spare Mancos Shale slopes and benches to the north and Mount Pennell to the northeast. The road trends to the south, passing by an interesting hill of Brushy Basin clay at 43.4 miles, and eventually enters sparse piñon-juniper forest and an area that infrequently enjoys a robust spring bloom of purple locoweed and dark rusty (from a distance) dock or canaigre. The junction with the Clay Point Road is at 47.1 miles. Here, the Burr Trail/Notom-Bullfrog Road turns to the right (south) and the pavement begins again (remember, however, that before reaching Highway 276, the crossing of Bullfrog Creek is at grade and may require high clearance or 4WD, and may not be passable at all during and after storms). Descriptions for travel in either direction are included in the Clay Point Circuit section.

Typical plant assemblage along the Burr Trail

Wolverine Loop Road and Little Death Hollow Road Trip

Distance: 27.7 miles

Wingate Sandstone cliff above the Chinle Formation

Most of Utah's renowned slot canyons lie within the Navajo Sandstone, a massive formation of wind-blown sand laid down in the Jurassic Period when this part of North America was a vast desert. While the Navajo is the thickest dune sand, both the Wingate Sandstone, which is earlier, and the Entrada Sandstone, which is later, represent similar periods of dry climate lasting a long time. Slots are much less common in the latter two formations, but Little Death Hollow and its companion canyon, Wolverine, are fine examples of Wingate narrows, and together they form a rare loop hike that is best done as a two-day backpack.

Little Death Hollow is located west of the southern end of Capitol Reef National Park, and east of the Escalante River and the town of Boulder. Access is from the Wolverine Loop Road that swings south off the Burr Trail that connects Boulder, Capitol Reef, and Bullfrog on Lake Powell. The Wolverine Loop is less than 30 miles in length, and its condition varies quite dramatically due to weather and irregular maintenance. We have traveled it at times when carefully driven sedans of at least average clearance might be able to make the trip, also when high clearance was necessary, and once when 4WD was required. The best information regarding its condition is available from the interagency visitor center on Highway 12 on the west edge of Escalante. Even small amounts of precipitation can render the road impassable until drying occurs.

The loop is interesting and scenic enough in its own right to serve as an alternate to the part of the Burr Trail between the loop's two ends. That Burr Trail section is the least interesting stretch on what is otherwise a truly spectacular drive from Boulder to Lake Powell. Wolverine is much, much slower, however, and really is enjoyable only when both road and weather conditions are good. Although as previously mentioned, there are times when cars might be able to make it, those times are not common, so high clearance is really the minimum, and sandy and/or wet spots make 4WD a nice comfort. Most Little Death Hollow hikers come from Boulder, and the slot is a little closer to the Burr Trail on the Boulder side, so the description of the loop that follows is counterclockwise from the western terminus.

The west end of the Wolverine Loop is 18.4 miles from the junction of the Burr Trail and Highway 12 in the town of Boulder. Turn right (south) and zero the odometer. (See the section above on the Burr Trail for more detail about this beautiful drive.)

The graded road traverses rolling hills in the brown Moenkopi Formation amidst typical piñon-juniper forest. For the first several miles the road is on high ground, but is very susceptible to even modest amounts of moisture, and the steep, short hills can be dangerous when wet. Then, when the route enters the wide sandy course of Horse Canyon, the threat is during dry conditions when everything softens up and two-wheel drive vehicles can bog down. After the road leaves Horse Canyon at mile 5.5, it meanders along generally higher ground until just before the Wolverine Creek trailhead at mile 10. A small, tight canyon here tends to collect run-off during and just after rain events, and once again, the soggy track may suggest 4WD. All this sounds worse than it usually is, but be prepared and informed.

Beyond the trailhead the road climbs steadily up the dip slope of the Shinarump Member of the Chinle Formation. Left (north) of the road and parallel to it is an interesting canyon worth exploring (there are at least two ways in from the road). To the right (south), big blocks of black petrified wood begin to appear, increasing in abundance up to the top of the hill at mile 11.3. On sunny days, entire hillsides sparkle with reflected light from chunks up to several feet in size. Rock collecting is not permitted in the national monument, but the sheer amount of the wood is impressive enough. The road then descends to an old corral and the signed Little Death Hollow trailhead at mile 12.8. The hike description for the slot is at the end of this section.

Petrified wood on the Wolverine Loop

From the trailhead it is just over 0.5 mile to an unsigned junction where a little used track goes to the left (north), leading to some good dispersed campsites (GSENM permit required) and back to the Wolverine Loop 2 miles from its eastern end at the Burr Trail. The main road continues straight ahead (east) and eventually climbs to a high point and cattleguard where the view back to the west is expansive. The sense of openness, along with good views, continues for the next 5 miles. At the 19.5-mile mark is a well-signed intersection. To the right (south) the road is usually good for 2.7 miles to Silver Falls Creek, and then of lesser quality on down to the Moody Canyons.

To continue on to the Burr Trail, turn left (north). Perhaps the best Wolverine Loop view is at 19.9 miles with a sweeping panorama to the west and south that includes Navajo Mountain near Arizona, the Aquarius Plateau to the northwest, and the mesas and cliffs east of the Escalante River. From this point to the Burr Trail the road alternately passes through nice piñon-juniper forest, small meadows, and dry washes. The upper end of the cut-off track that begins near the Little Death Hollow trailhead comes in from the left (southwest) at mile 25.7, and the pleasant pavement of the Burr Trail is at 27.7. A left (northwest) turn leads back to Boulder, and a right (southeast) to the Capitol Reef National Park boundary and a graded road surface in 1.7 miles.

Hiking Little Death Hollow and Wolverine Creek

Distance: 18 miles

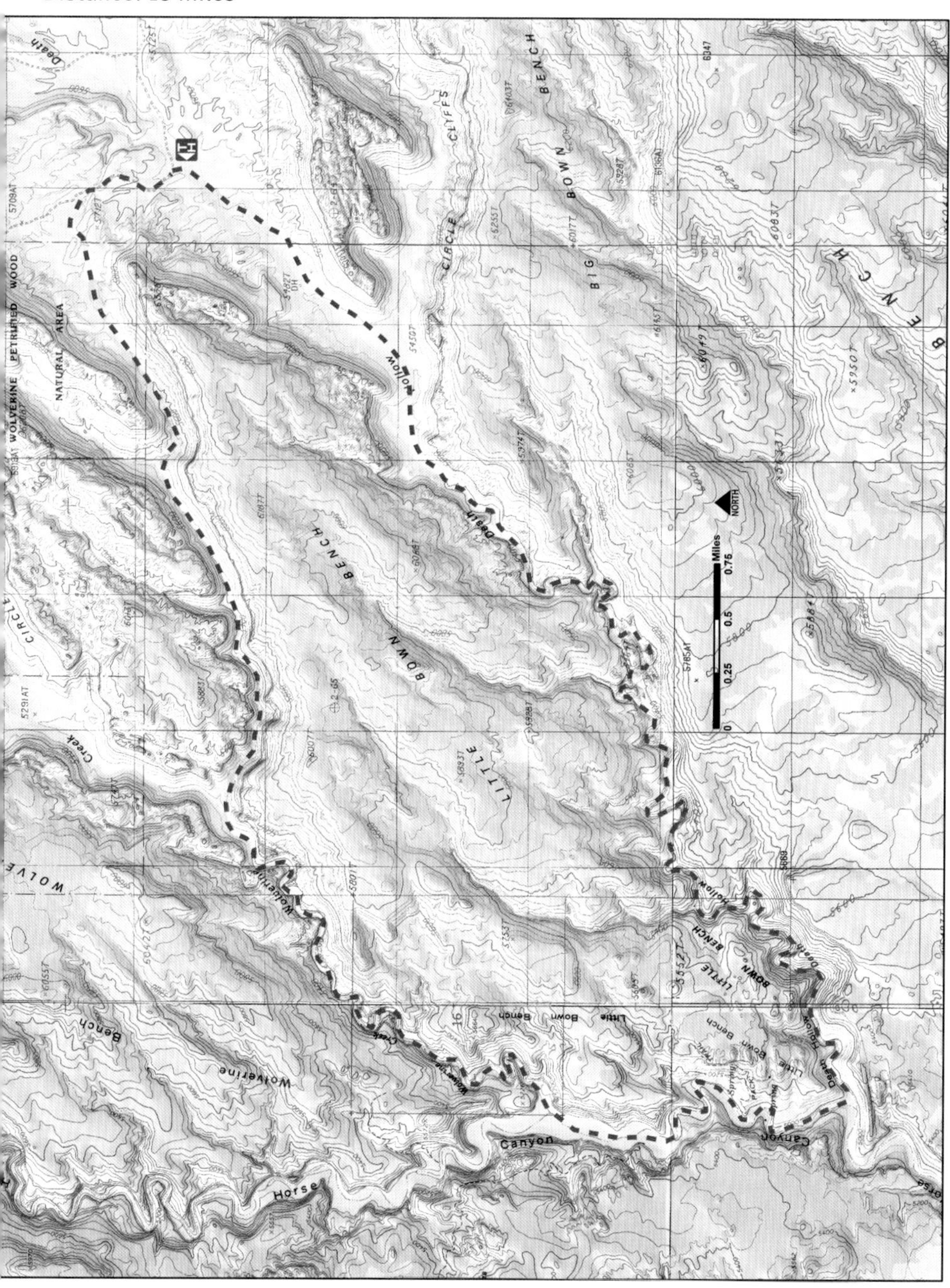

ittle Death Hollow and Wolverine Creek route

An 18-mile hike in a day is a significant undertaking for many, if not most, people. When the distance includes negotiating obstacles, taking a lot of photographs, and just generally enjoying a spectacular place, it is easy to run out of daylight, if not energy. Although getting through Little Death Hollow with a backpack is a bit of a chore, this loop really lends itself to a two-day pack, best during the long and cool days of spring, or during a dry and unusually cool stretch in early fall. There is ample parking for several vehicles at the trailhead (directions are included in the preceding section), where there is a sign-in register.

The beginning of the narrows of Little Death Hollow is about a 3 mile walk from the trailhead, mostly along a well-defined social trail. There is a natural tendency to try to get this part over with as soon as possible, but the hike is very pleasant, even mellow, and a fine way to ease into the day. The trail register is on the edge of a small thicket, and the path itself is subject to the vagaries of weather events, but should be easy to find by heading southwest into the very wide canyon. The trail generally follows a fairly straight path, cutting across the major and minor washes several times, but adhering to the higher ground and easier going. A large boulder to the right (west) of the trail marks the 1-mile point, and 0.3 mile farther on the route crosses the wash just upstream from its confluence with a major side drainage coming in from the east (left).

At 1.5 miles from the trailhead a short use trail leads to the right (northwest) to another large boulder, this one resting at the base of a steep slope leading up to the Wingate cliffs. This rock has a petroglyph panel on the east side, largely a line of bighorn sheep, but it has been vandalized in the past. Beyond, the social trail remains strong for almost a mile, with two wash crossings. After that it enters the wash for short distances and then cuts across meanders on the right (northwest) side. Fremont cottonwoods appear at 2.25 miles, and then Gambel oak. After a possible wet area, at 2.8 miles the canyon bends to the left (south) and the canyon becomes more scenic. A final meander cut-off trail is on the right (northwest) just beyond. As the canyon continues to narrow, the shade and slopes support a rich collection of high desert plants, including big sage, rabbitbrush, Mormon tea, Fremont barberry (mahonia), fishhook cactus, penstemons, prickly pear cactus, single leaf ash, skunkbush, piñons, and junipers.

With the Wingate Sandstone now down almost at wash level, the less permeable Chinle below forces water percolating through the porous sandstone to the surface. At the 3.2-mile mark, just after another probable wet section, a side canyon enters from the left (east), but the main canyon bends to the right (west). A social trail cuts across the meander. The canyon at this point is scenic, and the abundant vegetation nicely accents the red rock.

Good narrows begin 3.8 miles from the trailhead, with barberry (mahonia), Fremont cottonwoods, single leaf ash, and skunkbush persisting. Two side canyons quickly come in from the right (north). The first obstacle worthy of any note during our hike occurred at 5 miles, an easy to negotiate rock jam of two huge boulders. Good narrows follow, with a particularly fine stretch from 5.3 to 5.4 miles. The slot section begins 5.9 miles into the canyon, and gets even better 0.1 mile farther on.

Wingate Sandstone

Across south-central Utah, the Wingate Sandstone is a productive scenery producer. Although it is generally tan in color on fresh surfaces, it almost always sports a beautiful red iron oxide coating, giving it star power among the many formations on the Colorado Plateau. Another characteristic that is at least as important in terms of scenic impact: the Wingate tends to weather into soaring vertical cliffs above the pastel slopes of the Chinle Formation and below the ledgy Kayenta Formation and white domes of the Navajo Sandstone. In addition to the Circle Cliffs area (the cliffs are Wingate all the way around), the Wingate is the scenic climax along Highway 24 from Bicknell to Fruita, along the west side of the Maze, at the upper end of the San Rafael Reef slot canyons, and in upper Glen Canyon.

The Wingate rests atop an unconformity with the underlying Chinle Formation, which is not unexpected given the warm and moist climate during Chinle times, and the extreme aridity that typified Wingate deposition. The sandstone is very well sorted, and the uniform sand grains are fairly well cemented, both factors that lead to its propensity to weather into walls rather than slopes or domes. Like the older White Rim and Cedar Mesa Sandstones, and the later Navajo and Entrada Sandstones, the Wingate is eolian (wind blown) in nature, forming a vast erg over much of the Colorado Plateau.

The sand came from the north and northwest, where a huge flat plain bordered the ocean shoreline. When sea level fell, as it did perhaps six times during Wingate deposition, more sand was exposed to the wind and then transported to the south and southeast. (See the Navajo Sandstone sidebar in the Boulder Mail Trail hike section regarding the ultimate source of that sand.) When sea level rose, the sand supply would be cut off, as the water table would rise in the distant dune fields. Eventually, the top of the dunes would be leveled. When the sea receded again, the dunes would be regenerated on top of the preceding cycle.

In the area covered by this guidebook, the Wingate averages around 400 feet in thickness, but in Zion National Park it is absent. In its place is the Moenave Formation, a brown, slope-forming unit much like the older Moenkopi Formation. The Wingate and Moenave are contemporaneous, and at their margin, grade into one another. The Moenave was deposited by intermittent streams flowing north from highlands in present day Arizona. In places, thin sheets of Wingate sand intertongue with the river sediments of the Moenave.

Little Death Hollow and Wolverine Creek route

Little Death Hollow

For the next 1.5 miles, the slot is mostly tight enough to preclude GPS signals, clearly a good thing, so the distance is estimated by walking time with subtraction of the time spent getting through the obstacles. The slot widens briefly at 6.3 miles then tightens with several boulder chokes, a couple of which we passed through by crawling under the rocks. Backpackers should have a short rope to lower their packs over these rocks. The next big storm will no doubt alter, or perhaps fill, the tunnels, but there are other ways to get through. The 1.5-mile long, mostly slot section, is often sculpted and undulating, sometimes deep and dark. Even in Utah, its length and beauty stand out.

The interior canyon lowers and widens at 7.6 miles, with a feel much like Lower Muley Canyon in Capitol Reef. We were reminded of the need to be prepared for anything in a slot canyon when we came to a six-foot high boulder jam that dropped straight into what turned out to be an 18-inch deep pool of very cold water, even though there had been little rain in the previous several weeks. Soon after the long pool, the canyon enters the Kayenta Formation, a ledgy unit, and the slot ends. This is just beyond the 8.1-mile mark and makes a good turnaround point if you are going to retrace your steps back to your vehicle.

At 0.5 mile farther a cable crosses the canyon and a pipe comes down from the left (southeast), and goes underground to the right wall, just before the cliff turns toward Horse Canyon. The confluence of Little Death Hollow and Horse Canyon is 8.7 miles from the parking area and offers good shade from mature cottonwoods for camping.

To continue on the loop to Wolverine Creek, pass to the right (north) around the point (UTM 0477313mE, 4176559mN). Horse Canyon is wide and probably wet for the first

Little Death Hollow

0.5 mile to a fence and cabin on the left (west). Beyond the cabin it is considerably less interesting, but the road makes for better progress. The mouth of Wolverine Creek appears on the right (east) after just under 2 miles of walking in Horse Canyon. A sign prohibiting vehicles may mark the canyon, along with a face of interesting solution cavities on the north side. The GPS coordinates are UTM 0477244mE, 4178849mN. This hike can be easily done without a GPS, however, by simply staying to the right all the way around the loop.

The bottom of Wolverine canyon, while not as spectacular as Little Death Hollow, is nonetheless very handsome. The first mile is easy going on smooth gravel, with high Wingate walls on both sides, and high straight or even overhanging walls on the left (generally west) side. The walls close in to about five feet after the first mile, and the tread becomes rocky. At 1.5 miles is a high wall to the left (west), a lower undercut face to the right (east), and low angled and interesting sandstone closer to the wash on both sides. The appearance of water and cottonwoods 2 miles from Horse Canyon mark the presence of the Chinle Formation at wash level. The confluence with the canyon that leads to the Wolverine Trailhead is 0.75 mile ahead at UTM 0479350mE, 4181291mN; stay to the right (easterly) at this point.

After this junction the walking becomes a little more difficult, first on a bumpy Chinle bed, and then due to several large rocks in the wash that must be avoided. A short side canyon comes in from the left at 4.3 miles, again stay right, and the last major division is less than 1 mile beyond at UTM 0481955mE, 4181846mN, and as at all the other major canyon intersections, keep to the right (more easterly). From this point to the high point for the entire hike is 1.1 miles. As the high point is approached, the wash becomes small and side washes are confusing. We set a course to where the top seemed the lowest, and then followed a faint use trail down the other side. When that trail turned northerly, we went cross-country, bearing right (southeast) and following the terrain down to a large wash that leads to the trailhead. A high pour-off can be passed on the right (west), although we opted to go left (east) and soon found the road, which was easy walking at a time when that was most welcome.

This great canyon loop was a cautionary tale for us in another way. Having seen various print and Internet sites, it appeared that the distance would be about 16 miles, though one site indicated it was 20. We thought that 16 miles would be a long day hike, but well within our range. On a good trail, that is certainly the case, but with the slot, the obstacles, the sand, the rocks, and the actual 18-mile distance, it was hard enough that if we do the loop again it will definitely be as a backpack. By the time we reached Wolverine on almost an 11-hour day of hiking, and especially as we made our way up that canyon, it is fair to say that our appreciation of the scenery was substantially lessened. Thus, unless you routinely do extremely long and difficult hikes, our recommendation is to take two days to enjoy the loop.

Deer Creek Loop Hike

Distance: 5 miles

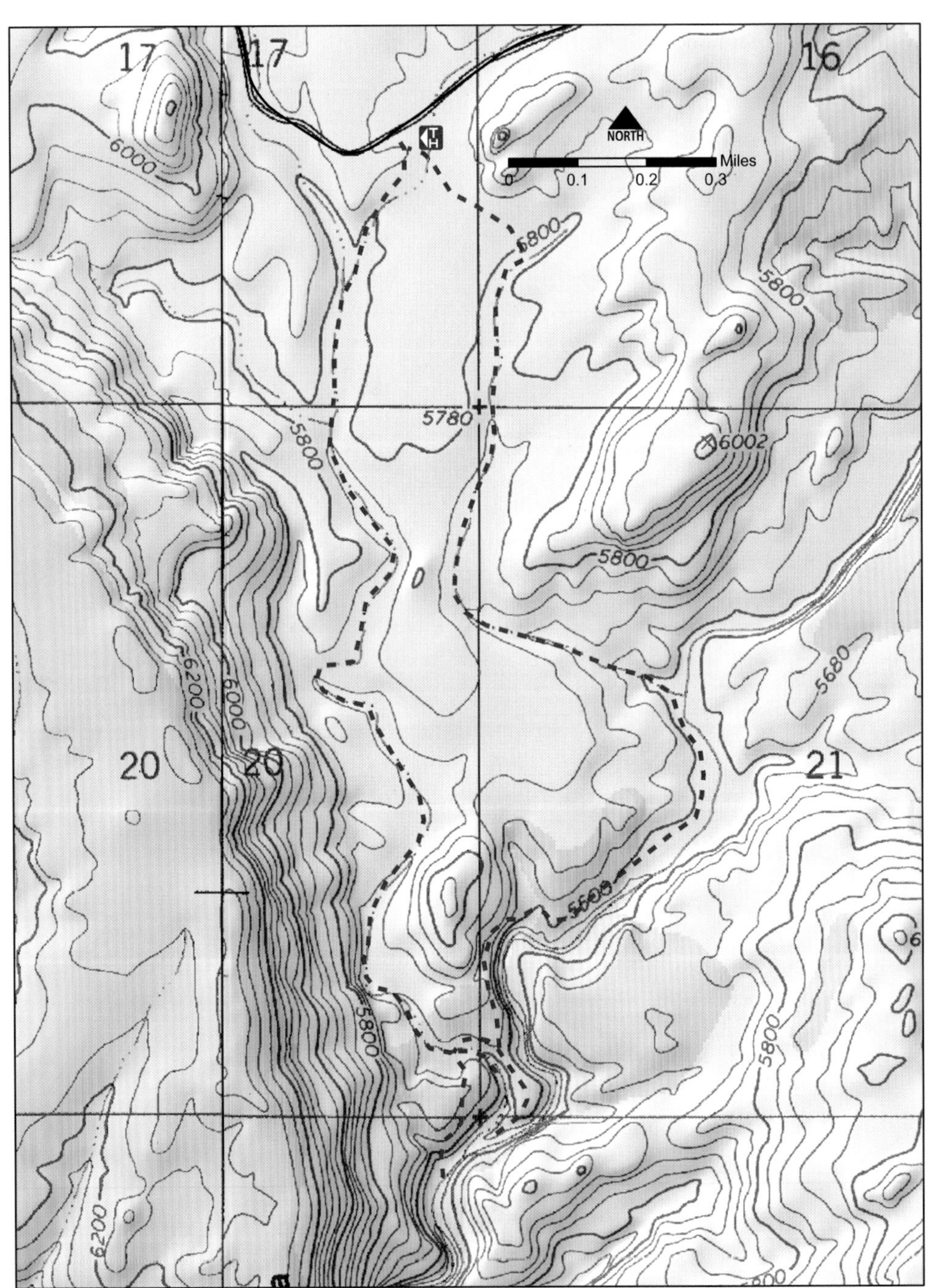

Deer Creek route

The western part of the Burr Trail near the town of Boulder passes through a sea of sand and slickrock, one from the other. Great slopes and cones of white Navajo Sandstone, accented by weathered crossbeds and joints, frame the road from Deer Creek almost to Boulder. They invite one to roam, perhaps to climb, and to marvel at the sheer expanse of bare rock. In summer the heat and brightness can be uncomfortable, but on cool spring and fall days this is a fine place to be.

The hike described here is not on formal trails, and therefore requires **very good route-finding skills**. It offers considerable variety, the opportunity—but not necessity—for a little challenge, and some pretty impressive natural features.

Getting There

For those coming from the southern end of Capitol Reef National Park on the Burr Trail, the starting point is 30.6 miles from the Notom-Bullfrog Road, and just barely over a mile west of the entrance to Deer Creek Campground. On the left (south) side of the road is a very large graded area that is a popular dispersed camping spot with a large ponderosa pine tree right in the middle. From the west, in the town of Boulder, turn east onto the Burr Trail from Highway 12 at milepost 86.3. It is 1.5 miles to the entrance sign for the Grand Staircase–Escalante National Monument, and a total of 5.4 miles from the highway to the parking area (on the right from this direction). Please be respectful of any campers here by parking away from their units; there is plenty of room for all.

The Hike

To begin the hike, simply enter the sandy wash that runs along the east and south margin of the parking area. The mileage for the hike begins in the wash near the farthest extension of the grading, toward the southwest, and marked by boulders placed to prevent driving into the wash. Walk in the sand to the right (southwest). At first, the going is very easy on a nice mix of sand and slickrock, with some black boulders to provide contrast. Ahead, the impressive slickrock flank of Durffey Mesa soars more than 400 feet above the wash. After 0.2 mile a dry tributary comes in from the right (north), followed by a very similar one at 0.4 mile. Continue straight ahead at both. At the second confluence there are two large ponderosas in the wash, an occurrence repeated several times during the initial 1.5 miles of the hike.

In many parts of the west, ponderosa forests thrive in an elevation band of about 6,500 feet to less than 8,000 feet, between piñon and juniper below and aspen and fir above. Ponderosas (*Pinus ponderosa*) are large, stately trees with long needles (around six inches) in bundles of three. Older trees have a distinctive orange bark divided into plates, and often have a pleasant aroma that reminds some of vanilla. Cones are also large, with sharp points on the scales; the seeds are the primary food of Abert squirrels, tassel-eared and with bright white fur on the underside of their tails. Ponderosas can grow in fairly dry climates, aided by a shallow root system that can take advantage of light rains that saturate only the top few inches of soil. In south-central Utah, ponderosas often grow at elevations that are lower than expected, especially where there is Navajo Sandstone slickrock and sand. The slickrock funnels extra water down to the sand, which then acts as an effective insulator that slows evaporation.

After the second dry wash comes in, the walking becomes considerably more difficult due to the amount of black boulders that often fill the wash. This condition lasts until the 1-mile mark. Sometimes the rocks can be avoided by walking on either side of the primary wash channel, but it is a nice relief when slickrock appears and continues for more than 0.3 mile. At this point the route passes to the right (west) of an interesting knob that is ribbed and lined on several different levels, and may be too enticing to resist climbing. As always, keep in mind that it is often more difficult to descend steep slickrock than it is to climb, and this cone is angled enough for that to matter. To continue the hike, stay to the left to avoid a short drop into a pool that ends the easy walking. After less than 200 yards of boulder hopping, cow trails lead up to an easy-going bench on the left (east) that avoids the wash. After a 0.1-mile break on the bench, re-enter the wash to the 1.7-mile mark. This is a quadruple decision point with coordinates of 0467533mE, and 4186807mN.

Straight ahead is an interesting narrows with obstacles; above and left of the narrows is the route to an impressive high finger between Deer Creek and the unnamed drainage you have been hiking; to the right is a route that goes all the way down to Deer Creek; and high above to the left is the return hiker-made path that eventually parallels Deer Creek on high benches. Each is described below.

The narrows are guarded as of this writing by two boulder chokes, neither of which is particularly difficult to descend, but harder to ascend. Beyond is an interesting series of chutes that may have water, some can be chimneyed, but others are too wide. This is a fun stretch for the adventurous, but a high dryfall prevents non-technical access to Deer Creek. A fairly reasonable class 3 exit from the narrows is on the left (northeast) side between the boulders and the chutes.

To avoid the narrows and access the point at the confluence with Deer Creek, contour across slickrock on the left (north). Choose a route that is comfortable, but not higher than necessary. Once fully up on the sandy bench, a clear social trail leads along the rim of the narrows, with good views back down and into them. The largely bare rock finger that towers above the confluence will be visible ahead and below to the right (south) after about 200 yards. The way down crosses a moderate slope of sand and small

Durffey Mesa

Deer Creek route

rocks and there are several faint paths that help prevent destruction of the biological soil crust. In all, it is 0.3 mile from the decision point out to the end of the finger. This is a nice place for a break or lunch, with Deer Creek visible far ahead, but audible as it rushes by unseen in a deep canyon directly below.

Downstream, the creek walls rise and tighten as the watercourse becomes pinned against the high wall of Durffey Mesa. Across the canyon to the right (the terminus of the unnamed wash) a trail can be seen that leads farther downstream and eventually to creek level. To take that short spur, return to the decision point.

In the wash bed just above the start of the narrows there is a wide, sandy wash entering from the south (right, looking down into the narrows). Walk south into the mouth of the wash less than 50 yards and look to the left (east) to spot a trail ascending the steep, sandy and rocky slope. A short climb attains a flat, followed by a very short uphill and then a long descent. This use trail is well defined and easy to follow. It crosses a shallow drainage and then ascends a sandy hill onto a gentle slope. Even from this point it doesn't appear that the path can lead down to Deer Creek, but it eventually reaches a small gully next to the big Durffey Mesa wall just over 0.3 mile from the decision point. A short descent follows, with a four-foot drop down to the willows fringing Deer Creek. The stream moves from wall to wall in the narrow and sheer canyon, so water shoes are necessary beyond this point. The tangle of vegetation wards off all but the very determined beyond the first crossing. It is just under 0.4 mile each way from the top of the narrows to stream level at Deer Creek.

Excluding exploration of the narrows, the two side trips above add about 1.4 miles to the round trip distance for the hike. To complete the loop back to your vehicle, look north from the decision point. Aim for a visible track that ascends eastward across the sandy slope from the highest exposed slickrock north of the narrows (a higher route than the one out to the finger at the confluence). A large black boulder marks the way as the route over the slickrock passes just above it. Once on the path, it soon rises to a flat and curves around to the left (eventually north). This is a good clear social trail that passes between a hill on the left (west) and high above Deer Creek, which remains deeply incised to the east.

Less than 0.2 mile from the decision point, the path drops off the sandy flat and crosses a gully on slickrock. It then makes a nifty traverse on a small break in the slope of the slickrock until that edge peters out, forcing the route to drop down a little to eventually pass by a saddle on the left (northwest). The path turns southeast to pass

Deer Creek side canyon

Deer Creek

Secondary iron

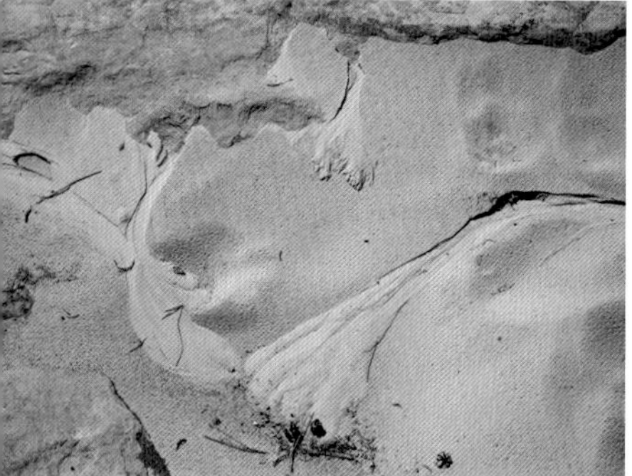

Sand detail

Harrimans yucca

over a sandy bench before bending back to the northeast, where it runs just above Deer Creek. The trail is close enough to the stream to see large trout feeding in the current, but there is no way down to the water at this point. Farther along, almost 0.9 mile from the narrows, there is a route down to Deer Creek at the confluence with a drainage joining from the west. A moderately steep, but short slickrock slope leads down to a small flat just above creek level. Tall clumps of water birch keep the willows at bay so there is room to move around. A spring-fed flow adds to Deer Creek, and across the main stream, seeps support a colony of mosses and ferns.

The main trail bends to the northwest just above, and climbs up to pass over a streaked pour-off above the spring. The social trail crosses the dryfall and bends back toward Deer Creek (and ultimately to the Burr Trail just west of the entrance to the Deer Creek Campground), but the route back to your vehicle stays in the shallow drainage to the left (west). A pillar with a waistline on the intermediate horizon is a good target. The going is easy, first on slickrock, then mostly sand. At 1.2 miles from the decision point, the valley bends to the right (north) and the walking is again mostly on gentle slickrock.

After the bend it is about 0.2 mile to a modest Y junction of very minor slickrock valleys. Stay to the left (northwest) in the slightly deeper channel, hiking on sand or slickrock. Another 0.2 mile will bring you to a cascade of black iron oxide mineralization that has tumbled down the white rock and is scattered on the slope. The source layer is visible near the top of the slickrock. The wash bends to the northwest at this point and soon ends at the base of a low, sandy ridge. Head up the slope, bearing just to the left of a large double-headed cone. The coordinates at the top of the little ridge are 0467654mE, 4188613mN. Continue walking to the west, south of the cone, which will lose one of its heads as you go. The ponderosa in the parking area, along with the several that are around it, are visible; simply head toward them to return to your vehicle. The total distance from the decision point is just under 2 miles, making the hike about 5 miles if you walk all the options.

Boulder Mail Trail Hike

Hiking distance is 12 miles round trip.

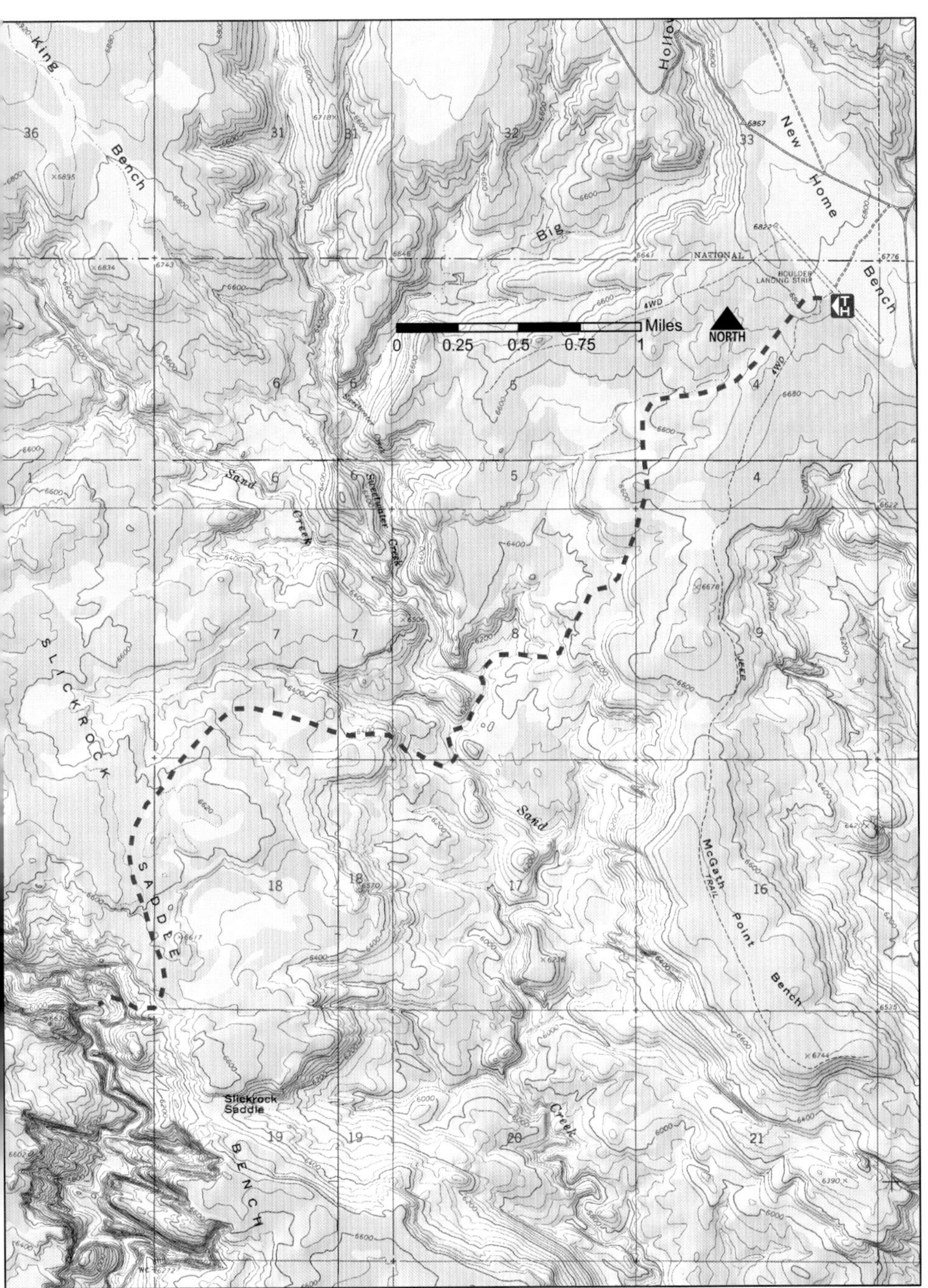

Boulder Mail Trail route

Boulder Mail trail

The east end of the Boulder Mail Trail is unlike any other trail in this book. For much of the way, the route is on bare slickrock, but not on top of the world—the effect is quite different than, say, the open feel above timberline. The two drainages that are accessible on a long and difficult day hike are flanked by spectacular Navajo Sandstone slopes both convoluted and steep, so the dominant impression is that of being down and in. Still, even for Utah, the long slickrock pitches are about as good as it gets.

It is not unusual to encounter historic artifacts while hiking in redrock country, many of which attest to the almost unimaginable (to modern sensibilities) efforts of early settlers in this harsh land. Corrals, cabins, fences, dugways, and irrigation ditches hang on in the dry climate. In this case, the trail itself is both a tangible remnant and a sobering reminder of what life was like a century ago in this part of the United States.

As members of the Church of Jesus Christ of Latter Day Saints moved to settle every corner of Utah following the charge of Brigham Young, it made sense to first develop the best valleys with the best water nearest to Salt Lake City. As the nineteenth century waned, new ground was hard to find, but families nonetheless made their way to a small area on the south side of the Aquarius Plateau where there was good pasture ground and ample water from Boulder Creek. The remoteness of the settlement is hard to conceive even now, but early Boulder truly defined what it meant to live on the frontier.

Frontiers are absorbed into the larger existing culture as goods and services become more easily available, security improves, and communication with that culture becomes routine. In 1902 the nearest bastion of civilization to Boulder was Escalante to the southwest, although that small town was no threat to Salt Lake or even Cedar City in terms of modern amenities. In that year a major step was taken with the "construction" of the Mail Trail, which offered the shortest and most efficient route from Escalante for the mules that brought the mail a couple of times a week. When the phone line, still visible along much of the hike, was added in 1910, Boulder's link to the world, tenuous as it might be, became established. The Mail Trail fell into disuse after Highway 12 reached Boulder at the beginning of the Second World War, but current day hikers can still experience much of the route and imagine along the way what it would have been like to reside in Boulder a hundred years ago.

The hike described here is 12 miles round trip, but will take a much bigger toll on most people than a similar length on a more standard trail. Do not underestimate the effect of knee-wrenching descents and quadriceps-burning ascents on the body. If you go all the way down to Death Hollow before turning around, expect to take much longer than you normally would. Fortunately, stopping at Sand Creek or on the rim of Death Hollow are good alternatives for shorter and much easier hikes.

Even though slickrock is rarely slick unless wet or polished, this trek really does demand good boots that don't cause blisters even on very steep rock. Additionally, the Mail Trail is best hiked during cool weather, and with sunglasses on clear days. The white, occasionally golden or reddish Navajo Sandstone is exceedingly bright and headache-inducing in bright sun (which is the default setting in south-central Utah!). Thunderstorms routinely cause both creeks to flash flood, which could cut off a return trip. Choose another hike if storms are in the forecast, since lightning is also a considerable hazard.

Getting There

To access the trailhead, start at the junction of Highway 12 and the Burr Trail in Boulder, and proceed west on Highway 12 for 3.1 miles to the well-signed Hells Backbone Road at milepost 83.3. Turn right (north) onto this good gravel road and as it curves around to the northwest, begin to look immediately for a track on the left (southwest), about 150 yards from the highway. At this writing, there are no signs to identify this road. Take the left turn, watching for a big rock or two right at the junction, and proceed carefully for 0.5 mile to the Boulder Airport. Cars should be parked well off the runway, which is a well-graded gravel strip through the sagebrush. Trucks can continue straight across the runway, negotiate a short rocky stretch, and park just beyond the trailhead on a track parallel to the road.

The Hike

The walk to the trailhead from the airstrip is less than 100 yards. A steel box contains a register and at the time of our visit, also had the permits that are required for overnight stays within the Grand Staircase–Escalante National Monument. The trail begins to the right of and adjacent to the register, and is faint at first. In general, the route to Death Hollow is clearly marked or is obvious, but there may be

Boulder Mail trail

times after wind or rain when the portions that are sandy may be obscured. The country here is big and confusing, so if you are unsure of the trail, it would be a good idea to turn back, but under normal circumstances, the way should be clear.

From the register, the trail climbs very gently and then descends on rocky tread to the 0.25-mile mark. Thankfully, this rocky section is short, and not repeated. The route winds through typical piñon-juniper forest, though at this relatively high elevation (6,750 feet), the pines dominate. Just over 0.5 mile along, and after following a gravelly wash bottom, the trail passes to the left (southeast) of an unexpected pour-off, and then winds through a pleasant open area of big sage. At the 1-mile mark, the route bends a little more southerly and largely ascends very gently for 0.4 mile before dropping slightly to a minor rim at 1.5 miles. This point is less than 200 feet lower than the trailhead, a reflection of the almost non-existent grade over that stretch.

The descent to Sand Creek begins in earnest here. The introductory slickrock pitch is benign, with a relatively gentle grade of short duration. At 1.8 miles the route enters another sage flat, and then proceeds to the inner rim of the Sand Creek canyon at 2 miles. Here (UTM 0457492mE; 4190819mN), begin to follow cairns down a chute to the left (south), where some old boards may still be piled up. Open slickrock hiking for 0.4 mile leads to a minor side canyon, and continues on down to Sand Creek at 2.6 miles. To the north (hiker's right) the cross-bedding in the Navajo Sandstone is quite obvious, evidence that the sand accumulated as dunes.

Sand Creek is a perennial spring-fed stream that supports lush vegetation within its narrow cut in the sandstone. The route turns left (south, downstream) and soon crosses the creek where it divides into two channels, at least until the next flood rearranges everything. About 100 yards downstream a cairn on the right (west) marks where the trail ascends briefly to a bench; it returns streamside shortly. At 2.9 miles an inviting side canyon appears on the right (northwest), but the route passes by its mouth. Less than 100 yards beyond (UTM 0456730mE; 4190068mN), cairns identify the route, which climbs steeply on slickrock for a 0.1 mile, heading just to the right (north) of a hoodoo-topped dome. The grade moderates when the tread returns to sand. Manzanita grows thickly along this mellow stretch on the shoulder above the canyon that was passed along Sand Creek.

As this pleasant section begins to steepen again, look ahead to the right (and up) to spot the old telephone line, amazingly, still often in place. Near the trail it is attached to a dead tree with an old insulator, but in most cases it just runs across branches. The single wire trends along the route, passing over it several times, and continuing into Death Hollow. When one spool of wire was exhausted, the next one was simply attached by winding the two together. As the trail again takes to slickrock, the pitch is steep at first, then moderates over 200 yards or so. The ponderosa pines here seem to be living on the bare rock, but their roots have penetrated the joints in the sandstone to significant depths. If there is sand around the tree, it acts effectively as insulation against evaporation, which further helps the pines and other plants survive long periods of drought.

Death Hollow

After leaving the rock, the trail continues to ascend almost to the 4-mile mark where there are fine views to the south and back to the east and northeast. The next mile is very gentle in gradient and is mostly on sand except for a couple hundred yards in the middle where there is interesting ribbed slickrock to cross. After the trail returns to sand, heavy rain or wind have the potential to obscure the route, and at least two old and now unused paths could be confusing. (Generally, however, it will be easy to follow the footprints of other hikers.) If conditions have made route-finding difficult, aim for a highpoint to the southwest where the trail climbs up a small hill. The shoulder of this rise (UTM: 0455018mE; 4188382mN) is also the rim of Death Hollow.

Death Hollow

It is all downhill from here to Death Hollow! For the first 0.3 mile, the gradient is moderate. A short drop to a large ponderosa is followed by a right turn to the north and a sandy pitch that is also short. From here almost to the stream is entirely on slickrock. Initially, the well-cairned route descends gently on an angled slope; following the cairns closely avoids steeper grades that typify a straight line route. At 5.4 miles a fairly discernible prominence just left (south) of the cairns is a fine viewpoint right down into Death Hollow. Many people stop here and turn around after lingering to enjoy the spectacular view.

Navajo Sandstone

Navajo Sandstone

Utah is graced with many colorful and spectacular rocks, but it is the Navajo Sandstone that tops them all. It can be snow white, or it can be red, and sometimes it can be both, either in streaks, or by wholesale change on a single vertical face. The Navajo is relatively hard, and it is often jointed heavily, resulting in common checkerboard slopes. The jointing also provides linear zones of weakness that can be exploited by run-off that over time can cut narrow slot canyons. By virtue of its resistance to erosion, it also forms huge domes, sometimes in great, impenetrable masses.

Many of the most scenic or exciting areas described in this book are on, or in, the Navajo Sandstone. The San Rafael Reef, from Ding and Dang Canyons all the way to the Black Dragon pictograph site, is a prime example. The Great Gallery in Horseshoe Canyon is painted on the sandstone, and the first part of Swett Creek is cut in the Navajo. The view west from the Henry Mountains is dominated by the Waterpocket Fold of Capitol Reef, which in turn owes its beauty and existence to the formation. It is here, however, between Boulder and Escalante, where the Navajo exposure is most extensive for hikers on the Mail Trail, or drivers on Highway 12.

The sandstone was originally laid down as huge dunes in a massive erg (dunefield) that covered almost all of present day Utah during the early Jurassic Period. The windblown deposition is recorded spectacularly in large scale crossbeds that are widely visible in Navajo Sandstone exposures. Modern day weathering and erosion often enhances the crossbeds so that they are obvious to anyone. Crossbeds form at the lee side of the dune. Well-sorted sand is carried up the gentle windward part of the dune, and falls out of the flow at the steep downwind lip, where it tumbles down the slope. As the winds change speed, a different size of sand grain is transported and deposited over the edge. In this way, steeply tilted layers of sorted sand build up over one another. In most ergs, there is a prevailing direction for the wind, and that is nicely preserved in the dip of the steeper beds.

The cross beds show that the sand was largely blown in from the north, similar to the direction of sand transport during Wingate Sandstone deposition. Since the Navajo erg has been proposed as the largest ever to appear on earth, the source of the sand is an interesting question. Recent research on zircon grains scattered among the quartz sand suggest that the source area was the core of the Appalachian Mountains that were elevated during the much earlier Pennsylvanian Period. Huge rivers then flushed the sand to the northwest, where it settled along the western shoreline of that time, in current day Montana and Alberta. Ocean currents then moved the grains south along the shore.

During the early Jurassic, Utah was on the west edge of the Pangaean supercontinent, which was beginning to break up. The global position meant that the paleoenvironment was extremely dry. Any time that sea level fell, vast flats of sand to the north would be exposed to arid winds, which were northerly during the annual monsoonal change in direction. Unimaginable amounts of sand were transported to the south to pile up to truly incredible depths of more than a thousand feet in much of south-central Utah, and two thousand feet in Zion National Park.

Navajo Sandstone along the Boulder Mail Trail

The siren call of the water may be too much to resist for some, however, just as it is very hard to stop just short of a summit. Additionally, it is on the plunge into Death Hollow that the actual remnants of the Mail Trail can be seen and appreciated. From the viewpoint the cairns seem to lead right off the edge of the cliff and into the air. Of course, this is not the case. Hidden ahead is a drop and then a traverse to the north which appears to take advantage of a natural shelf in the Navajo Sandstone that was probably enhanced when the trail was built. For people with strong aversions to exposure, almost the entire way down will be a challenge, or even not possible. If it is the latter, you will know right away. Many experienced slickrock hikers will find the route easy, even tame, while those in the middle will take a deep breath and continue. Everyone should obviously pay attention to what they are doing!

After the northerly traverse the route switchbacks very steeply down the wall. Along the way are steps and ramps cut into the sandstone, although it is hard to imagine mules willingly walking either up or down. The view into the chasm is always changing, and eventually the sound of running water will signal that the descent is nearly over. Before that happens, however, there is one final short and steep sandy pitch down to creek level.

The stream in Death Hollow is more robust than Sand Creek, and the resulting riparian environment is more lush and supports large trees of several species. Where the trail approaches the creek, a short step over a side channel leads to a section of the creek where rocks make it easy (at times of low to moderate flow) to get a good perspective upstream to a long pool. Water-loving plants cling to the cliff wall that forms the west bank. The main trail leads downstream for 75 yards to the 6-mile mark and a crossing that requires wading. Good campsites abound in that direction.

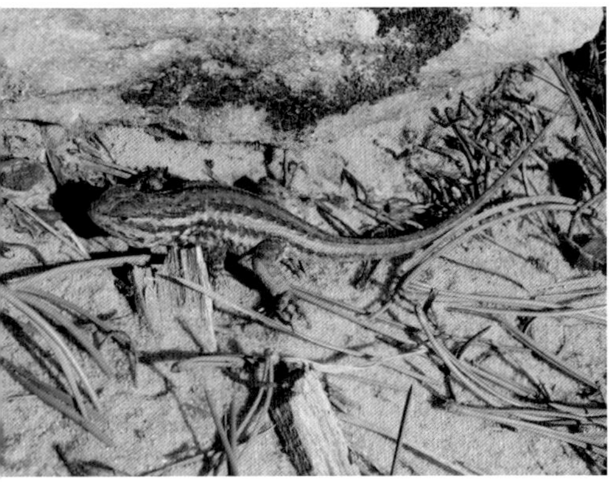

Lizard

The vegetation in this protected and well-watered place is dense and varied. Large specimens of box elder, Gambel oak, and ponderosa pine are abundant. Slightly smaller willows, red osier dogwood, rocky mountain and Utah juniper, and Utah serviceberry fill in any gaps that are not already occupied by ferns, rushes, or tall grasses. Poison ivy of a size that can be intimidating to many is also common, as it is in nearby drainages such as Calf Creek. The contrast between the riparian area and the slopes immediately above is very stark.

Day hikers set to return to the trailhead can get a miniature sense of what people at the bottom of the Grand Canyon feel when they look up and contemplate their hike out. The rim of Death Hollow is 640 feet above, with a large percentage of that elevation gain in the first 0.6 mile. With 6 miles yet to go, the prospect of the climb back up, and a second one (just under 500 feet) out of Sand Creek can be daunting. There is no shame in hiking to the inner rim of Sand Creek (round trip of 4 miles), or to Sand Creek itself (round trip of 5.2 miles), or to the viewpoint just above Death Hollow (round trip of 10.8 miles). Any hike in this slickrock gulf will be memorable.

Piñon branches along the Boulder Mail Trail

Lower Falls of Calf Creek Hike

Hiking distance is 6.1 miles round trip.

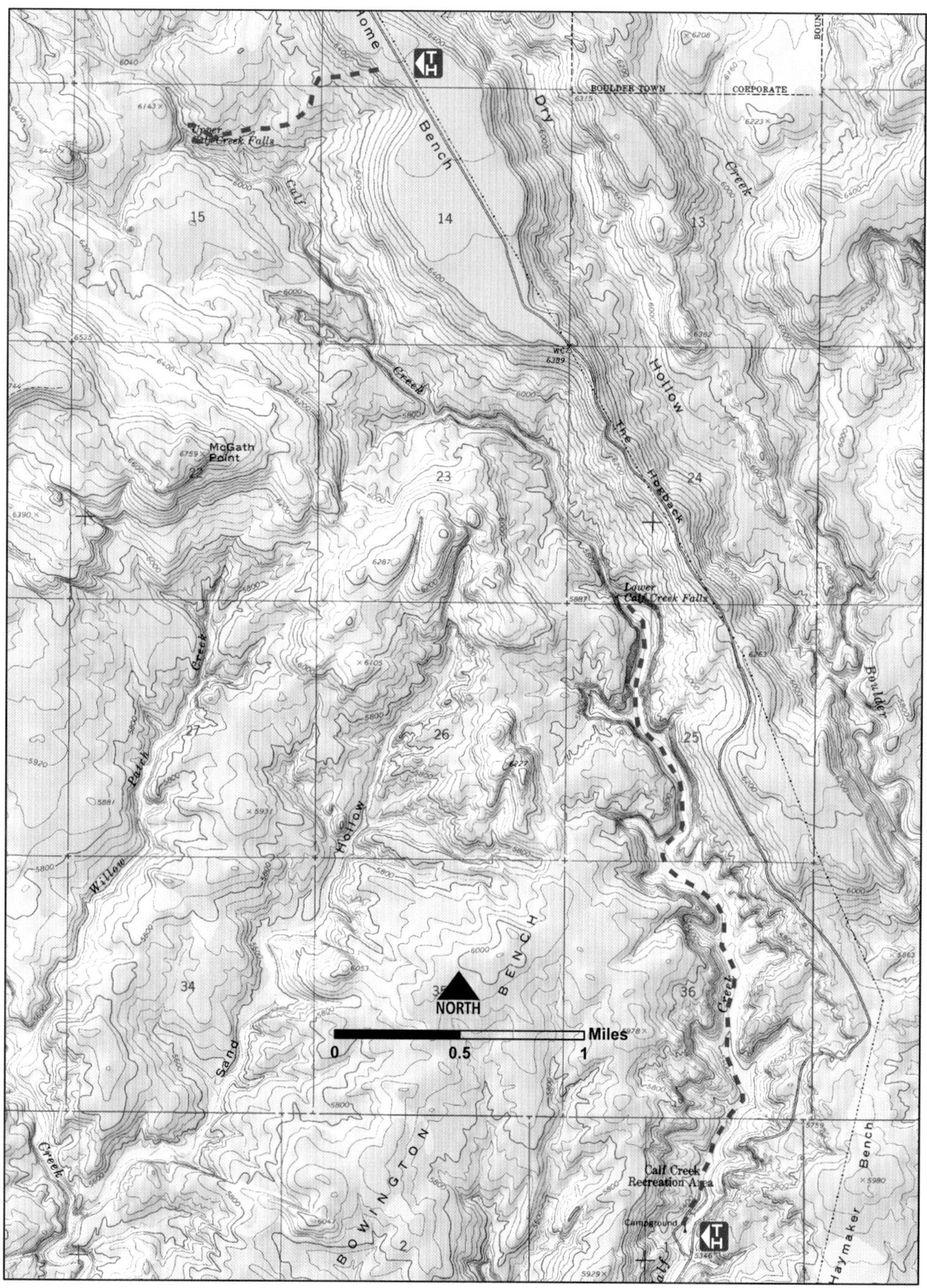

Lower Calf Creek Falls route (bottom) and Upper Calf Creek Falls route (top)

This may have happened to you: a hike that seemed only moderately scenic or interesting the first time comes to life on the second, or vice versa. Lower Calf Creek Falls may be a hike just like that. While it is hard to visualize many situations where the waterfall itself would fail to impress, the walk to it can be a bit of a trudge when conditions fall well short of ideal. The beauty and cool spray of the falls may be insufficient to compensate for an overheated hike in the height of summer, especially given the walk back to the car. On the other hand, in mid-October when the canyon is a riot of color and the weather pleasant, the entire affair can be hard to beat.

Getting There

The hike to the Lower Falls begins at the Calf Creek Recreation Area on Highway 12 in the Grand Staircase–Escalante National Monument. Roughly halfway between the towns of Boulder and Escalante, the entrance is well marked just east of milepost 75 on Highway 12 very near the bottom of the descent from the precipitous hogback at the end of New Home Bench. Parking in the narrow canyon is quite limited (about 30 spaces) and can be a problem at busy times and in the middle of the day. The BLM charges a fee (currently $2) for parking; holders of federal lands passes do not have to pay. Drinking water and a toilet are available, and the group camping area doubles as a picnic area when not occupied. A handful of mostly very small camping sites are scattered among the lush riparian vegetation. With lovely Calf Creek coursing through the area, they are very popular and often fill early in the day.

The Hike

From the parking area walk north on the road through the campground, following the signs to the trail, which bears to the left (northeast) just before the road crosses the creek on a concrete ford. Immediately on the left is a trail register, along with a box containing interesting trail guides that add to the enjoyment of the hike. The short, rocky climb is an indicator of what lies ahead. The gradient of the creek is modest, and the 550-foot gain in elevation between the trailhead and the falls, spread over 3 miles, would hardly be noticeable were it not for the presence of numerous short climbs and descents along the way. Not at all high by Colorado Plateau standards, Calf Creek does lie more than a mile above sea level, an elevation that may have an impact. Much of the route is in full sun, and during summer the combination of heat, elevation, sand, and the many hills may sap a lot of the pleasure out of the hike for some.

The density and variety of plants that border the trail are unusual for southern Utah, but expected here due to the nearby creek that is spring fed and flows all year. Early in the hike the path goes right through thickets of four-wing saltbush, Gambel oak, rubber rabbitbrush, and big sage in rapid succession. On the slopes, typical desert species like skunkbush, roundleaf buffaloberry, green ephedra, Fremont mahonia (barberry), and prickly pear cactus do very well. With good spring rains, the flower show can be spectacular in late April and early May, and fall can bring stunning color from mid to late October.

Calf Creek Falls

An added bonus along Calf Creek is evidence of the Fremont Culture that thrived in most of Utah for about six hundred years beginning roughly in 650 AD. Three of the numerous stops in the trail guide are devoted to Fremont sites, though all are distant from the trail (photographers will need a very long lens). At number six (1.1 miles from the trailhead), directly across the canyon and high on the far wall just below the top cliff band, is a granary. Almost exactly midway in the hike and just after a welcome Gambel oak tunnel, are three painted figures at the base of a huge, sheer Navajo Sandstone wall, again across the canyon. At the next stop (ten), another granary is barely apparent on the wall of a tributary entering from the left (northwest).

After passing the 2-mile mark, a measure of relief from the sun is afforded by another oak canopy, and then abundant box elder trees with their distinctive three-lobed leaves. The box elders turn a saturated pure yellow in the fall, competing with the Fremont cottonwoods near the campground for top color billing. At 2.4 miles the trail descends to the creek level, and the clear, smooth water is home to trout, big and small, positioned against the flow and moving with serious speed when startled. The canyon walls are close enough from this point to the falls that there is quite a forest along the stream. A quick glimpse of the top of the falls quickens the pace, and just over 3 miles from the trailhead is a worthy climax.

From the lip, Calf Creek takes a small preliminary jump, and then freefalls more than 100 feet almost directly into a beautiful, sand-rimmed pool at its base. The cliff glistens in the mist, and dark green algae covers the rock under and near the falls. High above the pool a series of seeps support small hanging gardens, and the beach is backed by a fringe of trees. The effect is more south sea island than Utah desert, and while the actual location enhances the impact, the falls would be noteworthy anywhere as they plunge over the red wall.

Fast hikers can make it to the falls and back in a couple of hours, but most people may take an hour and a half or more each way, and want to spend plenty of time enjoying the cascade and maybe finding a spot downstream to watch the trout. The return walk can also seem easier by following the trail guide on the way back, and/or studying the rich flora along the trail. In the fall, the foliage should be nicely backlit on a sunny day during the return hike, and there are several places along the trail that offer excellent and colorful vistas.

Upper Falls of Calf Creek Hike

Hiking distance is 2.2 miles round trip.

The hikes to Lower and Upper Calf Creek Falls are different in almost every respect, including the number of people on the trails. The Lower Calf Creek walk begins in an often crowded parking lot and is a wide, undulating trail suitable for almost anyone. Access to the Upper Falls is unmarked on Highway 12, and begins as a steep descent on slickrock that can be formidable to those who are not comfortable with that sort of thing.

Getting There

The trailhead for the Upper Falls is at the end of a short (0.1 mile) track off Highway 12 on the New Home Bench just southwest of the town of Boulder. From the junction of Highway 12 and the Hells Backbone Road about 3 miles west of Boulder, continue southeast on the highway for 2.2 miles to milepost 80.8, and turn right (southwest) onto a short track. From the Lower Falls drive 5.8 miles up to and over the famous hogback to milepost 80.8 and turn left.

The Hike

The trail begins as a sandy path that leaves from almost all the way around the parking circle (when driven counterclockwise). After a couple of hundred feet, there is a trail register among the piñons at the rim. The initial descent from this point drops 300 vertical feet in just 0.2 mile. The very top is especially steep on Navajo Sandstone slickrock.

Good boots with good traction soles are important here. The friction downclimb will seem easy or trivial to some, and for others it will be enough to stop the hike. We have seen people electing to sit on the rim while others in their group went down. In general, the rock is just rough enough to provide sufficient grip for most hikers, and there are numerous joints that add a little extra traction. The route is fairly easy to follow, often outlined by black boulders. After the first bare slickrock, there are some sandy spots and more black boulders, although the way is still steep. When the trail flattens and becomes a mild sandy track though the piñon-juniper "forest," it is a bit of a relief.

Once the grade settles to the point where it is possible to look around, the surroundings are quite interesting. Alternate stretches of slickrock, sometimes dotted with iron-rich masses, and small pockets of sandy soil offer considerable variety. The plant community is representative of the slickrock/sand environment in this part of Utah. While the dominant trees are the ubiquitous piñon and juniper, occasional small groupings of the much larger ponderosa pine occur in protected areas. Gambel oak, mountain mahogany, manzanita, and single leaf ash are other woody species, complemented by rabbitbrush, buckwheat, rice grass, yucca, and prickly pear. Near Calf Creek, in the riparian zone, stately Fremont cottonwood, boxelder, and willow thrive, and the lush growth in the canyon is often in view during the hike down.

Unlike the Lower Falls, both the top and bottom of the Upper Falls are easily accessed. The trail divides in a Y junction just over 0.8 mile from the rim. There should be cairns to mark this point, which is on a slickrock bench about 100 feet above the stream. To go to the bottom of the falls, take the left (more westerly) route. The first view of the falls is about 100 yards farther along, in combination with a fine view of a cavernous amphitheater on the other side of the creek. The trail descends quickly, including one short ledge drop, into a sandy undercut above the pool at the base of the falls. This alcove is noteworthy for providing a good look at the cascade, but also for its impressive stand of five-foot high poison ivy with its very large and actually handsome dark green leaves (leaflets, actually) of three.

Poison ivy near Upper Calf Creek Falls

The western species of poison ivy is *Toxicodendron rydbergii*, more likely to be a shrub than its eastern relative *T. radicans.* The plant contains a compound called urushiol in all of its parts, and 70 to 85 percent of people are susceptible to its effects, primarily sores that itch ferociously. Early in the spring and then again in the fall the leaflets may be red, but in summer they are dark and shiny green. The most likely plant that would be confused with poison ivy is box elder, a small tree in the maple (*Acer*) genus, since it has similar appearing leaflets, occasionally in threes. The difference is in the darker, shinier poison ivy leaflets, and that they are arranged alternately on stems, while box elder leaflets are opposite. While most Americans are quite familiar with poison ivy, if you are from Europe, where it is largely unknown, take care to learn what it looks like. There is plenty of room to avoid touching any of the poison ivy at the upper falls.

The trail down to the pool is to the left (northwest corner) at the entrance to the sandy alcove. Here the poison ivy is pretty close, but can be avoided. The last woody plant through which the trail passes before the foliage gives way to the pool is a fairly unusual species. Red-osier dogwood (*Cornus stolonifera,* or *C. sericea*) forms a dense clump of woody growth up to twelve feet high. Living up to its name, the smaller branches and even the trunks are bright red, and in the fall the large leaves turn a rich reddish-maroon color. In the late spring and early summer the dogwood blooms in a flat umbel of off-white, small, four-petal flowers. Redosier dogwood prefers moist, well-drained soils, pretty much the definition of a sand bank near a perennial waterfall.

The Upper Falls are not quite as impressive as their downstream counterpart, but the long freefall and pool are still very nice. Downstream the creek flows into a densely vegetated corridor that is especially pretty in the fall. The top of the falls is reached by returning to the junction and taking the other fork. Along the way manzanita, especially when it is naturally espaliered on the Navajo slickrock, is handsome all year with its evergreen leaves. Above the falls are a couple of pools in depressions in the rock, with the stream flowing smoothly between them and then plunging over the falls. Prudence and good sense are important here. The walk back to the rim involves about 650 vertical feet of climbing (including the gain from the base of the falls), but even those who found it a little unnerving during the descent should be more confident going up.

Hells Backbone Road Trip

Driving distance from Highway 12 near Boulder to Highway 12 in Escalante is 39 miles.

Boulder, Utah was a hard place to get to in 1932. The Boulder Mail Trail zigged across vast gulfs of slickrock, zagged down and down into Death Hollow and up and out again, before eventually plunging down into Escalante. It was not for the timid, neither mule nor rider. Thus, when Franklin D. Roosevelt created the Civilian Conservation Corps (CCC) as a way for families to weather the depth of the Depression, there was a natural demand in Utah for their services. Over time four CCC camps were established not far from Escalante. The first order of business was to build a proper road connecting Boulder with the world. Hand tools, horses, dynamite, hard toil, and ingenuity got the job done, and the Hells Backbone Road was passable by 1933. Today the lure of traveling that same route is irresistible to a surprisingly large number of visitors, including many Europeans.

Hells Backbone and Highway 12 can both get you from Boulder to Escalante in good weather. For those on the Grand Circle of national parks in Utah and Arizona it can be a hard choice, and the vast majority, of course, opt to stay on the highway as it crosses some of the most spectacular scenery on earth. If a full day has been allotted for the journey from Capitol Reef to Bryce, however, there need not be an agonizing decision. The best of Highway 12 covers only 14 miles from the Hells Backbone turn-off on the Boulder end to the Head of Rocks viewpoint about 10 miles east of Escalante. To have your cake and eat it too, drive this stretch first as an out and back (thereby greatly increasing the scenic splendor by seeing it in both directions) of just 28 miles round trip. This could be done quickly but Highway 12 is the last road where haste has any place at all, so allow at least a couple of hours. Consult the Highway 12 section for details.

Once on Hells Backbone Road it is more than 35 miles of graded gravel back to pavement just north of Escalante (an alternative is to return to Capitol Reef on the Posey Lake Road described later in this section). Much of the middle of this route has moderate grades, but both ends are quite steep. Experienced gravel road travelers know what this means: unless the grader's dust is visible ahead, the road is most likely severely washboarded, to the point that the incessant jarring can be unpleasant, and perhaps even dangerous when the vehicle gets too far off line. There are many places where the driver or passenger will be gazing down into an abyss along the shelf road sections, and during wet weather an added element of concern immediately arises. In good weather the enjoyment of a trip over Hells Backbone is more about expectations and driver confidence than it is about the difficulty of the drive. With stops, pictures, and lunch, allow at least three or four hours pavement to pavement.

From Capitol Reef, drive over the shoulder of Boulder Mountain on Highway 12 to the town of Boulder. Continue 3.1 miles past the Burr Trail turn-off to the sign for Salt Gulch and Hell's Backbone at milepost 83.3. Make a sharp right (north) onto a good gravel road. In 150 yards a sign pointing straight ahead identifies three destinations: McGath Trailhead, Hell's Backbone Bridge, and Blue Spruce Campground; to the left (west) is the dirt road to the Boulder Airport and the beginning of the Boulder Mail Trail hike described previously. The road quickly enters the boundary of the Dixie National Forest.

After almost 4 miles, irrigated fields begin to appear, along with several residences. Note the different fence styles at this point. Ranches continue for a couple of miles, and then the road grade steepens sharply and the washboard begins. The forest is typical piñon-juniper until the first ponderosa appears at 6.7 miles. A lesser track goes right at 8.3 miles, and at 9.4 is a signed junction, with Hells Backbone Bridge straight ahead and McGath Trailhead to the right (north). The latter is a very worthwhile side trip, especially when the aspen are in fall color.

McGath Road

The McGath Road, FR 566, is suitable for carefully driven cars much of the time. Heavy rains can produce ruts, but the road is usually well maintained. Set the odometer to zero. After passing over a flat, the route climbs steeply, becoming a one-lane wide shelf road. At the 1.1-mile mark are big views to the south of the Straight Cliffs and Navajo Mountain, with vast expanses of slickrock. Gambel oak covers the hillside. Another flat occurs at 2.8, with a sign for McGath Lake straight and Boulder Swale ATV Trailhead to the right (northeast). The road to the lake is rough, requiring high clearance. Keep to the right on FR 566 and soon emerge into a pretty section of aspen groves and meadows. At 4.5 miles a four-wheel drive road splits off to the right (east) to Road Draw, Haws Pasture, and Kings Pasture, while the Boulder Swale ATV Trailhead is straight ahead and only 0.1 mile away. A loop and information board are the terminus for standard vehicles.

Back on the Hells Backbone Road, mileages will be given from Highway 12 and in parentheses from the McGath Road. Continuing west, cross Lake Creek and soon begin a long, switchbacking descent to Sand Creek at 11.7 (2.3) miles. Sand Creek drops sharply down to the Boulder Mail Trail and an eventual confluence with the Escalante River. The forest at this elevation is a nice mix of ponderosa and piñon pine, Douglas fir, white fir, and juniper. From Sand Creek to the bridge is a steep climb. Manzanita begins to appear at mile 13.4 (4.0), and the bridge is at 14.4 (5.0). There are several places to pull over before the bridge, including one right at its downhill end.

At first it might be a little disappointing to find out that the bridge merely crosses a short gap, but it is the setting that matters. To the southwest the slickrock drops off spectacularly (alarmingly, perhaps, to some), plunging hundreds of feet nearly straight down

Hells Backbone bridge

into the reassuringly named Death Hollow. A slightly less impressive cleft is to the east, with the higher slopes of Boulder Mountain above. The ground-hugging manzanita on the white Navajo Sandstone provides great contrast and foreground for photographers. As might be expected, this is a place where a split second lack of concentration or a rockfall could be fatal, so take great care in exploring the area. Above the bridge parking is limited, but it is worth a short walk to get a sense of the morphology of the backbone and how easily just a little more erosion could have made it impossible to cross.

A Box Death Hollow Wilderness sign and Death Hollow access point are at 16.4 (7.0) miles. The multi-day trip down Death Hollow is only for the able and prepared hiker. After a long descent, the Hells Backbone Road approaches pleasant Pine Creek. Just before the crossing at mile 20.8 (11.4), a side road leads up the creek to the very pleasant Blue Spruce Campground, just 0.3 mile away. The campground ($8 per night at this writing) is modest, with only six small sites, but the mature blue spruce, red osier dogwood, river birch, and murmuring stream combine to create a refuge for the weary. The campground cannot accommodate large rigs, and there is no turnaround at the end of the road. Blue Spruce is a fine place to spend the night before hiking into the Upper Box, or simply to escape summer heat on the slickrock. The spur road continues past the campground, roughens, passes the entrance to the Cowpuncher Guard Station, and emerges into a nice linear meadow with Pine Creek to the west.

Just 0.2 mile beyond the road to the campground is informal parking on the left (southeast) for the trailhead to the Upper Box, a fine point-to-point hike down to the lower trailhead north of Escalante. An easy-to-miss plaque commemorating the CCC work on Hells Backbone is on the right (north) at mile 21.5 (12.1) on a right hand bend in the road. Deep Creek and Hungry Creek cross the road before it intersects with the Posey Lake Road at 25.4 (16.0). The sign at this intersection points to the right (north) for Posey Lake Campground and Loa, and to the left for Escalante. Forest Road 153 continues down to Highway 12, while FR 154 heads up and over the Aquarius Plateau to Highway 24 (see below for details).

Posey Lake Road Side Trip

Driving distance from Escalante to Highway 24 at Bicknell Bottoms is 49 miles.

The Posey Lake Road is a scenic connection between Escalante on the south and Bicknell and Loa to the north. It is a well-maintained gravel road for most of its length; there are short paved sections at each endpoint. In addition to accessing the west end of the Hells Backbone Road described above, it also is the easiest way to the top of Boulder Mountain (see that section for details). From Highway 12 to Highway 24 at Bicknell Bottoms is approximately 49 miles, of which about 7 are paved; the distance to Highway 24 in Loa is around 52 miles of which about 6 are paved. The stretch from the Hells Backbone Road to Escalante is discussed at the end of this section.

From the junction of Forest Roads 153 and 154 (at the west end of the Hells Backbone Road), the Posey Lake Road (FR 154) climbs to the northwest. Zero the odometer at this point and follow the sign to Loa and Posey Lake Campground. At 1.3 miles the Whites Flat Road branches off to the left (south), winding over to North Creek and the Barker Campground. The Posey Lake Campground entrance road is 0.5 mile farther on FR 154. Posey Lake is a pretty mountain pond, shallow with abundant vegetation in the clear water and good fishing. The campground has been recently upgraded and its 23 sites offer considerable variety. There is a boat ramp, picnic area, and short trail to an old lookout tower. At 8,200 feet, Posey Lake offers a nice respite from summer heat, especially at the sites that are completely shaded.

Past the lake, the road rises through pretty terrain. At the 3.5-mile mark there is a poignant plaque on the left (west) side of the road commemorating Asenith Roundy who died of exposure at this point when the family truck broke down on Christmas Eve day in 1939. As her husband walked more than 15 miles to Escalante in a snowstorm for help, Asenith perished while protecting their infant daughter, who was later rescued.

At 4 miles FR 154 cuts through a handsome, dense spruce, fir, and aspen forest, and at 5 miles passes over the indistinct rim of the Aquarius Plateau. This flat ridge connects Boulder Mountain to the east with Griffin Top to the west. At a general elevation of 10,000 feet, the Aquarius is a nice assortment of mixed forest, meadows, and shallow lakes or wetlands. Cyclone Lake is on the right (southeast) at 5.8 miles. The usually good road to Griffin Top goes to the left (west) at a signed intersection in a very large meadow at 8.1 miles.

After Roundy Reservoir at mile 11.4, the next junction is with FR 162 at 12.2. A 4WD trip over Boulder Mountain to this point is covered in the Boulder Mountain section. FR 154 continues straight, passing through scattered aspen groves that are brilliant in the fall. The aspen fall away 7 miles from FR 162, and the Posey Lake Road descends gently across open country for 8.2 miles, with huge views to the north. At this point a right (southeast) turn at an inverted Y intersection leads to the easiest access to the top of Boulder Mountain, also described in its namesake section. In another 1.2 miles is the dividing point for Highway 24 at Bicknell Bottoms (bear right, northeast) or to go straight to reach Loa and Highway 24. To return to Capitol Reef bear right, and then left at the pavement in 3 miles.

Hells Backbone Road Trip—continued

To complete the Hells Backbone loop back to Highway 12, turn left at the intersection (southwest) and stay on FR 153. Take it easy on the washboard descent to the Lower Box Trailhead spur road on the left (northeast) at mile 31.6 (22.2) as the piñon-juniper forest takes over quickly with the loss of elevation. The national forest boundary lies just beyond, and the next few miles are bordered to the east by the very steeply dipping beds of Navajo Sandstone that highlight the Escalante Monocline that tilts to the west. Short, precipitous canyons cut into the sandstone, which is beautifully cross-bedded, befitting its windblown origin.

Pavement begins 35.6 miles from the beginning of the Hell's Backbone Road and 26.2 miles from the McGath Road. Highway 12 is just 3.4 miles farther south. If doing Hells Backbone in the opposite direction, turn north off Highway 12 onto 300E at the elementary school in Escalante. This turn is well signed. The out and back tour of the best of Highway 12 can then be done at the conclusion of the Hells Backbone Road trip.

Escalante Monocline

Escalante Petrified Forest State Park

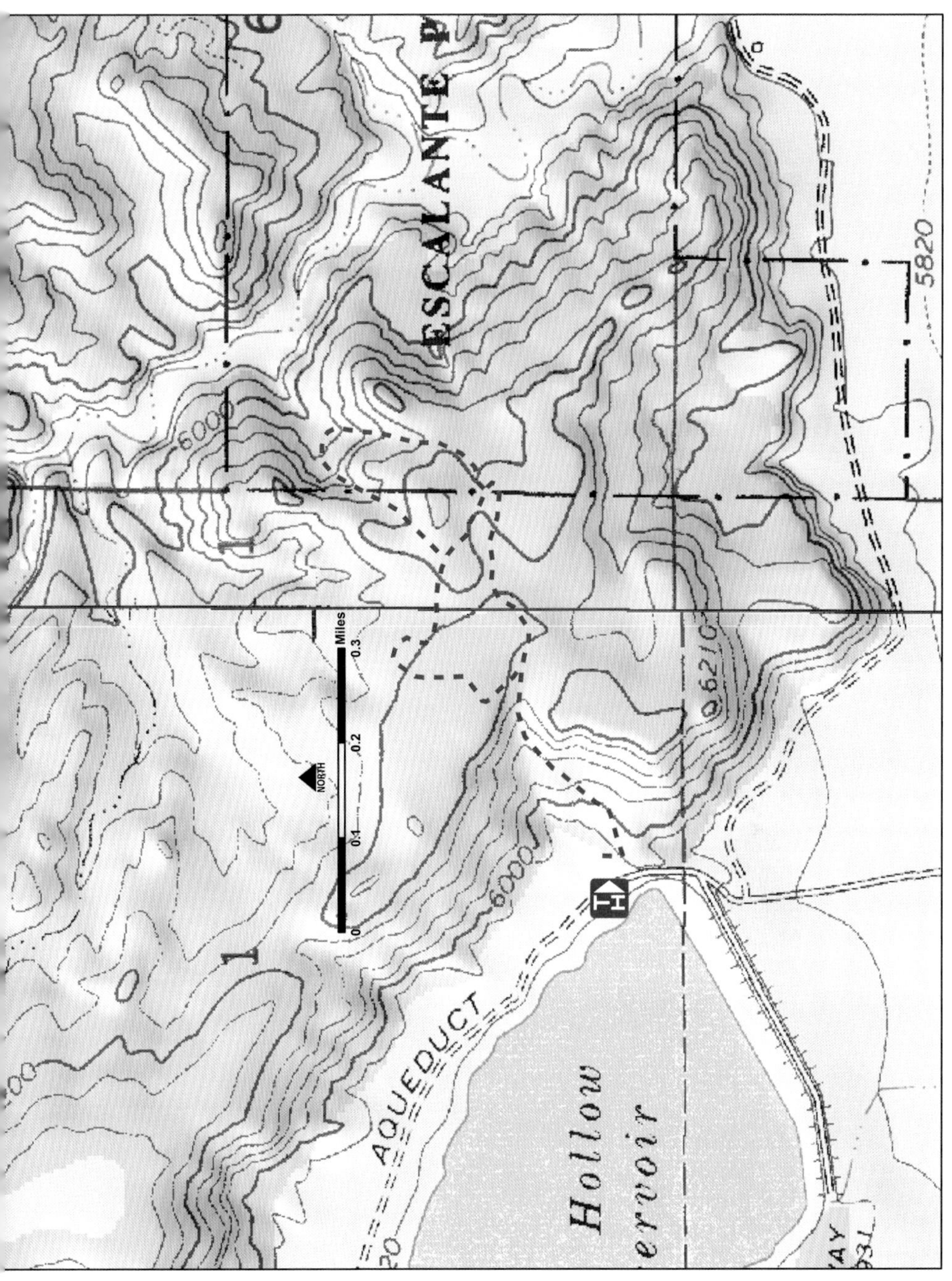

Escalante State Park route

Escalante Petrified Forest State Park

As this guide indicates, it is not hard to find petrified wood in many areas across south-central Utah. Along the Wolverine Loop there are tons of petrified wood scattered over a wide area of Chinle Formation sediments. Pieces pop up at many of the agate locations commonly visited, and wood is the mainstay of area rock shops. It would therefore be easy to dismiss Escalante Petrified Forest State Park in favor of some other wonderful parts of the Colorado Plateau. We might have been guilty of this ourselves, but *you* need not be. This small and often overlooked park is a true gem.

Getting There

The access road turns north (right, coming from the town of Escalante) off Highway 12, 1.7 miles west of Center Street in Escalante, and 0.6 mile west of the interagency visitor center on the west edge of town. The entrance road was largely paved at the time of our visit. The entrance station is 0.6 mile north of the highway. Fees are $6 per car for day visits; camping is $16 without hook-ups, and $20 with them. The campground is compact and most of the paved sites are a little small for big rigs, but the newer gravel sites with hook-ups can accommodate larger RVs. There are two group sites, and the park has showers and wireless Internet. It is also located right on the shore of Wide Hollow Reservoir and has a swimming area. For many travelers, though, the main attraction is petrified wood, and for good reason.

The Hike
Distance: 2.2 miles

Petrified wood log

The Petrified Forest Trail is a stem and loop, and steep enough to be strenuous for some people. The stem portion rises directly from the parking area, which is a sharp right (east) immediately after the entrance station. There are steep slopes and a few steps on the way up to the loop. By far the best, and most, petrified wood is on a significantly steeper and rougher loop that goes off the main trail. Total hiking distance for both trails is just under 2.2 miles, but it would be good to allow a couple of hours in order to find and enjoy all the wood. Collecting is prohibited in the state park. There is an informative trail guide for the main trail that is worth getting out of the box at the trailhead.

An interpretive panel at the trailhead explains how petrified wood is formed, and points out the rock unit in which it is found. The Upper Jurassic Morrison Formation is the source—it is much younger rock than the Chinle on the Wolverine Loop. In both cases, however, the paleoenvironment was much the same, consisting of river-borne clays and volcanic ash being deposited in oxygen-poor waters, primarily swamps. The abundant organic material, including large trees, periodically fell into the swamp where decomposition was delayed by the lack of oxygen. After subsequent burial, silica supplied by the ash and contained in groundwater eventually replaced the cells of the wood, sometimes so finely that growth rings, knots, and bark can be seen.

The main trail switchbacks sharply up from the parking lot, offering increasingly good views of the campground and reservoir. To the north, across the parking area, the three members of the Morrison Formation are easily distinguished. The lower one, consisting of red shales, is the Tidwell, and the light-colored resistant layer on top of it is the Salt Wash. The rest of the slope is the Brushy Basin, which is also the bed that produces the petrified wood. Along the trail is the usual assortment of shrubs that are found in the piñon-juniper forest: roundleaf buffaloberry, Mormon tea, Utah serviceberry, Apache plume, and skunkbush. After 0.4 mile of steady climbing, there is a junction with the loop portion of the main trail; bear to the right (southeast) here.

The trail soon reaches the top of the mesa and levels out among the piñon-juniper, rice grass, and basalt boulders. A fine view of Escalante, bordered to the southwest by

Petrified wood

Petrified wood

the Straight Cliffs, opens up to the right (southeast), and beyond, the first petrified wood logs are embedded next to the trail. There are four logs from 5 to 10 feet long, and typically (for the park) colorful, especially red and yellow. Another trail junction occurs 0.6 mile from the start. The sign says, "Sleeping Rainbow Trail, ¾ mile, very steep," with an arrow pointing to the right. Those who are only casually interested in petrified wood, and/or those who found the ascent to the loop trail difficult, would probably want to continue to the left on the main trail, where there are a couple more very good wood sites.

The Sleeping Rainbow Trail drops off the edge of the mesa, precipitously descending into a canyon, and then climbing back up a parallel canyon almost as steeply. It rejoins the main trail less than 100 yards from where it starts. The amount of petrified wood along this route is quite impressive, and its color and form are also excellent. The trail stays on the mesa for 150 yards as the number of scattered pieces of wood increases to the point that people have been unable to resist the urge to create little displays, usually on bigger rocks. When the trail begins its descent, it does so in earnest. Gambel oaks have found a niche just over the rim. Log segments appear everywhere. Many pieces are over 3 feet in diameter, and cascade in groups down each little side wash. Bright red and golden yellow chunks catch the eye at every turn.

The bottom of the canyon and turnaround point is 0.3 mile from the junction with the main trail. The turn is on top of a pour-off, on which two nice pieces of petrified wood rest. Right after reversing direction, the host rock contains so many small iron concretions that it looks as if it were made of marbles cemented together. Just above, the rock is pockmarked with solution cavities, some covered with a dark green velvet-like

Petrified wood

Petrified wood

moss. There is plenty of petrified wood to enjoy during the steep ascent back to the mesa top.

After rejoining the Petrified Forest Trail, it is 0.25 mile to a large cluster of logs and chunks, most with saturated red and yellow color. The route turns back to the east, climbs a gentle hill, and after less than 0.2 mile comes to a single log segment that is about four feet in diameter and very well preserved. The end of the loop and junction with the trail back down to the parking area is visible just ahead.

Once down, it is worth visiting the native plant display garden built in part by local elementary school students. Amid many good-sized pieces of petrified wood are scattered a good selection of shrubs and flowers that are common to the Colorado Plateau, and the signs offer a good way to learn what they are. A short stop in the visitor center in the back of the entrance station is also worthwhile.

Not all Utah arches are red

The Plateaus

The lower elevations of south-central Utah are hot in the summer. Most of the places described in this book are at those lower elevations (anything lower than 7,000 feet above sea level passes for low when it comes to summer temperatures in this part of the world). While visitation to the national parks has evened out over the years, and in fact is heaviest in some places in the spring and fall, many people are limited to the summer for the extended vacation time necessary to cover the vast distances on the Colorado Plateau. Even for those in standard passenger cars, there is relief from the heat, and, to a large extent, relief from crowds as well. This chapter covers high ground, cool(er) air, wide vistas, and a completely different ecological environment.

The mountains near Capitol Reef are not nearly as well known as the Wasatch and Uintas of northern Utah. The Wasatch is dotted with world famous ski areas and lies next to a major urban corridor, while the Uintas contain the state's high point and a vast and beautiful wilderness area. A single day hiking any popular trail in either will probably result in more contact with people than a week or two driving and hiking in the southern mountains, with the exception of hunting season.

The three mountains west of Capitol Reef are managed by the U.S. Forest Service (USFS). The roads, especially the rougher ones, are subject to significant changes in condition, sometimes due to continued use combined with infrequent maintenance, and sometimes due to weather events such as monsoonal thunderstorms. Passenger cars can usually be driven up Thousand Lakes Mountain, often to the edge of the vast flat top of Boulder Mountain, and around the Fish Lake Loop unless it is closed by snow. Other roads require high clearance, and some are difficult four-wheel drive tracks. Before leaving the pavement on any of them, make sure to get good and current information about road conditions from the appropriate managing office.

A very helpful tool in getting around safely is the travel map that each national forest provides free of charge. Most of the forested area covered in this book is administered by the Fremont Ranger District, located on Highway 24 in Loa. Some of the routes included may not be traveled by anyone else for a day, or even several days. There may not be cell phone coverage. Always, and without fail, take sufficient food, water, clothing, and equipment to spend a night or more if your vehicle breaks down. Think about what you would do if two tires failed when you were ten miles from the next nearest person.

The plateau mountains are at their best during two time periods. The first is the height of the subalpine flower bloom, which usually occurs sometime in late June, or early to middle July. Of course, winter moisture and spring temperatures have a great deal to do with determining the peak period, but good flower shows are far more reliable up high than they are in the desert. Many of the high elevation roads and tracks are closed until the middle of June, and later if necessary, to prevent road damage during snowmelt. In good years, the vast open areas above 10,000 feet in elevation may be covered with a carpet of flowers. The other sensational time to drive and/or hike the mountains is during the peak of fall color, namely that week, perhaps two, when the aspen shine like the sun itself. The last week of September and first of October are frequently that period. In good years all the mountains are dazzling with the gold, and sometimes orange or red, leaves of huge aspen clones edging into dark spruce/fir forests, or open sagebrush meadows.

The mountains described here are high. For each, at least one short hike is included that reaches above 11,000 feet in elevation. Even a brief walk to a viewpoint can be a struggle at this elevation for many, and the longer and steeper climbs can be outright dangerous. Know your limitations before you even drive to these heights. Just changing a flat tire could be a serious physical challenge. If you are unfamiliar with, or unsure of, your ability to handle exertion at two miles above sea level, it is best to work your way up, so to speak, gradually. See how you fare at 7,000 feet at Torrey, Flagstaff, Santa Fe, or the South Rim of the Grand Canyon, and then at the 8,000 to 9,000-foot elevation at Bryce Canyon. Cedar Breaks National Monument is largely above 10,000' on the rim where visitors look into the amphitheater. Only you can determine whether it would be safe and comfortable to spend a day just below treeline.

To be sure, most travelers come to southern Utah to bask in the reflected red rock glow, or test themselves in the confines of slot canyons, but if you can do it, a diversion to the mountains may be just the tonic for the crowds and heat down below.

Highway 12 (Scenic Byway 12)

The Federal Highway Administration manages a program to identify National Scenic Byways in the United States. Among the approximately 120 currently designated scenic byways, thirty-one routes stand out and are also designated All-American Roads. These include such stalwarts as the Natchez Trace Parkway in the Southeast, Colorado's San Juan Skyway, and the Seward Highway in Alaska. Every All-American Road is spectacular, but in terms of both jaw-dropping beauty and diversity, Scenic Byway 12 is second to none of them. Hardly a day goes by in the Capitol Reef visitor center without several travelers exclaiming about the amazing drive from Bryce Canyon National Park. The Scenic Byway includes all of Highway 12 from Highway 24 in Torrey to U.S. 89 south of Panguitch. The portion within the area encompassed by this guidebook, Torrey to Escalante, is covered below.

Highway 12

Torrey to Escalante

Distance: 64 miles

Highway 12 on Boulder Mountain in mid-April

For most of the distance between Highway 24 and Escalante, Highway 12 is a wide, modern, two-lane road. South of Boulder, however, the highway winds along the top of a narrow and very high hogback, and then plunges down steep grades with sharp curves to Calf Creek. This stretch of about 4 miles is a bit of a challenge for acrophobic drivers and those piloting big rigs. Nonetheless, tanker trucks, buses, and large RVs travel it every day in the high travel months. The other legitimate concern is snow on Boulder Mountain where the road crests at 9,600 feet above sea level. Snowstorms are not at all uncommon during April and October, and may even occur in May and September. The road is plowed all winter, though in serious storms it may not be passable at times, especially at night.

The eastern terminus of Highway 12 is at the junction with Highway 24, just west of Capitol Reef in the town of Torrey. Zero the odometer and turn south. The highway passes through private land for the first 8 miles, with irrigated pastures alternating with private homes, second homes, and small lodging businesses. At 2.7 miles the road crosses the Fremont River as it exits the agricultural region to the west and begins a rapid descent into the Fremont Gorge and on through Fruita in Capitol Reef. The settlement of Grover passes by largely unnoticed at mile 6.6, and the boundary of the Dixie National Forest is at mile 8. On the northeast-facing slope of Boulder Mountain the change from piñon-juniper forest to ponderosa pine occurs within a short distance as the highway gains elevation. Small groups of aspen also make an appearance. For travelers coming from the east across Utah in the summer, the immersion into forest and departure from the heat are usually very welcome events.

The Dixie NF operates three campgrounds during the summer along Highway 12 on the mountain. The first, Singletree, is the largest and lowest at 8,600 feet. It also is usually the last to close for the season, offering full services through September 15, and staying open through hunting season or until closed by snow. Sites are scattered among the ponderosas and are generally fairly large, and there are two huge group sites. The entrance road is to the left (east) at the 12-mile mark, and the campground is well off Highway 12.

After a steep hill just beyond the entrance to Singletree Campground, the highway undulates gently or contours along the side of Boulder Mountain. There are glimpses off to the east that portend big views, and a fine place to stop is the Larb Hollow Overlook at 14.3 miles. The short loop road to the viewpoint is on the left (southeast) and leads to ample parking, interpretive signs, and a vault toilet. The view is expansive. The prominences along the Waterpocket Fold, including the Golden Throne, are beautifully illuminated just before the sun falls behind the mountain in late afternoon. The Mancos Shale mesas near Caineville, the San Rafael Swell, the Henry Mountains, and even the distant La Sal Mountains east of Moab are visible on clear days.

Back on Highway 12, a short downhill leads to a very pretty area, beginning at mile 16.5. There is a rest area just before the entrance to the Wildcat Information Station, which is usually open from Memorial Day to Labor Day. Staffed by volunteers, the facility is an old Forest Service guard station, worth a visit on its own. This is the place to get information and maps for the hikes that begin nearby. Just to the southwest, on the right (northwest) side of the highway, is a wet meadow that supports a population of shooting stars (*Dodecatheon pulchellum*). These summer bloomers are pretty pink and yellow flowers with petals that turn back from the black stamens, which protrude in a tight cluster. The flower head is nodding; these shooting stars are falling to earth. At 16.8 miles from Highway 24 (milepost 106.4 on Highway 12), and immediately after the meadow, there is a dirt road to the west (right) that is signed for the Great Western Trail. Just off the highway is a convenient place to park for the Terrace Trail Loop.

A very short distance farther south along Highway 12, the USFS Pleasant Creek Campground has two sections, both on the left (east), with the first at mile 17.2 and the second soon after. Both offer pleasant shaded sites, but the more southerly unit is right on the highway and subject to more traffic sounds. Just beyond the campground, and on the same side of Highway 12, is the road to Lower Bowns Reservoir, a popular fishing spot that also has a developed campground. This road is usually in fairly good condition and passable by cars to the lake, beyond which it becomes a rough 4WD track. After the Lower Bowns Reservoir intersection, Highway 12 passes by a lovely meadow on the left (southeast) and offers a good view of the aspen-conifer slopes of Boulder Mountain ahead. Oak Creek Campground, at 8,800 feet, is on the left (east) at 18.3 miles. Its sites lie in a small bowl close to the road but far enough below to lessen highway noise. Large RVs and trailers should camp at Singletree, and some can fit in the more northerly Pleasant Creek section.

The next 10 miles or so are beautiful, both in the forested sections and when the road crosses vast open meadows with huge views to the east and south. Near Oak Creek, spruce and firs have invaded the aspen groves and, absent disturbance such as fire, will eventually become the climax species. Nearer to the highpoint and beyond on the south-facing slopes the aspen stands are almost monocultures, but several groves exhibit high mortality, perhaps due to Sudden Aspen Decline. The road tops out at mile 22.9 where a sign notes the elevation as 9,600 feet. The Steep Creek Overlook is on the left (southeast) 1 mile beyond the summit.

A side road drops down to the left (south) to the Homestead Overlook at mile 25.3. The view over the Frisky Creek drainage to the south is expansive. The white and red slickrock of the Grand Staircase–Escalante National Monument stands out below, and the scene extends to the Straight Cliffs that form the northeast wall of the Kaiparowits Plateau. The cliffs end at Navajo Point, and the rounded form of much higher Navajo Mountain is almost in line with the point. There is a vault toilet at the viewpoint. Turnoffs to the right (north) for the Deer Creek Trailhead and the Chriss Lake Road are at miles 26.5 and 27.8 respectively.

A tight left hand curve at the end of a long descent and 30.5 miles from Torrey begins a change in topography, ecosystem, and land ownership. A series of ranches begin along the East Fork of Boulder Creek, and the ponderosa soon give way to piñon-juniper (PJ). The road heads directly down a gentle bench slope toward the town of Boulder. The administrative boundary of the Dixie NF is at mile 35.8. Anasazi State Park is 0.5 mile farther on the left (east) side of the road.

The state park is both museum and archaeological site. In general, the Colorado River served as the dividing line between the Ancestral Puebloan culture to the southeast and the contemporaneous Fremont culture that occupied most of Utah northwest of the Colorado River. The Puebloan village at Boulder is therefore a bit of an anomaly within Fremont territory. The museum is very good, detailing the lifeways of the people who resided here. There are exhibits on housing, food, raw materials, tools, and the possible reasons the occupants left the site (which was occupied from 1125 to 1175). An open storage area displays pottery reconstruction, and many pieces recovered from the site are also exhibited. In back of the museum is the Coombs Site, named for the owner of the land before it became public. A roof protects the remaining low walls of an L-shaped cluster of rooms and a kiva, and there are interpretive signs to help visitors understand what is before them. The fee to visit the museum and site is $3 per adult as of this writing. The park also has a gift shop and knowledgeable staff who are very helpful.

Anasazi State Park

Boulder is a tiny community, but there are two small stores with gas pumps, both on Highway 12, and a handful of lodging and dining options. The junction with the Burr Trail is on the left (east) at mile 37.0 where the highway swings to the west and descends through the remaining homes and ranches to Boulder Creek. The character of the highway abruptly changes as it cuts into the side of steep Navajo Sandstone slopes and winds around sharp curves. A scenic turnout at mile 38.9 offers a last view of the green fields of Boulder. At 40.1 miles Highway 12 reaches the upper end of New Home Bench and the junction with the road to Hells Backbone.

The next 4 miles or so give little indication of what is to come. The unsigned turn for the trailhead for the hike to Upper Calf Creek Falls is at mile 42.6. The road passes through sparse PJ as it courses along the flat, and initially wide, New Home Bench. This point of land between Boulder Creek to the east and Calf Creek to the west suddenly narrows, with breathtaking views that seem almost straight down on both sides. In a couple of places the top of the ridge is wide enough only for the road—no shoulders and no guardrails. These are good places for the driver to pay attention to driving, but there are several pullouts to stop and get out to enjoy this spectacular place.

The end of the high point is at mile 45 where Highway 12 begins its descent to Calf Creek. At first the grade and turns are routine. A sign indicating a 4-mile 14 percent downgrade is an attention-grabber, but much of the descent is much gentler than that, and there is even an uphill section. The lower part of the grade is indeed steep, however, with very sharp curves, so caution and low gear are necessary. Brief glimpses of deeply incised Calf Creek occur on the way down, but opportunities to pull off are limited. Just before the road reaches creek level, the signed entrance to Calf Creek Recreation Area is on the right (northwest). This is a very worthwhile stop for those with the energy to hike to Lower Calf Creek Falls (described, along with Upper Calf Creek Falls, in the Circle Cliffs and Slickrock section), which is one of the highlights of south-central Utah.

Calf Creek flows through a narrow and winding canyon with just about enough room for the highway and stream. Near the creek's confluence with the Escalante River is the parking area on the right (west) at mile 49.6 for the Escalante River hiking route that follows the river west (upstream) to the town of Escalante. Highway 12 does not linger in the valley, climbing steeply on a roundhouse curve. At mile 50.5 there is a good viewpoint on the right (north).

For the next 4 miles the environment is sand and rock, mostly the latter, as the highway passes through and then climbs over the Navajo Sandstone. The white sandstone is heavily patterned and the entire scene is unique. There is an absence of formal pullouts, but there are a few wide spots to park and take a walk over the interesting terrain. The ability of a fair variety of plants to take root and find sustenance here gives perspective to hard times. By means of a couple of switchbacks the road rises to the Head of the Rocks turnout, a large parking area with interpretive signs and a fine view back to the east over the slickrock gulf. Shortly beyond, the character of the countryside again abruptly changes, the road straightens and begins a long gentle descent across Big Flat. The Hole in the Rock Road leading to the very popular slot and narrow canyons on the west side of the Escalante River branches off to the left (southeast) at mile 59.3.

Approaching the town of Escalante there are views of irrigated fields to the southwest, a reminder of this small town's origins. The story of early settlement is well told at the

View over Capitol Reef from highway 12

Boulder Mountain aspen

Highway 12 road hazard

Hole in the Rock Escalante Heritage Center, on the right (northeast) at mile 62.9, where there are also restrooms. When Mary Alice Barker stepped off the wagon near here in 1876, she was the first female settler in the Escalante valley.

Escalante is a pleasant, airy town with several old brick homes dating from the early Mormon settlement period. The creation of the Grand Staircase–Escalante National Monument in 1996, not widely welcomed by the residents at the time, has changed the complexion of the community. There are guides and outfitters, motels, restaurants, gas stations, and a grocery store. At the west end of town is the interagency visitor center, well worth a visit, and staffed by employees of the Park Service, BLM, and Forest Service. Farther west is the road to Escalante Petrified Forest State Park. Beyond the area covered in this guide, Highway 12 dials down the scenery to merely wonderful, especially at the Powell Point Overlook, the east side of Bryce Canyon National Park, and, just before reaching U.S. 89, Red Canyon.

Boulder Mountain

Boulder Mountain towers over Capitol Reef, the Escalante region, and the Fremont River valley, its vast bulk and 11,300-foot elevation serving as counterpoints to the narrow slot canyons, farm fields, and desert below. Boulder Mountain has much more area above 11,000 feet than the Henry Mountains, Thousand Lake Mountain, and Fish Lake Hightop combined, and much of it is accessible with a good high-clearance vehicle. While there is certainly some low relief on the plateau, the top clearly reflects its origin as a series of largely flat-lying ash flow tuffs. Lovely stands of spruce and fir are interspersed with wide meadows and a surprising number of lakes. During good years subalpine flowers warm the summer landscape, but after cool weather arrives Boulder Top can be a little bleak even as the aspen flame out on the slopes leading up to the summit.

West flank of Boulder Mountain

Terrace Trail Loop Hike

Hiking distance is 7.3 miles (9.3 miles including side trip to Chokecherry Point)

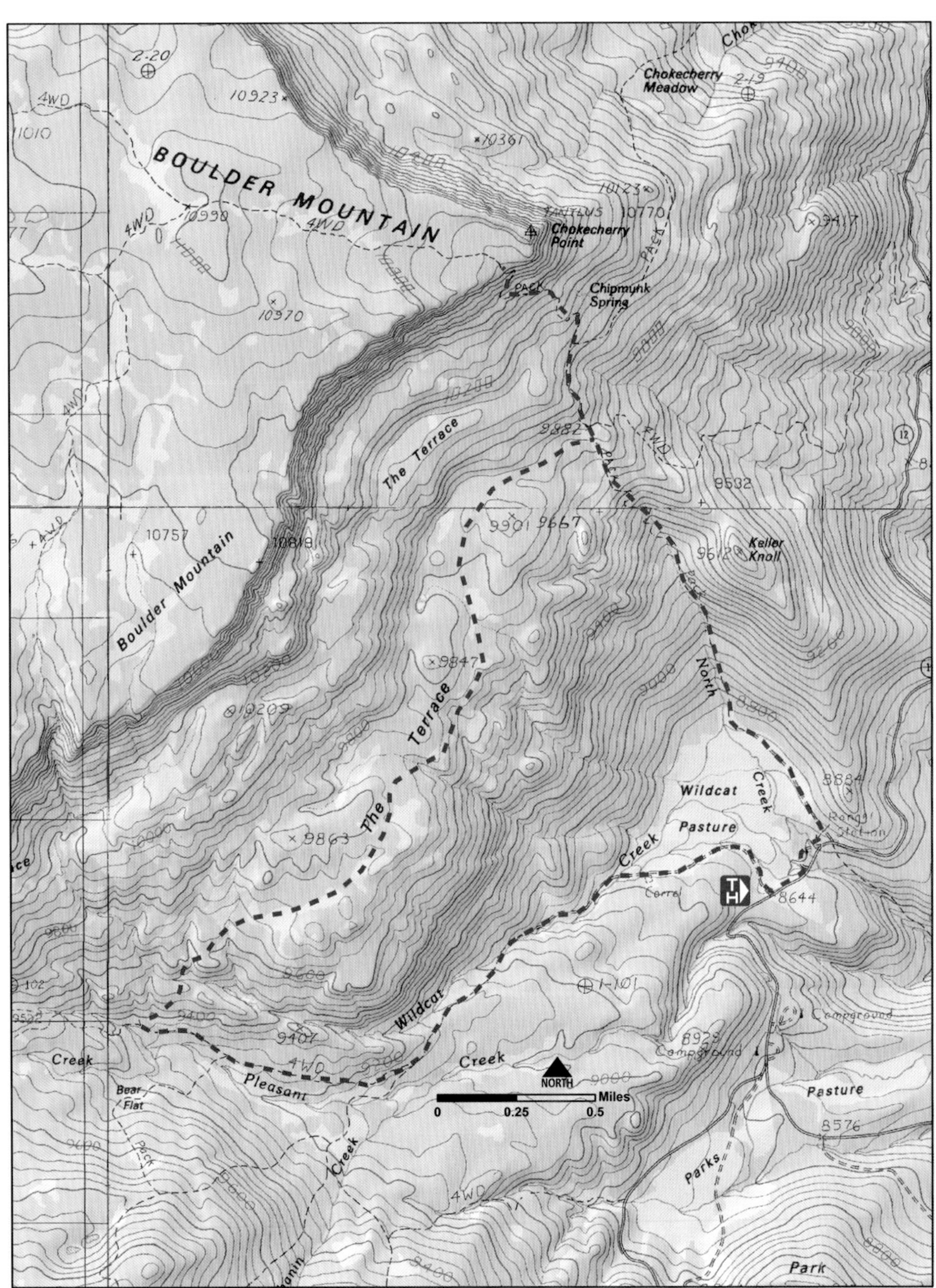

Terrace Trail route

Before venturing on top of Boulder Mountain it might be a good idea to explore a trail or take a drive on the flanks of the plateau. Ironically, the two trails described below both have much more vertical gain than the trails on top, but both are very good forest walks. For some reason, neither sees a lot of use, making it possible to enjoy a measure of solitude amidst the beautiful surroundings.

The Terrace Trail loop hike of about 7.3 miles offers that beauty and solitude, along with a good workout. Route-finding skills are necessary for this hike as there are several places where the trail is indistinct or not discernible. Note that the loop includes road walking and a long climb on the Wildcat Trail; the route is called the Terrace Trail loop to highlight the best part of the hike.

Getting There

We suggest starting at the Great Western Trail road and getting the short walk along the highway out of the way first. Drive 16.8 miles south from Highway 24 in Torrey on Highway 12 to a dirt road on the right (west) at milepost 106.4, signed for the Great Western Trail. Park in the broad flat area just off the pavement.

The Hike

Walk back to the northeast on the shoulder of Highway 12. Keep an eye out in July and August for the purple flowers of Parrys harebell scattered about the low and wet area north of the highway. If you have hiked extensively in the mountains of the Southwest or, indeed, almost anywhere in the northern states from Washington to Maine, you are probably familiar with common harebells. These nodding, bell-shaped blooms are extremely common and abundant enough locally to color entire hillsides in blue. Parrys harebell, however, is much less common, and occurs as a single flower about ¾ inch across atop a thin stem up to a foot long. *Campanula parryi* has long and narrow basal leaves, while common harebells (*C. rotundifolia*), as the Latin name implies, have round basal leaves. Sepals on the Parrys are much longer, extending to the openings between the fused petals. The primary way to tell the species apart, however, is the solitary nature of Parrys harebell against the clumps and sweeps of its much more common cousin. At the entrance road to the Wildcat Information Station, turn left (west) and walk in to have a look at the old guard station and a chat with the pleasant volunteers who staff it, typically from Memorial Day weekend into September at freeze up. After the hummingbird hatch near the beginning of August, there may be quite a frenzy if there are feeders outside the guard station. A useful map is available for the trails in the area, including the Terrace loop.

Parrys harebell

Terrace Trail

The eyes have it

From the station, continue northeast on the loop road for 0.1 mile to a T intersection with another dirt road. The restroom at the rest area is easily accessible down to the right (east) just before the junction. Turn left at the T, and walk northwest on Forest Road 323. At 0.75 mile from the GWT parking area is the older guard station, painted red, along with a corral and crumbling barn. There is also a large parking area here for those doing, say, an out and back hike up to Chokecherry Point.

The road forks just beyond the old guard station, with a sign right in the middle of the arms of the Y. It announces the Wildcat Trail, which is a long and lovely trek along the east and northeast flanks of Boulder Mountain; the Blind Lake hike described below also incorporates part of the Wildcat Trail. Keep to the right of the sign on the more easterly road. In another 0.1 mile a single track trail, marked by a sign and a cairn, angles off to the right (northeast). This is the Wildcat Trail, and it is the path up to the Terrace Trail. At the 1-mile mark the work begins, as the gradient steepens.

In just over 1 mile, you will gain about 1,100 feet in elevation. We generally hike along level ground on decent tread at around 2.8 miles an hour, but when elevation gains become significant, we figure on an hour per 1,000 feet of rise. If you live at lower elevation, keep in mind that this part of the hike will take you from just under 9,000 feet to nearly 10,000 feet. Since it is not at all uncommon for some people to show signs of altitude sickness much lower than 9,000 feet, this is not a hike to be taken lightly. It is also important to be at least partially acclimated to the elevation, and it is helpful that much of this part of Utah is fairly high. This might also be a good place to think about hiking strategy.

This hike can, of course, be done in the opposite direction than described, thereby spreading out the ascent, and leaving the descent of the steep part for near the end of the walk. If there is a choice, we will almost always go up the steepest part of a hike, and descend the more gentle leg. This is especially true if the steep part would be early or late in the hike. Going up we rest as necessary and really look around, and the risk of a serious fall is pretty minimal. On the other hand, after even a moderately long walk such as this one, coming down a steep grade when already tired, on a trail with plenty of loose rock, is far more likely to result in a fall, is hard on the feet, and can be pretty tedious.

The trail quickly enters a diverse forest with stately ponderosa pine intermingling with aspen and Engelmann spruce, and, later, Douglas fir. A tiny stream on the left (northwest) creates a lush little ribbon of grass on the otherwise dry slope. What appears to be an old road goes right up the fall line, but several sections of path with short switchbacks stay to the left (west) and are much easier to ascend. The trail parallels a fence line on the left (west) for a short distance after the 1.5-mile mark, and then passes through a gate to a short and welcome flat. After this all too brief respite, it is back to climbing. An open aspen grove with many dead and downed trunks signals that you are within 0.25 mile of the Terrace Trail. The trees end at the base of a meadow. At this point there are cairns to the left (west), but the trail continues straight ahead and is reasonably clear. The junction of the Wildcat Trail and the Terrace Trail is at UTM 0469606mE, 4219925mN, 2.1 miles from the start of the hike.

Just a few yards beyond the trail intersection is the ATV road that goes from Highway 12 up to Chokecherry Point and the Boulder Mountain plateau. The Wildcat Trail joins the road for a short distance here. Across the road is a good place for a break, with views to the east across Dirty Devil country and south to Navajo Mountain. It is not unusual in early August for monsoon rains to bring about a secondary bloom of lupines, skyrockets, wire lettuce, and groundsels, producing big swatches of color in the meadow.

Just for the fun of it, let's say that the climb to this point really didn't fulfill your fitness goal for the day. If that is the case, it is about 700 more vertical feet and another mile of walking to get up to the rim of Boulder Mountain. Simply stay on the road as it winds up through long stretches of aspen, with occasional views, mostly to the south, but also, in 0.3 miles, a nice look east at the Henry Mountains and the red sandstone of Capitol Reef. Just after this view is a signpost indicating the Wildcat Trail where it drops down to the right (east, then north). For Chokecherry Point, continue on the ATV track for another 0.7 mile until it reaches the rim and morphs into a 4WD road across the top of Boulder Mountain. There is abundant signage here, with the first announcing that you are at Chokecherry Point. This is reasonably accurate, but not impressive. The rim is non-distinct and views are obscured by the trees. The actual point is about 200 yards to the northeast.

In the event that your exercise goal is on track upon reaching the start of the Terrace Trail, go back to the sign marking the junction (it faces the road, but is in danger of toppling at this writing). The tread to the southwest is visible from the sign. The Terrace Trail crosses a meadow and drops down into the forest near a small pond, which is passed on the left (south). There are several tracks through the boulders here, so keep an eye out for cut logs that show the way. After emerging from the rocks the trail is clear, marked with blazes and many mostly recent arborglyphs. The trail passes through an area with some red volcanic rocks followed by a small meadow strewn with dead aspen trunks. Just after the 2.5-mile point the route follows a grassy break through a nice aspen forest; there is no easily discernible tread, but the opening, blazes, and cut logs make it easy to stay on track.

The Terrace is a broad bench across the southeast slope of the mountain. It is by no means flat, but the hills are short, and the trail stays near the 9,800-foot contour for 2 miles. Aspen or aspen-fir forest is broken by several lovely meadows. At the height of fall color, usually around the end of September, this part of the hike becomes very special. Aspen groves have a distinct aroma all the time, but in the fall it intensifies. If it is your first time among *Populus tremuloides*, that musty and earthy smell will stick with you. As usual in this part of Utah, lightly used trails are pretty clear in the forest, but can disappear in the meadows. On either side of the 2.9-mile mark are meadows. For the first meadow, aim for the gap between a small clump of aspen on the left (southeast) and the forest edge on the right (northwest). A couple of cut logs will confirm the route, and the tread becomes clear at the first cairn. For the second, and larger, meadow, simply stay to the right (northwest) along the forest margin. As the meadow narrows, the trail descends into the trees and then a small opening with jackstrawed dead aspen trunks. A muddy crossing of a tiny rivulet precedes a rough and rocky ascent. Forest succession is clearly occurring here as the conifers are invading the aspen.

Another meadow is entered after 3.8 miles, and a little farther on the trail tops a short steep rise to emerge into a long, narrow opening that stretches for more than 0.25 mile, with aspen around the margin all the way. Upon re-entering the trees, the distance to the next meadow is short. After crossing a very small stream the trail becomes obscure. Bear left (south) and downhill, and keep an eye out for two big cairns ahead; after the second the tread becomes clear again. At the 4.25-mile mark, the route crosses a pretty stream tumbling through lush vegetation, including yellow monkeyflowers. The path drops into the trees, crosses a small watercourse, and passes through a fence, all in just over 200 yards.

Yellow monkeyflowers

A descending traverse follows along a south-facing slope with abundant wild rose and skunkbush shrubs. From here it is not far to an old road, where there is a sign for hikers coming the other way, pointing out the Meeks Lake Trail and the Terrace Trail. Turn left (east) on the road, and in only a few yards pass by the formal stopping point for approaching motorized travel. The rest of the hike is on this track, which ends in just over 2.4 miles at the parking area just off Highway 12 where this description begins.

The walk down the road is mellow and easy-going for more than 1 mile. A slight, almost indiscernible downgrade and smooth tread are just the ticket for this stage of the hike. The route offers glimpses down into the Pleasant Creek drainage and to the high country beyond, along with many flowers in open aspen cover during early summer and then again when the rains come. The aspen on the slopes to the south have largely succumbed to Sudden Aspen Decline, a region-wide die-off apparently initiated by the drought of 2002 working on fully mature groves near the end of their growing span. The signed junction with the Behanin Creek Trail is on the right (south) at 5.8 miles, and 0.25 mile beyond that the road descends more abruptly and is very rocky. A large boulder in the middle of the track is an obstacle to 4WDs attempting to drive up the road, but there is room to park at the base of the pitch for hikers climbing up and back to Meeks Lake or taking the Behanin Creek Trail.

The track crosses Wildcat Creek at 6.25 miles and continues in this drainage down to Highway 12. Less than 300 yards later the road enters the top of a long meadow with many flowers even in early August. The stands of redroot buckwheat among the blue penstemons, skyrockets, and asters can be especially impressive. *Eriogonum racemosum* is a common plant at mid to high elevations in the Four Corners states, but is easily ignored when plants are widely scattered as they usually are. The buckwheat genus is quite varied, but all the members have tiny flowers. Redroot buckwheat is distinctive. Long (to 18 inches) leafless stems rise from a basal rosette of oval gray-green leaves and are topped with a tight spike of clustered white and pink flowers.

As the road traverses the meadow it crosses a cattleguard and then goes over Wildcat Creek at a culvert. Just beyond the culvert a road branches off and back to the right (southwest). The last 0.6 mile is a mostly easy-going walk past a corral, an area used for dispersed camping, and the junction with a road that goes to the southwest (right). Keep an eye out for tall pinedrops near this intersection. The loop closes at the parking area for a total hiking distance of 7.3 miles or 9.3 miles if you include the side trip up to Chokecherry Point.

Blind Lake Loop Hike

Driving distance from Highway 12 to the Blind Lake Trailhead is 8.5 miles one way.
Hiking distance is 4.2 miles round trip.

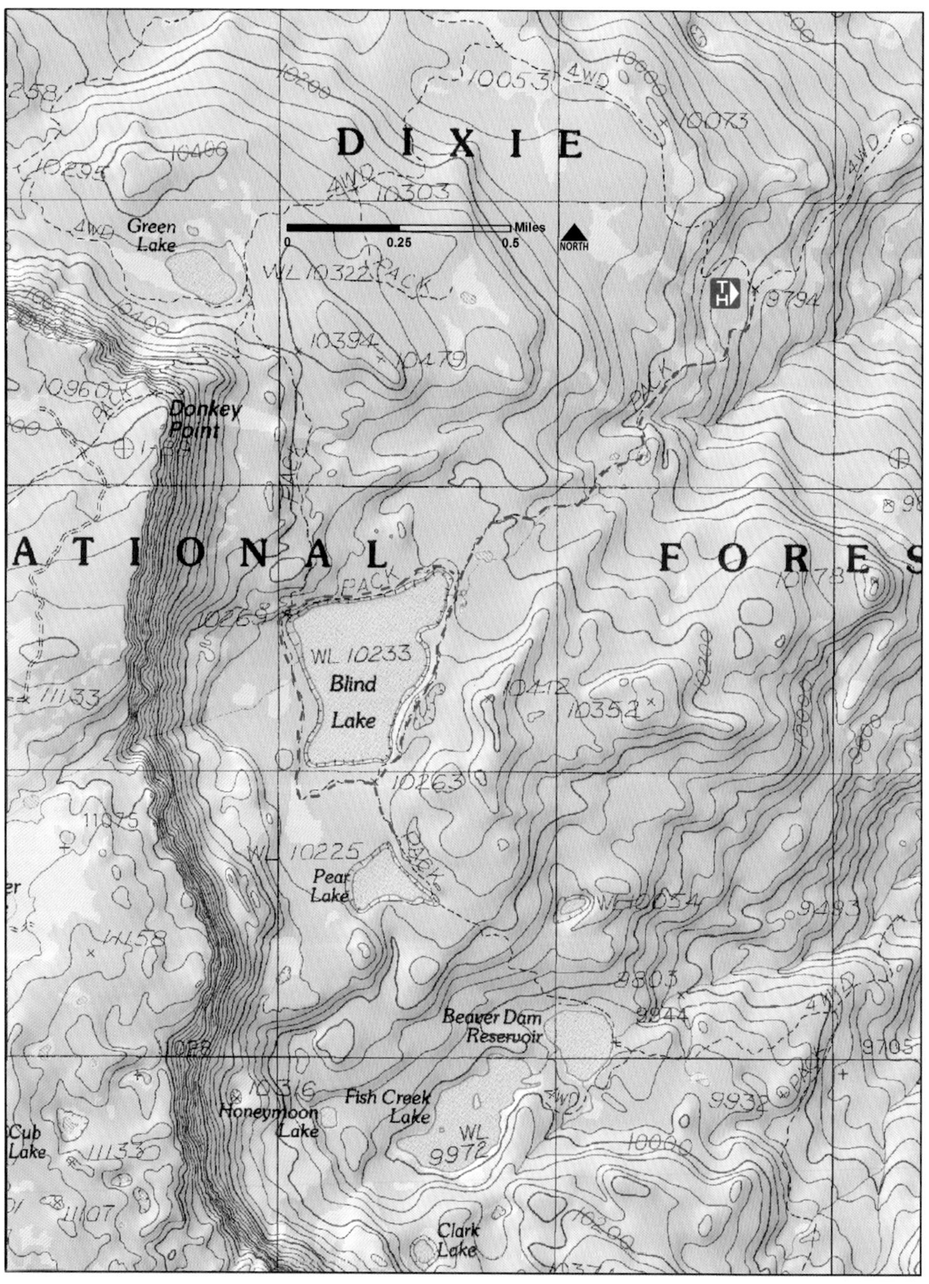

Blind Lake Trail route

Blind Lake

If you have a high-clearance 2WD or 4WD vehicle to get you to the trailhead, the hike to Blind Lake under the northeast corner of Boulder Mountain is a winner. If you have a passenger car and don't mind driving on a decent gravel road, the hike is a little longer, but still a winner. There is just something about alpine lakes backed by high cliffs and fringed with aspen and spruce that soothes the soul—especially if down below the temperature is pushing triple digits.

In addition to its scenic merits, Blind Lake is a prime fishing spot. It is well noted for its brook trout and splake fisheries, and also hosts rainbow and cutthroat trout. Because it is accessible only by trail, fishing pressure is a little less than it might otherwise be. Fishing from the shoreline is possible in many places; the most serious anglers will pack in a float tube.

Getting There

From Torrey, drive south on Highway 12 to mile marker 118, which is just beyond (south of) the paved road to Teasdale. (This junction is unsigned when approached from the north.) Turn right (southwest) onto 2275 South, the North Slope Road, and zero the odometer. A sign at this intersection indicates that Blind Lake is 9 miles, and Green Lake and Fish Creek Reservoir are each 10 miles, all to the right. After the turn, there is also a sign for Forest Road (FR) 179. The road is good gravel, subject to washboarding, especially as it climbs. After 0.6 mile there is a Y. Bear left (southwest) following the signs for the North Slope Road and FR 179. From this point the road gains more than 2,500 feet before reaching the Blind Lake trailhead.

The drive provides several sweeping views to the north or east, and if the washboard isn't too bad, the gravel portion is quite pleasant. At 4.9 miles is a huge view over the green fields of Grover to the east, including Capitol Reef, and from the left (northeast) the San Rafael Swell, Temple Mountain, Factory Butte, the Flat Top Buttes, and the Henry Mountains. On very clear days the La Sal Mountains east of Moab are visible. At the 5.6-mile mark is an aspen grove with associated Douglas firs and several dispersed camping sites. At 0.3 mile beyond is the junction with FR 520, which goes to the left (south), providing access to Fish Creek Reservoir. The sign points in that direction for the Fish Creek Trailhead and Great Western Trail (GWT).

For Blind Lake continue straight ahead, quickly coming to the end of the improved road. The track is then graded for another 0.7 mile, but may require high clearance. Just beyond the junction where FR 1330 goes to the right (northeast), the rest of the road to the trailhead at 8.5 miles has been roto-milled, and should be passable with 2WD high-clearance vehicles. Those in passenger cars should park and walk whenever the road becomes too rough.

The initial rocky pitch is quite steep, the first of several places where low range gearing is very handy. There are large boulders occasionally, but in general the track is wide enough that they can be avoided. Most of the ascent occurs in the next mile as the road twists back and forth up the slope through open meadow and lightly treed areas. At mile 8 it crosses the crest of the ridge and flattens considerably with views down into the Spring Creek drainage. The last 0.5 mile is much easier and faster. The trailhead is a large, flat, grassy area marked by a message sign at a point where the road makes a sharp right-hand curve and begins another ascent. There is a flexible plastic sign marking the beginning of the trail, but as of this writing, there is nothing that mentions Blind Lake.

The Hike

The elevation at the trailhead is just under 9,800 feet, and Blind Lake is at 10,233 feet, easily high enough to cause possible problems for those who are not acclimated to the elevation or are susceptible to altitude-related symptoms. The elevation also means that the scenery on the hike changes significantly during the short season between snowmelt and new snow. The former varies widely; it can be well into June before the road is even open, or it might be dry by early May. New snow can close things down in October.

There are four distinct mini-seasons for hiking. The first is soon after the road is dry, but when snow lingers on the north and east facing cliffs above the lakes. Second is just a few weeks later when the aspen green up and spring wildflowers are at their peak, and the third is high summer when the subalpine flowers are at peak and the aspen in deep summer green. This is also the usual time for monsoon thunderstorms, so attention needs to be paid to the forecast. Finally, sometime around the end of September, the aspen turn yellow and gold and the hike can be magical. The caution at this time is to be fully aware of which hunting season is in effect, and to dress accordingly.

The trail starts to the left (south) of the message board and a lone spruce tree. It appears to be headed into aspen forest, but quickly bends left and down, to run through a meadow with a fence to the east (left). After the short warm-up, the route climbs moderately to the 0.3-mile mark where it levels off and enters engaging spruce-aspen woods. In a lean snow year the open slope has small, ground-hugging cinquefoils already in bloom in early May. A shorter climb follows a sharp left turn of the path at 0.5 mile, and the flat above has several small ponds, at least during the period right after snowmelt.

The trail undulates mostly through forest and alongside small depressions up to the 1-mile mark, where it passes over two humps and then swings to the right (west) to pass a small lake on the left. Beyond the small lake it is only about another 500 feet to an unmarked trail to the right (northwest). This is the route around Blind Lake, but it is only a couple hundred feet more to Blind Lake via the main trail. The view from this northeast corner of the lake is very good, so it makes sense to go ahead and walk on up to the shoreline.

Blind Lake moraine

Blind Lake is the largest lake on and around Boulder Mountain, and it is natural. The north and east sides are impounded by a glacial moraine deposited just over 20,000 years ago. This time period represents what is called the last glacial maximum (LGM), and is correlated with the most recent continental glaciation in North America. Boulder Mountain and the Fishlake Hightop across the valley to the north were capped by ice during this period, with small glaciers spilling off the flat plateau and extending short distances down valley.

Moving ice can transport massive amounts of material, and when forward movement and melt back of the snout of the glacier cancel each other out, piles of rough, unsorted sediments can accumulate in terminal moraines. Similar elongate piles of glacial debris can be deposited along the sides of a glacier as lateral moraines. The natural dam that creates Blind Lake is a textbook example of a terminal moraine, and the trail follows the crest of the moraine along the north and east sides of the lake.

Glacial features are not the only geological contribution to the scenery at this first view area. Not far to the west of the lake is a massive wall of andesite, a type of igneous rock. Boulder Mountain, Fishlake Hightop, and Thousand Lake Mountain all owe their relatively flat and featureless surfaces to a roughly 26-million-year-old eruption that came from a vent near the town of Marysvale, to the west. The flow probably covered all or most of the ground to the east from the vent for 40 miles, but erosion has since removed substantial portions. On Boulder Mountain, the andesite is about 450 to 500 feet thick, forming a fine backdrop for Blind Lake.

Igneous material will sometimes cool in columns (think Devils Tower in Wyoming), and that is the case in the cliffs near Blind Lake. A good reason to do this hike soon after the road is dry is that there should still be snow on the east and north facing cliffs above the lake (this can be confirmed by looking south from many of the motel and restaurant parking areas in Torrey). The contrast of lake, forest, rock, snow, and sky is very striking, especially in the morning.

The best views of the lake and cliffs are from the north shore, and we recommend hiking in a counterclockwise direction to keep them in front of you. To do this, return to the unmarked path about 200 feet back down the main trail and turn sharply left (northwest). After just a short distance that trail emerges onto the top of the rocky moraine, affording great views across Blind Lake from a surprisingly high vantage point. Small spruce and aspen dot the moraine, but there are plenty of gaps in the cover. About halfway across the north edge of the lake the trail drops off the top of the moraine to contour along the south side of the ridge, and the views are even less impeded. It is less than 0.5 mile to the northwest corner of the lake, and a signed junction with the Wildcat Trail.

The Wildcat Trail connects many of the lakes that dot the northeast slope of Boulder Mountain. At this point the sign indicates that it is 1 mile to Green Lake and 4 miles to Donkey Lake, both up the hill to the north, and 2 miles to Fish Creek Lake and 10 miles to Grover, both back across the moraine. To continue around the lake, however, stay to the left, and drop down to the south, quickly passing through an opening in an old zigzag fence, the first of several on the west side of Blind Lake. The ambiance of the hike changes as the path meanders through dense spruce forest at some distance from the water. After a few minutes a wet meadow opens up on the right (west), providing a close view of the cliffs. In early spring the trail may be covered in a few spots with meltwater puddles, easily avoided, and there may be a waterfall coursing down the cleft that leads up to the Boulder Mountain plateau.

At 2 miles from the trailhead, the path passes the southwest tip of the lake and then emerges at the north end of a long, south-trending meadow. After 150 feet in the open, the trail turns sharply left (east) and re-enters the forest, bends left (north) again toward the lakeshore, and passes by several well-used camping spots. The trail becomes a little indistinct here, but passes just to the south (right) of a very low rise between it and the lake; an old double blaze on a spruce is helpful. The walk past the more narrow southern end of Blind Lake is only about 0.2 mile, ending at a T junction with the trail that runs along the east side. There is a sign here as well, the back of which greets hikers coming from the west, as described here. All the directions on the sign are to the south: Wildcat Trail No. 140, Beaver Dam Reservoir, Fish Creek Lake, and the junction with the Great Western Trail No. 001.

Not mentioned on the sign is nearby Pear Lake, so close that it takes less than five minutes to walk to it. Turn right (south), and shortly the lake will appear straight ahead down a gently sloping open area, at a point where the trail goes slightly left and climbs moderately. Just walk down to the shore and enjoy this smaller, but still significant, lake. The view is mostly to the south, where the high cliffs in that direction are closer than seen from the north end of Blind Lake. During the week, this very peaceful place will probably be entirely yours to absorb and enjoy.

To complete the loop of Blind Lake and return to the trailhead, reverse path back to the last sign and continue straight ahead (north and northeast) at that point. Soon, the trail climbs to the top of the east moraine that contains the lake, with occasional peeks of water and cliffs to the west. At 0.2 mile from the last sign the trail descends briefly and enters an open area that extends down to the right (south) and has been heavily used for camping. In this direction the trail is easy to follow, but for hikers coming the other way, the turn up into the trees is far less clear. Another six or seven minutes of walking reveals a man-made cut in the moraine, with an old rusty outlet down to the right (east) of the trail, apparently an early attempt to direct water for irrigation far below. Less than 100 yards beyond, the trail closes the loop around the lake, and it is a pleasant walk of a little over 1 mile back to the trailhead.

Pond along the Blind Lake Trail

Donkey Reservoir Road Trip

Driving distance from Teasdale is 11.2 miles.

Although perhaps slightly less scenic than Blind Lake, Donkey Reservoir is nonetheless a very pretty destination, tucked right up against the summit block of Boulder Mountain. Fishing for brook and cutthroat trout is a popular activity here, as well. A rough road leads right to the small dam that impounds a large body of water; there are quite spectacular views along the road, especially on the descent. Immediately following the rain events of September 2013, the road was somewhat battered and bruised. Even at that, it was an easy 4WD excursion, and if conditions improve after maintenance, the road could be negotiated in high clearance two-wheel drive. Several steep and rocky pitches make 4WD preferable at any time, however.

Lost Lake Fire area

To begin, drive to the center of Teasdale, on either of the access roads from Highway 24. Zero the odometer at the intersection of Center and Main Streets and head south, away from Highway 24. The road will quickly bear left (southeast) and pass through an interesting mix of fields and houses, many of which are tucked into the rock walls to the left. At 1.5 miles from the center of town turn right onto a good gravel road (675 East, Donkey Reservoir Road), which is signed for Coleman Reservoir 3½, Bullberry Lakes 5, and Donkey Reservoir 9. At 2.1 miles bear right (southwest) at a Y intersection, staying on 900 South. Turn left (south) at mile 2.7, passing through a fence on a cattleguard; the sign here gives distances for Coleman Reservoir, Round Lake, Wildcat Trail, and Donkey Reservoir. Bear right at 3.1 miles where a sign offers cautions about travel in the Lost Lake burn area.

Soon after this sign the road begins to pass through a part of the 2,000-acre Lost Lake Fire that occurred in June of 2012. It will be interesting to watch the recovery of the forest over time in this area, which is close to the upper elevation limit for piñon-juniper. In September of 2013 the blackened trunks of most burned trees were still standing and there was limited development of understory plants. In the one spot where there had been aspen, however, the saplings were already three or four feet high, illustrating clearly how aspen respond quickly

Red rocks viewed through fire-killed trees

after disturbance by suckering off existing roots. Above the burn, the grade of the road flattens for a short distance, representative of the many benches that are traversed on the frequently steep climb up the flank of the mountain.

Continue straight on the left fork at the next two junctions in the 1.5 miles after the burn sign, and again near the Boulder Creek Enclosure at 6.7 miles. The road steepens and roughens until it dips to run along the side of the aptly named Bobs Hole, seasonally complete with a pond of varying size, on the left (east) at 7.1. Gradually the road moves into more solid forest as it climbs, with short steep sections, until the drop down to Round Lake, a pretty, small pond to the right (south, then west) of the road. Bear right (west), staying on Forest Road 521 at mile 10.1; FR 526 goes straight ahead to Left Hand Reservoir. The Wildcat Trail joins the road from the left (southeast) at 10.3; it follows the road to Donkey Reservoir. A breached dam and subsequent wetland soon appear on the left (south), followed by the final climb up to Donkey Reservoir and a large parking area at 11.2 miles. A sign at the dam points straight ahead for the Wildcat Trail and Lost Lake.

Donkey Reservoir sits 800 vertical feet below the Boulder Mountain Plateau, which forms a nice backdrop for views from the north shore. The Wildcat Trail offers access to the northeast side of the reservoir on a rocky route that initially stays close to the water, but then climbs a gentle ridge before descending on the way to Lost Lake. The south shore is easier to reach as a track runs parallel to it toward the west. The lake is surrounded by a mix of aspen and conifer, making it a prime destination during the fall color season, although it is also quite scenic with a dusting of new snow a bit later. After enjoying the peace, beauty, and likely solitude of Donkey Reservoir, the trip back down the mountain, especially in late afternoon light, will offer sweeping views of the red rock country and green fields far below.

Donkey Reservoir

Boulder Mountain Summit Plateau Road Trip

Driving distance from Highway 24 at Bicknell Bottoms to the northwest edge of the Boulder Mountain summit plateau is 21.5 miles one way.

Although passenger cars can often be driven right up to the northwest edge of the plateau, the top of Boulder Mountain is a place for high-clearance vehicles. Navigation to the mountain and along the top is sometimes complex and can be confusing. At this writing the signs on the way up are good, though one is missing. Signs come and go, however, route numbers change and may not be consistent from map to map, and, importantly, management of lightly used roads and tracks may change. For example, many maps show roads leading to Donkey Point on the northeast flank, but they are closed to motorized travel at Raft Lake. Before heading out, take the time to stop at the Forest Service office in Loa to get the most current information and travel maps, including those for both the Fishlake and Dixie National Forest districts covered in this book.

Bicknell Bottoms

Pine Creek

Access to Boulder Top is easiest by a wide margin from Highway 24 at Bicknell Bottoms, Bicknell town, or Loa. The former offers the least off-pavement driving and is the best option for travelers coming from Capitol Reef, Torrey, or Highway 12. South of the town of Bicknell, the Fremont River passes through an extensive wetland administered by the state of Utah as the Bicknell Bottoms Wildlife Management Area and the K. E. Bullock Waterfowl Management Area. A paved road, signed 2175 South, Hatchery Road, intersects Highway 24 at milepost 63.2, which is 2.2 miles west of the more western road into Teasdale. Turn south here (left if coming from Torrey and Capitol Reef) and set the odometer to zero. Follow the paved road past the fish hatchery at 2.3 miles to a junction at 3.7 miles. A sign points straight ahead to the King Ranch and right to Escalante and Boulder, and there is also a street sign for 3925 South, Pine Creek Road. Bear right (west) on the gravel road and climb to a reverse Y intersection at 6.7 miles. Description of the rest of the route continues three paragraphs below.

There are two alternate routes to this point. If coming from the west on Highway 24, or from the north on Highway 72, pass through Loa on Highway 24 (this is also Main Street, which runs north-south). When Highway 24 makes a sweeping 90-degree turn to the east (left, heading toward Capitol Reef) at the south end of Loa, continue straight ahead on Main Street that is paved to the south, and zero the odometer. At 2.2 miles, where the pavement, now called Big Rocks Road, bends to the east (left), stay straight (south) on 2110S (Big Hollow Road), which is gravelled, and usually in good condition. A BLM sign at the 2.8-mile mark announces the Big Rocks special recreation management area, where off road travel is permitted in limited (and signed) areas.

The geologically recent Osiris Tuff here has weathered into a maze of rounded forms, offering plenty of opportunity for the kids to expend some energy. After leaving this area, the road crosses open, rolling, sage-covered ground before dropping into Big Hollow at 6.9 miles. A crossroads is passed at 8.1 miles, and the reverse Y intersection described at the end of the preceding paragraph comes up at 10.1 miles. Description of the rest of the route continues two paragraphs below.

A third possibility for accessing this junction is best for anyone staying or starting in Bicknell. Drive to the west end of town on Highway 24, and when the road begins to curve to the right (if heading west toward Loa), turn left (south) on 400W and zero the odometer. At 0.9 mile, turn right (west) on Bicknell Bottoms Road (850S). The pavement ends just after the small bridge over the Fremont River at 1.7 miles, and there is a Y junction at 2.1 miles. Stay right and continue to another intersection at 5.5 miles. Turn left (south) here, joining the route from Loa. It is another 2 miles to the common reverse Y junction described in this and the preceding paragraphs.

The point where the three routes described above come together is signed by the BLM for Boulder Top and Escalante, both straight ahead (south). Zero the odometer again and continue on the good gravel road across a wide open sagebrush and grass plain. In just over 0.5 mile stay left at the next Y (signed to the right for Antelope Spring and Pollywog Lake) and stay left again at the next Y at mile 1.3 where the sign indicates that it is 6 miles to the Aquarius Ranger Station and 12 miles to Boulder Top, on the left (southeast) fork, and 20 miles to Posey Lake and 44 miles to Escalante, on the right (southwest) fork. Keep to the left; the quality of the road stays quite good even after this junction where much of the traffic stays on the other fork (Road 154).

Posey Lake Road

The road now winds through a dense piñon forest and, upon entering the Dixie

National Forest at a cattleguard at mile 2.9, becomes Forest Road (FR) 178. Views open toward the mountain slopes that are dotted with brilliant aspen groves in the fall. Cattle on the open range amble along the road, generally indifferent to passing vehicles, though the calves are easily spooked. At mile 6.6 continue straight at a junction where FR 517 goes left (northeast) to the Pine Creek Trail.

After another 0.25 mile keep to the right when the signed road to the Aquarius Guard Station goes to the left (east) for 0.3 mile to the facility. The old ranger station, renovated in 2013, is now set up for overnight visitors who don't mind spartan accommodations. It sleeps four with a double bed and bunks and has a woodstove for warmth and a propane stove for cooking. Bedding is not provided, and while water is available, flush toilets are not: a nearby vault toilet serves the purpose. Limited RV and tent camping is permitted on the grounds for people in the same group. At this writing the cost to rent the station is a very reasonable $30 per night. More information and the opportunity to make reservations can be found at www.recreation.gov. Enter Aquarius in the "Park" or "Facility" name box and click on search. The cabin is generally available beginning around the middle of May until October 15.

Forest Road 178 continues south along the west flank of the mountain. Keep right at mile 7.6 when a track (FR 3328) goes to the left, and pass the Pot Holes Enclosure at mile 8.2. At 0.2 mile beyond the enclosure is a junction signed for the Miller Creek Trail 2, and Dark Valley 3, straight ahead, and Boulder Top 6, to the left (east). A second sign notes that the road to Boulder Top is closed 5.4 miles ahead from November 15 to June 15 annually. The main road swings around to the left and soon begins a long ascent to the northeast through several very pretty aspen groves before emerging onto the shoulder of the mountain with big views to the west and northwest.

After a couple more miles the road doubles back to the south to a junction where FR 542 goes left (northeast) to Cook Lake ½, and the Wildcat Trailhead 1. The main road continues straight ahead to the final significant intersection before the top of the rim. At 14.1 on the odometer is a sign for Boulder Top straight ahead and Miller Lake 1/2 to the right. This junction is in a pretty linear meadow near a cattleguard and fence. The closure dates at this location are listed as November 1 through June 15. After leaving the meadow the road roughens substantially and climbs steeply, passes through the closure gate, and reaches the plateau and a signboard with a map of Boulder Top at mile 14.8.

The side trip to Miller Lake is short and rough, but the lake is very nice. To get there, turn right (south) at the signed junction. The track bears to the right until making a right angle turn to the left at 0.2 mile where there is a sign. Rocks are especially numerous on the descent to the lake and high clearance is necessary. A somewhat faint turnaround circle in the meadow just north of the lake is 0.8 mile from road FR 178. There is a picnic table to the west of the circle. The lake is nicely framed by timber and a handsome talus slope on the east side. The west slope of Boulder Mountain rises above this pleasant spot.

Boulder Top has a unique feel—a combination of isolation and elevation and space.

It is big and the roads are rough, making it seem even more expansive. High clearance is necessary for travel beyond the initial signboard (reset your odometer here, as well) and good tires able to fend off the ubiquitous rocks, some sharp, are necessary. The main spine road extends southeast to Bowns Point, a long trek with a lot of slow going, but one that traverses the entire plateau. As the Forest Service closes roads to motorized travel, a wealth of possibilities open up in terms of walking, which is a fine way to experience solitude and quiet. With terrain that is gently rolling and often quite level, walking is generally easy, though the very high elevation will preclude it for some.

The descriptions that follow are merely a sampler of travel on Boulder Mountain; this is a place that rewards exploration. Just make sure to pay attention to your surroundings and route, since the absence of prominent landforms makes navigation more difficult. From the signboard continue straight ahead (east) for 100 yards to another sign that gives distances to a number of destinations on Boulder Top. Immediately beyond, the road condition drops another notch as it winds through a rolling flat dotted with spruce-fir groves and a multitude of boulders. At 0.2 mile the former road toward Government Point has been closed and is now a hiking trail. Continue straight ahead at 0.8 mile where a track (FR 541) leads up (right) to a fenced corral. The road climbs up to the highest bench on the mountain, and at 2.3 miles there used to be an old sign on the left that said Teasdale Ranger District, Highest pt., Bluebell Knoll, 11322. As of this writing, it was missing, but may be replaced before your visit. The post remains in place.

The short climb to the summit is worthwhile for the expansive views it offers. Pull off the road somewhere near the 2.3-mile mark and simply walk up the hill to the north. There are a couple of barely discernible old roads that can be followed, but the grade is reasonable and it may be just as easy to follow the path of least resistance. Without a formal trail, it is especially important to watch your step, avoiding vegetation when possible. If there are several hikers, spread out so that a use trail does not develop. Near the top of Bluebell Knoll a slightly more obvious old track cuts to the right (northeast) to the rocky summit that is dotted with trees but offers fine views from the northeast clockwise around to the southwest. Raft Lake lies below to the northeast, while directly east the Henry Mountain summits rise in the distance, just above the plateau. The expanse of Boulder Top is evident to the southeast. The climb up the hill might take ten minutes for people in good shape and acclimated to the elevation, or considerably longer for others.

Back on the road it is 0.3 mile to a junction signed to the left (north) for Raft Lake 1, Donkey Meadows 2½, Donkey Point 4½, and straight ahead for Elbow Lake 1. The side trip to Raft Lake is scenic and short on FR 1324. The road passes through open meadow and then contours through forest before dropping down to the ledgy ground west of the lake. During the summer, the mix of scattered spruces and many wildflowers makes this a good spot for a picnic. The road continues to the northern shore of the lake where motorized travel ends at a very informal parking area and hiking or horseback riding is necessary to continue on to Donkey Meadows and Donkey Point.

Donkey Point Hike

Hiking distance is 6 miles round trip.

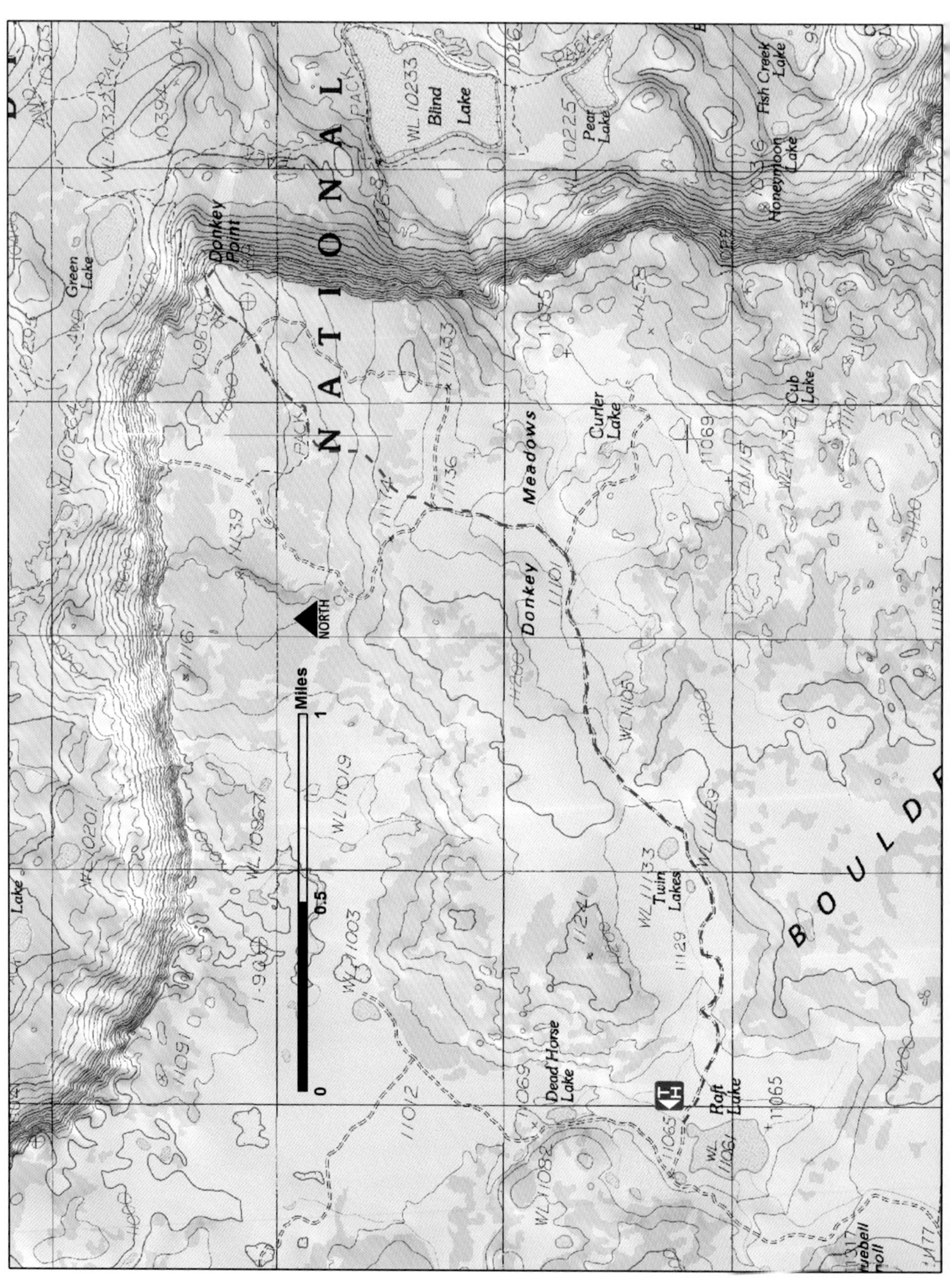

Donkey Point route

The view from Donkey Point is well worth the 6-mile out and back walk. Route finding is easy for the first couple of miles, then a bit difficult after the trail leaves the old road and before it enters the forest. The likelihood of having the entire trail to yourself is greater than the chances of meeting anyone (and they might well be on a horse). One late October, five days after a snowfall, there was not a single track that marked the snow in shaded areas where it covered the road up to Boulder Top. That might pretty much be the definition of solitude.

Getting There

The hike begins at the road closure on the north end of Raft Lake, directions to which are above. A sign for the Donkey Point Trail gives distances to Donkey Point 2, and Green Lake 3. The actual distance to Donkey Point is almost exactly 3 miles.

The Hike

The old road is the trail for much of the way and it is obvious as it ascends the gentle hill to the east. When the old track curves around, faint use trails cutting the bends are often present. They don't save much time or distance, however, and might as well be avoided. The walk through the meadow, with spruce-fir forest close by to the south is pleasant and easy going. Over the 0.75 mile from Raft Lake to Twin Lakes there are only about 60 feet of elevation gain, but, of course, just the last several hundred yards of the hike are below 11,000 feet, and that loss of about 150 feet must be regained on the return. The Twin Lakes may dry up after snowmelt unless the monsoon rains are heavy.

After passing by Twin Lakes on the south, the old road climbs a very gentle hill to a low and wide saddle at mile 1.1, and then drops almost imperceptibly into Donkey Meadows. An interesting S-shaped lake is on the right (south), and just over 1.5 miles from the trailhead the route goes by a circular channel surrounded by a nice grassy wetland, also on the south. Beyond the wetland, the track begins to bend around to the north. Several wet areas retain the multiple ruts of vehicles attempting to get through in the past, and the route becomes a little less obvious. An important marker is a sign well off to the right (east) of the tracks at the 2-mile mark. It is for the Donkey Point Trail and Green Lake; a distance of 1 mile is given for the latter. The arrow on the sign, which is correct, points between groups of trees toward denser forest beyond. Since there is no tread at all, it may be counterintuitive to leave the old road, but follow the sign and eventually trail will appear in the woods. Should anything happen to the sign it would be very difficult to stay on route without a GPS: the sign is at UTM 0459574mE, 4225240mN.

At the sign look carefully to the north and locate a cairn made of the same black volcanic rocks that litter the ground. The first is perhaps the most difficult to see; after finding it, more will appear in a fairly straight line to the solid forest. The gentle ascent ends at 2.2 miles, and the trail is quite well marked by cairns and blazes in the trees. Only very small openings break the canopy, and the walk through the spruce and fir is very nice. A stack of old cut logs is at 2.8 miles, and Donkey Point is at mile 3; the coordinates are UTM 0460542mE and 4226323mN.

The opening at the edge of the Boulder Top escarpment is not large, but it offers a bird's eye view from the northwest around to the southeast. The rock (Johnson Valley trachyandesite) is the oldest of the three ashflows that presumably came from the Marysvale center from 26 million years ago (ma) to 23 ma. Donkey Point is just a few feet below 11,000 feet in elevation, about 650 feet higher than Green Lake, which is plainly visible beneath the rim. An extremely steep trail leads down to it and the Wildcat Trail.

The view encompasses the other three mountains included in this book and the red-rock country on their flanks. Clockwise from the northwest (left) are the Rabbit Valley towns of Loa, Lyman, and Bicknell in front of Fish Lake Hightop; the Red Gate where the Fremont River exits the Rabbit Valley; the towns of Teasdale and Torrey west and east of Thousand Lake Mountain; the long red Wingate Sandstone cliff that descends to Fruita in Capitol Reef along Highway 24; the San Rafael Swell over the Wingate and white Navajo Sandstone; Factory Butte and the Caineville Mesas in the middle distance with Navajo Knobs, Ferns Nipple, and the Golden Throne in the foreground; and the Henry Mountains at the southern limit of the vista. On clear days the La Sal Mountains east of Moab will appear over the Golden Throne.

Green Lake below Donkey Point

Road Trip—continued

To continue across Boulder Top from Raft Lake, return to the previous junction with FR 178, reset the odometer, and head southeast toward Elbow Lake. At 1 mile is a junction, signed to the right (southwest) for Riddle Flat 1, Bakeskillet 2, and Spectacle Reservoir 6, all on road FR 1277.

Side Trip to Spectacle Lake and 4WD Road Trip

Distance: Driving distance from FR 178 to Spectacle Lake is 6.9 miles one way; 4WD driving distance from FR 178 to the Posey Lake Road (FR 154) is 20.5 miles.

High clearance vehicles can, as of this writing, make the side trip to Spectacle Lake on a very rough road with very little likelihood of seeing another vehicle (most likely an ATV, if anything). Two-wheel drive high-clearance vehicles will have to retrace their route back to FR 178 if they make it as far as Spectacle Lake. To take the spur route, turn right onto FR 1277, which is rocky and generally worsens along the way to Spectacle Lake. Elbow Lake will be on the left (east), as will Bakeskillet Lake farther on, though it may be dry. At mile 3.1 is a sign for Surveyors Lake 3 and Chuck Lake 4, both straight ahead, and Spectacle Lake 5 to the left; stay with the latter as the track becomes even less distinct. It is slow going to the remains of an old cabin at 4.7 miles and then to the top of a small ridge at 5.5 miles.

A steep rocky ascent at 6.1 is the first time that low range is truly helpful to manage speed. FR 1277 ends on the southwest flank of the dam that forms the two-lobed Spectacle Lake, which provides irrigation water for ranches far below. An abandoned cabin is well preserved at this point, but should not be entered due to the threat of hantavirus. The earthen dam is quite large and seems almost implausible in such an isolated spot, but reflects the value of water in what is mostly a high desert environment at lower elevations.

Adventurous drivers with robust 4WD vehicles and an understanding of how far away help might be, can descend from the mountain by a different route and loop back to the Posey Lake/Loa Road by turning right (west) onto FR 162 west of the cabin. If driving the 4WD track, reset the odometer to zero at the dam. FR 162 has three short, steep, and bouldery ascents, the first not far from the lake. This first pitch is the worst of the three and it has definitely deteriorated during the past several years. Four-wheel drive tracks rarely stay the same for any length of time, so be prepared for anything. If it looks too rough, simply turn around and retrace your route.

At 0.3 mile from the dam is a junction where FR 333 goes left to nearby Rim Lake. The sign is placed for oncoming vehicles and accurately gives the distance to Rim Lake as 0.25 mile, but is less correct in giving a distance of 1 mile to Spectacle Reservoir—although it may seem like at least that much. The track traverses surprisingly hilly terrain, passing through meadows and small stretches of forest. After 2.3 miles it passes by a series of lakes in an open area. They may be dry, which is good for driving since the road goes through several low spots, or they may be full, which is scenically preferred. As is true almost everywhere in the Utah backcountry, wet weather is to be avoided.

At 4.3 miles from Spectacle Lake (perhaps an hour of driving if no shoveling is necessary), the road crosses a cattleguard and fence, and a sign, again for oncoming vehicles, states the same closure dates as those posted on the approach to Boulder Top described in the previous pages. This point marks the edge of the Boulder Top plateau, and a long descent follows, almost all within dense forest. The track is still rough, but conditions are generally easier unless a recent weather event has created gullies or cut banks. FR 491 joins from the right (north) at 5.7 miles; keep left on FR 162. At a three-way intersection at mile 6.1, turn right (north) staying on FR 162.

A cattleguard and corral are at mile 7.2, amid small meadows covered in flowers in the late spring or early summer. The road surface improves to gravel at 7.4 miles at a junction with FR 176 that leads right (north) to the Row Lakes. Stay straight on FR 162, passing the track to Jacobs Reservoir on the left at 7.8, a second track (FR 262) to the Row Lakes on the right at 8.5, and then enjoying a long stretch of aspen-fringed meadows until the T intersection with FR 154 at mile 13.6. To return to Highway 24 and Capitol Reef, turn right (north) here on the good gravel Posey Lake/Loa Road, which is described in the Hells Backbone section. The total distance from the junction of FR 162 and FR 154 to Highway 24 at Bicknell Bottoms is 23.1 miles.

Columbine on Boulder Mountain

Road Trip—continued

The main stem route across the plateau, FR 178, continues along the north side of Elbow Lake, beyond which is a stretch where wet weather can soften the road considerably (in contrast to much of the route on Boulder Top which is generally rocky). A mile from the Spectacle Lake junction the road briefly enters the trees, then in 0.5 mile reaches another junction and potential side trip.

4WD Side Trip to Trail Point Hike

Driving distance is 3.9-mile difficult 4WD drive.
Hiking distance is 4.6-mile round trip.

A sign at this intersection gives distances to Crater Lake 3, Horseshoe Lake 4, Crescent Lake 5, and Trail Point 6. The road, FR 528, ends at a trailhead on the north shore of Horseshoe Lake. From there it is a beautiful 4.6-mile round trip hike to Trail Point over mostly gentle terrain. **Do not underestimate** the difficulty of the 3.9-mile drive to the trailhead. The track has many, many boulder patches that require very good clearance and careful wheel placement. During wet periods there are also several mudholes that are exceedingly slippery. Travel, though it may not seem like it, is mostly downhill on the way to Horseshoe Lake, and the return trip has enough steep ascents to make 4WD and low range necessary. Plan on an hour to drive each way, and it is likely that this road will do nothing except get worse over time. Strong hikers with standard SUVs might opt to hike the entire road to the trail, making for a round trip walk of 12.4 miles.

It doesn't take long to get the flavor of the road, with rocks littering the track almost from the start. Much of the route crosses open meadow, with copses of spruce nearby. A sign at 0.9 mile lists points that lie ahead. A lake appears on the right (west) at 2.1, with a likely dry lake a mile beyond. A small, reed-ringed pond on the left (east) at the 3.5-mile mark is just 0.4 mile from the end of the road at the trailhead. A short, steep bedrock ledge edges the parking area, though it is easy to park just short of this last obstacle.

Road to Trail Point trailhead

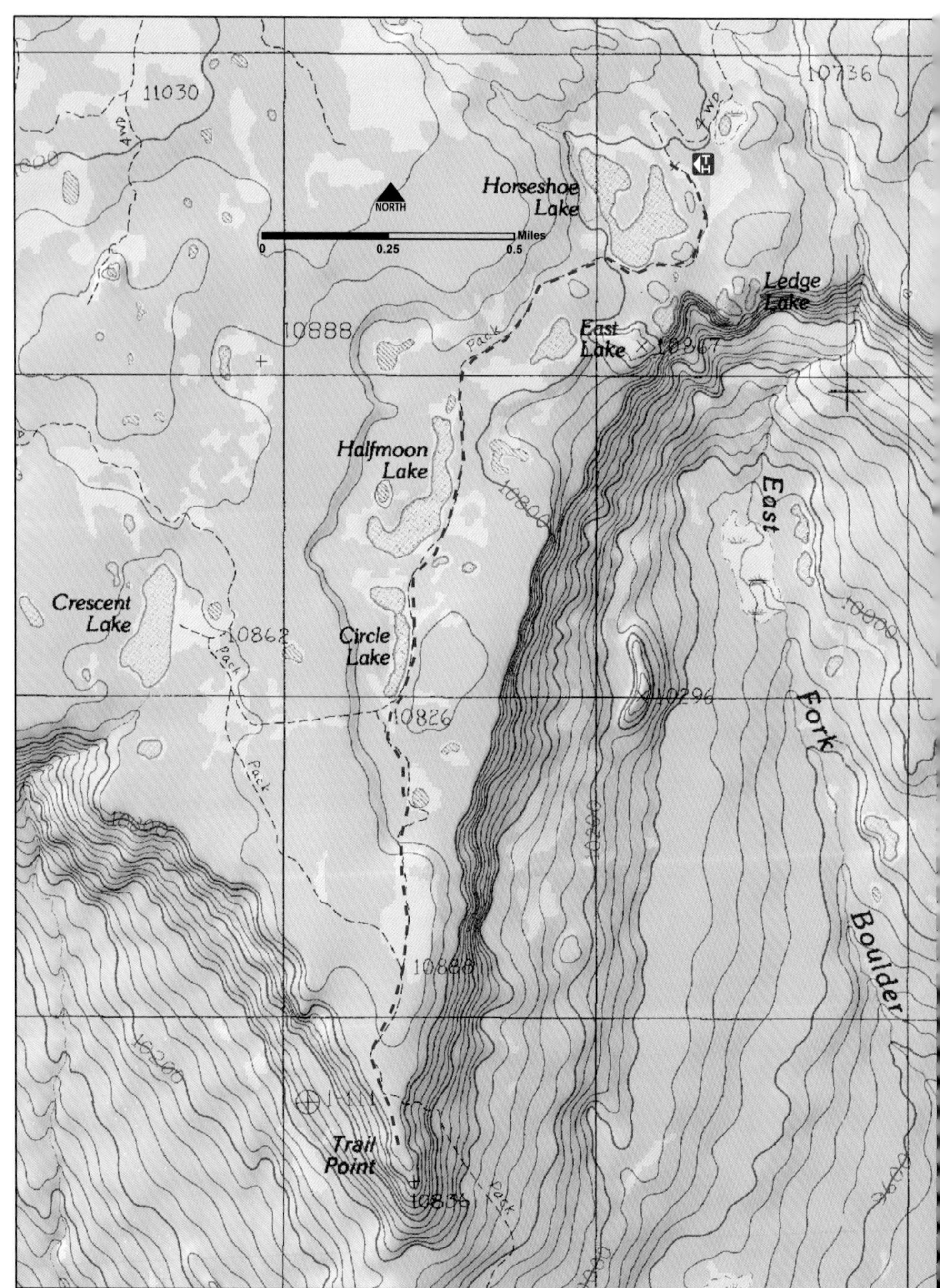

Trail Point route

The Hike

The hike to Trail Point is a beautiful walk that passes by four lakes and ends near a spectacular viewpoint on the south rim of Boulder Mountain. If the trail had paved road access, it would be one of the most popular high elevation hikes in Utah, but as it is, the chances of seeing anyone else, except perhaps during hunting season, are almost nil. With the exception of a couple of short hills, the path is easy all the way to the bouldery approach to Trail Point. A word of appreciation is in order for the trail crew that did an excellent job of clearing the route, making sure the cairns are adequate, and renewing the abundant double blazes on the trees. For a trail that is so remote and lightly traveled this level of maintenance is unexpected (and, of course, may change by the time you get here!).

The sign at the trailhead lists the lakes ahead, but the distances given are longer than they actually are. A nice vantage point for Horseshoe Lake is just beyond the southwest corner of the trailhead parking area. Looking down on the lake, the exposed rock ledge on the right side conjures up a New England lake, or even, with a little imagination, the Maine coast. The trail begins directly behind the sign and quickly drops down to shore level. As it rounds the south end of the lake the New England comparison is strengthened by the resemblance to many sections of the Appalachian Trail. The western arm of the horseshoe comes into view, with a strange rectangular void in the ledge on the far shore.

Horseshoe Lake

Lupines along the Trail Point trail

Just over 0.25 mile from the trailhead the path curves south (left) and away from the lake and begins to ascend toward a ridge crossing. The Johnson Valley trachyandesite is fully exposed here, and the trail down the other side is steep and loose. At the bottom of the slope the route bears to the right (west) and soon emerges onto the shore of East Lake at the 0.5-mile mark. (Note: The map on P. 282 does not reflect that the trail has been relocated to the east and south of East Lake.) This is by far the smallest lake along this trail, but interesting reflection patterns along the east shore can be very good if the light is right. Beyond East Lake the trail crosses a long meadow that retains water for some time after snowmelt. Initially there are two cairns that seem contradictory, but the one to the left (south) is merely an alternative route if the swale ahead is too muddy to pass through comfortably.

The meadow narrows and then opens again, and one of the cairns is actually perched on a big rock in the middle of what is a small pond during wet times. At the 0.75-mile mark the trail enters the forest and begins to climb. The divide before Halfmoon Lake is low and soon the shore comes into view and the trail descends to it. The lake is nicely fringed with spruce and fir, along with a light green perimeter of grasses.

Halfmoon Lake is nearly 0.3 mile long and the trail is scenic all the way along the shore. From the south end, it is only 100 yards or so to the next pond, Circle Lake.

Chances are that a very high percentage of hikes on Boulder Top are done during the summer. The road doesn't open until the middle of June, and by late August most of the meadows are somewhat bland after the gentians have bloomed. While the monsoons are definitely a lightning/severe weather concern, they also bring some spectacular cloud scenes on most days in July and August. The four lakes on the way to Trail Point are often calm, giving mirror images of the surrounding treetops and beautiful reflections of the towering cumulus. Somewhere along the walk, a break to sit on the shore and enjoy the solitude and the artistry of the natural world would seem to be in order.

After passing Circle Lake, at the south end, 1.5 miles from the trailhead is a junction; when last seen, the sign was lying down, but still there. The left (south) arrow is for Trail Point, and the right (west) is for Crescent Lake, which is about 0.5 mile away. Keep to the left (south) and pass by a wetland before beginning a short ascent 250 yards from the trail junction. The path tops out in a big meadow, following cairns. The open area narrows and the route re-enters the forest where it begins to dodge around mature spruce trees.

The ground cover here is a little unusual, consisting in very large part of silvery lupine (*Lupinus argenteus*). Lupines have a long bloom period during which they produce tall racemes of bluish purple, pea-like flowers. The leaves are palmate, with leaflets that are long and thin. Standing from knee to almost hip high, they put on quite a show among the conifers. The downside, especially for ranchers, is that all parts of some lupines contain alkaloids that are toxic to livestock. Given the abundance of both healthy-looking lupines and cattle on the mountain, however, it appears that peaceful coexistence is in effect.

The last 300 yards of the route to the point where it drops off the plateau are interesting and a bit of a challenge in terms of staying on track. The trail negotiates a field of boulders with little dirt tread to show the way. Small, two- or three-rock cairns are usually abundant, but may topple with the snowmelt. The trail is necessarily convoluted, so it is important to pay attention. At 2.3 miles from the trailhead the path begins to descend sharply, just to the east of Trail Point itself.

Since views are obstructed from the trail, and, of course, since the promontory is so obvious and inviting and nearby, the tendency will be to try to find a way up onto the andesite. This is not too difficult, but be very careful, since the large rocks are sometimes loose and can tip under a step. A little scrambling is necessary to get up on the main rib; again, it shouldn't be too hard if you find a good place, but remember that help is really far away. The views toward South Point to the west and Bowns Point to the east are good, and the entire panorama of Escalante country stretches off to the south beyond Kings Pasture directly below. Navajo Peak is clearly visible in the distance to the south-southeast. When the views have been absorbed, clear-thinking hikers will be pleased that they took care to remember the way back to the trail.

East Lake

Road Trip—continued

To complete the drive across Boulder Mountain to Bowns Point from the northern terminus of the Horseshoe Lake Road, continue east on the main spine road (FR 178). In 0.7 mile FR 1001 bears off to the left (east, then north) to Bess Lake. At 1.5 miles, in an open meadow, is the last major junction, which is signed for Beef Meadows 1½, Willow Draw 3, and Chokecherry Point 6, all to the left, and Pleasant Creek Meadow 4, and Bowns Point 9, both straight ahead. Zero the odometer one last time at this junction and go straight. From this point, the road gradually worsens, and approaching Bowns Point it nearly disappears in a rocky meadow. Lots of clearance is required and 4WD highly recommended. The views from the point are very good, especially on a clear day late in the afternoon, but it is a long trip out there; it should take over an hour to negotiate the 9 miles. Many stops to enjoy the solitude and beauty help to soften the bouncing and banging that the "road" engenders.

While the road is now rough, for the first mile there are signs of maintenance, most notably rock fills across potentially wet areas. Keep an eye out for marmots here, and indeed, anywhere on Boulder Mountain. Marmots are in the same genus as eastern woodchucks, and are actually large ground squirrels. The species on Boulder Top, and over most of the high country of the American West, is the yellow-bellied marmot, *Marmota flaviventris*. Conditions on the plateaus are perfect for them, with large meadows frequently dotted with boulder fields well suited for burrows. Marmots are very social, and when conditions are good, they live in colonies of up to twenty animals. Males share their burrows with up to four females. Mating occurs almost immediately after the long eight-month hibernation period ends, and litters of about four pups are born a month later. After a year, all males and most females depart the colony.

Road to Bowns Point

Marmots generally eat plants and seeds, but will consume insects and bird eggs as well. It is very important for them to bulk up prior to hibernation, since they will lose about half of their body weight during that period. They are most active above ground mid morning and late in the afternoon while they are feeding. Well known for their whistling, which is usually a signal for danger, they have quite an extensive array of communication sounds. Marmots can live up to fifteen years in the wild, succumbing primarily during hibernation in the winter and by predation in the summer. In the latter category, coyotes are most efficient, but badgers also will take marmots. While badger sightings are quite rare, they have happened in this area.

In just under 2 miles FR 1305 bears to the left (east) to Big Lake, and a little farther on, pretty Noon Lake is to the right (west). A large meadow appears at the 2.8-mile mark, with an identifying sign (Pleasant Creek Meadow) at 3 miles. The road passes through the southeast part of the meadow where a trickle of water represents the source of Pleasant Creek. A curve to the south (right) leads to a short, sharp uphill section with a bit of a difficult obstacle, best passed on the left at last reconnaissance. The next 2.5 miles to an old cabin are rocky and tedious. A culvert is a major speed bump at 6.1 miles; it can be avoided on the left (northeast). Very rough tread precedes a Y where the old track to the right has been closed. In the meadows the road is very faint, but generally can be discerned by looking far ahead.

A short distance after a sign for Bowns Point to the left and Deer Lakes to the right at 7.6 miles, it is truly difficult to pick out a line across a very large open area. The route is largely straight ahead, but is so obscure and boulder strewn that it would be difficult to drive. From this point it is better to hike the remaining 1.3 miles to Bowns Point. A group of dead trees at the far forest edge may serve as a marker for a few years; eventually you will need to enter the woods just to their left (north) to find the old two-track road. A newer sign for the Frisky Trail is at 8.4 miles, and Bowns Point is a pleasant 0.5 mile farther on.

At the point is a zigzag fence and the upper end of a cattle stock route to the plateau. The view is primarily from the northeast to the southeast, and best in afternoon to early evening. Given the time required to drive back across Boulder Top and down to the Rabbit Valley, those seeking good light for photography should consider camping at or near the point; chances are very high that you will have total solitude. From the left (northeast), the Golden Throne and other prominences in Capitol Reef can be seen in front of the Caineville Mesas, with Lower Bowns Reservoir and short stretches of Highway12 in the foreground. Directly east, the Henry Mountains rise above the red rock of the Waterpocket Fold. To the southeast are the Little Rockies beyond the red Circle Cliffs.

Speed bump on the road to Bowns Point

Fish Lake

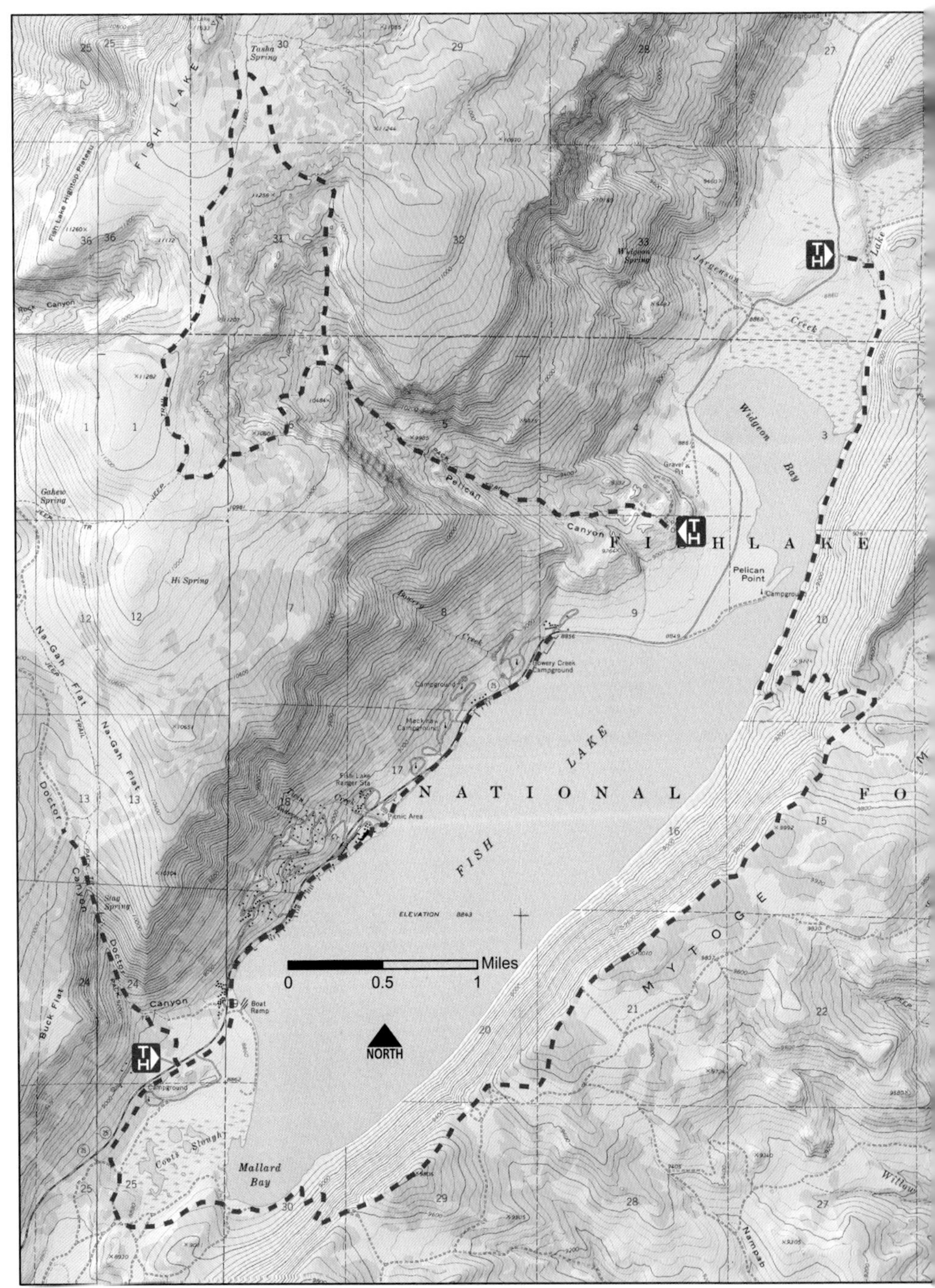

Doctor Creek Trail (lower left); Lakeshore Trail (around the lake); Pelican Canyon Trail (upper left)

Fish Lake and Fish Lake Hightop

Maybe in a state that boasts both the Great Salt Lake and Lake Powell it might be expected that a gorgeous high elevation natural fresh water lake with beautiful surroundings, excellent fishing, and a spectacular aspen color extravaganza each fall would receive less than its due. Still, it is hard to imagine how little notice Fish Lake gets compared to what it deserves. In addition to its abundant natural beauty, the area has a relaxed vibe even during the high season of summer (with the exception of the three holiday weekends), and is nearly deserted most of the rest of the year. A trio of modest, locally owned resorts provides lodging, but many visitors enjoy a stay at one of the Fishlake National Forest campgrounds, two within a stone's throw of the lake, and the other nestled in aspen on the multi-use trail only a few minutes by bike from the shore.

The lake is sandwiched in a graben between Fish Lake Hightop and Mytoge Mountain at an elevation of more than 8,800 feet. Running from southwest to northeast, Fish Lake is five miles long and a mile wide. The northwest shore is developed along Highway 25, but the southeast side is an unblemished forested slope rising to more than 10,000 feet. There are more than 100 private residences above Highway 25, but most are shielded from view by the forest, and the resorts are of older vintage and fit seamlessly into the environment. All are under special use permits with the USFS. The shoreline is on public land and there are many access points along the road. Best of all, the Lakeshore National Recreation Trail circles the lake, flat and very family friendly on the northwest side, and rough and wild on the other.

Fish Lake from Highway 25

Fish Lake Loop Road Trip

Driving distance is 51 miles.

For hot and tired desert visitors, the easy loop drive, all on paved roads, from Loa offers a real change of scenery and much cooler temperatures. Loa, the seat of Wayne County, is 27 miles west of the Capitol Reef visitor center on Highway 24. Proceed west and then north through town, zeroing the odometer at the junction with Highway 72. Stay on Highway 24 as it winds west past the mouth of Riley Canyon and then goes on a straight roller coaster course along the northern edge of the sagebrush-covered Awapa Plateau. After a summit (8,385 feet), the road descends about a mile to Highway 25 to Fish Lake. This junction is 12.7 miles from Highway 72 in Loa, and within sight of mile marker 39. Turn right (northeast), reset the odometer to zero and begin a long climb.

Not every sight that a traveler might encounter is awe inspiring, preposterously beautiful, or intensely exciting. No, some are, well, obscure. Such is most definitely the case with the rock "sculptures" of Lorenzo Larsen, a sheepherder in the area from after World War II until about 1980. These works of toil are noteworthy for their whimsy and austere location rather than artistry, but if you have a few minutes, dry weather, and a high-clearance vehicle, why not make a visit? At milepost 2.4 on Highway 25 (also the distance from Highway 24), a track leaves the road on the right (southeast) at a point where there is a large pullout on the northwest side of the highway. Take the track across the sagebrush high ground for 0.4 mile. Stop and look 100 yards to the northwest, where a four-foot tall rock figure resembles a woman carrying a frying pan.

Continuing on the track, it is just another 0.1 mile to a lesser track to the right (west). Park at the junction to avoid further damage to the ground and plants, and walk less than 200 yards to an elaborate collection of often indiscernible figures and a long, low wall that has suffered the ravages of time, but that will still probably conjure up some thought of Stonehenge. Return to Highway 25 by retracing your route, or continuing on down the main track, staying to the right and eventually descending a sharp and rough drop back to the paved road at milepost 1.5. In either case, turn right (northeast) on Highway 25 to continue on the Fish Lake Loop.

Continuing northeast on Highway 25, the route passes near a scattering of private homes and then tops out at an elevation of 9,036 feet. The Fishlake National Forest begins here, and almost immediately (milepost and odometer reading at 4.2 miles) a gravel road on the left (north) leads to a very large parking area from which two forest roads diverge. The one that drops down to the northwest (bear left) is FR 057, which leads to a spectacular fall aspen tour for all vehicles and then continues up to and along the summit of Fish Lake Hightop for those with four-wheel drive. This side trip is described later in this section.

Beyond this junction Highway 25 drops gently and at 5.6 miles a large pull-out on the right (south) offers an impressive first view of Fish Lake. From this vantage point not only are the lake and surroundings well displayed, but the sweep of aspen between the parking area and the lake is noteworthy as well. Aspen generally reproduce clonally in dry climates (new stems sprout from extensive root systems), and some clones in Utah and other western states have reached prodigious size. The clone visible from the viewpoint and through which Highway 25 proceeds is so big that some claim it may be the world's heaviest organism at more than 6,000 tons. It may also be very old, having first sprouted some tens of thousands of years ago. It even has a name—Pando—meaning "I spread" in Latin.

Aspen near Zedds Meadow

Aspen clones can often be discerned by the most casual of observers in both the spring and the fall, since the stems in each clone green up and leaf out at the same time, and change to the same shade of yellow, orange, or, rarely, red, simultaneously in the fall. Thus, one clone may be nice and green in the spring while an adjacent one may still be bare. On the northwest side of Fish Lake a heart-shaped clone turns a sharp red in the fall, while most of its neighbors are bright yellow.

After passing right through Pando, at mile 6.9 there is an exhibit on the right (southeast) that describes the Old Spanish Trail, an arm of which passed this point. This is also the trailhead for the Doctor Creek Trail and the Lakeshore Trail. Just beyond is the entrance to the Doctor Creek Campground, which has a group camp area as well as individual sites nestled in the aspen. The lake stretches ahead at the base of a gentle grade, and then the road parallels the shore a short distance from the water. There are several roadside access points to the shoreline trail, each with either a vault or flush toilet. The Twin Creeks Picnic Area is on the right, 8.7 miles from Highway 24. A very pretty spot right on the lake, Twin Creeks is a good place to begin a leisurely stroll or bike ride along the Lakeshore Trail.

Beyond Twin Creeks the road stays near the lake, passing by the several entrances to the Mackinaw Campground, the Bowery Campground, and a resort, the last of the

The Old Spanish Trail

The Old Spanish Trail, so named by John C. Fremont after his 1844 trip from California to Santa Fe, was a short-lived pack route across some of the most inhospitable country the American Southwest has to offer. After Coronado's incursion into what is now New Mexico in 1540, more than two centuries passed before active attempts were made to locate a viable trade route between the Spanish settlement of Santa Fe and Los Angeles. Initial exploration in 1765 identified a route from Santa Fe across southwestern Colorado and well into Utah. Perhaps the most famous of the early expeditions was led by two priests, Fathers Dominguez and Escalante in 1776. They traveled through the Grand Valley south of Moab, crossed the Colorado and Green Rivers, made their way around the San Rafael Swell, and eventually emerged from the Wasatch near present day Provo. At that point they decided to return to Santa Fe, and did so by circling south and then east, finding, after considerable difficulty, a place to cross the Colorado near Page, Arizona. The "Crossing of the Fathers" is now submerged under Lake Powell.

After trapper Jedediah Smith stitched together the middle portion of the route in 1827, a risk-taking merchant in Santa Fe named Antonio Armijo assembled the first pack train to make a successful trip to the West Coast and back. New Mexican woolens were generally traded for California stock, preferably mules. The trip could only be made in the cooler and wetter months, with the return to Santa Fe completed before the onset of snowmelt in the high country of Colorado. While the primary route of the Old Spanish Trail in Utah was to the north through Salina Canyon, a 72-mile long secondary trail traversed the difficult, but more hospitable, country by Fish Lake. After the Mexican-American War and the settlement of Utah and points west along the route, the Old Spanish Trail was replaced by easier wagon roads and reverted to more local use.

Old Spanish Trail exhibit

developed area along the shore. At this point Highway 25 morphs imperceptibly into Forest Road 640, and later FR 36; simply stay on the paved road to complete the loop. At mile 11.9 the spur road to Pelican Overlook leaves the highway on the left (west). This track is rocky and rough and requires a high-clearance vehicle as of this writing. The spur road stays left past the gravel pit and bears right and uphill at the next junction. It ends in a mile at a large parking area at the viewpoint.

Pelican Overlook (a sign provides an alternative name: Pelican Promontory) lives up to its name, with expansive views of the entire lake and Mytoge Mountain across the way. In summer, Fish Lake usually hosts a large population of resident white pelicans, which often can be seen in Widgeon Bay below the overlook. The parking area is on a shelf at the mouth of Pelican Canyon, well above the lake and it is a little difficult to figure out how that bench was formed. The answer relates to recent (in geologic terms) glaciations that covered Fish Lake Hightop with ice. As valley glaciers descended the canyon, they left terminal moraines behind, including the large one on top of which the viewpoint is located. The trail to the flat plateau high above leaves from the west side of the parking lot; the Pelican Canyon hike is described below.

Common sight near Widgeon Bay

Back on the paved road, keep an eye out for cattle that wander freely between prime grazing areas on both sides of the highway. At mile 13.3 on the right (east) is the signed spur road to the Lake Creek Trailhead, covered in the Circumnavigating Fish Lake section that follows. The road passes by extensive wetlands, along with Frying Pan and Piute Campgrounds. Between the latter two is the access road to the Tasha Equestrian Campground. The turn-off for the Gooseberry (also called Seven Mile) Road is beyond on the left. This good gravel road (soon to be paved) traverses very pretty high country to the west of mounts Marvine and Terrill, eventually descending to Interstate 70 east of Salina. The Fish Lake loop bends around the Johnson Valley Reservoir to begin a mostly southeasterly course toward Highway 72.

Along the northeast shore of the Johnson Valley Reservoir is a very good viewpoint. The road soon descends to a crossing of the Fremont River; just beyond the bridge is a parking area and pit toilet. Downstream from the road the Fremont wanders through Zedd's Meadow, a lovely wetland tucked in between steep, forested slopes on both sides. A long slope rises to a brief flat where a grove of contorted aspen is accented by small spruces that are often dotted with fallen leaves during the color change in the fall. The road then enters mostly open country for a long and winding descent among sagebrush-covered hills.

Far below, the Fremont River meanders along and small groves of aspen and evergreen provide variety. When the road eventually reaches the bottom of the valley, the Forest Service has provided large pullouts where overnight camping is allowed; a couple of these spots have pit toilets. Tent camping is even permitted on the grassy areas off the road. The attraction here is an excellent fishery in a truly beautiful setting. Summer weekends can be a little busy by rural Utah standards, but generally this is a quiet place.

As the valley widens, the upper reaches of Mill Meadow Reservoir come into view. Along the east side of this impoundment there are many places to camp, some with a pit toilet. Once again, fishing is the primary activity, and small boats are the usual choice. When the road turns east, away from the lake, a short ascent leads to Highway 72. A right turn (southwest) leads to the small town of Fremont and then on to Loa, while to the left (north) it is 2.2 miles to the turnoff to Thousand Lake Mountain.

Hancock Flat

Fish Lake Hightop Aspen Tour Road Trip

Driving distance from Highway 25 to the end of the road is 12.3 miles one way; 4WD is necessary for the last 3.6 miles.

Fish Lake Hightop

At the height of the fall color season, the drive to Hancock Flat, normally accessible to most passenger cars, is hard to beat. High-clearance 2WD vehicles can continue to the upper limit of the aspen show, but high-clearance 4WDs are necessary to reach the top of the mountain. In most years the peak color will occur at the highest elevations during the last week of September or first week of October, but many factors influence the timing and intensity of the show. A quick call to the Forest Service office in Loa (435-836-2811) is probably the best way to get a current update.

The improved gravel road to Hancock Flat leaves Highway 25 just beyond (east of) the 9,036-foot summit, which in turn is 4.2 miles northeast of the junction of Highways 24 and 25. Turn left (north) at the sign for Hancock Flat and immediately enter a huge gravel staging area. Most of the ATV traffic will be using a rough track that continues to the northeast, but the better road goes northwest from the parking area. Zero the odometer as this point. Forest Road 057 descends as a broad shelf road for about a mile, then begins a long flat or ascending contour for several miles. At the 1.8-mile mark the road circles around a steep drainage that offers the first brilliant aspen and from here on, there is color either next to the road or visible from it. When FR 057 passes through mature aspen stands, low-growing common junipers provide a nice contrast in color and form. As elevation increases, so too does the aspen abundance. After a couple of switchbacks the road leaves the forest and at mile 6 enters the south end of vast Hancock Flat.

More like a gentle bowl than a flat, the sagebrush and grassy open area is surrounded by spruce and aspen trees, the latter not only yellow, but also orange in some clones. The road winds down to the bottom and shortly comes to a signed junction that marks the end of travel for passenger cars. High-clearance vehicles can continue up through a particularly pretty part of the meadow by turning right (north) onto FR 329, following the sign for Hancock Spring and Fish Lake Hightop. The aspen groves are both scattered within the open area and surround it, making for a very attractive scene. The spring is developed with long troughs and is a focal point for the sheep that graze in this area. If they happen to be around they add not only visual interest, but engaging audio as well. Just beyond the spring is a particularly spectacular grove of mature aspen, and the road then switchbacks up the slope offering big views back over the meadow. At 8.7 miles from Highway 25 is another junction and the beginning of the four-wheel drive track up to the top of the ridge.

The junction is in a benign, flat, and somewhat open area. FR 329 ends here, while FR 352 bears left (east) to Fish Lake Hightop and also continues straight ahead (southeast, then south). (See the Doctor Creek hike section for important information about the FR 352 section that goes straight ahead here.) A wooden sign points to Fish Lake Hightop and Tasha Spring, both 4 miles at the end of the road. Additionally, a lettered rock shows the way to the Hightop (it says "Hilltop" on the rock) and Gahew Spring. The track up to the ridge is primarily used by ATVs, but can be negotiated by high-clearance 4WDs. Almost immediately the road becomes rocky, steep, and twisting, with the worst stretch in the first few tenths of a mile after the junction. The surface is largely hard, but a few soft areas test traction. By the time the road gets above the heavy forest, the grade lessens a little and it becomes a matter of avoiding the many, many boulders along the way. Full-size vehicles barely fit between some of them since the evolving route is determined by ATV drivers.

Most of the climbing is done by the 9.5-mile mark, though the track remains very rocky. A series of large cairns appear at 9.9 miles, and 0.1 mile farther on is a sign for the Pelican Canyon Trail. The sign indicates that it is 2 miles along the road to the Rock Spring Trail, and 5 miles down to the "Fishlake Hiway." This is the southwest leg of the Pelican Canyon Trail that begins just above the lake at the Pelican Overlook (see below for a description of this hike). Hikers fortunate enough to be chauffeured to this point can hike down the open gentle slope to the cairns, turn left (northeast), and follow them into the woods and then down to the lake. Another hiking option is to be driven to the beginning of the 4WD road, and then hike the 1.2 miles to the cairns and on to the lake. The sweep of Fish Lake Hightop can be viewed from this area, and if the tedium of avoiding rocks has become annoying, it is a good place to turn around.

Beyond the sign, after 250 yards the road roughens for a short stretch, and it does so again at the 10.4-mile mark. There is a good view of Widgeon Bay, Mytoge Mountain, and Thousand Lake Mountain, with Boulder Mountain off to the right (southeast). The road descends into a broad swale, and then climbs gently to the last rough spot at 11 miles. The rest of the way to the information board and end of motorized travel is relatively smooth.

Another good view down Pelican Canyon comes up at mile 11.6, and at 12 miles is a sign on the right that is also for the Pelican Canyon Trail. It indicates that the Rock Spring Trail is 1 mile farther along, and the "Fishlake Hiway" is 5 miles. If you have been doing the math on the Rock Spring Trail you have probably already discovered that distances on the ground may be somewhat independent of those on signs. This is also a good place to reinforce the folly of total reliance on signs in the backcountry, since they are susceptible to the elements and time and may disappear between our hike and yours. The road ends at an information board. From this point a climb of about 300 yards up the slope and through the cliff band to the left (northwest) is necessary to reach the summit ridge of Fish Lake Hightop.

Mytoge Mountain Road Trip

Driving distance from Highway 25 is 8.7 miles one way.

Mytoge Mountain bounds the Fish Lake basin on the southeast side of the lake. The shoreline is undeveloped on that side, and the northwest exposure of the slope leading down to the water is therefore heavily forested, forming a fine backdrop. The mountain is a large fault block, with a steep slope on the lake side, and a more gradual slope on the southeast toward Thousand Lake Mountain. On top, intervals of forest occur among large sagebrush meadows that offer fine views to the east and south; a couple of these meadows extend to the crest of the ridge where Fish Lake and the Hightop to the northwest can be seen from more than a thousand feet above the lake.

A high-clearance vehicle is necessary to comfortably make the drive. The Mytoge Mountain Road (Forest Road 046) leaves the south side of Highway 25 at milepost 4.8 (the same distance from Highway 24), just over 2 miles southwest of the Doctor Creek Trailhead. At the intersection there is a sign for the road, with distances to Dog Spring 3, and Silas Spring 9. Zero the odometer when leaving the pavement, and drop down to the southwest and then back toward the mountain. At 1.6 miles enter the Aspen at Fish Lake development and follow FR 046 as it curves to the right. Just beyond, at 1.8 miles, turn left (east) at a four-way intersection. At a cattleguard at 2.3 miles continue straight ahead where road 0051 bears to the right.

The scenery abruptly changes from open sagebrush to boulders and aspen at 2.7 miles. An old cabin and corral add interest to this glade. A mile beyond, the road passes through a pretty section of young aspen and eventually re-enters the national forest at a cattleguard 4.2 miles from Highway 25. This is the beginning of a steep climb and short switchbacks, recently widened at the time of our visit to accommodate full-size logging trucks, one of which we watched in amazement as it negotiated the tight turns. The switchbacks pass through what could be considered a mountain mahogany forest that is impressive both during flowering time and especially once seed has been set and plumes established.

The mountain mahogany genus, *Cercocarpus*, has only a half dozen or so species, but they are often very important browse plants for ungulates in high and dry environments. The species here is *Cercocarpus ledifolius*, usually called curlleaf mountain mahogany. The plants on this rocky slope are true trees rather than the more shrub-like forms of other mountain mahogany species. The shiny dark evergreen leaves are elliptical, and true to the common name, are often curled under. Flowering is late in the summer, and though individual flowers are small and unspectacular, taken in total, the bloom can be noteworthy. The seed

Mountain mahogany

plumes also curl, and are covered with hairs which brighten the fall landscape when backlit. Although *Cercocarpus* members are not related to tropical mahogany, the term is justified by the hard and dark wood.

The grade tops out at 5.3 miles, and the track to the first overlook goes off to the left (northwest) at 6.1. It is about a 0.3 mile to the overlook, which offers a good view of the southwestern end of the lake and Mallard Bay, across to the Doctor Creek Campground, and up Doctor Creek to Fish Lake Hightop. Back on FR 046, follow the road through the meadow to a rock sign indicating Elias Wells straight ahead and Mytoge Mountain Road to the left; take the left to the northeast. The road climbs up to nearly 9,500 feet in elevation and then levels out as it passes through aspen forest with encroaching conifers. The forest is limited in extent, and the road enters yet another open meadow, descending slightly.

Continue straight ahead at 7.2 miles from the highway (excluding the spur road distance to the first overlook) where FR 1479 goes to the right and FR 046M goes to the left. About 100 yards beyond this intersection is another left (northwest) turn to the second overlook. This track (FR 046N) makes a loop, first dropping down to the viewpoint, then returning to FR 046. This is the place where the Lakeshore Trail leaves the ridgeline and descends steeply down to the lake. Views are somewhat limited, and similar to the first overlook described above.

FR 046 switches back to the east and ascends a moderately steep slope after leaving the loop track into the viewpoint. At the 8-mile mark a jeep trail, FR 1467, descends to the right (east), while FR 046 climbs once more. A good view of Thousand Lake Mountain is marked by a sign on the right side of the road. FR 322 to the best overlook goes to the left (northwest) at 8.4 miles. It is about 0.3 mile on this track to a tight loop at the edge of the ridge. It is rocky enough on the northeast part of the loop that it might be a good idea to turn around rather than complete the very short circle. There is a bench on the lichen-covered volcanic rock and a wide open view of the entire lake, the lodge directly across on the opposite shore, and Fish Lake Hightop and more distant mountains. At 9,900 feet in elevation this can be a very pleasant spot during the summer, but it can be windy as well. The Lakeshore Trail also passes right through this area. The return trip to Highway 25 is perhaps even more scenic as views open up when the road descends the south and southeast-facing slopes.

Viewpoint along the Mytoge Mountain Road

Lakeshore Trail Hike

Hiking distance is 4.5 miles round trip to the southwest; 2.5 miles round trip to the northeast.

Lakeshore Trail

Spring comes late to Fish Lake, but when the aspen flush light green in late May or early June it will often still be cool and pleasant while the desert below is hot and gnat infested. (The Pelican Canyon Trail and the Lakeshore Trail on the northwest side of Mytoge Mountain may be snow covered well into the summer.) The summer is blessed with warm days and cool evenings, but it is fall when beautiful turns spectacular. A fine way to take it all in is to hike or ride a bike along the Lakeshore Trail that parallels Highway 25. There are many parking areas along the trail, several with vault toilets. A good place to start a hike or ride is at the Twin Creeks Picnic Area and amphitheater (milepost and odometer reading of 8.7 miles). There are several additional access points for the trail in either direction along the highway, including one at milepost 8 that is in the middle of perhaps the best section.

In reality, the path is better suited for hiking than for riding, even along the developed and much flatter northwest shore. Especially to the southwest from Twin Creeks the trailbed is often studded with numerous rocks, and the path makes sharp turns and has narrow bridges without railings. Real care needs to be exercised by bikers. This is the most scenic part of the trail on this side of the lake. From the picnic area it is only a few yards to the right (southwest) to the crossing of Twin Creeks and an interpretive sign describing Kit Carson's reaction to the mass of fish here during spawning season.

Fish Lake Lodge

The route follows a dirt road on the lake side of the Fish Lake Lodge before resuming as a trail beyond. The main building at the lodge is a rambling log structure consisting not of rooms for rent, but rather of two large ballroom spaces separated by a dining area. The historic building bespeaks an earlier age, but time is taking its toll on it.

Lakeshore Trail

Beyond the lodge, the trail passes quickly by some cabins and then enters a long passage through young aspen. Seeps along the way provide interesting plant diversity, and the lake is never far away. When the aspen leaves are turning, this part of the trail is breathtaking, especially walking southwest in the late afternoon when the sun backlights the trees. Two short sections of tread are built up right along the shoreline and offer the most challenges to bicycle riders—probably a good time to dismount and walk so the views can be enjoyed.

When the edge of the lake bends to the south, the trail emerges into an open sagebrush expanse, and begins a gentle climb. It is worth continuing up the hill and eventually back into the aspen around the Doctor Creek Campground, which is usually closed for the season prior to the fall color. The mix of larger aspen and ground-hugging common juniper is very pretty. It is about 2.25 miles from Twin Creeks to the gate just west of the campground. An easier stroll or ride is the 1.25 miles in the opposite direction from the picnic area to where the trail crosses the highway. This part of the trail is almost dead flat and right next to the lake. For a (much) longer trip on the Lakeshore Trail, see the Circumnavigating Fish Lake section that follows.

Circumnavigating Fish Lake Hike and Bike

Distance is 17.2 miles.

For the fit and agile, a fine all-day adventure is the self-powered circumnavigation of Fish Lake. While circling the lake is more easily done with a car shuttle, it is satisfying and scenic to do it on your own power. Depending on where you stay, this involves a hike of at least 10.2 miles, including the ascent of Mytoge Mountain, and a bike ride of about 7 miles. A good way to do this is to camp at the Doctor Creek Campground at the southwest end of the lake, or stay at a nearby resort. Leave bikes at your campsite or cabin and drive northeast on Highway 25. Zero the odometer as you pass the entrance to the Twin Creeks Picnic Area, and continue 4.6 miles to the signed Lake Creek Trailhead access road on the right (east). Parking is ample and there is a vault toilet. The information board has a map of the Fishlake National Forest, and there is also a map of the Lakeshore National Recreation Trail. Alas, at the time of our hike the latter did not show a trail on the southeast side of the lake, but take heart—it definitely exists and is a fine hike.

The trail begins by passing through the single log fence, descends, and heads across the meadow and wetland flat. It bends left (east) and crosses the bridge over Lake Creek, and 0.25 mile from the trailhead reaches a signed junction. The Crater Lake and Ivie Canyon Trail goes straight ahead, but turn right (south) at the vertical Lakeshore Trail sign. The path is reasonably visible as it passes through the grass, but don't expect anything more than a faint single track. In mid-summer the pretty purple flowers of Parrys harebells dot the greenery.

The trail curves to the right (southeast, toward the lake) at the 0.5-mile mark while still in the meadow, but with aspen off to the left. Beaver-chewed aspen stumps are next to the path 0.1 mile beyond. During the summer, this part of the route, and perhaps well up onto Mytoge Mountain, can be abuzz with mosquitoes. They are pesky enough

South end of Fish Lake from the Lakeshore Trail

that repellant and long sleeves make the walk much more enjoyable. Once on top of the mountain and even along the south end of the lake, mosquitoes are typically not as bothersome.

A mile along the route the trail enters a small group of spruce and fir trees and approaches the open water of Widgeon Bay. At a place named for a duck, one might expect to see ducks, and there may be a lot of them. White pelicans also like to fish in Widgeon Bay, and there are times when their molting feathers speckle the water. Another vertical trail sign appears as the trail passes through the forest on rocky tread. Near 1.5 miles the path jogs away from the shore to avoid a rock field, and then passes through a gate in a fence. For the next mile the trail generally is near the shore, only occasionally moving away to avoid an obstacle. The northeast end of the main body of Fish Lake is reached at 2.2 miles from the trailhead, and a small pebble beach is just beyond. Seagulls, great blue herons, bald eagles, and pelicans are potential sightings at this spot. Another bit of open shoreline is at 2.5 miles, after which the trail crosses a second rock field and then enters a grove of subalpine fir.

At high elevations, these trees are the sidekicks to the more stately Engelmann spruce with which they often mingle. True firs (the genus *Abies*) can be easily differentiated from the spruces by their cones. Fir cones, usually dark purple to almost red when viewed in certain kinds of light, sit upright on the branch; additionally, they fall apart on the tree and do not accumulate on the ground. Spruce (*Picea*) cones are usually tan, papery, pendant, and fall to the ground whole. Young firs, such as those here along the trail, have smooth gray bark with many small resin pockets. The needles of firs are soft to the touch, while spruce needles are sharp.

Morphologically, subalpine firs are often extremely skinny, sharply pointed at the top, and have branches that trend upward, never sagging. While we lay people often think that botanists have trees as common as subalpine firs all figured out, in fact there is considerable disagreement about whether or not there might be two separate species (*Abies lasiocarpa* and *Abies bifolia*). The former would be subalpine fir, and the latter Rocky Mountain subalpine fir. Since the vast majority of people simply refer to firs, spruces, Douglas firs, larches, and hemlocks as "pines," we think subalpine fir is good enough.

Not long after entering the firs, the trail bears to the left (southeast) and begins its steep ascent of Mytoge Mountain. Another Lakeshore Trail sign lets you know you are on track. The short pitch ends when the path goes left (northeast) again and begins to more gently ascend parallel to the shoreline. After 0.2 mile an open knob provides a glimpse of the lake, already quite far below. From this point to the top of the slope is another 0.8 mile. The easily followed path switchbacks many times, making the gradient gentle to moderate. Beetle kill among the Douglas firs has left swatches of standing dead trees; the extra sunlight reaching the forest floor has resulted in lush and diverse understory plants.

This first climb ends at the 3.6-mile mark. The trail passes through a gate in a zigzag fence and emerges onto an open sage flat, ringed in the distance by mature aspen. The

Lakeshore Trail

contrast with the trek up the slope of the mountain is stark. There is one of the typical vertical Lakeshore Trail signs near the fence, though it is aimed at hikers coming from the opposite direction. Follow the faint tread to the southwest, along the right (northwest) side of the open flat, soon passing another sign, this one a two-way. The tread disappears at an old two-track road. From this point look southwest (basically straight ahead) to the edge of the forest. In a fairly obvious opening in the trees there is another sign that marks the trail. Once back in the woods, the path is clear and easy to follow.

Along the crest of the Mytoge ridge, aspen generally are the predominant species, but the forest is most beautiful when spruce or fir provide dark green contrast. Of course, those conifers eventually will take over and force out the aspen unless fire, disease, or insects take out the evergreens first. The trail generally ascends, but at a gentle grade that allows plenty of opportunity to enjoy the forest and the solitude. After a lake view at mile 4, the groundcover is dominated by Oregon grape, with its holly-like leaves, pretty yellow flowers in late spring, and in late summer, grape-like fruit. The fruit is unappealing until after frost, when it is less unappealing!

At 0.5 mile after the lake view, the trail reaches an intermediate high point and descends nicely for 0.25 mile. At this point it enters another very large sage meadow surrounded by aspen, and there is a trail sign, again oriented for hikers coming the other way. Continue walking in the open, bearing right (west) along the edge of the meadow to and past a post. The route joins a faint two-track road for 50 feet. Leave it on the right (west) and head for another post at the margin of the forest. As before, the trail is clear in the woods and ascends gently.

Just short of the 5-mile mark there is a large cairn on the right (northwest), with a notably huge Douglas fir a few steps beyond. Shortly, pass through another gate and enjoy the fact that just about all of the climbing is done. Two hundred yards farther on is the first of three immense views of Fish Lake. Watch your step here as there are several small cacti that are difficult to see. At the next open viewpoint an old road comes in from the left (southeast), but the trail passes through the open area and into small aspens. Just over 5.25 miles from the trailhead is a third aerie, and by virtue of the shade from an old trooper of a Douglas fir, perhaps the best place for lunch.

Shortly after the three viewpoints the trail veers left (southeast) away from the rim, returning to it in about 0.25 mile. The walk continues to be very pleasant, passing by the edge of another huge sagebrush flat that offers distant looks at Boulder Mountain to the southeast, and to its left, the closer Thousand Lake Mountain. Just before the 6-mile mark, the path enters the sagebrush and the lake is again visible. The trail joins the tip of the loop of a road coming in from the left (southeast) for a few feet, then continues on to the southwest, as usual, roughly straight ahead. Right on the rim there is a bench, perfectly situated directly across from the Fish Lake Lodge and offering a fine look at much of the Fish Lake basin.

At 0.1 mile from the bench, a trail sign confirms the route, with a brief grade up to a mini-highpoint. At 6.5 miles the trail descends sharply for a short distance, then passes by another sage meadow, with a road visible below. After another good view of the lake and lodge is a second steep grade, this one on loose tread. At 7.2 miles the trail passes through a zigzag fence. There is road access at this point, and a bench on the far slope at the forest edge.

From here, the trail wastes little time in getting down to lake level, accomplishing the task in almost exactly 1 mile. To start the descent, turn toward the lake (northwest) and go through the gate in yet another wooden fence. Shortly there is a bench with a good view of the Doctor Creek drainage across the lake, followed by steep trail with loose tread. The grade is helped a little by several switchbacks. A huge osprey nest sits atop a truncated tree at one of the switchbacks, with a bench directly beneath. Please keep moving here, especially if there are two angry birds caterwauling above. When the descent is complete, the shoreline bench at 8.2 miles is a pleasant stop.

The next 0.6 mile is a comfortable walk over flat terrain and somewhat smooth tread, with the lake nearby to the right (northwest). Not long after passing a small building, the trail leaves the forest and enters a grassy meadow. The vertical wooden Lakeshore Trail signs are done, and this short stretch is perhaps the least clear part of the hike. Keep going on what is now a very old two-track, heading directly toward the outside corner of a wooden rail fence. A couple of no motor vehicle signs are on the route, which stays just outside the fence and parallel to it. The trail ahead becomes visible as it ascends into pretty aspen trees, and there is a plastic trail sign here.

The low ridge is sublime with mature aspen framing lake views. After topping out, the trail enters a sagebrush meadow and descends very gradually past beautiful wetlands to the right (northwest). At 9.4 miles there is an unsigned Y junction. Continue southwest on the right arm of the Y and then follow the path around to the right (northwest) to enter another aspen grove. After leaving the aspen, the route passes a row of old fence posts on the left (southwest) and briefly joins a dirt road for 100 feet before breaking off to the right (north) at an obvious and signed junction. This is the home stretch, especially if you are camping at Doctor Creek. The trail follows some of the Old Spanish

Trail route as it winds through aspen and common juniper. At 10.2 miles there is a final gate and the path runs along the north side of the campground; although there doesn't appear to be a formal route into the campground, there are several places where it can be accessed. If you started from a cabin, continue on the trail, cross the entrance road to the campground, and descend across open sagebrush, finally crossing Highway 25 to the resort.

The only thing left to do if you are making a non-motorized circuit of Fish Lake is to hop on your bike and retrieve your vehicle at the Lake Creek trailhead. From the campground, ride out the entrance road almost to the dump station and garbage container, and turn right (northeast) onto the portion of the Lakeshore Trail described in the previous section. Remember that the tread here quickly turns very rocky, and be prepared to walk a little to enjoy the lakeside scenery. When the trail connects with the road at the Bowery Haven Resort marina, ride along the pavement to Lake Creek. There is some room outside of the white shoulder line, and traffic is usually very light, making for a very pleasant ride of about 7 miles from the campground.

Aspen and common juniper near Doctor Creek Campground

Pelican Canyon Hike

Hiking distance is 10 miles round trip.

The Pelican Canyon hike is a fine way to access Fish Lake Hightop and is a beautiful walk in its own right for fit hikers who are accustomed to the uncertainty of route-finding conundrums. The trailhead is on top of a huge glacial moraine near the northeast end of the lake, and can be reached by high-clearance vehicle or by mountain bike. For the latter simply get on the Lakeshore Trail wherever it is convenient and ride northeast past the Bowery Haven Resort. Here, the trail leaves the shoreline and ascends across the sagebrush slope to the parking area. The trail tread is much rougher than along the lake and is suitable really only for mountain bikes, if that.

To drive, once again zero the odometer at the Twin Creeks Picnic Area and proceed northeast for 3.2 miles to a left (west) turn onto the one-mile, high-clearance road to the Pelican Overlook, where there are no facilities. At this writing there is no sign marking the junction for vehicles coming from the lake. Stay left past the debris dump and bear right and uphill at a Y junction before entering the trees.

As described here, the trail is a stem and loop that includes more than 2 miles of walking on the rough track (Forest Road 352) that runs near the top of the mountain. The road walk is very scenic, and the chances of encountering a vehicle are slim. The recommended route is to do the loop in a counterclockwise direction. This results in steeper climbing on the way up, more than offset by longer easy downhill striding on the way back. This is a strenuous day hike of 10 miles, including about 2,300 feet of vertical gain.

The trail begins on the northwest side of the broad parking area at Pelican Overlook. A sign for the Pelican Canyon Trailhead indicates that it is 5 miles to Fish Lake Hightop and 6 miles to Tasha Spring. Happily, it is actually closer to 4 miles for the climb to the road, and only about 2.5 of those miles include steep ascents. The trail passes through open sagebrush for more than 100 yards to what appears to be a Y junction. An old sign points straight ahead to Rock Spring 5 and Gahew Spring 6. Stay left and walk gently uphill; the right fork shortly fades out. The first part of the hike has a gentle gradient and passes through beautiful aspen with several meadows alongside. Kinnikinnik, Douglas fir, Oregon grape, and low-growing common juniper provide contrast to

Pelican Canyon Trail junction

Kinnikinnik

the aspen, and flowers abound throughout the summer.

In the fall when the aspen are resplendent in yellow, kinnikinnik, or common bearberry, provides a nice contrast with its alternate, deep green leaves and bright red berries. Kinnikinnik is a circumpolar species, growing at high latitudes all across the northern hemisphere, and it is also found at high elevation in the Southwest. It essentially forms a groundcover under the right conditions of moderate shade and fairly coarse soils. Kinnikinnik (*Arctostaphylos uva-ursi*) is in the manzanita genus, and its small, bell-shaped flowers in pink or white are very much like those of greenleaf manzanita. The term "kinnikinnik" also refers to a smoking mixture used by Native Americans; bearberry was sometimes part of the mix, while red osier dogwood was a more common constituent.

After 0.6 mile a sign marks a trail to the left (southwest) to the Bowery Haven Resort, but the path appears to be overgrown and littered with fallen trees. The gradient increases slightly, but remains easy for just over 1 mile from the trailhead. At this point a large Douglas fir tree right next to the path on the east (right) side is a good place to turn around for those seeking a less strenuous, yet beautiful stroll in peaceful surroundings.

The next 1.2 miles are generally steep and rocky, with only a few short breaks. The route follows the canyon floor or runs along the base of the sloped east wall. The first flat, after 0.25 mile of climbing, is densely covered with bright green meadow rue, particularly impressive in the fall when the aspen are turning. The sheltered and shaded canyon hosts many flowers, including tall larkspur, chiming bells, geraniums, yarrow, and Rocky Mountain beeplant. To the east the tree cover is occasionally broken by small meadows, and larger boulder fields. At the 2.25-mile mark the path emerges into the bottom of a larger meadow where the routes divide. This is a good turnaround point for anyone wanting a moderate length hike that includes a bit of a workout as well. From the top of the meadow there are good views, and there is a pretty pond on the southwest corner of the opening, which is just below 10,500 feet in elevation.

The junction of the main route to the end of the road and base of the summit ridge and the southwest route of the Pelican Canyon system is marked by signs, one of which had fallen from its post on our last visit. The fallen sign to the right (east) is for the Right Fork Pelican Canyon Trail #4368 and gives the distance to Fishlake Hightop as 2 miles and 3 miles to Tasha Springs. It also mentions the Tasha Creek Trail #126. The other sign is for the Pelican Canyon Trail #4125, with distances of 2 miles to Fishlake Hightop and 3 miles to Gahew Spring. The actual distance to the road via Trail #4125 is about 1.3 miles. It is worth noting that the Fishlake National Forest map and the Fremont District travel map both identify the trails as numbers 368 and 125 respectively (with the stem trail down to the trailhead as 125), while the Trails Illustrated map reverses them, sending 125 to the end of road FR 352, and 368 to the southwest.

As mentioned above, if you are going to complete the loop back to this junction, we think it is better to stay to the right on the Right Fork, which trends northerly. The path through the meadow is very faint, so it is important to pick out the cairns that lead the way up into the trees. In the forest there are blazes to mark the route, one short one above a longer slash. For the next mile the route combines steep sections with nice flats, along with a mix of meadow and forest. Even in the fall there may be lupine, dwarf goldenrod, aster, and cinquefoil in bloom. The last real work is a set of steep switchbacks at the 3-mile mark. After these the gradient lessens and the last 0.5 mile to the road is a very pleasant stroll across open grasslands dotted with small spruce trees. Alpine flowers such as bistort and alpine avens color the landscape.

This last 0.5 mile is sparsely marked with cairns made of a few large rocks and usually there is no visible tread. Stray cairns pop up occasionally as well; the best course is to follow the cairns on a straight line toward the southwest end of the summit ridge. The route we followed intersected with FR 352 near a steel fencepost, and, just a few steps to the east, a sign for the Tasha Creek Trail #4126. The latter was hanging by a thread, however, and only the post is likely to remain in the future. To the north (right) the information board at the end of the road was visible a little more than 200 yards away. To the left (south) along the road, also a few hundred yards away, is a sign for the Pelican Canyon Trail, indicating that the Rock Spring Trail is 1 mile to the left, and the Fishlake Hiway is 5 miles. The confusion created by this situation is an additional reason to hike the loop in the direction described, since the route from either starting point to the trail down the canyon is difficult to find.

Cairns along the Pelican Canyon Trail

The elevation at the information board at the end of the road is about 11,420 feet. The GPS coordinates here are UTM 0435939mE, 4273092mN. The top of the summit ridge is about 200 feet higher, and can be reached by threading a route up through the obvious cliff band to the northwest of the information kiosk. To continue on the loop part of the hike, simply follow the road to the southwest. Aside from one short uphill climb, the 2.3-mile walk on FR 352 is flat or gently downhill, with good views most of

Pelican Overlook road

the way. The first is 0.7 mile from road's end, where Fish Lake is visible below with Mytoge Mountain and Thousand Lakes Mountain to the east, and Bouldertop to the southeast. At the 1.3-mile mark the view opens to the other side of Fishlake Hightop, and after the short uphill there is another good view of Fish Lake, the mountains beyond, and the agricultural Rabbit Valley.

After the road bends to the right following a moderate descent, the Pelican Canyon Trail sign is on the left (southeast) side. It gives the distance to the Rock Spring Trail as 2 miles and the Fishlake Hiway as 5 miles, but it is only just over 3.5 miles back to the parking lot. As with the upper trailhead area, confusion is possible here if driving up FR 352 (described in the Fish Lake Hightop Aspen Tour section) since there are cairns 200 yards to the southwest. It is best to leave the road at the sign (UTM 0435444mE, 4269757mN). There are two cairns within view downslope. The route bends left around a small rise, and meanders down the meadow. Another bend to the east leads to the forest. The trail tread appears just to the left (north) of a rock outcrop, almost 0.3 mile from the road.

Pelican Canyon Trail

The next mile is sublime, passing through mature subalpine forest consisting mostly of Engelmann spruce. Even though the gradient is steep in places, the trail is usually covered in soft duff composed of spruce needles, making it much more comfortable than the rocky tread beyond the trail junction. Just before closing the loop, the trail skirts the small pond on the edge of the meadow. From here it is more than 1 mile of steep descent and then 1 mile of easy walking to the parking lot.

Doctor Creek Hike

Hiking distance is 3 miles round trip.

Aspen love on the Doctor Creek Trail

This is a pretty hike, very suitable for those who would find the Pelican Canyon hike a little too much, but who still want to get a bit of a workout. The trailhead is on the southeast side of Highway 25, 6.9 miles from Highway 24, and just before the entrance to the Doctor Creek Campground. At the trailhead is one of the two Fish Lake basin exhibits on the Old Spanish Trail, including metal cutouts of a pack train emerging from the aspen. The trail begins next to the sign on the left (east) side of the parking area, soon crosses Highway 25, and heads into the canyon that is prominently visible uphill to the northwest.

Initially, the grade is gentle, and the well-defined trail soon enters scattered aspen dotted with just enough evergreens for contrast. As usual around Fish Lake, the aspen make for a spectacular scene in late September or early October when the color is at peak. Just under 0.4 mile from the trailhead is a small building; the trail continues behind it where there is a sign for the Doctor Creek Trail, Big Flat 2, and Hancock Spring 4. It is a good idea here to turn around and note where the trail back to the car leaves the open area by the building. Only a small "trail" sign marks the spot.

As the gradient steepens, the trail gradually enters the canyon of Doctor Creek. Engelmann spruce and subalpine fir increase in number. The ground is often covered with the holly-like leaves of Oregon grape, and beautiful clumps of tall grass set off the aspen trunks even after the leaves have fallen. At the 0.9-mile mark an open talus slope to the left (southwest) consists of platy pieces of Lake Creek Trachyte, the middle ash flow tuff laid down during the explosive volcanic period that affected this area from 26 to 23 million years ago. Shortly after passing the talus, the trail begins the first of four switchbacks up the northeast side of the canyon, and openings provide a glimpse of the southwest end of Fish Lake. Douglas fir and common juniper have made inroads among the dominant aspen on the slope.

The grade, fairly steep to this point, lessens at 1.2 miles, and a couple hundred yards later the trail emerges from the forest into the bottom of a large meadow that extends up to the southwest end of the Hightop. Take note of the small trail sign for the return.

The tread across the meadow may be faint or non-existent. The route continues basically straight ahead to cross a shallow draw studded with rocks. On the far side of the draw the tread is more visible and is marked with cairns.

After a short ascent the trail crosses another opening and ends at FR 352 after passing through a double cairn. The GPS coordinates here are UTM 0434389mE, 4266696mN, and the elevation is 10,035 feet. The Doctor Creek Trail terminus is in a flat, rock-strewn meadow with good views up to the summit ridge, and a partial view back to the southeast that includes Boulder Mountain. A zigzag fence is a nifty tie-up, and there are signs of an earlier piping system for livestock watering. Exploration opportunities abound, either up or down the road, or up the meadow, making sure, of course, to be able to find your way back to the trail for the hike back down to the lake.

If you have an intrepid driver with a good high-clearance vehicle, the Doctor Creek hike can be configured so that it is entirely downhill. This might make it a lot more fun for the non-marathoners among us. For directions, go to the Fish Lake Hightop Aspen Tour section and follow the route to Hancock Flat and beyond to the junction with FR 352. For Doctor Creek, instead of bearing left on 352 to the summit, continue straight ahead (southeast).

The road is fairly good at first, reaching the north end of a meadow 0.5 mile from the intersection, and remaining good across the open area for another 0.3 mile; go straight ahead here when a lesser track goes to the left (southeast). After another 0.1 mile leave the south end of the meadow where the road quality begins to decline; hikers could be dropped off at this point. A good high-clearance vehicle can continue for just over another 0.5 mile, staying left each time a track goes to the right (southwest) into a timber sale area. Several stretches with very large and unavoidable rocks preclude further travel 1.4 miles (or sooner) from the junction with FR 352.

The walk to the upper trailhead for Doctor Creek is an easy amble on down the road, either 0.8 mile from the end of the passable road, or 1.3 miles from the south end of the meadow. The trail begins just after the zigzag fence where the road bends to the right in another meadow and begins to go slightly uphill. It is signed and further marked by two cairns next to the road. The GPS coordinates are given above, and make sure to read the trail description carefully since you will have to find the path in the forest after crossing the open area with the rocky draw. The small trail sign is hard to find from a distance. Reconnect with your helpful driver at the trailhead on Highway 25 at the Old Spanish Trail interpretive site.

Thousand Lake Mountain and Torrey Area

Thousand Lake Mountain rises to 11,306 feet above sea level just to the west of Upper Cathedral Valley in Capitol Reef National Park. Of the four major mountains described in this guidebook, it has the easiest road access, and under normal conditions passenger cars may be driven above 10,500 feet. Elkhorn Campground is the highest Forest Service or BLM campground on any of the mountains near Capitol Reef, and it offers an excellent exploration base for Thousand Lake and even down into Cathedral Valley. Dispersed camping is also very popular, and there are many numbered roads or tracks that lead to beautiful spots in the aspen or conifers. The Thousand Lake Mountain section ends with two hikes on the mountain's southeast flank, both accessed from Highway 24 near the town of Torrey.

Cathedral Valley view from Thousand Lake Mountain

Thousand Lake Mountain Road Trip

Driving distance from Highway 72 to Wiffs Pasture is 12.5 miles one way.

The primary access is a generally good, but quite steep, road that leads east from Highway 72 northeast of Fremont. From Capitol Reef or the northern terminus of Highway 12, take Highway 24 west out of Torrey, passing through the small agricultural communities of Bicknell and Lyman. They are situated in the high elevation (approximately 7,000 feet) Rabbit Valley, a pastoral mix of irrigated alfalfa, a little grain, sheep, horses, and cattle. Many of the sheep and cattle spend idyllic summers grazing at even higher elevations in the national forest. On the north edge of Lyman, Highway 24 bends due west, heading straight for Loa. Less than two miles from Lyman a county road, signed only for Fremont, goes right (north), joining Highway 72 in 1 mile. If approaching from the west on Highway 24, turn east on 72 at the north end of Loa and proceed just over a mile to the point where 72 makes a right angle turn to the north. The two routes come together at this point.

From this convergence, reset the odometer and drive north, through the tiny town of Fremont, for 8.1 miles to a cattleguard and signed boundary of the Fishlake National Forest. Just beyond is the turn for the Fish Lake circuit, but continue on Highway 72 for another 2.2 miles to a gravel road on the right (east) at milepost 11.4. (For travelers coming from the north and Highway 10 or Interstate 70, this turn will be to the left, just over 0.5 mile south of milepost 12.) The only notice on Highway 72 for this junction is for Elkhorn Campground on a brown sign. Immediately after making the turn, however, the distances to Riley Spring 3, Elkhorn Campground 8, Baker Ranch 11, and Cathedral Valley 13 are listed. The gravel road is designated as Forest Road 206.

Zero the trip odometer and head up the steep, and then very steep, sometimes washboarded road, which is FR 206. The elevation gain is sufficient to ascend from a vast expanse of sagebrush into scattered aspen groves in only a couple of miles. At the 2.7-mile mark is a large parking area on the right (south) that serves as the Riley Spring trailhead for the Great Western Trail, open to vehicles no more than 50 inches wide. There is a pit toilet, along with a map of the various foot and vehicle trails on Thousand Lake Mountain. The aspen grove here is very pretty and easy to walk through. Riley Spring itself is just above the parking area, and is surrounded by a protective fence.

The road continues to climb, but at a much reduced gradient. Several tracks, marked with route numbers that are 206 and then a letter, lead off to the edge of the forest and dispersed camping sites. At 4.6 miles from Highway 72 is a junction with the road to Meeks Lake. (An interesting and pretty drive up to this point from just north of Cathedral Valley is described below in the Baker Ranch Access subsection.) Stay right (southeast) as 206 climbs above the often dry Heart Lake.

After a short steep climb, at mile 4.7 there is a small parking area for the Desert Overlook, a worthwhile stop. A short walk past the Douglas firs leads to an open area

Wiffs Pasture

and a huge view to the east. Light is especially good near sunset before the mountain shadows envelop Cathedral Valley. From the right (southeast) the vista includes the Henry Mountains, the deep valley of the South Desert, the distinctive form of Factory Butte, Cathedral Valley directly below, and the San Rafael Swell to the northeast. When the air is clear, the La Sal Mountains east of Moab are visible in the far distance.

An intersection with the Polk Creek Road (FR 022) is just 0.2 mile past the overlook. The sign indicates that it is 2 miles to the left (east) to Round Lake and 8 miles to Cathedral Valley, and straight ahead 3 miles to Elkhorn Campground and 6 miles to Deep Creek Lake. The Polk Creek Road (FR 022) into Capitol Reef National Park is steep, especially on the lower slopes and always requires a high-clearance vehicle. Four-wheel drive is handy for the trip back up, both for traction and in a few places where low-range gearing makes it easier to maneuver around the many rocks. Several good camping sites are available in the national forest before the road descends below the aspen-fir zone. See the companion book to this guide, *Capitol Reef National Park, The Complete Hiking and Touring Guide*, for information on Cathedral Valley, including important differences in camping regulations.

To continue up Thousand Lake Mountain, stay straight (south) at the junction. Shortly the road passes through a burn area that was replanted with ponderosa pines in 1999. Even in this relatively wet high-elevation environment, the burned trunks and stumps of the original forest persist today. The road ascends in earnest through aspen and spruce-fir stands, with the grade steep enough that storm run-off can cut small channels in the gravel surface, requiring careful driving of regular passenger cars. In late September and often into early October, the aspen put on quite a show along this stretch, especially when backlit by the low-angle fall sun.

At the 7.6-mile mark is a sign for Elkhorn Campground (straight ahead), and Snow Lake, 4 miles to the left (southeast). The latter is the main road. The campground is located in small to medium size trees and is very pleasant. There are seven sites and there are many times when they are all open, including during the prime

Elkhorn Ranger Station

aspen fall color season. A nice group site is also available. Adjacent to the campground is the old Elkhorn Ranger Station, set on the west edge of a meadow under the plateau that caps the mountain.

From the spur road into the campground, the route continues south below the flat summit. At 8.9 miles is a T intersection, which is signed for Tubb Flat to the left and Snow Lake to the right. The short 0.4-mile drive on FR 1576 to Tubb Flat is worth the time, and the road is generally good. Tubb Flat is a vast meadow on a bench that extends to the east. Great views are enhanced by the surrounding aspen groves.

The main road generally climbs beyond the junction. Ten miles from the highway is a small sign for the Flat Top Trail on the right (west) side of the road. This short and very steep hike is rewarding and is discussed in detail at the end of this section. A couple of tenths farther on is a sign for Deep Creek Lake, along with a picnic table and vault toilet. At this writing there is no sign for Snow Lake, but it can be seen from a very short walk to the right (west) at about the 11.5-mile mark, and just before another intersection, this one signed to the left (southeast) for Deep Creek Overlook. The road down to the viewpoint is sometimes in good shape, but the last time we went there it was very rough, requiring good high clearance. At the end of the 0.6-mile long spur, walk along an indistinct trail just to the right (south) of a small knob to the overlook. The view is much like Tubb Flat and Desert Overlook and can be skipped if the road is in poor condition.

The condition of the primary road declines a little beyond the Deep Creek junction, but is worth following to Wiffs Pasture, 12.5 miles from Highway 72. Here, the road emerges into another large meadow, again surrounded by aspen that are spectacular at the height of fall color. A small grove on the southeast edge of the opening is especially photogenic; on the west edge more mature aspen tower over young spruce, ornamenting them with fallen leaves in fine holiday fashion. Wiffs Pasture is at the south end of the long bench below the plateau to the west, and offers a good view of the latter and Boulder Mountain to the south. The road continues down off the bench, but is rougher and dead-ends beyond, making this a good place to turn around.

Thousand Lake Mountain Road

Baker Ranch Access Road Trip

Driving distance as described is 18 miles.

Windy Ridge

In addition to the primary access on FR 206 and secondary access on the Polk Creek Road (FR 022) described above, there is a third way to get to the high country of Thousand Lake Mountain in a standard high-clearance vehicle. Like the Polk Creek Road, FR 020 from the Baker Ranch climbs up the east side of the mountain, beginning in piñon-juniper forest and winding up through open meadows with great views and occasional groves of aspen and conifer. As a bonus, short side trips lead to pleasant mountain ponds.

Directions to the start of this route are in the Last Chance Desert section, in the Last Chance Desert Access from Highway 24 part. The intersection noted in the third paragraph from the end is the specific point. From this junction zero the odometer and travel west on the Baker Ranch Road, following the sign to the ranch and Thousand Lake Mountain. The ranch house and outbuildings are on the right (north) in 2.2 miles, and the Fishlake National Forest boundary is just under 1 mile beyond. The road is now designated as Forest Road 020, and a sign for the Baker Ranch Road gives distances to Meeks Lake 6, Elkhorn Campground 12, and Loa 25, all to the right (ahead, up the mountain), and Cathedral Valley 8, back down past the ranch. A second, newer sign points to Riley Spring 9, Elkhorn Campground 12, and U-72 11.

The road winds up at moderate to steep grades, and though rocky, is generally a little less rough than the lower Polk Creek Road above Capitol Reef NP. At mile 5.4 is the well-signed junction with FR 019 to Meeks Lake and Morrell Pond. This side trip is very pleasant on roads that are usually at least as good as FR 020. To visit the lakes, turn right (northwest). The spur road to Morrell Pond is at 6.2 and is signed.

For now, continue straight ahead on 019, and pass by an unnamed pond and dispersed campsite at 6.6 miles. The road descends nearly down to Farrell Pond, at 8.0. This small pond is popular with ducks and there are good views up to the ridge that extends north from Geyser Peak, the high point to

Meeks Lake

the southwest. The road ends at 8.8 miles, just above the east end of Meeks Lake, expanded during our visit by a beaver dam comprised mostly of aspen branches. The lakeshore, visible from the turn-around, can be reached by a short walk down the old road. All the lakes here in the Solomon Basin are carefully managed by the Utah Division of Wildlife Resources, and contain a variety of stocked trout.

On the way back to FR 020, another very short side trip leads to Morrell Pond. The turn is 2.6 miles from the end of the road above Meeks Lake; turn left (north) and drive less than 0.5 mile to a small hill above the lake. A picnic table is a pleasant place to pause and enjoy this lightly visited place, and a vault toilet is nearby.

Above the east shore of the lake and next to the road are several silver buffaloberry plants large enough to be called small trees. Observant high desert travelers are generally familiar with roundleaf buffaloberry, a gray-green shrub with densely packed round leaves that usually curl under at the margins. This plant is common in Capitol Reef National Park, the east end of Grand Canyon NP, and along Utah Highway 95 near Natural Bridges National Monument. At a casual glance, about the only thing that roundleaf and silver buffaloberry have in common is the characteristic color of the foliage, shared with the widespread, invasive, Russian olive.

Silver buffaloberry

Silver buffaloberry, *Shepherdia argentea*, prefers a cooler and moister climate. It is common on the northern Great Plains, and in Utah generally grows in an elevation range of 5,000 to 7,000 feet. Here, near Morrell Pond, it is thriving at more than 8,000 feet. The leaves are oval, about 2 inches long, and covered with silver hairs, especially on the underside of the leaf. Branches have abundant thorn-like twigs that keep browsing by livestock to a minimum but do not deter mule deer, pronghorns, and elk. Silver buffaloberry is most easily identified after its bright red fruit forms in late summer, following a bloom of small yellow flowers in April or May. The fruit persists well past frost, and is a mainstay in the diet of several game bird species.

Back at the junction with FR 020, reset the odometer to zero and bear right (southwest); the sign is for Baker Ranch to the left, and Heart Lake and U-72 to the right. After about 2 miles great views to the east begin. The Henry Mountains, Caineville Mesas, Factory Butte, and the San Rafael Swell are in the middle distance, with Upper Cathedral Valley and the Upper South Desert in the foreground below. The road winds through largely open meadow along Windy Ridge (the sign is at 3.1 miles), with aspen fringes that are spectacular in the fall. At 4 miles the road passes through the first aspen and spruce-fir forest, and then connects with the main access road, FR 206, at 4.9 miles, above Heart Lake. A left (south) turn here leads up onto Thousand Lake Mountain, Elkhorn Campground, and the Flat Top hike, or to the Polk Creek Road back down to Capitol Reef NP; a right (northwest) turn will take you down to Highway 72.

Flat Top Trail Hike

Hiking distance is 2.4 miles round trip.

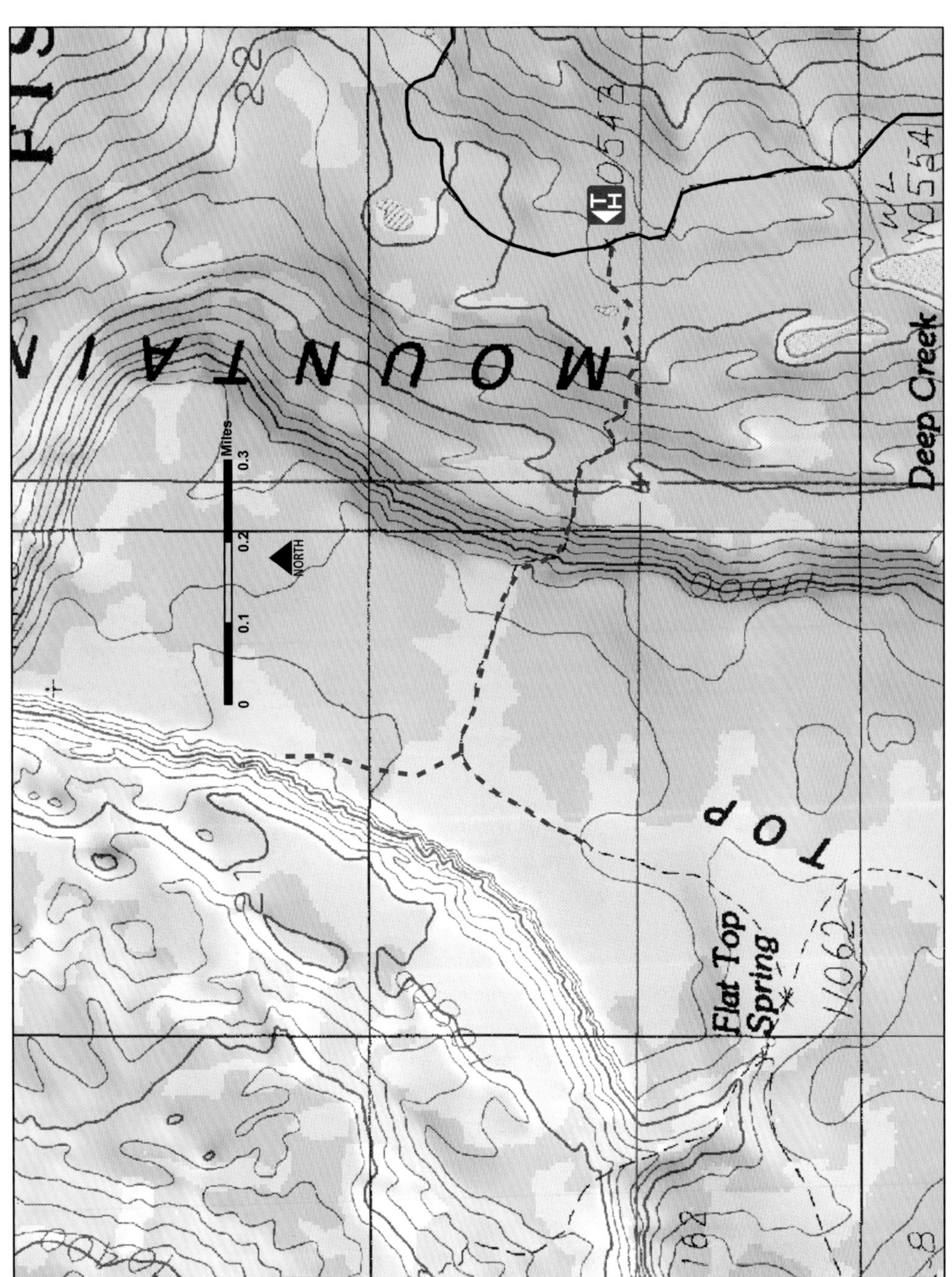

Flat Top Trail

The summit plateau of Thousand Lake Mountain is called Flat Top, a name that is highly accurate in describing the topography. The mountain, like nearby Boulder Mountain and Fish Lake Hightop, is capped by relatively recent lava flows which protect the softer sedimentary rocks at its base. Most of the volcanic rocks on all three mountains have been dated to an age of about 26 to 23 million years. A more recent episode of volcanism on Thousand Lake Mountain has been determined to be about 5 million years old. The Flat Top Trail ascends the east face of the summit plateau and passes through a variety of volcanic rocks.

Flat Top Trail

Flat Top Trail

The trailhead is 10 miles from Highway 72. See the Thousand Lake Mountain Road Trip section above for specific directions. The small sign on the right (west) side of the road is marked for the Flat Top Trail, and gives distances for Flat Top 1, Flat Top Spring 2, and Bull Run Flat 4. There is enough room for a vehicle to park off the road to the left (east) across from the sign. The Flat Top Trail is very lightly used, but aside from one spot is reasonably easy to follow up to the plateau where it disappears entirely.

The hike begins as an easy-going walk through pretty forest consisting of Engelmann spruce and subalpine fir. Compared to the sparse vegetation in the redrock country below, the moist lushness of thick forest is a welcome change for summer travelers. After about 250 yards of pleasant walking on obvious tread, there is a confusing spot where a small trough straight ahead appears to be the likely location for the trail, but is not. The track actually bends slightly to the right to the top of a small rise, and then turns right again (westerly) and drops to a rocky water crossing. The water is part of a small wetland that connects to Deep Creek Lake that is just to the south. There are several easy ways to rock hop across. The first steep climb starts immediately beyond the crossing, at one point passing next to a mossy rivulet. The sharp grade moderates 0.3 mile from the road, climbing gently and then descending to the edge of a large talus slope to the south (left).

When the trail again begins to go up, it is only 0.2 mile to the plateau, but it will seem longer. The path is both steep and loose, requiring good footwear, especially on the descent. The top comes suddenly as the trail emerges from the trees into an open area that stretches all the way across Flat Top to the west. Here, the trail essentially disappears, although large old cairns, difficult to see, mark the way across the bench. The point where the trail leaves the trees is an important one to remember or to GPS (UTM 0458915mE, 4254723mN) if you are going to explore along the plateau.

Walking on Flat Top is certainly easy (as long as the 11,100-foot elevation isn't a problem) and it is worth doing in the summer to enjoy the flowers, and any time to take in the view from the west side. The open area bisects the largely forested ridge on a line that trends just north of west. Either search for and follow the cairns, or just head across the middle of the boulder-strewn meadow for 0.25 mile to a fairly discernible track that runs more north and south. You may find the remains of a sign lying on the ground along that trail. When it was standing in correct position, the right arrow pointed back across the plateau to the trail from the road, and the left arrows for Neff's Reservoir and Lyman pointed south.

The majority of the few people who use this trail system go south across a larger meadow, but the best view off the west side is to the north. To do that, follow the trail to the right (north) as it enters the forest where there may be some fallen trees to avoid. Shortly the path leaves the trees (again, pay attention to this point for the return trip) and disappears after going along the edge of the meadow for a few yards. Ahead and to the northwest the west edge of the summit block rises gently toward a copse of small trees. A sharp cliff drops off to the west, and the view is grand. The lip of the cliff is dangerous, but there are plenty of safe places to sit and take in the view of the town of Fremont far below, Mytoge Mountain and Fish Lake Hightop to the northwest with the Sevier Plateau beyond, and the Tushar Mountains and Delano Peak just south of due west. The walk to the viewpoint from the intersection with the north-south trail is 0.3 mile each way.

Flat Top Trail

Flat Top is an interesting place, with the secluded feel of being on an island, which in effect is the case in terms of topography and the ecosystem. It is also, however, a place where it would be easy to get lost, and the chances of meeting anyone else are very slim. Make sure that you can find your way back to the trail and your vehicle.

Hells Hole and the Torrey Petrified Wood Site

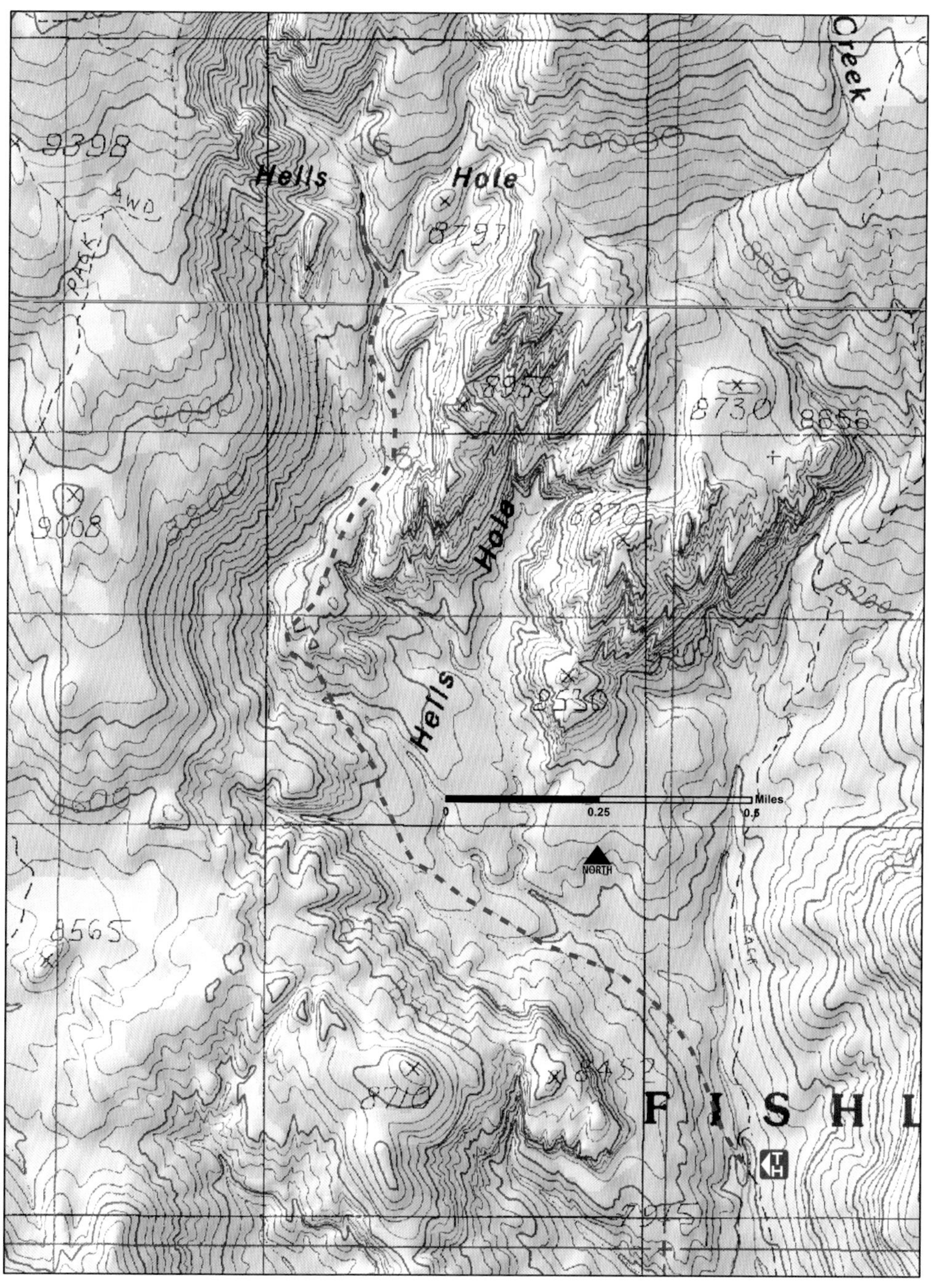

Hells Hole route

This is an intermediate elevation drive and hike that combines very well with the Torrey petrified wood site, which is described at the end of this section. Access to the Hells Hole trailhead usually requires 4WD to get through some sand drifts that often span the road. The direct route to the petrified wood area generally requires high clearance, but not 4WD.

Hells Hole is red rock elevated. Here, the Navajo Sandstone is exposed in jagged cliffs well above 8,000 feet. The Navajo is stunningly divided about midway up the exposure: dark red in color below and bright white above. The trail, actually an ATV route, passes right by some of the best vantage points, and the entire scene is spectacular. For many hikers, however, it is the hidden canyon just after the best views that will be most memorable. This incised drainage is handsome, with tall vertical walls on alternating sides, but the main attraction is the bristlecone pine forest along the way, nicely accented by Douglas fir, Engelmann spruce, ponderosa pine, huge mountain mahogany, and the standard piñon and juniper.

Road to Hells Hole

Hells Hole Hike

Driving distance (sometimes requiring 4WD) from Highway 24 is 5.1 miles one way

Hiking distance is 4.4 miles round trip.

For the trailhead to Hells Hole, turn north off Highway 24 onto the Sand Creek Road at the west edge of Torrey, just west of milepost 68. The turn is well marked with brown signs on the highway for Torrey Trailhead and the Great Western Trail, and by a street sign for 520 West. Zero the odometer at this point. At the end of the pavement in 0.75 mile, bear left (northwest) on Forest Road 146, and cross a cattleguard, entering the Fishlake National Forest. An information board will be on the right. Although the road now crosses essentially flat terrain, it is quite rough and rocky, and the going is slow.

At 1.4 miles the road passes three large water tanks, and then drops down to cross Sand Creek 1.5 miles from Highway 24. There is usually a little water at the creek. After a steep climb up the far bank, it is a short distance to a junction where Forest Road 207 (FR 207) bears left (west) and FR 146 goes north. Either direction can lead to Hells Hole, but neither avoids the sand later on. FR 207 is slightly shorter, but it is a nice loop to use both, so this description will follow a clockwise loop of FR 207, with the return on FR 146.

FR 207 heads west through gently rolling ground, paralleling Sand Creek, which is crossed at 2.2 miles, with a steep exit from the drainage. At 2.5 miles is a Y junction where FR 1598 goes to the left. Stay right (northwest) on FR 207. Another junction is at 3.2 miles where FR 1584 goes sharply left (southwest). Continue straight ahead to a rough, boulder-strewn crossing of Sand Creek. FR 1597, the return route, comes in from the right (east) at 3.4 miles; stay straight. The sand drifts are just ahead. For more than 0.1 mile, sand blows into the slightly incised roadbed, and can accumulate to significant depth. Even with 4WD, this stretch can be daunting, although sometimes the sand doesn't go all the way across the road, allowing for traction to resume. Momentum is a good thing here. If the sand is especially bad, it isn't a long walk to the trailhead, though it will add about 3.2 miles of round trip hiking.

Stay left in the wash at 3.7 miles and enjoy relatively easy driving. The route divides at 4.5 miles, and as of this writing it was better to stay straight (north), quickly bending to the left (west) for the final crossing of Sand Creek. Narrow leaf cottonwoods are present near the wash, but only 0.1 mile farther on, the road passes through a nice aspen grove. Another 0.5 mile of easy driving ends at the trailhead. Here, the old road, open to ATVs no more than 50 inches in width, goes up a steep and very rough and rocky slope ahead. There is room to park a vehicle or two in front of the sign that gives distances on the Great Western Trail (GWT): Torrey is listed as 3 miles to the south (it is actually over 5), and Wiffs Pasture and Elkhorn Campground are listed as 3 miles and 10 miles respectively. The sign marks the trailhead for hikers, but remember to walk up the ATV trail rather than pass through the steel posts that block motorized vehicles on this arm of the GWT.

The hike to Hells Hole follows the ATV route up the steep hill. On weekends and during hunting season there is a good chance that you might meet four-wheelers on the trail, but during the week the chances are that you will have it to yourself. The elevation at the trailhead is just over 7,800 feet, so elevation may be a factor for some. After the initial ascent, the road climbs moderately, and the tread is frequently just sandy enough to be very comfortable on the return trip. There are peeks at the sandstone from the trail, with a good view opening up after 0.3 mile of walking. Even from a distance, the dividing line between the white rock on top and the red rock below is distinctive. The abrupt color change may reflect leaching of iron out of the white section, while the red color is due to iron oxides.

Alongside the trail are scattered ponderosa and piñon pine, Utah juniper, Douglas fir, and healthy examples of roundleaf buffaloberry. Between the trees the sandy soil is often completely covered with a biological soil crust, which consists of mosses, fungi, lichen, and cyanobacteria. The latter are especially important, as they are filaments that enlarge when it rains, coiling around sand grains and the other constituents of the crust. The resulting black, sometimes brown, interlocking material looks like drip castles in miniature. This soil crust performs many duties, including preventing wind erosion and providing a nutrient-rich mat in which seeds can germinate and grow. The crust is a living thing, easily crushed and killed by careless footsteps. Because the crust takes several to many years to regenerate, please stay on the trail.

Just over 1 mile from the trailhead, the ATV trail drops down to cross a wash, and then climbs steeply. At the top of the rise is a nice stand of greenleaf manzanita, which might be covered in small, bell-shaped pink to white blossoms in May. Just as it does at Hells Backbone, the manzanita clings to small bits of sandy soil on the sandstone bedrock. The trail soon passes by the tip of a redrock outcrop, and then turns sharply to the right (east) and ascends steeply on slickrock. When it bends back to the north (left), it is a short walk up a small cleft (beyond the black boulders that define the curve) to a fine view into the heart of Hells Hole.

The ATV trail ascends more rock after the left-hand curve, then flattens before another short stretch of slickrock at 1.35 miles. Just beyond is a nice view off the road to the right (southeast) into a small basin studded with Douglas fir, and to the left of the trail are several very large mountain mahoganys. After another 300 feet there is a small grove of mature ponderosa pine on the right (east), and a short walk through them and along the sandstone wall on the left (north) accesses another good view of Hells Hole. Manzanita flourishes in the sand at the base of the cliff.

After the pines, the trail drops down into a moderately deep drainage. At the bottom, a large pipe high above spans the entrance to a very interesting canyon. This canyon is scenic, cut into the sandstone, and also hosts a nice mix of forest along the way. Pass under the pipe, and immediately on the right is a large bristlecone pine tree. We often think of bristlecones as living right at treeline in the harshest conditions of any tree, but they can also thrive in more benign environments. They are five needle pines, like many other species, but their short, dense, and very dark green needles set them apart. Many descriptions suggest that the branches look like bottle brushes, and indeed they do. The branches, especially lower ones, often hang down in pendants. Cones are about three inches long, and the scales have small but sharp points. The species in Utah is the intermountain bristlecone pine (*Pinus longaeva*); individual trees in Nevada are almost five thousand years old. Bristlecones are not common across the West, but in this unnamed canyon they are quite abundant.

As with all narrow canyons in southern Utah, this one should not be entered if there is even a chance of rain. If the weather is fair, however, the walking is easy except for a

Canyon above Hells Hole

Bristlecone pine

couple of obstacles. While there are a few short sections where there are vertical walls on each side, more often the intermittent stream has cut a wall on one side, and there is a slope on the other. Bristlecones continue, mixed in with ponderosa and piñon pine, Douglas fir, juniper, and mountain mahogany. In the spring, at least, there may be a small flow of water (or, during snowmelt, too much to do the hike) that appears at some point up the canyon above where it sinks into the sandy streambed.

Small pieces of white or orange gypsum become more frequent up canyon, with a large chunk in the wash 0.2 mile beyond the pipe. Aside from stepping over or crawling under a few logs, the going is easy and pleasant until the most significant barrier is reached 0.5 mile into the canyon. A huge boulder is wedged between the walls and as of this writing, either the climb on the right side or the scramble up the very steep slope on the left is fairly difficult. There is no foul in turning around here if you don't want to attempt either option.

Above the boulder choke the canyon eventually divides in a Y confluence. The arm to the right (northeast) is filled with dense vegetation, notably the bright red-stemmed red osier dogwood. At the top of the Y is a stand of mature Engelmann spruce trees, and the ground is littered with their papery cones. These spruces are normally found at higher elevations, but the cooler and wetter conditions in the canyon are sufficient for them to thrive. A simple touch of the branch tips confirms that the sharp needles belong to a spruce.

The left (northwest) arm is short and worth exploring. The wash is littered with huge pieces of gypsum. The source is the Carmel Formation, which can be seen as the wash rises quickly into the base of a large amphitheater. The Navajo-Carmel contact is about halfway up the far wall. The Carmel is Jurassic in age, and was laid down on a very flat coastal plain. Layers of gypsum are abundant in between silt strata. From the base of the amphitheater, the view back to the south includes a high cliff of sandstone where bristlecone pines cling to precarious footholds more in keeping with their image. The return trip down canyon provides a different perspective, and is worthy of slow and attentive passage.

After the nice downhill walk back to the trailhead, reset the odometer of your vehicle if you wish to return to Torrey by a partial loop. At 0.5 mile down FR 207 the road passes out of the Kayenta Formation (which is just below the Navajo) and enters the Wingate, which forms the red cliffs on the left (east, then north) all the way to FR 146. The sand drifts are easier on the down grade. At 1.8 miles from the trailhead, bear left (southeast) on FR 1597. The road parallels a wash as it trends to the southeast, then bends left (northeast). At 2.8 miles is a junction with the access road to the petrified wood site going left (north), while the road to Torrey continues straight ahead. The latter passes over ledge at 3 miles, and comes to another junction 0.1 mile later. The sign is for opposing traffic. Turn right (south) onto FR 146, and proceed 0.8 mile to the junction with 207. To return to Highway 24, turn left (southeast), cross Sand Creek and negotiate the rough road across the flat back to the pavement at Sand Creek Road.

Torrey Petrified Wood Site

Driving distance from Highway 24 is 3 miles.

Torrey petrified wood site

Petrified wood weathers out of the Chinle Formation over a large area northwest of Torrey. To get to the site from Highway 24, follow the directions at the beginning of the Hells Hole hike section to the junction of Forest Roads 207 and 146. At that point, bear right (northeast) on FR 146, and continue on the rough road for 0.8 mile to a signed intersection. Though rough, high-clearance 2WD vehicles can usually manage this stretch. The sign points left to Sand Creek and the Great Western Trail horse and foot route, and right to Sulphur Basin and the GWT ATV route. Turn left (west), and soon drive over slickrock. From the sign it is just 0.3 mile to a triangular junction. Turn right here, either up the steep first option, or sharply right (north) on a more gentle grade just beyond. If coming from Hells Hole, follow the return description to 2.8 miles from the trailhead and turn left (north) at that point.

The track heads north toward the prominent cliff fronted by the gray Chinle slopes. As it nears the base of the slope, it bends to the west. Petrified wood weathers out of the ground all along the road and up the slope. Simply stop along the track and walk around to find it. One good place is about 0.4 mile from the junction, and just before the road crosses a broad wash. Even the berm left by the grader contains many pieces of wood.

By some standards, the material here is somewhat pedestrian in nature, since the predominant color is black. Nonetheless, patient searching should be able to turn up pieces with good red streaking, and others with drusy quartz linings. Over the past decade the Torrey site has been heavily collected, and the petrified wood is best enjoyed in its natural environment. Collecting requires a free permit, available at the Fremont River District office on Highway 24 in Loa. To return to Highway 24, return the way you came, following the directions at the end of the Hells Hole Hike.

Torrey petrified wood

Cooks and Meeks Mesas Loop Hike

Hiking distance, including the spur to Meeks Mesa, is 7.3 miles.

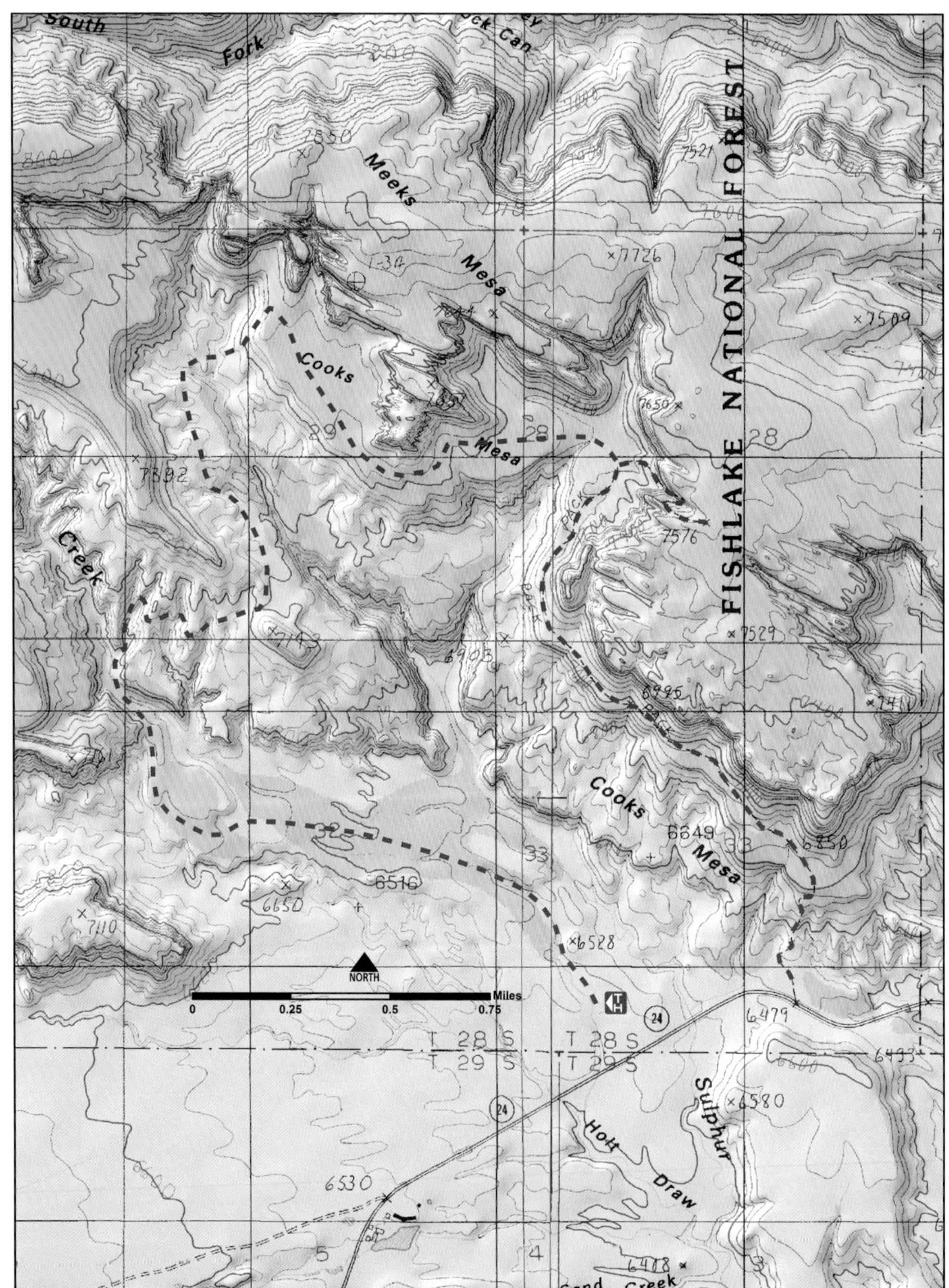

Cooks and Meeks Mesas route

Cooks Mesa route

Meeks Mesa route

Let's say it is April, a fine time to be at Capitol Reef, but the day is to be unseasonably warm. You are, of course, still hooked on the red rocks, but would like to get up a little higher and perhaps find some solitude. If there were whole tree trunks of petrified wood, that would be nice, too. Oh, and views, if possible. Cooks and Meeks Mesas fit the bill. There is a caveat: this hike is really for experienced route finders who are comfortable with a little uncertainty and relish, rather than worry about, solitude.

Meeks Mesa towers over Highway 24 from west of Capitol Reef National Park to east of Chimney Rock in the park. Cooks Mesa is a bench that wraps around Meeks' southwest flank. The route is on hiker- and horse-made trails, and cross country. The climb up to Meeks is very steep, but follows an old dugway developed to provide a way to bring cattle up to graze on the broad mesa. The description below may be sufficient for some hikers without a GPS unit, but having one may be comforting to others. Most of the route, including the ascent to Meeks Mesa, is shown on the Twin Rocks 7.5 minute USGS quadrangle map, but the westernmost part is on the Torrey quad. All of the hike as described lies in the Fishlake National Forest, but exploration atop Meeks Mesa can extend into the national park, where quite different regulations apply to many activities.

The hike is a loop that can be done in either direction. We think that route-finding is more easily accomplished by walking in a clockwise direction, and that is followed here. With a GPS, a counterclockwise path is fine as well. If you have two vehicles, even the short road walk to complete the loop can be avoided. The trailheads are both adjacent to

Highway 24 on the north side of the road and just west of the entrance to Capitol Reef National Park. If you do have two vehicles or a bike, leave one at the informal camping area at milepost 72.9. Here a rocky, then smooth road leads into an area with several short spurs. After turning off the highway the road immediately splits; as of this writing the rocks are a little less high on the right fork. The two roads quickly rejoin, and after they do, continue to the northwest by staying to the left. Go to a large pine tree on the left (west) and look for a trail leading up a gray clay slope to the north. Park here.

The turnoff to the trailhead where this description begins is 0.5 mile farther to the west at milepost 72.4. If you are driving from the park, the road to the right is largely hidden by a roadcut and comes up unexpectedly quickly. Drive in the short distance to a fence and park. If the dirt track is too rough, simply park nearer to the highway. The hike begins by passing through the gate and securing it behind you. For the first 1.1 miles the route follows the old Holt Draw Road and is very easy walking. At that distance the road becomes a little less obvious and a path diverges at an acute angle from it. This point is at UTM 0466107mE, and 4242609mN.

Take the path (right, more northerly) and in 0.25 mile arrive at Sulphur Creek. Depending on recent rains, there may or may not be a little flowing water. Although the more obvious hiker-made trail continues to the left and stays above the wash, go straight, cross the creek bed and find what may be an obscure trail up the far bank. Before doing this, look ahead to the north and spot a single large ponderosa pine tree to confirm that you are on track, and note a prominent point not far behind it. After crossing Sulphur Creek the use trail bears a little left (northwest) but soon comes around to pass just to the right of the point, which consists of a brown Moenkopi Formation cliff capped by a solid piece of Shinarump sandstone. It is only about 500 feet from the creek bed to this point, which is at UTM 0465741mE, 4242911mN.

On higher ground, the trail becomes more clear as it climbs alongside the point. Once in the Shinarump it follows a gully through interesting terrain and eventually climbs onto the gray clay of the Chinle Formation. After a switchback, it is 0.25 mile to the base of a short, steep climb. When the grade becomes more gentle (UTM 0465942mE, 4243266mN), there is a junction just under 2 miles from the trailhead. The right (east) fork climbs steadily up to a nice viewpoint in 0.2 mile, but to continue on to the mesas, stay to the left in a northerly direction. The route bends to the northeast, and soon tops a low divide. From here almost all of the rest of the hike is visible: first up the wide drainage, exiting on the right (east) side, then east, south, and southeast along the prominent shelf in the middle of the Chinle (and well below the base of the prominent red Wingate Sandstone cliff).

After the divide, the path bears left (north) and proceeds over very gently rolling ground. There are abundant pieces of petrified wood scattered about, generally black and sometimes with small quartz crystals that formed in openings. The multi-hued clays of the Chinle add to the scenic impact. Occasionally, vegetation in the Chinle swamps was buried during flood events. Later, silica, largely from volcanic ash mixed in with the

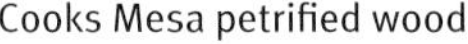

Cooks Mesa petrified wood

Cooks Mesa petrified wood

clays, replaced the woody tissue and the logs were preserved as petrified wood. Although the color is usually unspectacular, the preservation of bark, rings, and knots can be very impressive. The more glamorous material typical of Petrified Forest National Park is also found in the Chinle Formation. As at the Torrey site, any collecting requires a free permit that can be obtained at the Forest Service office in Loa.

At 0.7 mile beyond the trail junction the route traverses a gray flat with abundant petrified wood, and very colorful, largely pink, Chinle sediments just off to the left (west). In another 0.25 mile the track, which is easy to follow at this point, crosses a wash, and begins a steep climb for 0.2 mile. At first, this ascent is on an obvious old road, but near the top the route is a little less clear. The serene, flat bench of Cooks Mesa is reached at just over the 3-mile mark. There may be some cairns here to mark the trail for hikers proceeding in the opposite direction, but it would be better to have a GPS if you are doing that. The point is UTM 0466080mE, 4244541mN, at an elevation of about 7,320 feet.

The next section of the hike is essentially cross country, though there may be short stretches of weak hiker-made track. Simply continue to the east (bearing right after climbing onto the bench) along the wide, easy-going flat. Piñons and junipers dot the landscape during the pleasant walk. After about 0.6 mile on the bench, it narrows and there may be a piece of trail to follow. Along this track is the first really large petrified log, followed by many others scattered all over the flat. With so many trees to look at, passing through this area may take some time.

Eventually the bench is cut by a drainage that forces hikers a little north of east, to a crossing of a sandy wash about 4.4 miles from the trailhead. This (UTM 0467391mE, 4244092mN) is a nice place to stop for lunch and contemplate whether to climb up to Meeks Mesa. There may be another short stretch of trail, but it soon disappears, leaving a circuitous small wash trending east as the best route to avoid abundant biological soil crust. The wash ascends gently to a clear trail at UTM 0467445mE, 4243889mN. For Meeks, turn north (left) on this track, or to complete the loop along Cooks Mesa, turn right (south).

The hike up to Meeks Mesa is an interesting one. It is steep, sometimes on slickrock, and at other times on loose dirt and rock. Once on the clear hiker-made trail heading north, cross over a low rise, through a swale, and then up a steep slope littered with huge Wingate Sandstone boulders fallen from the soaring cliffs above. When the trail reaches the base of the wall, it contours through a nice section of boulders and shrubs, providing a break before the main ascent.

It may be a little hard to even imagine, but the route up to the mesa top is an old cattle dugway. Cows were herded up this serpentine corkscrew to graze on the large expanse above. There are several places where the ranchers cut steps in the sandstone to give the cattle more purchase on the rock, and there are holes where fence posts or other guides were placed. Some of these holes are right at the start up the slickrock. Though generally not marked by cairns, the route is usually fairly clear, though after about 0.1 mile it switchbacks to the west and descends before turning again to the east at a point where currently a little fencing remains. Steps are cut in the rock just after this switchback. Near the top the route follows a natural bench, emerging onto the sandy, cactus and biological soil crust–laced Meeks Mesa after about 0.3 mile of climbing. This is the higher end of the tableland at about 7,600 feet above sea level.

Much of Meeks is rather uninteresting, and it is big enough to even lose your way. There are no trails, and the aforementioned cactus and soil crust can make just walking around a bit of a trial. Once on top, the Capitol Reef National Park boundary is only about 0.5 mile to the east. The views from the edges of the mesa can be very good, however, including the one just to the right (south) of the point where the trail emerges onto the mesa. Absolutely make very certain that you can find the beginning of the route back down, which is at UTM 0467838mE, 4243725mN. Rescues have been required for hikers who have found their way on to Meeks Mesa and then couldn't find their way back down. The bones that you might see near the bottom of the descent are those of a horse that paid insufficient attention to the need for caution while going down the steep rock and slopes. The distance for the side trip up to Meeks Mesa is about 0.5 mile each way, with an elevation gain of around 400 feet.

Once down, and back on the trail at the point where the cross country route joins it, the walk down Cooks Mesa is very mellow, with a slight downgrade, big views, and the high Wingate wall to the left (northeast). In about 0.3 mile the path rounds a broken Wingate knob, detached from the main cliff, on the left (east). Only scattered pieces of petrified wood remain, seemingly less each year, once again testimony to the need to enjoy and leave it in place. The trail is quite clear, including short stretches on slickrock. The 1.5-mile stroll to the exit point from Cooks Mesa to the informal camping area is very pleasant.

For clockwise hikers, finding the trail off the bench is the only difficult route finding concern. From the broken point described above, the hike is in a southeastern direction, paralleling the cliff above. The bench widens significantly where it, and the cliff, sweep around to the northeast. The exit route is right at the southern tip of this point, usually marked with cairns. Even up close, the little passage through the upper rock band may not be obvious, but should be apparent after some searching. The GPS point is UTM 0468309mE, 4242303mN. After the first drop, the trail is easy to follow as it trends northwest on a bench, and then drops through a rib onto the Chinle slope. At 0.3 mile after leaving Cooks Mesa, the path arrives at the parking area. If you do not have a shuttle vehicle, it is easiest to walk back to the start along Highway 24.

Wingate Sandstone, Chinle Formation, and petrified wood

Resources

Additional information and resources are available from the travel councils and land management agencies listed.

Traveler Services

Wayne County (towns of Loa, Fremont, Lyman, Bicknell, Teasdale, Torrey, Caineville, Hanksville): www.capitolreef.org
Sevier County (Fish Lake area): www.sevierutah.net
Emery County (San Rafael Swell, towns along Highway 10, and Green River): www.emerycounty.com/travel
Carbon County (Price area, northern San Rafael Swell): www.castlecountry.com
Garfield County (towns of Escalante and Boulder): www.Brycecanyoncountry.com
Road Conditions: www.udottraffic.utah.gov

Utah State Parks

Goblin Valley: Phone 435/275-4584 (office is in Green River) https://stateparks.utah.gov/parks/goblin-valley/
Escalante Petrified Forest: Phone 435/826-4466 https://stateparks.utah.gov/parks/escalante-petrified-forest/
Anasazi: Phone 435/335-7308 https://stateparks.utah.gov/parks/anasazi/
Millsite: Phone 435/384-2552 https://stateparks.utah.gov/parks/millsite/

Bureau of Land Management (BLM)

Price office (administers public land in the San Rafael Swell): Phone 435/636-3600 https://www.blm.gov/office/price-field-office
Cleveland Lloyd Dinosaur Quarry: Phone 435/636-3600 (the Price office) https://www.blm.gov/learn/interpretive-centers/cleveland-lloyd-dinosaur-quarry
Henry Mountains Field Station (Hanksville; administers public land south of the San Rafael Swell, including the Henry Mountains): Phone 435/542-3461 https://www.blm.gov/office/henry-mountains-field-station
Grand Staircase Escalante National Monument: Phone 435/826-5600 (Escalante office) https://www.blm.gov/programs/national-conservation-lands/utah/grand-staircase-escalante-national-monument

Forest Service

Fishlake National Forest (administers public land on Boulder, Fishlake, and Thousand Lake Mountains): Phone 435/836-2800 (Fremont River Ranger District office in Loa) www.fs.usda.gov/fishlake

Dixie National Forest (administers public land on the south side of Boulder Mountain): Phone 435/826-5499 (Escalante Ranger District office in Escalante) https://www.fs.usda.gov/dixie

National Park Service

Capitol Reef National Park: Phone 435/425-3791 www.nps.gov/care

Capitol Reef Natural History Association: Phone 435/425-4106 www.capitolreefnha.org

Canyonlands National Park (administers Horseshoe Canyon and the Maze District): Phone 435/259-2652 (Maze District) www.nps.gov/cany

Glen Canyon National Recreation Area: Phone 928/608-6200 (Page, AZ) www.nps.gov/glca

Region Cross-Indexed by Activity

Canyons

Desert Rambles

Fall Color

Geology

Human History

Mountains

Perennial Water

Rock Art

Rocks, Minerals, and Fossils

Slickrock

Slot Canyons

Sweeping Views

About the Authors

Rick and Lynne Stinchfield have volunteered at Capitol Reef National Park for three months in each of the last eleven years. During that time they have explored not only the park, but also a considerable portion of the public land that surrounds it. With each passing year their to-do list grows longer rather than shorter.

Upon their retirement in 2001 (Rick from higher education administration and Lynne from the antiques business) they worked at the Grand Canyon for more than a year and a half, spending as much time as possible below the rim. After beginning their volunteer work at Capitol Reef, they also managed a venue at the annual Tucson mineral show.

Rick is the author of *Capitol Reef National Park, The Complete Hiking and Touring Guide,* and several articles on mineral collecting and other subjects. He and Lynne led field classes for University of Northern Iowa students to various locations in the West. Their work at Capitol Reef has finally allowed them to put their geology degrees to use.

The Stinchfields live in Pagosa Springs, Colorado, when they are not at the park, and enjoy volunteering there for the Pagosa District of the San Juan National Forest.